Complete Book
of Distance
Learning Schools

The Princeton Review

Complete Book of Distance Learning Schools

Everything You Need to Earn Your Degree Without Leaving Home

Dr. Jerry Ice and Dr. Paul Jay Edelson

Random House, Inc.
New York
www.review.com

Princeton Review Publishing, L.L.C.
2315 Broadway
New York, NY 10024
E-mail: comments@review.com

ISBN: 0-375-76204-3

Editor: Erik Olson
Designer: Greta Englert
Production Editors: Kristen Azzara, Julieanna Lambert
Production Coordinator: Greta Englert

CONTENTS

Chapter One

Why Distance Learning?

Distance learning, e-learning, degrees from a distance . . . you may already be familiar with these and other terms in the language of distance and online learning. For those interested in earning a degree without the constraints of classroom attendance, online education is becoming an increasingly important and workable option. As reported by the National Center for Education Statistics (NCES), the number of institutions offering online and other forms of distance education has seen explosive growth in recent years. Nearly one-third of all colleges and universities reported that as of 1997, they offered some form of distance learning.

As a growing number of colleges and universities promotes new ways of pursuing degrees and taking college courses, people seeking a quality education from a distance are challenged by the broad range of choices available. Potential students must decipher a new educational language, assess program standards, and select learning options.

This expanded guide, The Princeton Review's *Complete Book of Distance Learning Schools*, will help you identify the institution and program that will meet your needs. Our goal is to help you sort through the terminology, identify the important factors in selecting a degree program, and understand the process of completing your degree from a distance.

This chapter presents the scope of distance learning offerings, introduces you to the kind of students you are likely to find in distance or online programs, and explains the need for advanced study in a knowledge-based economy.

Distance Learning Is Exploding

The distance learning field is rapidly gaining new players. More institutions are offering more courses, and many more students are enrolling.

Here are the numbers, courtesy of the NCES (www.nces.ed.gov).

- An estimated 54,470 distance education courses were offered in the 12-month 1997–1998 academic year by 2-year and 4-year post-secondary institutions.
- There were 1,661,100 enrollments in all distance education courses.
- There were 1,363,670 enrollments in college-level, credit-granting distance education courses, most at the undergraduate level.

The Students You Will Meet

Today's students are busy with work and family. Completing a college education is *not* their only priority. According to *Lifelong Learning Trends,* a fact book published annually by the University Continuing Education Association (www.nucea.edu), present-day students are faced with many demands. They are also armed with the technology to make use of Web-based services, and operate in an environment that makes Web-based services increasingly inviting. In brief, *Lifelong Learning Trends* states:

- 42 percent of baccalaureate-seeking students attend part time.
- 60 percent of graduate students attend part time.
- 50 percent of households in the United States own a computer.
- 40 percent of the U.S. population is online.
- 20 percent of corporate training is expected to include distance education by 2001.

Trends in the way students live and work indicate that online and distance learning will become increasingly popular strategies for pursuing higher education.

Increased Knowledge Feeds the Economy

Meeting the challenge and making the choice to advance your education is important—perhaps more so in the new Knowledge Economy. Companies count employees' knowledge as intellectual capital. To see how much value companies can gain from their employees' knowledge and talent, take the example of the comparative value of General Motors and Dell Computers. GM has a total market value of $65 billion, which can be roughly broken down into the amounts it has invested in people, plants, and materials. Dell Computers also has a market value of $65 billion. The difference between the two companies is that while most of GM's worth is in plants and materials, Dell's people—and their very special knowledge—are its most valuable "commodity."

Not too many years ago, high school or college graduates could join a company after graduation and remain at that company for their entire career. Today, mergers are commonplace and companies frequently change strategies. Consequently, long-term employment with the same company is less and less common. Employees need to look ahead at their own personal and professional development in order to stay competitive and in demand. For some, this will mean taking a number of short-term courses leading to a certificate; others will need to enroll in a degree program at the undergraduate or graduate level.

Earnings Increase with More Education

Lifelong Learning Trends states simply that education beyond high school is financially rewarding. Individuals with college training can expect to earn higher salaries than those without post-secondary education. In 1998, the average annual salary of all college graduates was more than $40,000. This was twice the amount those individuals would have earned with only high school diplomas. Today, a college degree is becoming an important credential, a passport to jobs requiring higher-level skills, and the minimum level of education expected in many professional positions.

Since the early 1970s, the number of students attending colleges and universities has risen. The demand for a smarter and better-trained workforce has changed the higher-education landscape. No longer is college attendance meant solely for 18- to 22-year-olds, for whom a college degree might come in "handy" some day. In 1979, less than half of all high school graduates went directly to college. Compare that to 1997, when two-thirds of high school graduates entered college upon graduation. The difference: the greater need in competitive fields for graduates with very specific skills. The information age has increased the demand for strong skills in communication, problem solving, and working with others.

In order for colleges and universities to serve the increased demand for college education, distance education is becoming a major form of delivering instruction to students. Though distance education is not a new approach for colleges, the emerging technologies have made it very practical and cost effective. The interactive nature of video and e-mail can bring students and teachers together in a rich learning environment.

Distance learning is here to stay. The new, online approach combines quality and rigor, as well as providing "anytime" access to the electronic classroom for both students and faculty. Like any decision, choosing a distance learning program must be approached in a deliberate manner; this publication will provide a road map for student-employees seeking to advance their careers and personal development.

Chapter Two

What Is Distance Education?

Modes of Instruction

Distance education has steadily evolved over the past hundred years. The term *distance learning* can be used to describe any form of education in which the teacher and student are not physically present in the same room. Popular modes of distance learning include correspondence, radio, television (closed circuit, satellite, and network), audio- and videocassettes, computer-assisted, and now, in a huge way, Web-based. Interestingly, in many programs these approaches not only coexist, but complement one another. Students may find it advantageous to enroll in a school that offers the added flexibility of multiple approaches. Moreover, some distance learning students might want to take a traditional face-to-face course as part of their curriculum, either in the evening or during the summer. A "full-service" institution can offer most of these options.

In the nineteenth century, the advent of education through correspondence was perceived as revolutionary, extending opportunity to adults in ways never before anticipated and promoting a greater democratization of learning. Today, computer networking technology has spread the boundaries of education even further. Without question, online instruction has led to significant breakthroughs and brought a new luster to part-time distance education. The U.S. Department of Education's estimate of 2 million online students by the year 2001 suggests the appeal of this educational phenomenon. Let's analyze its features in greater depth.

E-Learning and Synchronous/Asynchronous Instruction

The root of asynchronous distance learning (ADL) is asynchronous communication. In its simplest form, asynchronous communication occurs when someone sends you an electronic message to which you respond at a later time. Students who are enrolled in an ADL class have their own passwords to reach the course site on the Internet. An interactive software program such as Blackboard, Caucus, or Lotus Notes Learning Space then allows all students to post messages to one another and follow the thread of conversation.

As with e-mail programs, all entries are submitted and distributed electronically, but these interactive software programs differ from conventional e-mail in several important respects. First, all students have simultaneous access to all other students in the class through the conference program. Student submissions are displayed sequentially in what is called a "threaded conversation," which preserves a historical record of all submissions. For example, the instructor may distribute a copy of the syllabus and reading list to all students, and for the first assignment may post a question based on those readings, such as, "If effective leadership behavior can be analyzed into a number of measurable traits or abilities, why not select leaders based on test performance?" As students contribute their responses, a thread of conversation is posted and developed. Ideally, each student reflects upon and comments on the other students' submissions.

Unlike a traditional class, which may meet once or twice a week, students in electronic courses drop in to class and participate many times over the period of a week. Instructors may require that students in the course log on for a minimum of one hour three times a week. The instructor does the same, contributing his or her thoughts and observations to the discussion, helping to move it along, and ensuring that important curricular issues are covered. Bear in mind that all parties log on at times convenient for them, which vary by participant. The instructor may log on Tuesday and Thursday evenings and perhaps one morning on the weekend. Many students log on most often over the weekend. Students log on from home or work or, if they travel, from their hotel rooms. In a one-week period, a class of 20 students usually contributes upwards of 60 messages for each discussion theme. This is a lot of interaction, maybe even more than in the conventional classroom, where oftentimes not all students participate.

After a week, the class can move on to the next item in the syllabus, following the same format. The instructor can also introduce the modification of volunteer student discussion leaders who take responsibility for moving the discussion along. Each week a different discussion leader would put his or her spin on the material.

The most commonly used software programs permit instructors to create a syllabus with many subunits, develop and distribute exams, and facilitate group projects. As the level of technology in both software and hardware continues to improve, electronic courses will become more sophisticated, integrating video, voice, and graphics in imaginative and highly productive ways.

The biggest intellectual and behavioral hurdle for faculty and students to clear is overcoming the anxiety caused by the disunities of time, space, and action. In the ideal face-to-face learning environment, being present in the same physical room (and being able to see each other) provides visual cues that can be reassuring and familiar. In a short period of time the participants create a sustaining educational community and achieve a type of symphony of learning.

In truth, reality can fall short of the mark. Large classes meeting at inconvenient times; rooms that are too hot, cold, or stuffy; indifferent fellow students; rigid and unimaginative pedagogy; and many other variables conspire to deflate expectations and value. Even in small classes it's hard to be in top form as an instructor at all times, and for students, scheduling difficulties and inhibitions to full participation are still problems. Moreover, gender, racial, economic, social, psychological, and behavioral differences—including students' ease with speaking in class—can combine to create an uneven playing field for students in face-to-face classes, where spontaneous behavior can overwhelm more thoughtful participation.

In contrast, imagine the electronic course as an opportunity for all members to participate at times convenient for them, without physically having to come to a college. Faculty do not have to stay late to teach in the evening after a full day of work, and students have time to read and craft their responses to the questions and comments posted. The result is a collaborative effort to achieve a common understanding of the subject material.

In addition to the online discussions, students complete the full complement of written assignments, including reports and term papers they can submit electronically, by fax, or by mail. These written assignments can also be posted electronically to other students in the class so each can see what the others have written, a feature not usually offered in traditional classes.

Students may also e-mail privately with the instructor or with each other one-to-one, and phone conversations and office meetings are also available.

Additional Advantages of E-Learning

- Students initially baffled by the differences between face-to-face and electronic courses quickly adapt, much as earlier generations adapted to the abstract feeling of telephone communication between parties at great distances.
- Technical problems are minimal, and since technology is portable, students can "attend" class by logging on at work, at home, or from the field.
- Student writing and research skills improve. Responses are carefully written and not just spontaneous "off the top of the head" utterances. Source material is more closely read and skillfully woven into comments.
- Students participate more. Psychological, physical, and social barriers can be mitigated.
- There is a permanent written record of all student and faculty contributions that can be studied and reviewed at any time by all participants. Professors can monitor the frequency of student log-ins because the software program in use indicates to what extent students have read the online postings of other students. The instructor can then follow up with students who do not appear to be participating.
- Sharing of projects helps other students broaden their understanding, promoting a true learning community.
- Students learn how to access the Internet directly from the electronic class and use the World Wide Web as a source of information. This promotes the development of "hypertextuality" because Internet links can be quickly distributed to and used by all class members.
- Guests can participate from other locations, even other countries.

- The combination of these factors promotes the creation of a high-quality learning environment.
- Administrative difficulties such as shortage of physical classroom space are eliminated, as are questions of adequate parking and facilities support, which tend to be problematic for part-time students and faculty.

Drawbacks of the Electronic Classroom

With any innovation, there is always a downside. For some students, the physical separation from the other students and the instructor can be a serious problem, giving rise to the common phrase "the loneliness of the long-distance learner." However, most students find that prolific e-mail exchanges are in fact a superior way of getting to know their fellow students (since they can't go out for a cup of coffee following class).

More significantly, distance learners must find ways to pace themselves and make sure they do not fall behind in their course work. Students who have gotten into the habit of doing readings and assignments the night before class will be at a disadvantage. Online education requires self-discipline and superior time management skills. Juggling multiple responsibilities is important for all part-time students, but it is even more so for those studying from a distance.

The heavy emphasis on writing, as opposed to talking, can be a problem for students who are weak in this area. Although all students will discover they are better writers by the end of the semester, initially the need to type all class contributions can be a burden.

Online education also demands a high level of interaction, meaning students will be expected to contribute to class discussions frequently and in depth. For students who have gotten into the habit of passively listening to others, the need to be an "active learner" can come as a shock. But the rewards are considerable, and most students and faculty members say they learn more within the enriched environment of online courses.

Naturally each student must have a sufficiently powered computer with a Web browser and an online service provider. Most colleges offering online courses will point students in the right direction and make helpful suggestions on how to get started. Students are also responsible for these connectivity charges as well as for the maintenance of their computers. These costs should be more than offset by savings in transportation (gas, parking) and, most of all, time expended in attending face-to-face courses.

I remember my own experience as an evening student attending college in New York City. Often I would fall asleep on the subway after attending my night class following a long day at work. I wish I'd had the option of online learning then! My fellow students and I were always rushing. Some commuted more than two hours (in each direction) just to attend class. Sad to say, a good number never finished their degrees; the obstacles to completion were just too great. The advent of online learning makes going to college easier for part-time students. Sure, you still have to be prepared to do the work and set aside the necessary time, and you may fall asleep at your computer. But when you wake up you will be within the comfort of your own home or workplace and not on the subway!

Chapter Three

How to Select a Program and School

Programs and Institutions

Selecting a program is usually the first critical decision a student makes. This may be within a traditional discipline (such as history, art, literature, or psychology), within a professional/occupational area (such as engineering, nursing, or education), or simply related to an area of general interest (like family studies, the culture of Italy, or environmental issues). Increasingly, the world of higher education, especially graduate education, is orienting itself more to addressing the broader categories, especially in part-time education, where students are searching for options that address their personal vocational or avocational aspirations.

Moreover, the expansion of opportunities in the workplace has created entirely new categories of employment, often with new education and training requirements. For example, the area of information technology, or IT, is a category of education that has burgeoned in the past few years. It would not even have been found in a college catalog a decade ago. The future is sure to hold further new and unknown opportunities.

Both online and traditional college catalogs are customarily organized by department, division, or school, and reflect the distribution of faculty within the college or university. A subject index may also indicate whether a particular curriculum is offered. Still, these "text" methods are incomplete and inadequate because many colleges and universities will allow students to shape, at least in part, their own programs. It is a rare program indeed that is entirely prescribed. When this is the case, it is usually owing to some professionally required course of study, and even then, once the minimal criteria are achieved students can add additional concentrations. For example, within "teaching foreign languages" a student might add a specialization in technology.

For many people, it may be helpful to think of the specialization and then create an appropriate field of study around it. You should feel free to make contact with academic advisors at the schools you are considering and seek answers to all your questions. Document and keep responses, because without the necessary paper trail you will have a difficult time if problems emerge. Remember that advisors speak to scores of students and, like all of us, can and do forget things. If you have retained the e-mail, fax, catalog page, or copy of the Web page, you will have an easier time buttressing your case than someone else who can allude only to "a phone conversation last April or May."

The Building-Block Approach to Curriculum Development

It may be useful to think of the curriculum development as a large edifice constructed out of individual building blocks arranged on the following levels: (1) courses, (2) specializations, (3) certificates, and (4) degrees. For your own benefit, it is important to ensure that your school is committed to explaining these elements completely. Schools understand your need to fully understand the curriculum development and see it as a way of enticing and then locking in students for a longer, more complex, and therefore more expensive program. It's a win-win situation for student and school as long as the arrangements are clear to all parties.

Another factor to consider in building your course of study is the ability to transfer courses or larger program segments from one institution to another. Bear in mind that not all schools will allow you to transfer all of your credits into their program. Often there are ceilings—six credits or two courses are typical at the graduate level. For undergraduates the allowances are more liberal and can be as much as 75 percent of a bachelor's degree program. As in all other areas of life, though, exceptions and flexible approaches may be possible, so it pays to speak to academic advisors and to ask questions about anything that is not to your liking. In our new era of student-focused education, the student, as the consumer, has greater leverage than ever before. As online choices continue to expand, institutions are competing with each other in many dimensions of service.

Accreditation

In the United States, higher education institutions participate in a system of voluntary peer accreditation as a means of establishing quality. Criteria are evaluated by accreditation teams composed of individuals selected from peer institutions. Accreditation is re-evaluated, generally on a five-year cycle, so no institutions are automatically reaccredited without going through the lengthy, detailed, and demanding accreditation process. The benefit of this system is that students (as well as those who may be paying students' tuition) are assured of quality in curriculum, staffing, facilities, and support systems, as well as compliance with various state and federal regulations such as equal opportunity, access for the disabled, health, and safety.

Accreditation in the United States is organized by the Council for Higher Education Accreditation (CHEA), which can be found on the Web at www.chea.org. CHEA is a nonprofit organization of colleges and universities that serves as the national advocate for voluntary self-regulation through accreditation. CHEA recognizes these six regional accrediting organizations:

Middle States Association of Colleges and Schools (MSA)
www.msache.org

Northwest Association of Schools and Colleges (NASC)
www.cocnasc.org

North Central Association of Colleges and Schools (NCA)
www.ncacihe.org

New England Association of Schools and Colleges (NEASC)
www.neasc.org

Southern Association of Colleges and Schools (SACS)
www.sacscoc.org

Western Association of Schools and Colleges (WASC)
www.wascweb.org

Being accredited means that a school's instruction, courses, degrees, and certificates will be recognized nationally and internationally and are potentially transferable from one school to another.

Institutions Outside the United States

Global recognition of an institution outside the United States is established through a set of guidelines based on generally accepted accrediting principles. These principles are listed in the Commonwealth Universities Yearbook (www.acu.ac.uk). An additional source is the International Handbook of Universities (IHU), published by the United Nations Educational, Scientific, and Cultural Organization (UNESCO), which can be found on the Web at www.unesco.org.

Proprietary and Career Schools

Not all institutions are accredited by these regional associations. This is especially true within the proprietary, or for-profit, sector of education, which includes a large number of career colleges and trade schools. This has always been a dynamic sector of educational entrepreneurship. Often these schools are state-regulated or may be members of their own professional associations, such as the Career College Association (www.career.org) or the Association of Proprietary Colleges in New York (www.apc-colleges.org). This is not the same as being accredited by the recognized accrediting bodies mentioned earlier, whose criteria are based on the goals of traditional colleges and universities. Proprietary colleges tend to be highly specialized and would not generally fit the model of traditional schools.

High-quality proprietary schools exist. They have long been a part of the higher education landscape, often filling niches that others ignore or avoid. Because these schools specialize in occupation-oriented curricula, their faculty are generally drawn directly from the field. What the instructors may lack in traditional credentials, they make up in practical experience. Also, the close relationships these schools may have with an industry can be an asset in job or internship placement.

Distance learning programs that focus on specialized instruction, such as training to become a master chef or a computer technician, as one criterion (which you don't necessarily have to meet) to determine whether you'll be able to successfully complete their courses may ask whether you have already shown accomplishment in a program recognized by the Distance Education and Training Council (DETC). For more than 75 years, the DETC (formerly the National Home Study Council) has been the standard-setting agency for distance education institutions. The Council has progressively raised its standards. Its accrediting program employs procedures similar to those of other nationally recognized educational accrediting associations.

Generally, institutions accredited by DETC are not regionally accredited. The American Council on Education (www.acenet.edu) reviews courses from DETC member institutions and makes course credit recommendations on a course-by-course basis. The credit recommendations appear annually in *The National Guide to Educational Credit for Training Programs*. There are more than 3,000 colleges and universities in the United States, and the decision to accept transfer credits from DETC-accredited institutions is made individually by each institution.

In assessing the quality of proprietary nonaccredited institutions, it is important to collect as much information as possible. Even if it's not required, an on-site visit gives you a chance to look around and meet with students, faculty, and administrators. Information on the school's industry ties, faculty credentials, and success of graduates is also important. In the absence of traditional accreditation, you should make a particular effort to find out whether the school's level of instruction meets industry standards. Without this knowledge, it will be difficult to make an intelligent choice.

Diploma Mills

Beyond the career colleges with well-established facilities and reputations, there is another class of institutions derogatively referred to as "diploma mills." Even lacking academic accreditation, these schools may have obtained, in some instances, a license to conduct business within a state. Their degrees are bogus, literally not worth the paper on which they're printed. In some advertisements they may make the claim that "you can earn a bachelor's in a week"—slightly longer for a master's and doctorate. These specious credentials will not pass muster in the workplace or in any other situation where colleagues and supervisors have a modicum of knowledge concerning academic quality. It is important to remember that institutional reputation *is* a valuable sign of quality. Your degree is only as good as the institution offering it. If you're unsure about a school's merit, contact recent graduates using names and addresses provided by the school's alumni office. After all, it is your money and time. As with any major purchase, it is wise to do as much up-front research as possible.

Accreditation Pending

In some cases, you may encounter institutions whose accreditation is "pending." This means that they have applied for accreditation and their credentials are in the process of being reviewed, which can take several years. While in some cases this claim may be legitimate, the only way to reasonably assess their status is to check with the appropriate regional association. The college should provide follow-up information willingly and should readily share further details on the status of its application. Schools that waffle or obfuscate should be avoided. In higher education, accreditation is the essential coin of the realm. Some degree-granting proprietary schools are regionally accredited by one of the six associations mentioned earlier in this section, and these schools are very clear in stating their credentials. Degrees from such institutions are as worthy of consideration as those offered by traditional public and private institutions.

Online Institutions

Within the past few years, an entirely new category of higher education institution has emerged: those specializing in online education. This may be an outgrowth of a school's existing commitment to earlier forms of distance education, or it may be a new institution with no track record. The earlier caveats concerning accreditation and reputation apply. State-of-the-art technology in itself is an insufficient criterion on which to base your decision.

Special Issues for Programs from a Distance

When choosing a distance learning program, you need to look at many of the traditional criteria, including the nature and type of program, the quality, and its fit with your personal and professional goals. You should also investigate important personal criteria, such as its convenience, the ability to control your own study schedule, and the time to degree completion. When you have narrowed your choices, you should then review the important issues specific to distance learning programs.

Expertise in Serving Students from a Distance

Although online and asynchronous education have made distance learning available at many respected schools, you should pay specific attention to the institution's track record in serving students away from campus. Assess the strength of both the academic and student support systems by asking questions about academic advising, consultations with faculty, and whether the help desk is available 24 hours a day, 7 days a week.

A Robust Academic Environment

A quality program should operate in an academic environment that provides you with easy access to the tools of learning: the faculty, a bookstore, and a library. Faculty may be asked to sign on two or more times a week—perhaps even daily. Easy electronic access can give you the chance to interact with faculty even more than you would in a traditional classroom. You should find out whether faculty members are easily available through online office hours, telephone, or fax, and whether you can meet with them in person—if your location permits and that is your preference.

You also should investigate whether the books will be available through an online outlet. Some programs may direct you to their own electronic bookstores or to one of the online mega-bookstores, such as Amazon.com or Barnes & Noble (www.bn.com).

Students should also have easy access to library resources. While a local university, workplace, or community library may meet your basic needs for supplemental resources, you should also have access to a library that offers additional research facilities and the privilege of checking out books. Often individual institutions will belong to a library consortium in which a number of schools across the country pool their resources, thereby expanding users' choices. Students may request these materials through interlibrary loan.

Student Support Services

The resources that engage you in learning are critical, but you will also want to investigate what student services the institution provides. In addition to knowing how to access the main programs, you should have a place to get any additional questions answered. What will happen, for example, if everything doesn't go as expected? Find out whom you will contact. You should have access to academic support processes such as registration and getting grade reports and transcripts. This may be done online or via telephone. You may also wish to investigate whether there are easy ways for you to contact other students from a distance if you choose to do so.

Technical Support

Having access to technical help is important for any online program. Technical problems seem to occur most often at startup, so you may wish to find out beforehand whether you'll get e-mail responses or be able to get a person on the telephone. Some institutions offer a service around the clock seven days a week, but such systems may rely heavily on e-mail solutions. Other institutions offer responses in one or two days.

Campus Residency

Will your program of study be entirely from a distance? Some programs designed for adult students use a combination of site-based and distance methodologies. In these settings, a site-based residency may be required. The residency may be as short as one or two days, may require week-long stays at selected intervals, or may be as long as several weeks. The face-to-face component fulfills the traditional value of helping people connect personally and operate in a classroom setting. Check to see that these residencies can be fit to your personal schedule.

Media Options

Earlier in this chapter we mentioned a number of different distance learning technologies. To get a handle on what your learning environment will be like, you should ask what combination of media will be used. Will you use just print? Video? Online computer technology? Or will it be a mix of media and methodologies?

Faculty

More important than the combination of media is the role of the faculty in assisting students to complete the course. Distance education courses are designed to allow students to learn on their own. Faculty are there to act as mentors and are assigned to specific courses based on their academic expertise, current teaching experience, and commitment to students taking courses through distance education. The faculty member's role changes from traditional classroom instructor to a mentor who determines the student's academic progress through written assignments and proctored examinations. You need to determine whether the faculty are prepared and trained to help you learn from a distance. They should have the appropriate academic credentials and degrees from accredited institutions.

Student Contact

It's equally important to determine what sort of interaction you will have with other students. Just as colleagues can help you learn in a traditional class, they can be instrumental in courses from a distance. You should ask how you will relate to other students and whether you will be asked to work with them in your distance learning program.

Prospective distance education students need to evaluate many aspects of an institution's program carefully before reaching a final decision. If it's possible, a good strategy may be to begin by taking a single course at the school without first matriculating for a degree. Then you can decide whether distance learning and the institution are right for you.

Chapter Four

Admissions

With nearly 80 percent of publicly supported institutions offering some kind of distance learning, the opportunities for students are enormous. With so many choices, the prospect of selecting and getting admitted to an institution can be daunting. Our goal in this chapter is to demystify the system by walking you through the key points of the admissions process, from application to acceptance. It's important to understand that although the programs are offered through alternate methods, the institution's review of an applicant for the off-campus program and the steps the candidate takes to apply will, in many cases, echo traditional admissions processes. We focus on the common elements of admissions. Differences between graduate and undergraduate admissions criteria and issues will be identified when appropriate.

Choose a Program

Our first piece of advice is simple: Start at the end. Determine everything you must do to complete your degree program requirements and how long it will take you—*then* go back and work on admissions.

Start by choosing a program that fits your personal and professional goals as well as your lifestyle needs. If you haven't yet taken this step, please review the institution listings and profiles in this book. When you find programs of interest to you, gather their Web-based and printed information for review, use these materials to help in assembling your questions, and get your answers from the institutions you're considering. Your goal is to determine how well the described programs meet your learning objectives and timeline for completion.

Check the Mechanics

When you are close to a decision, check out the components of the application.

1. **Check the due date.**

   Find out when your application is due.

2. **Know all the required pieces of the application.**

   You may need to complete several different sections, including essay, letters of recommendation, and demographic information. If you need standardized examination scores, make sure you take the tests far enough in advance of the application deadline.

3. **Choose references, and give them enough time to do a good job.**

   It is common for applications to request references from people who can comment on your academic and personal preparedness for a degree program. Choose people who will be thoughtful and honest. Make sure you give the people you ask enough time to do a good job.

4. **Have your transcripts and test scores sent to the admissions committee.**

   If you are seeking admission to a graduate degree program, you will have to ask your undergraduate school or schools to send an official transcript. If you are a recent high school graduate, you may need to send your high school transcripts.

5. **Write your essay thoughtfully.**

   Undergraduates can get a great deal of advice about how to write personal essays at www.review.com. In the essay, your goal is to distinguish yourself from the many other applicants. Graduate essays are typically more clearly focused on your fit with the particular program to which you are applying.

6. **Fill out the application form.**

   Find out if the application form can be completed online or if you must fill out a paper copy. If no online form is available, find out if you can fax the completed application or if it must be mailed.

7. **Pay by check or credit card.**

   If you need to send a check, allow enough time to meet any deadlines.

Your application establishes your academic profile. The application process allows you to describe your academic achievement and helps the admissions committee judge your fit with the program to which you are applying. Typically, the admissions process involves several considerations.

Understand How You'll Be Assessed

College and university applications—at both the graduate and undergraduate levels—provide you with a vehicle for demonstrating your preparedness for the program you seek to enter. The process probes your academic and personal readiness for completing a degree. Different programs and institutions request different information, and they may weigh the parts differently.

Your Academic Background

The academic background is requested and shown in a number of ways, but will most likely always include your prior schooling, grade point average (GPA), and ability to read and write English effectively. A qualitative review may include an evaluation of the quality of your writing on the application, an examination of your letters of recommendation, a review of your academic record and GPA, and a assessment of your relative work experience and potential for success.

Those who are not native speakers of English may need to demonstrate their proficiency in English through the Test of English as a Foreign Language (TOEFL).

The TOEFL evaluates the English proficiency of individuals whose native language is not English. Most people who take the TOEFL are planning to study at colleges and universities in the United States and Canada. TOEFL is also used by institutions in other countries where English is the language of instruction. In addition, many government agencies, scholarship programs, and licensing/certification agencies use TOEFL scores to evaluate English proficiency. TOEFL is administered under the direction of the Educational Testing Service (ETS). Since 1998, the TOEFL program has been gradually shifting from a traditional paper-and-pencil test to a computer-based test. In North America, many parts of Europe, and parts of Africa, the computer-based test replaced the paper test in 1998. More information may be obtained from www.toefl.org. Acceptable scores are set by institutions, and they are usually higher for graduate schools than for undergraduate schools.

Writing Assessment

Students are expected to write often and fluently when completing degree programs through distance education. The admissions committee is likely to use institutional writing standards in reviewing any writing required on the application. Sometimes this assessment is done in conjunction with a test score from the Graduate Record Examination (GRE) for graduate degree programs.

Because online and other distance education methodologies are so writing-intensive, many programs expect the student to complete a writing exercise online. This enables the institution to determine how effective a student is in understanding a question and its context as well as how comprehensive a response the student can provide in a specified time period. Institutions often ask students to describe how they expect to grow professionally by completing a graduate degree.

Letters of Reference

These letters attest to your ability to do well in the degree program. Ask for references from people who can speak of your academic and professional capabilities, with an emphasis on the experiences and characteristics that will help you succeed in completing your degree.

Departmental Proficiency Examination

Students may find that some institutions have a departmental proficiency exam in a particular subject or content area, taken either at the time of admission to a program or shortly after gaining admission. Institutions now focus on the growth and development of the student from initial admission to the program through graduation, and the departmental proficiency examination is one benchmark of where the student began.

Technical Proficiency

Online and distance programs require that you have the technological proficiency to flourish in an online environment. This requirement is most often stated in terms of required equipment. Programs that make extensive use of e-mail and Internet sites will expect students to have computer and Internet access. Sometimes, the program will ask you to communicate via e-mail or compose something online to test your initial computer preparation.

Undergraduate Requirements

Recent high school graduates—those who are 18 to 22 years old and are beginning their college programs—will need high school transcripts and, in some cases, must complete a standard entrance examination. The high school GPA and class standing are often critical components of the application for recent graduates. For older students, admissions committees often place less emphasis on grades and more on relevant experience in the workplace or success as a volunteer.

If you choose a traditional, on-site undergraduate institution that also offers distance learning courses, you may be able to register for individual distance courses, if not an entire degree or certificate program. Criteria vary. In some cases, any student admitted under the traditional criteria is eligible to enroll in a distance learning program. In others, students are required to complete on-campus work first. Check to see whether your institution offers departmental examinations that may fulfill these prerequisite requirements.

Some institutions limit distance learning to students who have earned some college credits—as much as 30 semester hours. The purpose of these policies is to ensure that students have succeeded in a traditional college classroom and have demonstrated the discipline and ability to meet academic standards required for independent and distance learning.

Conditional Admission

Some institutions will grant students conditional admission. Students are reconsidered for full and unqualified admission after they complete a limited number of initial courses and reapply for matriculated status. The purpose of conditional admission is for an institution to determine the ability of the student to complete college-level work before granting full-time status.

The SAT

Undergraduate candidates required to take standarized tests before applying to college most often take the SAT. They receive a verbal and a math score, each ranging from 200 to 800, which supposedly help predict the student's academic performance in college. In addition, some colleges require the SAT II examinations, a series of subject tests sometimes used for admissions or placement. SAT IIs are offered in English, history, mathematics, science, and languages.

The ACT

The ACT (American College Testing) Program tests students in English, mathematics, reading, and science reasoning. The ACT is now accepted by virtually all colleges and universities in the United States, including all of the Ivy League schools. The ACT is curriculum-based and is not an aptitude or IQ test; the questions on the ACT are directly related to what is taught in typical high school courses in English, mathematics, and science. Because of this, students are generally more comfortable with the ACT than they are with traditional aptitude tests.

The ACT includes 215 multiple-choice questions and takes approximately 3 hours and 30 minutes to complete with breaks. Actual testing time is 2 hours and 55 minutes. In the United States, the ACT is administered on five national test dates, one each in October, December, February, April, and June. In selected states, the ACT is also offered in late September. Information can be obtained at www.act.org/aap/faq/general.html.

Graduate Requirements

Once you have selected a program that meets your personal and professional goals, you must still consider whether you are prepared to address the required content in a degree program. While the specifics vary for adult students returning to graduate studies, a wide variety of graduate degrees do not require an undergraduate major in the same field. Master's degrees in supervision, management, liberal arts, or leadership, for example, may require at least three to five years of related work experience instead.

You may, however, find yourself facing additional academic prerequisites if you wish to study in an area different from your undergraduate major or if the program requires course work in specialized areas. A Master of Business Administration (MBA), for instance, may require an academic background in economics; an environmental science degree may require specific science prerequisites.

Where an undergraduate degree in the same field is expected as preparation for many graduate programs, applicants may often make up the prerequisites they do not have on a course-by-course basis. You may wish to begin as a nonmatriculated student, taking individual courses at the institution of your choice. Or you may be able to demonstrate your command of the required subjects through college-equivalency examinations.

One such test is the College-Level Examination Program (CLEP). The CLEP examinations are accepted by more than 2,800 accredited institutions of higher education. There are 5 general and 29 subject exams available through CLEP, giving applicants the opportunity to quickly fulfill prerequisites. For information on the CLEP, visit www.collegeboard.org/clep, or check out The Princeton Review's *Cracking the CLEP*, published annually.

Grade Point Average

Many graduate programs expect a grade point average of 3.0 (B) or better on a 4.0 scale. A 2.7 or higher is commonly accepted. The institution may review not only the overall GPA, but also the GPA for selected parts of undergraduate work, such as the last 60 semester hours (two years) of credit, or the GPA in the major. Applicants returning to college several years after obtaining a baccalaureate degree will find that less emphasis is placed on the undergraduate GPA and more is placed on experiences related to the desired field of study.

Professional Credentials

Professional programs, such as nursing, may require licenses such as the RN (Registered Nurse) or the LPN (Licensed Practical Nurse)—credentials that would be required regardless of the program delivery mode. Though professional study via distance learning is burgeoning in areas like engineering, nursing, and library science (we even know of one online JD program!), the greatest demand for distance learning remains that for nonprofessional graduate programs.

Graduate School Entrance Examinations

As with undergraduate programs, some institutions require a standardized examination as part of your application package. For graduate students, those examinations most commonly required are the GMAT, the GRE, the MAT, and departmental proficiency exams.

GMAT

The GMAT (Graduate Management Admission Test) is one measure of an applicant's ability to complete graduate work. Used in combination with undergraduate grades, the GMAT can help colleges determine an applicant's chance of success in an MBA program. The test measures general verbal, mathematical, and analytical writing skills that have been developed over a long period of time. The GMAT is given entirely in English. Scores range from 200 to 800, and many graduate programs expect scores to be well above 500. The GMAT is a computer-based exam that is offered year-round at test centers throughout the world. In 1999–2000 there were more than 200,000 test-takers and their scores were considered by more than 1,300 institutions. For more information visit www.gmac.com.

The GMAT is administered as follows:

Analytical Writing Assessment
Analysis of an Issue (30-minute testing period)
Analysis of an Argument (30-minute testing period)

Optional Break for 5 Minutes

GMAT Quantitative (75-minute testing period)
Problem Solving
Data Sufficiency

Optional Break for 5 Minutes

GMAT Verbal (75-minute testing period)
Reading Comprehension
Critical Reasoning
Sentence Correction

The GMAT is a standard exam for applicants pursuing an MBA and is generally not required for students interested in a Master of Science in Management (MSM) program, even though some colleges require applicants to take the GRE or Miller Analogies Test (see both below) regardless of their intended program of study. The MSM is intended for students who are employed in a management/supervisory position and desire a degree program that focuses on the practitioner side of management. It is geared toward people who will manage individuals in complex, dynamic organizations. It is structured for employed adults with professional responsibilities in management, technical, and administrative positions. While MBA programs typically focus on quantitative issue in management, MSM programs emphasize the human dynamics of management.

GRE: General and Subject Tests

The GRE General Test measures verbal, quantitative, and analytical skills that have been acquired over a long period of time and that are not related to any specific field of study. The test consists of three scored sections:

- Verbal: 30 minutes, 30 questions
- Quantitative: 45 minutes, 28 questions
- Analytical: 60 minutes, 35 questions

The verbal section measures the ability to analyze and evaluate written material and synthesize information obtained from it, analyze relationships among component parts of sentences, and recognize relationships between words and concepts. The quantitative section measures basic mathematical skills and understanding of elementary mathematical concepts, as well as the ability to reason quantitatively and solve problems in a quantitative setting. The analytical section measures the ability to understand structured sets of relationships, deduce new information from sets of relationships, analyze and evaluate arguments, identify central issues and hypotheses, draw sound inferences, and identify plausible causal explanations.

Because students have wide-ranging backgrounds, interests, and skills, the verbal section of the General Test uses questions from diverse areas of experience. The areas tested range from the activities of daily life to broad categories of academic interest such as the sciences, social studies, and the humanities. The quantitative section covers content areas usually studied in high school: arithmetic, algebra, geometry, and data analysis. Questions in the analytical section measure reasoning skills developed in virtually all fields of study.

The GRE Subject Tests are designed to help graduate school admissions committees and fellowship sponsors assess the qualifications of applicants in specific fields of study. The tests also provide students with an assessment of their own qualifications. Scores on the tests are designed to indicate the student's knowledge of the subject matter emphasized in many undergraduate programs. Because past achievement is usually a good indicator of future performance, the scores are helpful in predicting student success in graduate study. Since the tests are standardized, the scores permit comparison of students from institutions with different undergraduate programs. For some Subject Tests, subscores are provided in addition to the total score; these subscores indicate the strengths and weaknesses of an individual student's preparation, and they may help students plan their future studies. Subject Tests are currently available in 14 disciplines. Total testing time for each Subject Test is 2 hours and 50 minutes.

The GRE Writing Assessment is offered as a separate test, independent of the GRE General Test and GRE Subject Tests. It is available year-round at all ETS-authorized computer-based testing centers worldwide. Currently, graduate departments are evaluating whether to require applicants to take the test. Check with your prospective graduate schools for updates on whether this test is required. Further information can be obtained at www.gre.org.

MAT

The MAT (Miller Analogies Test) is a standardized test of verbal analogies used to assist graduate departments and schools in their admissions process. Students should check with the graduate departments of the schools in which they are interested to determine whether they require the MAT and what (if any) cutoff scores they use. The MAT consists of 100 analogies given in a 50-minute period. The test is given only at Controlled Test Centers (CTCs), typically located on college and university campuses throughout the United States. A detailed description of the test and testing procedures can be obtained at www.hbtpc.com/mat.

Chapter Five

Financing Your Education

Undergraduates

Shop, shop, shop—students need to be aware that the cost of completing an undergraduate degree will vary considerably between institutions. Private colleges will generally charge more than public colleges and universities. How much? Tuition and fees can vary from less than $50 per credit to more than $500 per credit. In-state residents will pay less than out-of-state residents at public colleges. Community college tuition will be less than baccalaureate tuition.

Shopping will be important because identical courses at several different types of institutions will have a broad range in price. Costs at many colleges will also vary by specific program of study and course delivery options. Many colleges are reviewing their tuition and fees to attract students to distance education programs. Therefore, for many distance programs, in-state/out-of-state differences are being eliminated and replaced with standard tuition to cover all students. Online course tuition may still have a higher overall cost, however, due to the round-the-clock support needed by students.

Graduates

Costs at the graduate level, as at the undergraduate level, will vary considerably between publicly supported institutions and private colleges and universities. Generally, out-of-state students can expect to spend $10,000 to $15,000 annually on tuition. Residents enrolling at their state institutions will encounter tuition below the $10,000 threshold. Graduate students need to be aware that, in some cases, additional fees are assessed for the required short residencies, access to library services, and academic advising.

Financial Aid

The current system of financial aid for undergraduate, graduate, and professional distance learning programs is far from perfect. The growth of distance education offerings has far outpaced the growth and development of government-backed student financial assistance.

A report published by the NCES released in December of 1999 reported a 34 percent increase in the number of higher education institutions offering course work via distance education from 1995 to 1998. Among the 34 percent of institutions that offered any distance education courses in 1995 to 1998, 25 percent offered degrees or certificates solely through distance education. A corresponding increase in government-backed financial aid for distance education, however, has yet to be witnessed.

College tuition rose an average of 6 percent per year in the last decade of the twentieth century—more than twice the rate of inflation. While distance education offers students the chance to save on expenses such as commuting and child care, be aware that it's not necessarily the cheaper option in the end. Some universities may charge "technological fees" to help cover the costs they incur in developing, implementing, and maintaining the technological infrastructure needed to deliver online programs. Overall, the NCES study mentioned above found that 57 percent of institutions are charging both comparable tuition and comparable fees for their distance education and on-campus courses.

Most distance learners are adults who work while attending college on a part-time basis and rely on a combination of their own savings, loans, and tuition reimbursement from employers or corporate sponsors. Not surprisingly, the number-one source of financial aid for adult learners is not government-backed student loans, but their own savings—or a combination of their savings and tuition reimbursement from company benefit plans.

Federal Government Aid—Undergraduate Level of Study

The federal government, through the U.S. Department of Education, has grant, scholarship, and student loan programs for undergraduate-level studies. However, these programs are definitely limited if the undergraduate degree or certificate is delivered entirely through distance learning. The reasons why government aid is not always available are addressed later in this chapter. Because not all aid programs are available to distance learners, we cannot stress enough the importance of contacting the financial aid office of the university of your choice. They will be able to verify that the distance learning program in which you are interested is eligible to participate in one or more federal aid programs. Colleges and universities may be approved to participate in the federal and state aid programs for on-campus degree programs and still have their distance learning degree programs excluded from this approval.

Government financial aid for undergraduates includes Federal Pell Grants, Direct and FFEL Stafford Loans, PLUS Loans (for parents of undergraduate students), and the campus-based programs that include the Federal Supplemental Educational Opportunity Grants, Federal Work-Study, and Perkins Loans.

For extensive information on the different types of government aid available, visit the Department of Education's online resource center at www.ed.gov.

The Department of Education also offers a free publication, *The Student Guide: Financial Aid for 2000–2001,* which explains government aid, types of student loans available, and how eligibility for government-backed loans is determined. You can download a copy of this free guide online at www.ed.gov/offices/OSFAP/Students; receive it in the mail by calling 800-433-3243; or write to the Federal Student Aid Information Center, PO Box 84, Washington, DC 20044 and request a copy.

On a positive note, Congress has recognized the potential of distance education to expand educational opportunities and has responded with several initiatives to consider the most effective way of providing financial aid to distance learners. Authorized under the amendments to the Higher Education of 1998 are the Learning Anytime Anywhere Partnerships (LAAP) and the Distance Education Demonstration Program. The LAAP project allowed the creation of Web-based programs to train financial aid administrators to manage the aid for distance education programs. The Demonstration Program allowed an initial 15 institutions or consortia of colleges and universities to offer government-backed financial aid for distance education programs. For more information on this project, you can visit the Department of Education's online resource center at www.ed.gov.

Federal Government Aid—Graduate Level of Study

Unlike those available for undergraduate-level studies, there are no government-sponsored direct grant, scholarship, or "free money" programs for graduate-level studies. For grad students, assistance is instead offered in the form of student loan programs. However, grad-level distance learning programs are even more likely to be exempt from student loans than the undergrad programs. Contact the financial aid office to determine whether the program you are interested in is eligible to participate in government student aid.

The federal government sponsors several loan programs to help graduate learners finance their education. The Federal Perkins Loan Program is a need-based, interest-subsidized loan that is available on an institutional basis to graduate and professional students. The graduate annual maximum in this program is $6,000, but most schools do not have adequate funding to award that much. *Never* refuse a Federal Perkins loan. Repayment begins nine months after the last day of study, and the rate is only 5 percent.

The Subsidized and Unsubsidized Federal Stafford Loans are another source of financial aid for many graduate or professional students. The annual loan limits are tied to the cost of attendance and individual eligibility, but may go as high as $18,500 a year. The interest rates on these loans are variable, but are currently capped at 8.25 percent. The Subsidized Stafford Loan is need-based, and for those who qualify, the loan does not accrue interest while the borrower is enrolled at least half time. The Unsubsidized Stafford Loan is not need-based, and the borrower is responsible for the interest that accrues while he or she is still in school. For both of these loans, repayment of principal does not start until six months from the last day of half-time attendance. For most graduate degree programs, six credits is considered half time.

The Taxpayer Relief Act of 1997 authorized a number of changes in the tax law that included the creation of the Hope Scholarship Credit and the Lifetime Learning Credit, as well as providing a deduction for student loan interest. Beginning January 1, 1998, taxpayers who have received loans in order to pay the cost of attending eligible educational institutions for themselves, their spouse, or their dependents generally may deduct interest they pay on these student loans. This includes interest paid on the Stafford and Perkins Loans for graduate students. For more information on this tax deduction, contact the Internal Revenue Service and request *Publication 970: Tax Benefits for Higher Education*, or download it at www.irs.gov/forms_pubs.

Federal Aid Eligibility Requirements

In order to be eligible for government-backed student financial aid, including loans, you must:

- Be a U.S. citizen or an eligible noncitizen. Those with alien registration cards, special asylum status, or temporary resident cards may not be eligible and need to speak to the financial aid office of the college they wish to attend.
- Attend a college approved for the government aid program. Not all universities or distance learning programs are eligible to participate in government loan programs.
- Be enrolled in a degree- or certificate-granting program. Individual courses taken outside a degree or certificate program are not covered.
- Be officially attending on at least a half-time status.
- Meet satisfactory academic progress standards. This generally means taking and passing a set number of courses each semester. Your university of choice will be able to provide additional information on this criterion.
- Demonstrate financial need (except for the Unsubsidized Stafford Loan). Financial need is determined by a standardized annual analysis of your income, assets, and liabilities versus the cost of the college you wish to attend. It is determined by the data you provide on the Free Application for Federal Student Aid (FAFSA) each year of your enrollment.
- Be in good standing with the government aid programs, with no defaults on previous loans or outstanding overdue payments in any other programs.
- Be registered with the selective service (if applicable).

The process for determining federal financial aid eligibility is the same for graduate and undergraduate aid. The level of your need will be officially calculated each year by the federal government's Department of Education, using the information you provide on the FAFSA. The FAFSA is a form that all learners must file each year so that colleges can determine the amount of their aid eligibility using a standard formula. Because application deadlines often apply to graduate or professional school aid, it is best to submit the forms as early as possible, even before you know whether you have been admitted. You can access and complete the FAFSA at the government aid resource center by visiting www.ed.gov/offices/OPE/express.html or www.fafsa.ed.gov. You can also obtain a paper copy directly from most financial aid offices or request a paper copy by calling 800-4-FED-AID.

When the FAFSA is submitted, each school or university you list on this form will receive an electronic report that has basically the same information as the paper Student Aid Report (SAR) you will receive in the mail. The FAFSA information you submitted about your annual income, number of dependents, assets and holdings, and liabilities will determine your level of aid eligibility. Another factor that may affect your eligibility includes the cost of attending the institution. This information will be used by the financial aid office at the university of your choice to calculate the different types of loans for which you may be eligible and the amounts of these loans.

We suggest you complete the FAFSA even if you think your income is too high to qualify you for federal student financial aid. Most state financial aid and private scholarship programs also use the data from the FAFSA/SAR to determine your eligibility for nonfederal aid such as state loans and private grants and scholarships.

State Government Aid

To supplement the federal government aid programs, individual states also administer their own financial aid programs. Supplemental loans or grant programs may be available for residents of certain states if they satisfy basic requirements of residency and academic program eligibility. Individual states offer various student incentive programs and most states offer the Robert C. Byrd Honors Scholarship Program, which distributes federal funds through the state financial aid process. Some states have a variety of adult aid programs. For example, New York State has special tuition assistance programs for part-time learners who attend college in state. It also supports a number of distance learning colleges and universities.

Since the aid available varies from state to state, the best thing to do is to check with the financial aid administrator at the college of your choice. The institution will send you financial aid information and application forms upon request and should be able to include a list of the agencies that administer aid programs. You can also access general information through the federal student aid website at www.ed.gov/offices/OSFAP/Students.

Remember that state aid is administered separately from federal student aid and that programs differ from state to state. Every state has a state office of student financial aid that administers the state aid programs. It would be wise to explore and investigate aid possibilities with the state agency or office to see whether you qualify for any special aid programs.

Why Government Aid Is Not Always Available

We again remind you that not all undergraduate or graduate distance learning programs are eligible to participate in the federal or state aid programs, even if their campus-based programs are eligible for aid. You must check with the financial aid office of the university of your choice to verify the availability of government assistance.

Government-sponsored aid programs have many requirements attached to them and were originally designed to be most beneficial to full-time students. The Federal Stafford Loan Program, for example, requires that the learner attend at least half time to be eligible. For most graduate programs, this means six credits per semester of study. Most adult learners work full time and study part time and may not meet this half-time requirement. Also, the full-time work income of most adult learners disqualifies them from all but the higher-interest, unsubsidized types of loans.

Some distance learning programs cannot participate in government-sponsored aid programs because these degree programs do not meet certain federal aid eligibility restrictions. In order to qualify to participate in government aid programs, universities are required to design degree programs that comply with a complex set of laws and regulations dealing with correspondence and distance learning. The one federal regulation that limits the eligibility of distance education students to receive government financial assistance is Section 600.7(1)(i) of the Department of Education's *Student Financial Aid Regulations through December 31, 1999,* which states simply that "institutions that offer more than 50 percent of their courses in correspondence/telecommunications format do not qualify as eligible institutions for purposes of federal student financial aid." In other words, if the majority of a school's courses aren't taught the old brick-and-mortar way, regardless of the quality of the courses themselves, that school doesn't have the opportunity to award federal financial aid.

The Distance Education Demonstration Program, which was authorized by the 1998 amendments to the Higher Education Act that governs all of these government student assistance programs, is clearly a step toward recognizing distance learning as an increasingly suitable option for students. This project recognizes that "distance education has great potential to broaden education opportunities universally, especially for working parents, students who live in rural areas, and students with disabilities that may limit their access to the traditional campus setting." The project was designed to test new ways of delivering and administering the federal aid program and has granted waivers on one or more of the statutory and regulatory requirements in its efforts to do so. The program, however, is still in its infancy and, as such, has very limited impact on the aid currently available to those in undergraduate and graduate distance learning programs. Again, check with the financial aid office of the universities in which you are interested.

Some universities will offer no organized aid to adult learners at all. They expect these students to fund their own education, and this policy has discouraged many potential students from pursuing these distance learning programs. Keep in mind, however, that government aid and loans are not the only option available. Most adult learners rely more heavily on the nongovernment aid alternatives that are available.

Corporate Tuition Benefit Information

Recent studies by the International Foundation of Employee Benefit Funds, as reported by the National University Continuing Education Council, show that more than 90 percent of American companies offer tuition reimbursement to their employees. Of these companies, 88 percent will pay for graduate-level studies, and 63 percent will pay for vocational or technical training. Yet less than 5 percent of the money earmarked for employee education in the United States is used each year. These statistics alone should encourage you to find out whether your company has an education benefit program and whether you are eligible.

Some companies may pay as much as 100 percent of university tuition, as long as the program is work-related. Many others will pay a maximum amount each calendar year, often up to $2,000. One way of approaching the issue with your employer is to argue that the investment in your knowledge is actually an investment in the knowledge base of the company. Never assume that your company has no such education benefits or that it will refuse to pay at least part of your tuition bill. If your employer cannot pay for the entire program, ask if the firm can pay for specific courses that are directly related to your work.

Most employers are more than willing to pay for continuing education that has the potential to increase employee productivity. Improvements in an employee's ability to design or use a better computer network, for example, are easily recognized as an improvement that is in the company's best interest. Also, many programs listed in this guide require work-based projects and case studies that may prove beneficial to the employer, and are therefore more likely to be covered by corporate tuition benefits.

Keep in mind, however, that recent changes in tax laws address qualifying education, as well as how to treat tuition benefits or reimbursements. The Internal Revenue Service has a comprehensive website that provides you with details on these changes at www.irs.gov. *Publication 508: Tax Benefits for Work-Related Education,* which is downloadable from this site, provides extensive information on how to treat reimbursements and what qualifies for tax-free educational assistance. You may also call 800-829-3676 to request a free copy of this publication. Whether your tuition benefits are tax-exempt or not, talk to your benefits manager as well as your tax accountant to determine your tax liability on graduate tuition payments made on your behalf.

Family Loans

Another often-overlooked option is family loans. In the summer of 2000, the average return on a bank-guaranteed certificate of deposit was 6 percent. If a bank will pay this percentage of interest for the use of your parents' money, offer them several percent more for the same privilege. You must, however, treat a loan from a relative just as you would one from the bank. At a minimum, the loan agreement should include written terms defining the amount loaned, the interest charged, the repayment schedule, and the total amount of payments.

If you need help figuring out loan repayment amounts and terms, consult an amortization handbook, which is readily available at your public library or local bank. It will provide you with a table of what your monthly payments will be for any amount you borrow for any length of time at any predetermined interest rate. Most spreadsheet programs such as Excel and QuatroPro also have amortization schedules that will let you plug in the interest rate and the principal (the initial amount you borrow) and provide you with the repayment amount based on the time schedule you choose.

Home Equity Loans

The equity in the home you own is still another asset you can use to leverage funds for your academic endeavor. Home equity loans usually carry lower interest rates than other types of commercial credit, such as credit card and personal loans. Call several lenders and ask to speak to a home equity loan officer. Lenders vary in what they offer, but most will loan up to 80 percent of the equity in your home at rates that are competitive with those of student loans. The interest is usually tax-deductible, and most homeowners easily qualify.

Education as a Business Deduction

Self-employed learners may be able to have the cost of education deducted as a business expense, much like office supplies. This is usually reported on income tax forms Schedules C, C-EZ, or F: Profit or Loss from Business. If you are employed by someone else, your educational expenses may also be deductible. They would be reported on Schedule A as itemized deductions.

Don't lose sight of the fact that not all education expenses are allowable deductions. Current qualifying education costs include education or training that is required by the employer or the law to keep present salary, status, or job and that maintains or improves skills needed in your present work. If the education is for purposes of meeting the minimum educational requirement of your present trade or business or if it is part of a program of study that can qualify you for a new trade or business, then the costs associated with it will not qualify as deductions.

For example, if you are working as a financial planner, you will not be allowed to deduct the education costs related to becoming a Web designer/Webmaster unless part of your job requires that you be able to build your own website to fulfill the financial planning of your clients. If you take courses that will allow you to have greater access to information on the Web and teach you how to use it to help with financial planning, the educational expenses related to those courses probably *would* be deductible.

Tax laws are complicated and ever-changing. It would be wise to check with your accountant or tax advisor and to contact the IRS for its latest publications before assuming that your educational expenses will be considered tax-deductible.

Pension Plan Borrowing

Some pension or retirement funds allow you to borrow from or against your pension or 401(k) assets. The interest rates vary, usually from 6 to 9 percent, and other limitations may apply, but this type of borrowing may still provide better rates than most commercial or personal loans. This is a loan that must be paid back, even if you own these 401(k) assets. Don't forget to take into account the tax-liability implications and the terms of repayment when considering this option.

A similar alternative is to borrow against life insurance or other investments. Consult your tax and investment advisor to determine what you can borrow from, the terms of repayment, and tax liability implications.

Military Aid—Active Duty Tuition Assistance

Military aid programs are just as complicated as any form of government aid. There are many rules for qualifying for military aid and even more rules for using that aid for distance learning. If you are on active duty, meet with your educational benefits advisor. Discuss the merits of using tuition assistance (which will pay up to 75 percent of the costs of tuition) versus using veteran educational benefits, which you may already have access to even if you are still on active duty. Get a complete orientation of your benefits package. Benefits can vary with branch of service, rank, dates of enlistment, and terms of active duty. Your educational benefits advisor can assist you in interpreting your benefits package regarding any distance program.

Your military educational advisor can also guide you to Servicemembers Opportunity Colleges (SOC). These colleges work with the military to maximize credits already earned through the American Council on Education (ACE) or other specialized military in-service training programs. Ask your advisor to provide you with a directory of all independent study or distance learning programs that are preapproved for military benefits under the Defense Activity for Non-Traditional Education Support (DANTES) program. Using a DANTES or SOC program may make your military tuition reimbursement process less cumbersome in the long run.

Military Aid—Veteran Educational Benefits

If you are a veteran of the U.S. armed forces, you may have educational benefits you could use to pay for distance learning programs. You can start by contacting your local Department of Veterans Affairs and speaking with an educational benefits officer (EBO). You can also call 888-442-4551 to be connected to the closest VA regional office. You can provide that office with basic information, including your Social Security number and the dates you served on active duty, and they will be able to check your service record to determine whether you have any education benefits available. The office will also be able to determine the amount of veteran educational entitlements, as well as the preset date at which they will expire. Keep in mind that because of this preset expiration date (usually 10 years after the date of separation), it would be advantageous for you to do this as soon as possible. Veteran educational benefits also exist for spouses and dependents of certain veterans.

You may also log on to the VA website at www.gibill.va.gov or contact the VA certification officer at your college or university. The certification officer will be able to tell you if your program of study is eligible for aid, as well as the terms under which each program is accepted by the Department of Veterans Affairs. Not all programs at a college will be approved for veteran tuition benefits payments, so you need to specify to the VA certification officer the program of study you wish to pursue.

Private Loans

The rate of tuition increases has created a need for financial aid that often cannot be met by the traditional federal- or state-sponsored aid programs. More and more universities have created and instituted their own private educational loans for working adult students, and may also create partnerships with independent lending institutions to provide accessible private educational loans.

The traditional lenders that participate in the federal loan programs have also created their own private educational loans in order to meet this need. Most of these private educational loans are patterned after the government loan programs' rates and repayment terms. They usually make loans based on creditworthiness of the applicant or the amount of debt vs. income. The one stipulation that most institutions require is that students maintain full-time status, typically 12 semester hours of credit at the undergraduate level. At the graduate level, students need to check with the institution in which they wish to enroll to determine what is considered full-time status. Other lenders design their private loan programs to behave more like lines of credit, with checks made payable to the university or college to ensure that they are used for educational costs only. Regardless of the lender or basis for the loan, always consider the repayment terms and costs of borrowing.

Tuition discounts are sometimes offered by colleges and universities to attract adults back to school. Spouse discounts, alumni discounts, and discounts for multiple-family-member enrollment are some examples of these tuition discount programs. Private colleges generally take the lead in offering tuition discounts. You should check with the admissions office of the college or university you plan to attend to determine whether tuition discounts are available.

Private Scholarships

Private scholarships award millions of dollars for college study every year. The key is to find these private scholarships in time to apply for them. While most of these private scholarships are targeted at high school seniors or promising students younger than 21, there are others that are aimed at specific interest groups or ethnic backgrounds. A good source of information is the website www.finaid.org. You provide information on your background, interests, hobbies, and educational goals, and the site will search for grants and scholarships that may be applicable to your situation. Unlike most other sites and services that provide the same information, this particular site, as of this printing, does not charge you for the service.

Private Scholarship Search Firms

This is a good opportunity to talk about private scholarship search firms. In our experience, these search firms may not be as helpful in finding scholarships for distance learning as they would be for traditional on-campus programs. You may very well be able to gather on your own the same information that they would send you in their "special report." There are more bogus scholarship search companies and financial aid search consultants than bogus mail-order colleges.

Once you find a scholarship that seems to meet your particular situation, contact the agency or organization that sponsors this scholarship to determine whether there are any restrictions or limitations with reference to distance learning.

Another resource for older adults on financing their education is the American Association of Retired Persons (AARP), whose website can be found at www.aarp.org. This site offers information on returning to college, including suggested reading materials, articles, etc. The Internet is a wonderful source of free information on financial aid. FastWeb (www.studentservices.com/fastweb) is a free, searchable database that archives listings and content information on more than 185,000 scholarship, loan, and gift aid programs.

Chapter Six

The Corporate Connection

Savvy Employees Can Learn While They Earn

Corporations are major players in both supporting and providing higher learning. Savvy employees can capitalize on the learning opportunities offered through tuition aid, on-the-job learning, and the formal education and training employers sponsor.

Tuition Aid

Tuition aid is an acknowledged and valued benefit of employment at many corporations. Through their own training programs—on-site and via distance technologies—corporations also build the knowledge and skills of their workforce. Many employers extend those educational programs even further through partnership and collaboration with higher education institutions. Sharp employees can benefit from their employers' interest in education—and build their own skills and knowledge.

Many employers create a learning environment by supporting their employees' advanced study at colleges and universities. *Fortune* magazine's "100 Best Companies to Work For" (Volume 141, No. 1, January 10, 2000) states, "The 100 Best also do their utmost to address their employees' intellectual needs. Some 53 offer on-site university courses, and 91 have tuition reimbursement, with 24 reimbursing more than $4,000 a year. One company offers up to $15,600 a year." To view the most current volume of the "100 Best Companies to Work For," visit www.fortune.com.

Tuition aid policies, like any other employee benefit, vary in what they cover, how much they pay for, and when they pay. Further, the legal environment affects whether tuition aid is treated as an employee benefit or as taxable income. While some generous employers pay 100 percent of tuition and fees, others cover tuition but not application fees or other student fees associated with campus life. Employers may also limit the amount paid based on the grades earned, using a payment scale keyed to the grade. They may choose to set a dollar limit for each employee based on the calendar or fiscal year. Employers also vary as to when they will pay the agreed-upon tuition. Some will pay tuition in advance and may deal directly with you, the employee. Others will forward a tuition voucher directly to the institution where you are enrolled, and all the fiscal transactions will occur between the employer and the educational institution. Others reimburse your costs after your course is completed, thus requiring you to fund the initial program costs.

Employers may set programmatic limits on what they will support. Most will support colleges and universities that are regionally accredited. Some will also support institutions with other specialized accreditation, such as the Distance Education and Training Council (www.detc.org) or recognition by the American Council on Education.

Legal issues may also affect corporate tuition aid policies. At times, the law defines tuition aid as a benefit free of tax implications only when the advanced education is job-related. Some employers then support only programs identified as job-related, a concept that is sometimes difficult to define. Accounting courses for an employee of the accounting department are clearly job-related, but the question of whether liberal arts courses are job-related is more ambiguous, and tuition reimbursement policies vary widely. In some legal environments, tuition aid is defined as additional income and is treated as taxable.

Despite the widespread availability of tuition aid plans, only about 5 percent of employees use tuition aid benefits each year. If you want to be one of the savvy employees who take advantage of this benefit, inquire at your human resources department to see whether your employer has a tuition aid program. If so, gather some basic information about what it pays and under what conditions.

Corporate-Sponsored Education and Training

Many corporations invest in their people—they offer formal company-sponsored education and instruction, provide on-the-job training, and partner with higher education institutions to offer specific programs. All of these ventures help create an environment that fosters learning, the key to productivity gains in the new economy. What employees know and are able to do can pay off for employers. A quick look at the website, materials, and journal published by the American Society of Training and Development (www.astd.org) highlights this new link. The ASTD emphasizes linking training to job performance, and terms such as *knowledge management* are gaining favor over formerly accepted terms such as *information systems*. Think about the difference in images. Information is just data; knowledge opens new vistas.

Corporate Universities

The Corporate University Xchange, Inc. (www.corpu.com), reports the following facts:

- More than 40 percent of Fortune 500 companies have corporate universities. They spend nearly $20 million, representing 2 percent of the average organization's payroll.

- Corporate universities have as their goal training courses with a demonstrated outcome. As such, partnerships with higher education institutions are a key strategy.
- By 2001, 60 percent of corporations are expected to use distance or computer-assisted instruction to achieve their goals.

The term *corporate university* refers to the area of a company or organization that focuses on training, education, and human capital development. In some cases, it may be an actual training/education center through which employees pass for orientation, specific training for their position, and ongoing professional development. A separate corporate university may be a site for colleges and universities to come to deliver classroom-based college degree programs, noncredit training courses, and tailored programs for the company on a contract basis. Employees might receive much of this training on-site, however.

Chapter Seven

The Student Perspective

Students today are entering, through distance education, into a new type of university. With the advent of affordable and accessible college courses offered over the Internet, today's student has more opportunities than ever to complete a course or a degree program without leaving home. No longer will the student need to focus on what Carol Twigg, former vice president of the University Consortium Educom (now Educause), refers to as "broadcast" education, where the professor broadcasts the curriculum, the student absorbs it, and then everyone moves on.

Student Services

When students enroll in a distance education program, a number of items are important in making the experience positive and meaningful. The checklist should include:

✓ **Access.** The student needs to be able to access all academic and support areas through e-mail, phone, or fax, and should be required to visit locations physically seldom or not at all. Students report that they are drawn to colleges with distance education programs that have few entrance requirements—at least eliminating those entrance requirements that are aimed at the traditional residential student.

✓ **Flexibility in Program Design.** The program should be flexible in enabling a student to utilize transfer credits; in obtaining college credit for successful outcomes on national examinations such as CLEP, DANTES, etc.; in having workplace training and education assessed for college credit; and in offering a specialization within a degree program designed to build on a student's educational objectives. Students prefer the opportunity to complete course work through a variety of distance education methodologies rather than relying on one method for the entire degree program, especially at the undergraduate level. Very few people would prefer to use only one method, such as the PC, to complete 40 courses online for a baccalaureate degree.

✓ **Academic Advisor.** An individual should be available to work with the student from start to finish, answer any questions that arise regarding the course or degree program in a timely manner, and serve as a positive influence during the process.

✓ **Financial Aid Assistance.** The student should have access to all applicable financial aid information regarding available programs and student eligibility, and should by assisted by financial aid staff in completing and processing required paperwork. The ability to finance one's education through loan, college scholarship, and grant programs as well as eligibility for federal, state, and private financial aid are all important to the student seeking financial assistance. Students must be given a clear understanding of what they are required to do if granted financial aid and have a source of information if any questions arise.

✓ **Registration Process.** There should be clear instructions regarding the registration process, with staff available to assist the student in completing this process quickly and easily from a distance. Registration methods that include online registration and toll-free numbers are more popular among students than on-site, arena-style registration.

✓ **Tuition and Fees.** Clearly defined tuition and fees, as well as any other expenses students will incur, are instrumental in allowing the students to determine the total annual cost of their education. Students need to be aware of hidden costs that many times are not reimbursed by employers that pay only tuition. There are many institutions that have dramatically increased fee areas while maintaining low annual tuition rates.

✓ **Library, Computer, and Other Support Structures.** The student needs to have the support structure necessary to complete the required course work, such as library access, Internet sites to obtain materials, and access to textbook providers via e-mail, phone, and fax. The student needs to be made aware of the exact computer specifications, both hardware and software, required for completion of the course work. A technical help desk should also be provided.

✓ **Sympathetic Faculty.** In most cases, students completing courses from a distance have professional and personal priorities that can get in front of their educational priorities. It is important, from a student standpoint, that faculty have experience mentoring students from a distance and realizing the full-time work responsibilities that many students have while engaged in such programs. Because of the demands on students, faculty may need to be flexible regarding assignment deadlines and requirements. Students are attracted to classes that allow them to utilize their work experience and apply it to the assignments they are asked to complete for a class.

Advice from Those Who Have Been There

Michael Cronin graduated from Empire State College with a Bachelor of Science in fire administration. Michael had a long career in the New York Fire Department and used this experience in pursuing a degree through distance education. He explains his motivation for pursuing and completing his degree:

Like many young people, I attended college when I graduated high school. However, I left school before graduating to start a career with the New York Fire Department. Advancement in rank was determined solely by highly competitive examinations. A college degree was not a requirement for promotion. During my career, I was promoted to the ranks of lieutenant, captain, battalion chief, deputy chief, deputy assistant chief, and assistant chief. Unlike most people who pursue a college degree to advance their careers, my career was already successful. Not having a degree left me with an unfulfilled feeling, though. I wanted a college degree not for what it might do for me professionally, but rather what it would do for my self-esteem.

External learning made it possible for me to finish my bachelor's degree. I enrolled at the Center for Distance Learning at Empire State College with 80 transfer credits, and over a period of several years earned a Bachelor of Science degree in fire administration. My mentors took a personal interest in my success. They were hard taskmasters who held me to a high standard of excellence, and I hold them both in high regard and deep affection.

My assignment before retirement from the fire department was chief of training. In collaboration with John Jay College, I had the New York Fire Department Training Academy designate a satellite campus where a Master of Science degree in protection management would be offered to members of the fire department. I enrolled in the program along with 25 firefighters of all ranks. Two years later, 21 of us received our Master of Science degrees. The program is ongoing, preparing the future leaders of the fire department to meet the challenges that face today's fire service effectively. The success of the program is an achievement of which I am most proud.

I am now president of Michael F. Cronin Associates, a fire consulting firm that provides expert witness testimony and litigation support to attorneys. This field of endeavor is neither uncompetitive nor uncrowded. While few people in the field share my experience, even fewer people match my formal education. It is my degrees that establish me as a credible person whose opinions should receive serious consideration. None of this would have been possible without the Empire State College's Center for Distance Learning.

Jason Bock completed his Bachelor of Arts degree in business administration in 1999 from The Union Institute's Center for Distance Learning, located in Cincinnati, Ohio. Jason describes his experience below:

I was not supposed to take 15 years to graduate from college. I began taking college courses when I was 15 at the University of Texas at Arlington. By 16, I was a full-time college student at St. Gregory's College in Shawnee, Oklahoma. Two years later, I graduated valedictorian with an associate's degree and a 4.0 grade point average. I received a full scholarship to complete my education at Our Lady of the Lake University in San Antonio. After my father died a year later, I bounced out to the University of Texas at San Antonio for several semesters. Finally, I got a full-time job and moved to Dallas.

With the support of an associate's degree, I was able to build a successful career in retail advertising. Unfortunately, it was difficult to take even part-time courses having a career with constant deadlines and requiring late nights. I did manage to grab a few more courses at Oklahoma State University before lack of funding gutted many of the evening and weekend courses in my degree program.

Three years ago, I accepted a senior advertising position with a small grocery retailer in Ohio. As part of my job package, I was offered support in completing my degree. Deadlines, late nights at work, and a lack of funds kept me out of the classroom for the first two years. In July of 1997, I realized that I needed to get serious about completing my degree. I had 131 credit hours . . . and no degree.

Initially, I investigated two nearby private universities and a public university. Both of the private universities had weekend college programs and some evening classes. Weekend classes were not much of a solution since I often worked or had activities with my family on the weekends. However, the majority of these classes were lower-level classes. Only a few upper-level classes were offered. It would take me four to five years to fill a degree plan at either of these schools. In addition, the cost was high. The public school didn't fare much better. While costs were lower, most of the upper-level classes were still offered infrequently at night, limiting my ability to earn a degree short of an additional four- to five-year span. Frustrated, I turned to the Internet. I had seen a banner advertisement on the World Wide Web for an online college. There are a variety of online baccalaureate programs. I was looking for a flexible business program at a school that would consider my prior coursework.

I chose The Union Institute (TUI). There were several important factors in my decision to choose TUI. First, Union was located in Ohio. I appreciated the fact that it was a nearby university. Union also included a face-to-face component. I appreciated the idea of meeting professors and other learners face to face, even for a weekend. The Union Institute also offered student-directed degree plans and course work, a reasonable residency requirement, and easy transfer of credit. These were all good reasons to select Union. However, one event sealed my decision to attend The Union Institute. At Union, the faculty is not insulated from students at all. On my first phone call to Union, I was put in direct contact with an advisor and faculty member for the Center for Distance Learning. Being able to talk directly with a member of the faculty made a huge impact on my decision.

One of the tremendous benefits of distance learning is the option of taking a full-time load—virtually impossible in the traditional setting with my job. It is difficult to get started with a distance learning course. Since there are no lectures, distance learning requires reading and writing well beyond a traditional college course. My first semester, I fell behind quickly in my studies and had to do some marathon weekends to get caught up.

To succeed, a distance learning student must be able to manage their time well. Managing time was critical. I did a lot of my course work late at night after my family was in bed, something impossible in a traditional environment. I also organized a lot of my courses around topics of interest to my business, allowing me to study and work during the day effectively. Each semester after my first, I made a schedule with projected completion dates for each assignment. I kept track of these target dates to ensure I wasn't falling too far behind. The system worked well and allowed me to take breaks from time to time. There wasn't a "typical day." I tend to cluster activities. So, I might not work on my schoolwork at all for a week (except for reading—I read constantly). The next week, I would work many hours completing assignments.

Distance learning is certainly not for everyone, but it can solve many problems that traditional course work cannot. Distance learning is self-driven learning. Someone who is typically self-motivated and able to figure things out on his or her own is an ideal candidate. While professors will gladly help and assist, they are not there to baby-sit. Distance learning was very challenging for me, where traditional college course work was relatively easy. Completing my degree in a challenging environment was much more rewarding. For a new student investigating distance learning, I would recommend spending a lot of time investigating the options. Make certain that you have good communication and friendship with at least one professor or your advisor. That will probably solve any problems you might have. If you are uncomfortable with writing a lot, spend a few weeks or months practicing before you begin.

Recently, Tina Greco, a New Jersey resident, received a Master of Science in management through Thomas Edison State College, located in Trenton, New Jersey. This program is aimed at mid-level managers who came into the management field without an undergraduate major in business. The program is offered almost entirely online. Tina outlines for us her motivation and experience in completing the graduate degree:

> Once I determined that a traditional classroom education was too disruptive to my lifestyle and that of my family, I began to explore distance education as an option. Obtaining a degree online afforded the option of completing assignments around the schedule of my commitments. Weekly assignments did not have to compete with my employers' expectations of me, the family dinner hour, or social commitments.
>
> There are many distance education programs to choose from, and it became important to list the factors that would determine a selection. I did not want my degree to be perceived as a correspondence degree without rigor or credibility. What was the point of obtaining a degree that was not respected? The yardstick that traditional institutions of higher education use to determine value is accreditation. The same is true for distance learning education programs. The primary question to ask is whether the institution delivering the education is accredited by a recognized accrediting body. In addition, one should ask whether the program of study has a discipline-specific accreditation. Answers to these questions addressed the issues of credibility, rigor, and respectability that I felt were crucial to the decision-making process.
>
> Once these questions were answered, the next issue was the choice of discipline and whether it truly was a program obtainable completely online via the Internet or a hybrid that required a "residency" of some short duration during the course of study. I knew that I wanted the vast majority of my study to be online and was not interested in weekend or monthly residencies. I also knew that I could not complete the degree over a long period of time—my family could only be patient so long. Therefore, I looked for a program that would let me earn a degree in less than three years. I also had concerns that I might feel disconnected from the process if I were too isolated. I was concerned that working alone on a laptop—in a distance learning environment—could somehow transverse the space/time continuum and create a cyber-learning classroom. By addressing these questions and making inquiries of several programs, I began to narrow the field of likely institutions.
>
> The next considerations were ranking and familiarity with delivering distance education. Many institutions were just beginning their distance learning education delivery systems and had few years of experience. I wanted a program that had worked out the "bugs," had a proven track record of accreditation, and was well established in the distance learning environment. In addition to program issues, I had concerns about student issues such as: How would I access a library? Where would I purchase my textbooks? Would I have technical support from the institution when it came to using my personal computer?

My exploration ended with the selection of Thomas Edison State College. *Forbes Magazine* had recently ranked it "one of the top 20 cyber-universities," and it had been delivering distance education since the early 1970s. It was fully accredited, had an established reputation of rigor and excellence, and offered a master's degree in the field of management that I could complete in two years or less. The College had an affiliation with the state library for borrowing and research privileges and a bookstore that delivered books to your doorstep.

Linda Brown Holt completed a Master of Arts in humanities through California State University at Dominguez Hills in 1993. Below, she describes her experiences with completing a degree, without campus attendance, through the use of correspondence study:

On several occasions in my thirties, I attempted to earn a graduate degree by commuting to a campus and taking classes. However, with a career, family responsibilities, and volunteer activities, I could not manage the long commutes and late hours. I knew distance education offered the solution I needed, but like many adults, I wanted to make sure the program I chose was of the highest quality and met my own academic, personal, and professional goals.

In the early 1990s, I was very happy to discover the Master of Arts in Humanities External Degree Program at California State University— Dominguez Hills (CSU-HUX). The CSU-HUX program was exactly what I was looking for: a well-rounded, academically impeccable program that allowed me to expand on my knowledge of the humanities while focusing in an area of special interest (in my case, philosophy). The program was flexible, but I was never coddled or spoon-fed education. In fact, I worked harder and had more direction and guidance from faculty than I did in some of my more traditional undergraduate classes many years before. At the end of each class, which followed the traditional college semester model, I had a sense of accomplishment and mastery. Several of the final papers I wrote for courses were subsequently published in a journal.

At the time, CSU-HUX offered what it termed "parallel instruction." While my professor was teaching graduate students in a classroom in California, I sat in my living room in New Jersey following a detailed syllabus, critical readings, and assigned texts. I was able to communicate frequently with my professor by phone or mail (today, it would be e-mail) and had numerous written assignments, which were always returned with instructive and sometimes motivational comments to help me stay on course. And because I chose a public university, the cost of my education was very affordable.

In about two and a half years of part-time study, I graduated with an MA from California State. The CSU-HUX program stimulated my mind, put me in touch with exciting faculty who challenged me and helped me think in new ways, and gave me an unmatched sense of achievement. Today, while continuing to work full time, I am also a doctoral student in a classroom-based program at Drew

University, one of the finest private liberal arts colleges in the Northeast. Using the knowledge I gained at CSU—Dominguez Hills and Drew, I am developing expertise that I can apply in a second career.

Clearly, there is a place for both distance and classroom-based education in our lives. Thanks to CSU-HUX, I have had the best of both of these wonderful worlds.

Students' course evaluations are becoming common for online teaching and learning. These evaluations are important in gaining student feedback on the success or obstacles encountered in completing a course. Listed below are selected student comments from evaluations received on a number of Internet courses offered by the State University of New York at Stony Brook. These comments have been grouped by specific topics to show student feedback on the various components incorporated into a distance learning experience.

Financial Considerations

"Online classes were the cheapest way to earn a degree." —*Frank L.*

"Less expensive than traditional courses." —*Sharon T.*

Students' Interaction with Faculty

Students surveyed regarding the faculty performance for the online experience responded as follows:

"Instructor very knowledgeable . . . shares a wealth of information." —*Henry V.*

"Instructor relates well to students, even though we were at a distance and never met face-to-face." —*Anna K.*

"Instructor good at focusing student's attention back to the main subject when online discussions go off of it." —*Mark W.*

"The instructor used current relevancies and was able to recommend and access Internet websites for new information. . . . The class was not restricted to textbooks only." —*Mary T.*

The Online Experience

In answer to the question, "If possible, would you take your entire degree online?" students told us the following:

"Absolutely. I would love to finish all courses online." —*David W.*

"The convenience is outstanding." —*Henry V.*

"Definitely. Fits my lifestyle best." —*Sue M.*

"I find it difficult to learn this way." —*Debbie L.*

"No. I don't want the machine to altogether replace the woman or man." —*Emily C.*

"I would take most courses online. When taking courses teaching hands-on skills, such as computer skills, I would prefer classroom courses." —*Philip S.*

"The flexibility is great for people who work at a full-time job." —*Sam G.*

"I love the freedom to log on and work on the course when the time is good for me." —*Dexter W.*

"It is really convenient to attend class at any hour—in my pajamas!" —*Mary T.*

"You obtain helpful feedback from other members of the class." —*Howard B.*

"Many students can give helpful suggestions they might not be comfortable giving in a face-to-face environment." —*Tameka N.*

"Since we were not face to face, there were fewer debates and arguments than if we were all in one room." —*James C.*

Chapter Eight

The Faculty

Faculty who are used to teaching face to face have tended to be skeptical of online teaching. This is partially because new waves of teaching technology, particularly the introduction of television and computers, have been greatly oversold in the past, resulting in unrealized expectations. The use of broadcast television led to large groups of students watching "canned" programs on a TV monitor. There was no opportunity for student-faculty interaction, and the production quality of these courses was often low, engendering the derogatory phrase "talking heads." The same was true of early versions of Computer-Based Teaching (CBT), which were based on the idea that the computer itself could serve as an expert teaching machine, without the intervention of a live faculty member. E-learning—using interactive Web-based and computer technology—has been unfairly saddled with the bad reputation of these prior experiments, which, unfortunately, still color many people's misunderstanding of modern distance education.

When judged on its own merits, online distance learning has gained esteem among experienced teachers. Consider the following features, which have contributed to the acceptance of electronic courses by hundreds of teaching faculty who have tried e-teaching:

- The intellectual model of the e-course is the electronic seminar, wherein relatively small groups of approximately 12 to 25 students interact with an instructor. With this low student/faculty ratio, the environment is quite intimate and personal. The electronic seminar is conducted in a nonsynchronous mode, allowing students to sign on and access the seminar over the course of a week or so. This helps busy, working students avoid the time constraint problems they would face with a "real time" exchange.

- E-classes require intense interaction between faculty and students—more than in many traditional face-to-face courses. Students are typically expected to log in and contribute three to five times each week. With this frequency of interaction, everyone gets to know one another very well. There are few opportunities for passivity.

- In the electronic classroom everyone must write. All assignments are typed, creating a permanent record of each person's contributions. This promotes careful, reflective submissions. Instructors can easily monitor student progress and communicate with those who need help or who have trouble keeping up. This is usually done privately by e-mail or phone.

- Because of the flexibility of the virtual classroom, punctuality is not a problem and students don't lose class time because of weather, traffic, or unforeseen scheduling conflicts, the bane of all working adults. Also, students who travel can log in from anywhere and therefore will not fall behind their classmates.

- In the electronic class, students interact with each other more than with the instructor. This promotes true peer-based discussion learning, a long-sought "holy grail" of higher education.

- Access to the World Wide Web places library and other research resources within reach of every desktop. Students can develop their ideas and carry out assignments using a host of sources that were previously inaccessible to distance learners.

For these reasons, e-learning has quickly earned numerous adherents among faculty, both nationally and internationally. The combination of the intellectual rigor of traditional education and the flexibility of cyberspace benefits both faculty and students and creates robust learning communities online. Students find that they learn more in this environment, adding to the satisfaction faculty experience when teaching electronic courses.

There are, however, some important caveats to this rosy picture of online learning. First, like the students, instructors must be fully trained and supported in the use of computer technology. They must be exposed to examples of "good practice" and mentored by colleagues with extensive prior experience in the electronic classroom. Successful e-teaching requires much more than simply placing one's lectures online; it mandates the careful rethinking of an entire course. All assignments must be reviewed and, if necessary, redesigned.

Dr. Edelson has taught several courses online. He has determined that for his classes to be successful, each element must be carefully spelled out in greater detail than in courses with conventional syllabi, where ambiguities could be "talked out" in class. He has also discovered that without the visual cues that are commonly taken for granted in the face-to-face classroom, he must pay greater attention to written comments and ask probing questions that require students to respond in greater detail. In the end, he found the results of teaching online very comparable to what students experienced in his face-to-face classes and was pleased at the high-quality learning environment. He also had to ensure that the campus bookstore would mail books to students and that all aspects of campus business could be done by students electronically without their having to visit the college personally.

The rapid growth of e-learning attests to its acceptance by students and faculty. Both groups have discovered that the many positive features of the electronic classroom outweigh the negative effects of not physically meeting as a class. As more powerful computers complement increasingly sophisticated software, things will only get better for those teaching and learning from a distance. Also, as technology and Internet costs drop, it is possible that additional barriers to learning will fall, further increasing access and opportunity for countless adults.

We have learned, after reviewing hundreds of cases, that good teaching and successful learning are independent of the medium of course delivery. Instead, they depend on the effort put forth by students and faculty. The success of online students in every walk of life shows that quality higher education is now literally at our fingertips. There is no reason why online students can't have the finest-quality higher education.

For more information on e-learning, consult the following resources:

Boaz, M., and Associates. *Teaching at a Distance: A Handbook for Instructors.* Mission Viejo, Calif.: League for Innovation in the Community College, 1999, www.league.org.

Cyrs, T., ed. *Teaching and Learning from a Distance: What It Takes to Effectively Design, Deliver, and Evaluate Programs.* New Directions for Teaching and Learning, no. 71. San Francisco: Jossey-Bass, 1997, www.josseybass.com.

Palloff, R., and K. Pratt. *Building Learning Communities in Cyberspace.* San Francisco: Jossey-Bass, 1999, www.josseybass.com.

Additionally, *The Chronicle of Higher Education* (www.chronicle.com) is a regular source of information about distance learning publications and conferences.

Chapter Nine

Some Final Thoughts

The number of online distance learning opportunities continues to grow. Students can now choose from an unprecedented range of new courses, certificates, and degrees. It's no exaggeration that anyone who uses e-mail and has access to the World Wide Web can consider taking a college course electronically. Consider these factors in making this important decision.

Your Learning Style

Learning from a distance requires discipline and commitment. Although the electronic classroom is a dynamic tool capable of engendering powerful feelings of identity and belonging, the experience is still a far cry from meeting in a classroom with fellow students. You must regularly set aside the time to do the work, which may require at least six to nine hours per week in addition to three to five hours of log-on time per week. Are you the kind of person who adheres to schedules? Do you need to be physically in the same place as other students and faculty? Will you do the work without anyone there to push and motivate you? Some students have difficulty adjusting to the anonymity of the virtual classroom and find the physical presence of other students, and especially faculty, essential. On the other hand, if you like to write and express your thoughts, online learning may be ideal for you.

Your Comfort with Technology

You don't have to be a computer whiz, but you do have to feel comfortable with technology and have access to the appropriate equipment. And even with the best equipment, things will still go wrong. When this happens, you need to get help. Are you patient and methodical enough to contact the appropriate resources? This could include the college help desk, your Internet provider, and even the company that manufactured your computer. You might even end up doing some troubleshooting yourself. Even though help is usually just a phone call away, it helps to be self-reliant and a little more panic-proof than the average person. If you are still unsure of your computer skills, don't worry; by the end of a single semester of online study you will have improved skills as well as the self-confidence that comes from meeting new challenges head-on.

The Support Level of Your Environment

Adult students with family and/or work responsibilities need to be able to juggle their workloads effectively in order to allow time for studying. A supportive family environment is essential. Families need to be flexible when Mom or Dad, husband or wife is on deadline for a term paper or studying for an important midterm. Adult students experience enough self-doubt; what they need from those around them are comfort and sometimes a little push in the right direction. Be sure to share your educational goals with the people you're closest to; you will need them throughout the process.

Your Time Frame

Remember the old phrase "Slow and steady wins the race"? It's definitely true when it comes to education. You might feel that you've already delayed your decision too long and are eager to make up for lost time. Well, hold on. Experience shows that even a single course is a heavy load for adult students who have been away from college for any length of time, and two courses is about the maximum for those who are working. Our 60 years of combined experience as adult educators has shown us that students who unrealistically overload on courses do not do as well as they could have with a lighter schedule. On the other hand, if you are on leave from work and have the rest of your life well in hand, you may be able to push the envelope with a third course. Just make sure to check your school's refund/cancellation policy in case you change your mind and scale back once the term has begun.

Going to school as an adult is fun. It is a chance to bring your maturity and hard-earned practical experience into a rigorous intellectual environment. An academic credential will also unlock doors for you as you continue to pursue a career. The Internet provides opportunities and choices unheard-of as recently as a decade ago. It makes sense to investigate distance learning as a possible learning option. This year approximately 60,000 electronic college courses will be scheduled in the United States alone. With a little searching, there's an excellent chance you'll find a program that's ideal for you. Best of luck as you begin (or continue) your journey toward a degree or certificate. Believe us when we say that this is one of the best investments you can make in your future.

Distance Learning Survey—Undergraduate Programs

American Military University

Operations
9104-P Manassas Drive
Manassas Park, VA 20111
Contact: James P. Peter, Chancellor
Department e-mail: jherhusky@amunet.edu
School Web address: www.amunet.edu
Institutional accreditation: Distance Education and
    Training Council

Subjects Offered

Military management, intelligence studies, criminal justice,
    military history, management, marketing, general studies

Admissions Requirements

Is a minimum high school GPA required? Yes
Is provisional admission available? Yes
Is an admissions interview required? No
Can pre-requisite course work be waived? Yes
Are international students eligible to apply? Yes
Is the TOEFL required for international students? Yes
What is the minimum TOEFL score required? 520

Program Delivery

Hardware requirements: Ability to connect with Internet
Software requirements: Internet Explorer (or other
    browser)
Is the library accessible to students? Yes
Are computers accessible to students? Yes

On-Campus Requirements

Is an on-campus component required? No

Tuition & Fees

In-state tuition per credit: $250
Out-of-state tuition per credit: $250
Average yearly cost of books: $50

Financial Aid

Is financial aid available to full-time students? Yes
Is financial aid available to part-time students? Yes
Are academic scholarships available? Yes
Assistance programs available to students: Veterans'
    assistance

American River College

Learning Resources
4700 College Oak Drive
Sacramento, CA 95481
Contact: Henry Burnett, Dean, Learning Resources
Department e-mail: burneth@arc.losrios.cc.ca.us
Department Web address: www.arc.losrios.cc.ca.us/
    learnres/distance.html
School Web address: www.arc.losrios.cc.ca.us
Institutional accreditation: Accrediting Commission for
    Community and Junior Colleges of the Western
    Association of Schools and Colleges

Subjects Offered

Biology, business, computer information science, English,
    health education, interdisciplinary studies, library,
    management, marketing

Admissions Requirements

Is a minimum high school GPA required? No
Is provisional admission available? Yes
Can pre-requisite course work be waived? Yes
Are international students eligible to apply? Yes
Is the TOEFL required for international students? Yes
What is the minimum TOEFL score required? 500

Program Delivery

Primary method of program delivery: Web
Two-way interactive video: No
Two-way audio, one-way video: No
One-way live video: No
One-way pre-recorded video: Yes
Is the library accessible to students? Yes
Are computers accessible to students? Yes

Remote Sites

Other branches of the institution: No
Other college campuses: No
Students' homes: Yes
Work sites: No
Libraries: Yes
Elementary/Secondary schools: No
Community-based organizations: No
Correctional institutions: No

On-Campus Requirements

Is an on-campus component required? Yes
On-campus program orientation: Yes
On-campus exams: Yes

Tuition & Fees

In-state tuition per credit: $11
Out-of-state tuition per credit: $134

Financial Aid

Is financial aid available to full-time students? Yes
Are academic scholarships available? Yes
Assistance programs available to students: Federal Stafford Loan, Federal Pell Grant, Federal Work-Study Program, in-state student aid programs, veterans' assistance

Andrew Jackson University

School of Undergraduate Studies
10 Old Montgomery Highway
Birmingham, AL 35209
Contact: James Lee Smith, Dean
Department e-mail: info@aju.edu
School Web address: www.aju.edu
Institutional accreditation: Distance Education and Training Council

Subjects Offered

General studies, business, communication, criminal justice

Admissions Requirements

Is a minimum high school GPA required? No
Is provisional admission available? No
Is an admissions interview required? No
Can pre-requisite course work be waived? No
Are international students eligible to apply? Yes
Is the TOEFL required for international students? Yes
What is the minimum TOEFL score required? 550

Program Delivery

Primary method of program delivery: Text
Two-way interactive video: No
Two-way audio, one-way video: No
One-way live video: No
One-way pre-recorded video: No
Audio graphics: No
Audio: No
Software requirements: Internet access, Microsoft Word or WordPerfect
Is the library accessible to students? No

Remote Sites

Other branches of the institution: No
Other college campuses: No
Students' homes: Yes
Work sites: No
Libraries: No

Elementary/Secondary schools: No
Community-based organizations: No
Correctional institutions: No

On-Campus Requirements

Is an on-campus component required? No

Tuition & Fees

In-state tuition per credit: $112
Out-of-state tuition per credit: $112
Application fee: $75
Can it be waived? No
Average yearly cost of books: $1,000

Financial Aid

Is financial aid available to full-time students? No
Is financial aid available to part-time students? No
Are academic scholarships available? No
Assistance programs available to students: Veterans' assistance

Anne Arundel Community College

Distance Learning Center
101 College Parkway
Arundel, MD 21012
Contact: Paul Warner, Director, Learning Technologies and Distance Learning
Department e-mail: dlcenter@mail.aacc.cc.md.us
Department Web address: www.aacc.cc.md.us/diseduc
School Web address: www.aacc.cc.md.us
Institutional accreditation: Middle States Association of Colleges and Schools

Subjects Offered

Biology, business, computer technologies, chemistry, communication arts technology, communications, economics, English, geography, health, history, paralegal studies, mathematics, physical science, political science, psychology, sociology, women's studies

Admissions Requirements

Is a minimum high school GPA required? No
Is provisional admission available? No
Is an admissions interview required? No
Can pre-requisite course work be waived? Yes
Are international students eligible to apply? Yes
Is the TOEFL required for international students? Yes
What is the minimum TOEFL score required? 550

Program Delivery

Two-way interactive video: Yes
Two-way audio, one-way video: Yes
One-way live video: Yes
One-way pre-recorded video: Yes
Audio: Yes
Hardware requirements: Macintosh with OS 8 or higher, or personal computer with Windows 95 or higher
Software requirements: Access to the Internet, an electronic mail address, Netscape 4.0 or higher, or Internet Explorer 4.0 or higher
Is the library accessible to students? Yes
Are computers accessible to students? Yes

Remote Sites

Other branches of the institution: Yes
Other college campuses: Yes
Students' homes: Yes
Work sites: Yes
Libraries: Yes

On-Campus Requirements

Is an on-campus component required? Yes
On-campus exams: Yes

Tuition & Fees

In-state tuition per credit: $60
Out-of-state tuition per credit: $204
Average yearly cost of books: $800

Financial Aid

Is financial aid available to full-time students? Yes
Is financial aid available to part-time students? Yes
Are academic scholarships available? Yes
Assistance programs available to students: Federal Stafford Loan, Federal Plus Loan, Federal Pell Grant, Federal Work-Study Program, in-state student aid programs, veterans' assistance

Arkansas Tech University

Office of Academic Affairs
Virtual Learning Center
Office of Academic Affairs
Russellville, AR 72801
Contact: John Gale, Director of the Virtual Learning Center
Department e-mail: gabriel.esteban@mail.atu.edu
Department Web address: www.vlc.atu.edu
School Web address: www.atu.edu
Institutional accreditation: North Central Association of Colleges and Schools

Subjects Offered

Biology, computer science, emergency management, English, parks, recreation and hospital administration, history, journalism, mathematics, management, music, physical science, political science, psychology, sociology, wellness

Admissions Requirements

Is a minimum high school GPA required? Yes
Is provisional admission available? Yes
Is an admissions interview required? No
Can pre-requisite course work be waived? No
Are international students eligible to apply? Yes
Is the TOEFL required for international students? Yes
What is the minimum TOEFL score required? 500

Program Delivery

Primary method of program delivery: Web
Two-way interactive video: Yes
Two-way audio, one-way video: No
One-way live video: No
One-way pre-recorded video: Yes
Audio graphics: No
Audio: No
Hardware requirements: IBM PC compatible 486-66 or Macintosh 68040
Software requirements: Netscape or Internet Explorer and Microsoft Word or WordPerfect
Is the library accessible to students? Yes
Are computers accessible to students? Yes

Remote Sites

Other branches of the institution: No
Other college campuses: Yes
Students' homes: No
Work sites: No
Libraries: No
Elementary/Secondary schools: Yes
Community-based organizations: Yes
Correctional institutions: No

Tuition & Fees

In-state tuition per credit: $114
Out-of-state tuition per credit: $228
Average yearly cost of books: $400

Financial Aid

Is financial aid available to full-time students? Yes
Is financial aid available to part-time students? Yes
Are academic scholarships available? Yes
Assistance programs available to students: Federal Stafford Loan, Federal Perkins Loan, Federal Plus Loan, Federal

Pell Grant, Federal Work-Study Program, in-state student aid programs, veterans' assistance

Athabasca University

Public Affairs
1 University Drive
Athabasca, AB, Canada T9S 3A3
Department e-mail: auinfo@athabasca.ca
School Web address: www.athabasca.ca
Institutional accreditation: Association of Universities and Colleges of Canada

Subjects Offered

Accounting, administration, anthropology, applied studies, art history, astronomy and astrophysics, biology, career development, chemistry, communications, computers and management information systems, computer science, criminal justice, economics, education/educational psychology, English/English as a second language, environmental science/studies, finance, French, geography, German, global studies, health administration/health studies, human resource management, human services, industrial relations, information systems, labour studies, legal studies, management science, marketing, mathematics, music, native studies

Admissions Requirements

Is a minimum high school GPA required? No
Is provisional admission available? No
Is an admissions interview required? No
Can pre-requisite course work be waived? No
Are international students eligible to apply? Yes
Is the TOEFL required for international students? No

Program Delivery

Primary method of program delivery: Text
One-way pre-recorded video: Yes
Audio: Yes
Hardware requirements: Pentium 100 or higher, 32MB of RAM, 50MB free disk space, 3.5" floppy disk drive, mouse, 28.8KBPS modem
Software requirements: Windows 95, Microsoft Word (v. 6 or higher) or Microsoft Works (v. 4 or higher), current version of Netscape or Internet Explorer
Is the library accessible to students? Yes
Are computers accessible to students? Yes

Remote Sites

Other branches of the institution: Yes
Other college campuses: Yes
Students' homes: Yes

On-Campus Requirements

Is an on-campus component required? No

Tuition & Fees

In-state tuition per credit: $444
Out-of-state tuition per credit: $694
Average yearly cost of books: $50

Financial Aid

Is financial aid available to full-time students? Yes
Is financial aid available to part-time students? Yes
Are academic scholarships available? Yes

Athens Technical College

Academic Affairs
800 US Highway 29 North
Athens, GA 30601-1500
Contact: Dr. Ken Jarrett, Vice President for Academic Affairs
Department e-mail: jarrett@aati.edu
Department Web address: www.aati.edu/edonline.html
School Web address: ww.aati.edu
Institutional accreditation: Southern Association of Colleges and Schools

Subjects Offered

English, math, economics, psychology, computer programming, marketing, general business, paralegal studies, electronics

Admissions Requirements

Is provisional admission available? Yes
Is an admissions interview required? No
Are international students eligible to apply? Yes

Program Delivery

Primary method of program delivery: Web
Hardware requirements: 32MB of RAM, Pentium 200 or higher, 50MB free disk space, 56K modem
Software requirements: Netscape 4.61 or higher, Windows 95 or higher
Is the library accessible to students? Yes
Are computers accessible to students? Yes

Remote Sites

Other branches of the institution: Yes
Other college campuses: Yes
Students' homes: Yes

On-Campus Requirements

Is an on-campus component required? No

Tuition & Fees

In-state tuition per credit: $24
Application fee: $15
Can it be waived? No
Average yearly additional fees: $35

Financial Aid

Is financial aid available to full-time students? Yes
Is financial aid available to part-time students? Yes
Are academic scholarships available? Yes
Assistance programs available to students: Federal Pell
Grant, Federal Work-Study Program, in-state student aid
programs

Atlantic Cape Community College

Academic Computing and Distance Education
5100 Black Horse Pike
Mays Landing, NJ 08330
Contact: Mary Hall, Dean
Department e-mail: wall@atlantic.edu
Department Web address: www.atlantic.edu/distance_ed/
index.html
School Web address: www.atlantic.edu
Institutional accreditation: Middle States Association of
Colleges and Schools

Subjects Offered

Accounting, business law, nutrition, anthropology, art,
information systems, business, marketing, criminology,
biology, computer information systems management,
economics, English, earth science, French, history,
hospital administration, physical education, mathematics, music, nursing, operating systems technology,
philosophy, psychology, sociology, Spanish

Admissions Requirements

Is a minimum high school GPA required? No
Is an admissions interview required? No
Are international students eligible to apply? Yes
Is the TOEFL required for international students? Yes

Program Delivery

Two-way interactive video: Yes
Software requirements: Students must have a computer
with a graphical user interface, a modem, and a
connection to an Internet service provider.
Is the library accessible to students? Yes

Remote Sites

Other branches of the institution: Yes

On-Campus Requirements

Is an on-campus component required? No

Tuition & Fees

In-state tuition per credit: $80
Out-of-state tuition per credit: $80
Average yearly cost of books: $50

Financial Aid

Is financial aid available to full-time students? Yes
Is financial aid available to part-time students? Yes
Are academic scholarships available? Yes

Atlantic Union College

Adult Degree Program
PO Box 1000
South Lancaster, MA 01561
Contact: Corina Parris, Associate Director
Department e-mail: auc@atlanticuc.edu
Department Web address: www.apoed.com
School Web address: www.atlanticuc.edu
Institutional accreditation: New England Association of
Schools and Colleges

Subjects Offered

Art, behavioral science, business administration, office
management, communications, computer science,
education, English, history, interior design, modern
language, personal ministry, physical education,
psychology, religion, theology, women's studies

Admissions Requirements

Is a minimum high school GPA required? No
Is provisional admission available? Yes
Is an admissions interview required? No
Can pre-requisite course work be waived? Yes
Are international students eligible to apply? Yes
Is the TOEFL required for international students? Yes
What is the minimum TOEFL score required? 550

Program Delivery

One-way live video: Yes
Audio graphics: Yes
Audio: Yes
Is the library accessible to students? Yes
Are computers accessible to students? Yes

Remote Sites

Students' homes: Yes
Work sites: Yes
Libraries: Yes

Elementary/Secondary schools: Yes
Correctional institutions: Yes

On-Campus Requirements

Is an on-campus component required? Yes
On-campus course work: Yes
On-campus program orientation: Yes

Tuition & Fees

Average yearly cost of books: $300

Financial Aid

Is financial aid available to full-time students? Yes
Is financial aid available to part-time students? Yes
Are academic scholarships available? Yes
Assistance programs available to students: Federal Stafford
    Loan, Federal Perkins Loan, Federal Pell Grant

Austin Community College

Distance Learning
OPC, 7728 West Highway 290
Austin, TX 78736
Contact: Mary L. Cummings, Director
Department e-mail: opc@austin.cc.tx.us
Department Web address: www.dl.austin.cc.tx.us
School Web address: www.austin.cc.tx.us
Institutional accreditation: Southern Association of
    Colleges and Schools

Subjects Offered

Anthropology, art, biology, business, chemistry, child
    development, computer sciences/computer studies,
    development studies, economics, English, geography,
    government, humanities, math, history, kinesiology,
    marketing, psychology, recreational therapy, real estate,
    sociology, social welfare, journalism, fashion design,
    Spanish, philosophy, technical communications, medical
    terminology, semi-conductor overview, speech, financial
    management

Admissions Requirements

Is a minimum high school GPA required? No
Is provisional admission available? Yes
Is an admissions interview required? No
Can pre-requisite course work be waived? No
Are international students eligible to apply? Yes

Program Delivery

Primary method of program delivery: Web
Two-way interactive video: Yes
Two-way audio, one-way video: Yes

One-way live video: Yes
One-way pre-recorded video: Yes
Audio: Yes
Is the library accessible to students? Yes
Are computers accessible to students? Yes

Remote Sites

Other branches of the institution: Yes
Students' homes: Yes
Work sites: Yes
Elementary/Secondary schools: Yes

On-Campus Requirements

Is an on-campus component required? No

Tuition & Fees

In-state tuition per credit: $33
Out-of-state tuition per credit: $162
Average yearly cost of books: $750

Financial Aid

Is financial aid available to full-time students? Yes
Is financial aid available to part-time students? Yes
Are academic scholarships available? Yes
Assistance programs available to students: Federal Stafford
    Loan, Federal Perkins Loan, Federal Plus Loan, Federal
    Pell Grant, Federal Work-Study Program, in-state
    student aid programs, veterans' assistance

Baker College On-Line

1050 West Bristol Road
Flint, MI 48507
Contact: Chuck Gurden, Director of On-Line Admissions
Department e-mail: gurden_c@coefl.baker.edu
Department Web address: online.baker.edu
School Web address: www.baker.edu
Institutional accreditation: North Central Association of
    Colleges and Schools

Subjects Offered

Web design, general business, business administration,
    human resources, health service administration

Admissions Requirements

Is a minimum high school GPA required? Yes
Is provisional admission available? Yes
Is an admissions interview required? No
Can pre-requisite course work be waived? Yes
Are international students eligible to apply? Yes
Is the TOEFL required for international students? Yes
What is the minimum TOEFL score required? 550

Program Delivery

Primary method of program delivery: Web
Two-way interactive video: No
Two-way audio, one-way video: No
One-way live video: No
One-way pre-recorded video: No
Audio graphics: No
Audio: No
Software requirements: Office programs with word processing package, Internet access
Is the library accessible to students? Yes
Are computers accessible to students? No

Remote Sites

Other branches of the institution: Yes
Other college campuses: No
Students' homes: Yes
Work sites: Yes
Libraries: Yes
Elementary/Secondary schools: No
Community-based organizations: No
Correctional institutions: No

On-Campus Requirements

Is an on-campus component required? No

Tuition & Fees

In-state tuition per credit: $150
Out-of-state tuition per credit: $150
Average yearly cost of books: $1,500

Financial Aid

Is financial aid available to full-time students? Yes
Is financial aid available to part-time students? Yes
Are academic scholarships available? No
Assistance programs available to students: Federal Stafford Loan, Federal Pell Grant, veterans' assistance

Bakersfield College

Distance Learning
1801 Panorama Drive
Bakersfield, CA 93305
Contact: Dr. Greg Chamberlain, Dean, Learning Resources & Information Technology
Department e-mail: kloomis@bc.cc.ca.us
Department Web address: online.bc.cc.ca.us/distance
School Web address: bc.cc.ca.us
Institutional accreditation: Western Association of Schools and Colleges

Subjects Offered

Astronomy, business, business administration, child development, computer studies, English, fire technology, geology, math

Admissions Requirements

Is a minimum high school GPA required? No
Is provisional admission available? Yes
Is an admissions interview required? No
Can pre-requisite course work be waived? Yes
Is the TOEFL required for international students? Yes
What is the minimum TOEFL score required? 500

Program Delivery

Primary method of program delivery: Web

Remote Sites

Students' homes: Yes
Work sites: Yes
Libraries: Yes

On-Campus Requirements

Is an on-campus component required? No

Tuition & Fees

In-state tuition per credit: $11
Out-of-state tuition per credit: $130

Financial Aid

Is financial aid available to full-time students? Yes
Is financial aid available to part-time students? Yes
Are academic scholarships available? Yes
Assistance programs available to students: Federal Stafford Loan, Federal Plus Loan, Federal Pell Grant, Federal Work-Study Program, in-state student aid programs, veterans' assistance

Baltimore City Community College

Academic Affairs Division
Evening, Weekend and Special Sessions Department
2901 Liberty Heights Avenue
Baltimore, MD 21215
Contact: Mrs. Synthia Jones-Green, Director Evening, Weekend and Special Sessions Deptartments
Department e-mail: distancelearning@bccc.state.md.us
Department Web address: bccc.state.md.us/educational.html/edograms.html
School Web address: bccc.state.md.us
Institutional accreditation: Middle States Association of Colleges and Schools

Subjects Offered

Biology, health care management, business, philosophy, dietary management, preparation for academics success, economics, psychology, English, remedial reading and writing, general law, science, gerontology, sociology, health, special education, history I and II, teacher certification, hospitality management, early childhood education, literature

Admissions Requirements

Is a minimum high school GPA required? No
Is provisional admission available? No
Is an admissions interview required? No
Can pre-requisite course work be waived? No
Are international students eligible to apply? Yes
Is the TOEFL required for international students? Yes

Program Delivery

Primary method of program delivery: Web
Two-way interactive video: Yes
One-way pre-recorded video: Yes
Hardware requirements: Computer with modem and Internet access
Software requirements: Microsoft Internet Explorer (4.0 or higher) or Netscape (Version 3.01 or higher)
Is the library accessible to students? Yes
Are computers accessible to students? Yes

Remote Sites

Other college campuses: Yes
Students' homes: Yes
Work sites: Yes
Elementary/Secondary schools: Yes

On-Campus Requirements

Is an on-campus component required? Yes
On-campus course work: Yes
On-campus program orientation: Yes
On-campus exams: Yes

Tuition & Fees

In-state tuition per credit: $60
Out-of-state tuition per credit: $150
Application fee: $20
Can it be waived? No
Average yearly cost of books: $700
Average yearly additional fees: $108

Financial Aid

Is financial aid available to full-time students? Yes
Is financial aid available to part-time students? Yes
Are academic scholarships available? Yes

Assistance programs available to students: Federal Pell Grant, Federal Work-Study Program, in-state student aid programs, veterans' assistance

Beufort County Community College

Learning Resources Center
PO Box 1069
Washington, NC 27889
Contact: Penny Sermons, Director Learning Resources Center
Department e-mail: pennys@e-mail.beufort.cc.nc.us
School Web address: beufort.cc.nc.us
Institutional accreditation: Southern Association of Colleges and Schools

Subjects Offered

Business, human services, drafting, English, criminal justice, early childhood, sociology, psychology, medical terminology

Admissions Requirements

Is a minimum high school GPA required? No
Is an admissions interview required? No
Can pre-requisite course work be waived? Yes
Are international students eligible to apply? No

Program Delivery

Primary method of program delivery: Web
Two-way interactive video: Yes
Hardware requirements: Multimedia PC with Windows 95 or 98, Netscape Communicator or Microsoft Internet Explorer
Software requirements: depends on course work
Is the library accessible to students? Yes
Are computers accessible to students? Yes

Remote Sites

Students' homes: Yes
Work sites: Yes
Libraries: Yes
Elementary/Secondary schools: Yes
Correctional institutions: Yes

On-Campus Requirements

Is an on-campus component required? Yes
On-campus program orientation: Yes
On-campus exams: Yes

Tuition & Fees

In-state tuition per credit: $27
Out-of-state tuition per credit: $170
Average yearly cost of books: $350

Financial Aid

Is financial aid available to full-time students? Yes
Is financial aid available to part-time students? Yes
Are academic scholarships available? Yes
Assistance programs available to students: Federal Stafford Loan, Federal Plus Loan, Federal Pell Grant, Federal Work-Study Program, in-state student aid programs, veterans' assistance

Bellevue University

Admission
College of Distributed Learning
1000 Galvin Road South
Bellevue, NE 68005
Contact: Dr. Christine Beische, Dean of College of Distributive Learning
Department e-mail: kathy@bellevue.edu
Department Web address: bellevue.edu
School Web address: bellevue.edu
Institutional accreditation: North Central Association of Colleges and Schools

Subjects Offered

Business administration, management, information systems

Admissions Requirements

Is a minimum high school GPA required? No
Is provisional admission available? Yes
Is an admissions interview required? No
Can pre-requisite course work be waived? Yes
Are international students eligible to apply? Yes
Is the TOEFL required for international students? Yes
What is the minimum TOEFL score required? 500

Program Delivery

Primary method of program delivery: Web
Two-way interactive video: No
Two-way audio, one-way video: No
One-way live video: No
One-way pre-recorded video: Yes
Audio graphics: Yes
Audio: Yes
Is the library accessible to students? Yes
Are computers accessible to students? Yes

Remote Sites

Other branches of the institution: Yes
Other college campuses: Yes
Students' homes: Yes
Work sites: Yes
Libraries: No
Elementary/Secondary schools: No
Community-based organizations: No
Correctional institutions: No

Tuition & Fees

In-state tuition per credit: $132
Out-of-state tuition per credit: $132
Average yearly cost of books: $35

Financial Aid

Is financial aid available to full-time students? Yes
Is financial aid available to part-time students? Yes
Are academic scholarships available? Yes
Assistance programs available to students: Federal Stafford Loan, Federal Perkins Loan, Federal Plus Loan, Federal Pell Grant, Federal Work-Study Program, in-state student aid programs, veterans' assistance

Bemidji State University

Center For Extended Learning
1500 Birchmont Avenue
Bemidji, MN 56601
Contact: Robert Griggs
Department e-mail: rjgriggs@vaxl.bemidji.msus.edu
Department Web address: cel.bemidji.msus.edu/cel
School Web address: www.bemidjistate.edu
Institutional accreditation: North Central Association of Colleges and Schools

Subjects Offered

Accounting, health, anthropology, history, biology, humanities, business administration, industrial education, chemistry, music, criminal justice, philosophy, economics, physical education, education, political science, English, psychology, environmental studies, religious studies, geography, social work, sociology

Admissions Requirements

Is a minimum high school GPA required? No
Is provisional admission available? Yes
Is an admissions interview required? No
Are international students eligible to apply? Yes
Is the TOEFL required for international students? Yes

Program Delivery

Primary method of program delivery: Remote site
Audio: Yes
Is the library accessible to students? Yes
Are computers accessible to students? No

Remote Sites

Other college campuses: Yes

On-Campus Requirements

Is an on-campus component required? No

Tuition & Fees

In-state tuition per credit: $122
Out-of-state tuition per credit: $225
Average yearly cost of books: $600

Financial Aid

Is financial aid available to full-time students? Yes
Is financial aid available to part-time students? Yes
Are academic scholarships available? Yes
Assistance programs available to students: Federal Stafford
    Loan, Federal Perkins Loan, Federal Plus Loan, Federal
    Pell Grant, Federal Work-Study Program, in-state
    student aid programs, veterans' assistance

Bergen Community College

Office of Distance Learning
400 Paramus Road
Paramus, NJ 07652
Contact: Dr. Mark Kassop, Coordinator of Distance
    Learning
Department e-mail: mkassop@bergen.cc.nj.us
Department Web address: www.bergen.cc.nj.us/dlearning
School Web address: www.bergen.cc.nj.us
Institutional accreditation: Middle States Association of
    Colleges and Schools

Subjects Offered

American language, cultural anthropology, general biology,
    introduction to human biology, introduction to
    business, business math, entrepreneurship, principles of
    business management, general chemistry, introduction
    to criminal justice, macroeconomics, microeconomics,
    introduction to education, principles and practice of
    education, history of Western civilization, United States
    history, information technology, Web publishing,
    introduction to Internet, American literature, world
    literature, elementary statistics, business communication,
    introduction to philosophy, ethics, basic logic, religions
    of the world, American government, state and local
government, general psychology, introduction to
    sociology, introduction to human resources, sociology of
    the family, social problems

Admissions Requirements

Is a minimum high school GPA required? No
Is provisional admission available? Yes
Is an admissions interview required? No
Can pre-requisite course work be waived? Yes
Are international students eligible to apply? Yes
Is the TOEFL required for international students? No

Program Delivery

Primary method of program delivery: Web
Two-way interactive video: Yes
One-way pre-recorded video: Yes
Audio: Yes
Is the library accessible to students? Yes
Are computers accessible to students? No

Remote Sites

Students' homes: Yes
Work sites: Yes
Libraries: Yes

On-Campus Requirements

Is an on-campus component required? No

Tuition & Fees

In-state tuition per credit: $80
Out-of-state tuition per credit: $80
Average yearly cost of books: $800

Financial Aid

Is financial aid available to full-time students? Yes
Is financial aid available to part-time students? Yes
Are academic scholarships available? Yes
Assistance programs available to students: Federal Stafford
    Loan, Federal Perkins Loan, Federal Pell Grant, Federal
    Work-Study Program, in-state student aid programs,
    veterans' assistance

Bethel College

Department of Nursing
RN Outreach
300 East 27 Street
North Newton, KS 67117
Contact: Verda Deckert, Director
Department e-mail: udeckert@bethelks.edu
Department Web address: bethelks.edu/academics/faculty/
    verdedeckerrnoutreach.html

School Web address: bethelks.edu
Institutional accreditation: North Central Association of
Colleges and Schools

Subjects Offered

Nursing

Admissions Requirements

Is provisional admission available? No
Is an admissions interview required? No
Can pre-requisite course work be waived? No
Are international students eligible to apply? Yes
Is the TOEFL required for international students? Yes
What is the minimum TOEFL score required? 540

Program Delivery

Primary method of program delivery: Remote site
One-way pre-recorded video: Yes
Audio: Yes
Hardware requirements: VCR, CD player
Software requirements: Internet
Is the library accessible to students? Yes

Remote Sites

Students' homes: Yes

On-Campus Requirements

Is an on-campus component required? No

Tuition & Fees

In-state tuition per credit: $215
Out-of-state tuition per credit: $215
Average yearly cost of books: $200

Financial Aid

Is financial aid available to full-time students? Yes
Is financial aid available to part-time students? Yes
Are academic scholarships available? Yes
Assistance programs available to students: Federal Stafford
Loan, Federal Perkins Loan, Federal Plus Loan, Federal
Pell Grant

Bluefield State College

Center for Extended Learning
219 Rock Street
Bluefield, WV 24701
Contact: Dr. Thomas E. Blevins
Department e-mail: tblevins@bluefield.wvnet.edu
Department Web address: www.bluefield.wvnet.edu/itc
School Web address: www.bluefield.wvnet.edu
Institutional accreditation: North Central Association of
Colleges and Schools

Subjects Offered

Medical assisting, health, business, education, computer
science, English, criminal justice, history, radiological
technology, geography

Admissions Requirements

Is a minimum high school GPA required? No
Is provisional admission available? Yes
Is an admissions interview required? No
Are international students eligible to apply? Yes

Program Delivery

Primary method of program delivery: Remote site
Two-way interactive video: Yes
Is the library accessible to students? Yes
Are computers accessible to students? Yes

On-Campus Requirements

Is an on-campus component required? No

Tuition & Fees

In-state tuition per credit: $96
Out-of-state tuition per credit: $233
Average yearly cost of books: $500

Financial Aid

Is financial aid available to full-time students? Yes
Is financial aid available to part-time students? Yes
Are academic scholarships available? Yes
Assistance programs available to students: Federal Stafford
Loan, Federal Pell Grant, Federal Work-Study Program,
veterans' assistance

Bossier Parish Community College

Institutional Advancement & Effectiveness
Educational Technology
2719 Airline Drive
Bossoer, LA 7111
Contact: Kathleen Gay, Director of Educational Technology
Department e-mail: kgay@bpcc.cc.la.us
School Web address: www.bpcc.cc.la.us
Institutional accreditation: Southern Association of
Colleges and Schools

Subjects Offered

English, speech, art, history, sociology, math, psychology,
business administration, health and physical education,
telecommunications, pharmacy technician program,
pharmacology for allied health, dosage and calculations,
introduction to pharmacy, pharmacy practice, applied

clinical pharmacology, trends in pharmacy, sterile products, introduction to computer, concepts, criminal justice, Web design, problem solving

Admissions Requirements

Is a minimum high school GPA required? No
Is provisional admission available? No
Is an admissions interview required? No
Can pre-requisite course work be waived? No
Are international students eligible to apply? Yes
Is the TOEFL required for international students? Yes
What is the minimum TOEFL score required? 500

Program Delivery

Primary method of program delivery: Remote site
Two-way interactive video: Yes
One-way pre-recorded video: Yes
Is the library accessible to students? Yes
Are computers accessible to students? No

Remote Sites

Other branches of the institution: Yes
Other college campuses: Yes
Students' homes: Yes
Community-based organizations: Yes
Correctional institutions: Yes

On-Campus Requirements

Is an on-campus component required? Yes
On-campus course work: Yes
On-campus admissions interview: No
On-campus program orientation: Yes
On-campus exams: Yes

Tuition & Fees

In-state tuition per credit: $230
Out-of-state tuition per credit: $390
Average yearly cost of books: $600

Financial Aid

Is financial aid available to full-time students? Yes
Is financial aid available to part-time students? Yes
Are academic scholarships available? Yes
Assistance programs available to students: Federal Stafford Loan, Federal Perkins Loan, Federal Pell Grant, Federal Work-Study Program, in-state student aid programs, veterans' assistance

Brenau University

Nursing
Online Education
One Centennial Circle
Gainesville, GA 30501
Contact: Judy Bradberry, Offsite Coordinator Nursing
Department e-mail: jbradberry@lib.brenau.edu
Department Web address: www.brenau.edu/nursing
School Web address: www.brenau.edu
Institutional accreditation: Southern Association of Colleges and Schools

Subjects Offered

Leadership, theory and concepts, health assessment, research, health promotion, community, cultural diversity, health care systems and policy, clinical practicioner

Admissions Requirements

Is a minimum high school GPA required? No
Is provisional admission available? Yes
Can pre-requisite course work be waived? No
Are international students eligible to apply? Yes
Is the TOEFL required for international students? Yes
What is the minimum TOEFL score required? 500

Program Delivery

Primary method of program delivery: Web
Two-way interactive video: No
Two-way audio, one-way video: No
One-way live video: No
One-way pre-recorded video: No
Audio graphics: No
Audio: No
Hardware requirements: Pentium processor, 56KBPS modem
Software requirements: Microsoft Office 97 or later, Internet service provider
Is the library accessible to students? Yes
Are computers accessible to students? Yes

Remote Sites

Other branches of the institution: No
Other college campuses: No
Students' homes: Yes
Work sites: Yes
Libraries: No
Elementary/Secondary schools: No
Community-based organizations: No
Correctional institutions: No

On-Campus Requirements

Is an on-campus component required? Yes
On-campus course work: No
On-campus admissions interview: No
On-campus program orientation: Yes
On-campus exams: No

Tuition & Fees

In-state tuition per credit: $335
Out-of-state tuition per credit: $335
Average yearly cost of books: $700

Financial Aid

Is financial aid available to full-time students? Yes
Is financial aid available to part-time students? Yes
Are academic scholarships available? Yes
Assistance programs available to students: Federal Stafford Loan, Federal Perkins Loan, Federal Plus Loan, Federal Pell Grant, Federal Work-Study Program, in-state student aid programs, veterans' assistance

Brevard Community College

Distance Learning
1519 Clearlake Road
Cocoa, FL 32922
Contact: Dr. Katherine M. Cobb, Dean of Distance Learning
Department e-mail: cobbk@cc.fl.us
School Web address: www.brevard.cc.fl.us
Institutional accreditation: Southern Association of Colleges and Schools

Subjects Offered

Behavioral science, biological science, business, community service learning, computer programming and analysis, criminal justice, dental assisting, English/communications, education, experiential learning, hospitality and tourism, humanities, Internet research, legal assisting, logistics, mathematics, nutrition, office of technology, office of educational vocational credit, physical education, physical science, social science

Admissions Requirements

Is a minimum high school GPA required? No
Is provisional admission available? Yes
Is an admissions interview required? No
Can pre-requisite course work be waived? Yes
Are international students eligible to apply? Yes
Is the TOEFL required for international students? Yes

Program Delivery

Primary method of program delivery: Remote site
Two-way interactive video: Yes
Hardware requirements: Pentium or Power Mac 133 MHz, 28.8KPBS modem, 64MB RAM
Software requirements: Internet Explorer 4.0 or higher, Netscape 4.0 or higher
Is the library accessible to students? Yes
Are computers accessible to students? Yes

Remote Sites

Other branches of the institution: Yes
Students' homes: Yes

On-Campus Requirements

Is an on-campus component required? No

Tuition & Fees

In-state tuition per credit: $53
Out-of-state tuition per credit: $179
Average yearly cost of books: $600

Financial Aid

Is financial aid available to full-time students? Yes
Are academic scholarships available? Yes
Assistance programs available to students: Federal Stafford Loan, Federal Perkins Loan, Federal Plus Loan, Federal Pell Grant, Federal Work-Study Program, in-state student aid programs, veterans' assistance

Brookdale Community College

Telecommunications Technologies
Distance Education Applications
765 Newman Springs Road
Lincroft, NJ 07738-1597
Contact: Norah Keer McCurry, Manager—Distance Education Applications
Department e-mail: nmccurry@brookdale.cc.nj.us
School Web address: www.brookdale.cc.nj.us
Institutional accreditation: Commission on Higher Education of the Middle States Association of Colleges and Schools

Subjects Offered

Anthroplogy, American and world civilization, biology, marketing, business, music appreciation, personal finance, philosophy, economics (macro and micro), ethics, English composition, psychology, American literature, human growth and development, children's literature, sociology, French communication, Spanish 1 and 2, here's to your health, musical theatre, human geography, communication media, world literature, medical terminology, career development, accounting 1 and 2, computer keyboard, mini/micro computers, computerized reservations

Admissions Requirements

Is a minimum high school GPA required? No
Is an admissions interview required? No
Can pre-requisite course work be waived? Yes
Are international students eligible to apply? Yes
Is the TOEFL required for international students? No

Program Delivery

Two-way interactive video: Yes
Two-way audio, one-way video: Yes
One-way live video: Yes
One-way pre-recorded video: Yes
Audio graphics: Yes
Audio: Yes
Is the library accessible to students? Yes
Are computers accessible to students? Yes

Remote Sites

Other branches of the institution: Yes
Other college campuses: Yes
Students' homes: Yes
Work sites: Yes
Libraries: Yes
Elementary/Secondary schools: No
Community-based organizations: No
Correctional institutions: No

On-Campus Requirements

Is an on-campus component required? No

Tuition & Fees

In-state tuition per credit: $75
Out-of-state tuition per credit: $150
Application fee: $26
Can it be waived? No

Financial Aid

Is financial aid available to full-time students? Yes
Is financial aid available to part-time students? Yes
Are academic scholarships available? Yes
Assistance programs available to students: Federal Stafford Loan, Federal Perkins Loan, Federal Plus Loan, Federal Pell Grant, Federal Work-Study Program, in-state student aid programs, veterans' assistance

Broward Community College

Continuing Studies
Distance Education
1002 North First Street
Vincennes, IN 47591
Contact: Vernon E. Houchins, Dean, Continuing Studies
Department e-mail: disted@indian.vinu.edu
Department Web address: www.vinu.edu/distance
School Web address: www.vinu.edu
Institutional accreditation: Southern Association of Colleges and Schools

Subjects Offered

Education, study skills, psychology, literature, sociology, history, computer information, recreation management, business, chemistry, English, math, speech, economics, law enforcement, government, corrections, portfolio development, health information management, fitness, wellness, surgical technology, earth science

Admissions Requirements

Is a minimum high school GPA required? No
Is provisional admission available? Yes
Is an admissions interview required? No
Can pre-requisite course work be waived? No
Are international students eligible to apply? Yes
Is the TOEFL required for international students? Yes

Program Delivery

Primary method of program delivery: Text
Two-way interactive video: Yes
Two-way audio, one-way video: Yes
One-way pre-recorded video: Yes
Hardware requirements: 90MHz processor (Intel, AMD, Cyrix), 16MB of RAM, 500MB hard drive, 15" monitor, 28.8KBPS modem
Software requirements: Netscape Navigator
Is the library accessible to students? Yes
Are computers accessible to students? Yes

Remote Sites

Other branches of the institution: Yes
Other college campuses: Yes
Students' homes: Yes
Work sites: Yes
Libraries: Yes
Elementary/Secondary schools: Yes
Community-based organizations: Yes
Correctional institutions: Yes

On-Campus Requirements

Is an on-campus component required? No

Tuition & Fees

In-state tuition per credit: $83
Out-of-state tuition per credit: $83
Application fee: $20
Average yearly cost of books: $700
Average yearly additional fees: $25

Financial Aid

Is financial aid available to full-time students? Yes
Is financial aid available to part-time students? Yes
Are academic scholarships available? Yes
Assistance programs available to students: Federal Stafford Loan, Federal Plus Loan, Federal Pell Grant, Federal Work-Study Program, in-state student aid programs, veterans' assistance

Bucks County Community College

Distance Learning
275 Swamp Road
Newtown, PA 18940-4106
Contact: Georglyn Davidson, Distance Learning Coordinator
Department e-mail: learning@bucks.edu
Department Web address: www.bucks.edu/~distance
School Web address: www.bucks.edu
Institutional accreditation: Middle States Association of Colleges and Schools

Subjects Offered

Abnormal psychology, accounting, administrative services, advertising, astronomy, biology, business/business administration/business law, chemistry, child psychology, communications, economics, education, English, ethics, foreign language, health, history, human resources management, Internet design/marketing, management, marketing, mathematics, medical transcription, music, nutrition, paralegal, philosophy, religion, secretarial services, sociology, statistics, teacher education, theater, women's studies

Admissions Requirements

Is a minimum high school GPA required? No
Is provisional admission available? No
Is an admissions interview required? No
Can pre-requisite course work be waived? Yes
Are international students eligible to apply? Yes

Is the TOEFL required for international students? Yes
What is the minimum TOEFL score required? 550

Program Delivery

Primary method of program delivery: Web
One-way pre-recorded video: Yes
Audio graphics: No
Audio: Yes
Hardware requirements: Depends on the course
Software requirements: Depends on the course
Is the library accessible to students? Yes
Are computers accessible to students? Yes

Remote Sites

Students' homes: Yes

On-Campus Requirements

On-campus course work: Yes
On-campus program orientation: Yes
On-campus exams: Yes

Tuition & Fees

In-state tuition per credit: $148
Out-of-state tuition per credit: $222
Average yearly cost of books: $650

Financial Aid

Is financial aid available to full-time students? Yes
Is financial aid available to part-time students? Yes
Are academic scholarships available? Yes
Assistance programs available to students: Federal Stafford Loan, Federal Perkins Loan, Federal Plus Loan, Federal Pell Grant, Federal Work-Study Program, in-state student aid programs, veterans' assistance

Burlington County College

Distance Learning
County Route 530
Pemberton, NJ 08068
Contact: Susan Espenshade, Coordinator of Distance Learning
School Web address: www.bcc.edu
Institutional accreditation: Middle States Association of Colleges and Schools

Subjects Offered

Anthropology, art, biology, business, cinema, computer information systems, communications, economics, education, English, French, food service management, geology, history, literature, mathematics, music, political science, psychology, sociology, Spanish, theater

Admissions Requirements

Is a minimum high school GPA required? No
Is an admissions interview required? No
Can pre-requisite course work be waived? Yes
Are international students eligible to apply? Yes

Program Delivery

Primary method of program delivery: Web
Two-way interactive video: Yes
Two-way audio, one-way video: No
One-way pre-recorded video: Yes
Audio graphics: Yes
Audio: Yes
Is the library accessible to students? Yes
Are computers accessible to students? Yes

Remote Sites

Other branches of the institution: Yes
Other college campuses: Yes
Students' homes: Yes
Work sites: Yes
Libraries: Yes
Elementary/Secondary schools: Yes
Community-based organizations: No
Correctional institutions: No

On-Campus Requirements

Is an on-campus component required? No

Tuition & Fees

In-state tuition per credit: $60
Out-of-state tuition per credit: $140
Average yearly cost of books: $1,000

Financial Aid

Is financial aid available to full-time students? Yes
Is financial aid available to part-time students? Yes
Are academic scholarships available? Yes
Assistance programs available to students: Federal Stafford Loan, Federal Perkins Loan, Federal Plus Loan, Federal Pell Grant, Federal Work-Study Program, in-state student aid programs, veterans' assistance

Caldwell College

External Degree Program
Department of Continuing Education
9 Ryerson Avenue
Caldwell, NJ 07003
Contact: Lisa D. Bisceglie, Dean of Continuing Education
Department Web address: www.caldwell.edu/adult-admissions

School Web address: www.caldwell.edu
Institutional accreditation: Middle States Association of Colleges and Schools

Subjects Offered

Accounting, business administration, communication arts, computer information systems, computer science, criminal justice, English, education, government services, history, international business, management, marketing, humanities, political science, psychology, religion, social studies, sociology

Admissions Requirements

Is a minimum high school GPA required? No
Is provisional admission available? No
Is an admissions interview required? No
Can pre-requisite course work be waived? Yes
Are international students eligible to apply? Yes
Is the TOEFL required for international students? No

Program Delivery

One-way pre-recorded video: Yes
Audio graphics: Yes
Audio: Yes
Software requirements: Windows 2000
Is the library accessible to students? Yes
Are computers accessible to students? No

Remote Sites

Students' homes: Yes
Work sites: Yes
Correctional institutions: Yes

On-Campus Requirements

Is an on-campus component required? Yes
On-campus admissions interview: Yes
On-campus program orientation: Yes

Tuition & Fees

In-state tuition per credit: $337
Out-of-state tuition per credit: $337
Average yearly cost of books: $300

Financial Aid

Is financial aid available to full-time students? Yes
Is financial aid available to part-time students? Yes
Are academic scholarships available? Yes
Assistance programs available to students: Federal Stafford Loan, Federal Perkins Loan, Federal Plus Loan, Federal Pell Grant, Federal Work-Study Program, in-state student aid programs, veterans' assistance

Caldwell Community College and Technical Institute

Distance Learning
2855 Hickory Boulevard
Hudson, NC 28638
Contact: Nancy Risch, Coordinator, Distance Learning
Department e-mail: nancyr@caldwell.cc.nc.us
Department Web address: www.caldwell.cc.nc.us/pages/curric.html
School Web address: www.caldwell.cc.nc.us
Institutional accreditation: Southern Association of Colleges and Schools

Subjects Offered

Accounting, art, biology, business, education, English, humanities, psychology, criminal justice, emergency preparedness technology, fire protection, history, information systems, networking, office systems technology, sociology

Admissions Requirements

Is a minimum high school GPA required? No
Is provisional admission available? Yes
Is an admissions interview required? No
Can pre-requisite course work be waived? No
Are international students eligible to apply? Yes

Program Delivery

Primary method of program delivery: Remote site
Two-way interactive video: No
Two-way audio, one-way video: No
One-way live video: No
One-way pre-recorded video: Yes
Audio graphics: No
Audio: No
Hardware requirements: Computer with Internet access
Software requirements: Internet Explorer or Netscape Navigator v4.0 or higher
Is the library accessible to students? Yes
Are computers accessible to students? Yes

Remote Sites

Other branches of the institution: Yes
Other college campuses: Yes
Students' homes: Yes
Elementary/Secondary schools: Yes
Community-based organizations: Yes
Correctional institutions: Yes

On-Campus Requirements

Is an on-campus component required? Yes
On-campus course work: No
On-campus admissions interview: No
On-campus program orientation: Yes
On-campus exams: Yes

Tuition & Fees

In-state tuition per credit: $27
Out-of-state tuition per credit: $170
Average yearly cost of books: $400

Financial Aid

Is financial aid available to full-time students? Yes
Is financial aid available to part-time students? Yes
Are academic scholarships available? Yes
Assistance programs available to students: Federal Perkins Loan, Federal Pell Grant, Federal Work-Study Program, in-state student aid programs, veterans' assistance

California College for Health Sciences

2423 Hoover Avenue
National City, CA 91950
Contact: Jeff Welsh, Director of Education
School Web address: www.cchs.edu
Institutional accreditation: Distance Education and Training Council

Subjects Offered

Respiratory therapy, advanced respiratory therapy, childhood education, EEG technology, medical transcription, allied health, business, management (health services), respiratory care (health services), accounting, management (business), finance, marketing, gerontology, community health education, health psychology, health care ethics, polysomnography

Admissions Requirements

Is a minimum high school GPA required? No
Is provisional admission available? Yes
Is an admissions interview required? No
Can pre-requisite course work be waived? No
Are international students eligible to apply? Yes
Is the TOEFL required for international students? No

Program Delivery

Primary method of program delivery: Text
Two-way interactive video: No
Two-way audio, one-way video: No

One-way live video: No
One-way pre-recorded video: No
Audio graphics: No
Audio: No
Is the library accessible to students? No
Are computers accessible to students? No

Remote Sites

Other branches of the institution: No
Other college campuses: No
Students' homes: Yes
Work sites: Yes
Libraries: No
Elementary/Secondary schools: No
Community-based organizations: No
Correctional institutions: No

On-Campus Requirements

Is an on-campus component required? No

Tuition & Fees

In-state tuition per credit: $133
Out-of-state tuition per credit: $133
Average yearly cost of books: $50

Financial Aid

Is financial aid available to full-time students? No
Is financial aid available to part-time students? No
Are academic scholarships available? No

California State University, Chico

Center for Regional and Continuing Education
California State University, Chico
Chico, CA 95929-0250
Contact: Jeffrey S. Layne, Telecommunications Specialist
Department e-mail: rce@csuchico.edu
School Web address: www.csuchico.edu
Institutional accreditation: Western Association of Schools and Colleges

Subjects Offered

Social science, religious studies, sociology, American studies, geography, English, history, math, anthropology, women studies, economics, education-special education, health and community services, nursing, political science, plant and soil science, psychology, paralegal, education-teacher evaluation, career and life planning, philosophy, family relations

Admissions Requirements

Is a minimum high school GPA required? No
Is provisional admission available? No
Is an admissions interview required? No
Can pre-requisite course work be waived? No
Are international students eligible to apply? Yes
Is the TOEFL required for international students? Yes
What is the minimum TOEFL score required? 550

Program Delivery

Primary method of program delivery: Web
Hardware requirements: Computer with 200 MHz processor or better, or Macintosh 200 MHz Power PC 604 or better
Software requirements: Netscape Communicator 4.8 or Internet Explorer 5.5, RealPlayer, Adobe Acrobat Reader, Shockwave, and Flash

Remote Sites

Students' homes: Yes
Work sites: Yes

On-Campus Requirements

Is an on-campus component required? No

Tuition & Fees

In-state tuition per credit: $246
Out-of-state tuition per credit: $246
Average yearly cost of books: $55

Financial Aid

Is financial aid available to full-time students? Yes
Is financial aid available to part-time students? Yes
Are academic scholarships available? Yes
Assistance programs available to students: Federal Stafford Loan, Federal Perkins Loan, Federal Plus Loan, Federal Pell Grant, Federal Work-Study Program, in-state student aid programs, veterans' assistance

Califorinia State University, Dominguez Hills

Division of Extended Education
Center for Mediate Instruction and Distance Learning
1000 East Victoria Street
Carson, CA 90747
Contact: Dr. Warren Ashley, Director, Center for Mediate Instruction and Distance Learning
Department e-mail: eereg@csudh.edu
Department Web address: www.csudh.edu/dominguezonline
School Web address: www.csudh.edu

Institutional accreditation: Western Association of Schools and Colleges

Subjects Offered

Nursing, assistive technology, purchasing, production and inventory control, quality assurance

Admissions Requirements

Is a minimum high school GPA required? No
Is provisional admission available? Yes
Is an admissions interview required? No
Can pre-requisite course work be waived? No
Are international students eligible to apply? Yes
Is the TOEFL required for international students? Yes
What is the minimum TOEFL score required? 550

Program Delivery

Primary method of program delivery: Web
Software requirements: Windows 95 or better, Pentium I or better, 32MB RAM or better, 28.8KBPS modem or better, Explorer Netscape 4.0 or better
Is the library accessible to students? Yes
Are computers accessible to students? Yes

Remote Sites

Students' homes: Yes

On-Campus Requirements

Is an on-campus component required? No

Tuition & Fees

In-state tuition per credit: $225
Out-of-state tuition per credit: $225
Average yearly cost of books: $55

Financial Aid

Is financial aid available to full-time students? Yes
Is financial aid available to part-time students? Yes
Are academic scholarships available? Yes
Assistance programs available to students: In-state student aid programs

California State University, San Marcos

Extended Studies
Center for Distance Learning
333 Twin Oaks Valley Road
California State University, San Marcos Extended Studies
San Marcos, CA 92096
Contact: Bryana Ramos, Registration Specialist & Online Coordinator.

Department Web address: www.csusm.edu/es
School Web address: www.csusm.edu
Institutional accreditation: Western Association of Schools and Colleges

Subjects Offered

Sociology, education, small business, personal enrichment, legal courses, large business, computer courses, Internet courses, foreign language, health, fire service

Admissions Requirements

Is a minimum high school GPA required? No
Can pre-requisite course work be waived? No
Are international students eligible to apply? Yes
Is the TOEFL required for international students? No

Program Delivery

Two-way interactive video: No
Two-way audio, one-way video: No
One-way live video: No
One-way pre-recorded video: No
Audio graphics: No
Audio: No
Hardware requirements: modem at least 28.8KBPS
Software requirements: Basic Internet access, e-mail, Netscape or Internet Explorer
Is the library accessible to students? Yes
Are computers accessible to students? Yes

Remote Sites

Other branches of the institution: Yes
Other college campuses: No
Students' homes: Yes
Work sites: Yes
Libraries: Yes
Elementary/Secondary schools: Yes
Community-based organizations: Yes

On-Campus Requirements

Is an on-campus component required? No

Tuition & Fees

In-state tuition per credit: $105

Financial Aid

Is financial aid available to full-time students? No
Is financial aid available to part-time students? No
Are academic scholarships available? No

Campbellsville University

1 University Drive
Campbellsville, KY 42718
School Web address: www.campbellsvile.edu

Subjects Offered

Principles of management

Admissions Requirements

Is a minimum high school GPA required? Yes
Is provisional admission available? Yes
Is an admissions interview required? No
Can pre-requisite course work be waived? Yes
Are international students eligible to apply? Yes
Is the TOEFL required for international students? Yes
What is the minimum TOEFL score required? 500

Program Delivery

Primary method of program delivery: Web

Tuition & Fees

In-state tuition per credit: $368
Out-of-state tuition per credit: $368
Average yearly cost of books: $120

Carl Sandburg College

2232 South Lake Storey Road
Galesburg, IL 61401
School Web address: www.csc.cc.il.us
Institutional accreditation: North Central Association of
    Colleges and Schools

Admissions Requirements

Is a minimum high school GPA required? No
Can pre-requisite course work be waived? Yes
Are international students eligible to apply? Yes
Is the TOEFL required for international students? No

Program Delivery

Two-way interactive video: Yes
One-way pre-recorded video: Yes
Is the library accessible to students? Yes
Are computers accessible to students? Yes

Remote Sites

Other branches of the institution: Yes
Other college campuses: Yes
Students' homes: No
Work sites: No
Libraries: No
Elementary/Secondary schools: Yes

Community-based organizations: No
Correctional institutions: No

On-Campus Requirements

Is an on-campus component required? No

Tuition & Fees

In-state tuition per credit: $54
Out-of-state tuition per credit: $150
Average yearly cost of books: $400

Financial Aid

Is financial aid available to full-time students? Yes
Is financial aid available to part-time students? Yes
Are academic scholarships available? Yes
Assistance programs available to students: Federal Stafford
    Loan, Federal Perkins Loan, Federal Plus Loan, Federal
    Pell Grant, Federal Work-Study Program, veterans'
    assistance

Cedarville University

PO Box 601
Cedarville, OH 45314
Contact: Chuck Allport, Assistant to Academic Vice
    President
Department e-mail: allportc@cedarville.edu
School Web address: cedarville.edu
Institutional accreditation: North Central Association of
    Colleges and Schools

Admissions Requirements

Is a minimum high school GPA required? No
Is provisional admission available? No
Can pre-requisite course work be waived? No
Are international students eligible to apply? Yes
Is the TOEFL required for international students? Yes

Program Delivery

Primary method of program delivery: Web
Two-way interactive video: Yes
Hardware requirements: There is a high-quality networked
    computer in each dorm room and several on-campus
    labs
Software requirements: Extensive products available on
    "Cedarnet"
Is the library accessible to students? Yes

On-Campus Requirements

Is an on-campus component required? Yes
On-campus course work: Yes

Tuition & Fees

In-state tuition per credit: $238
Out-of-state tuition per credit: $238
Average yearly cost of books: $30

Financial Aid

Is financial aid available to full-time students? Yes
Is financial aid available to part-time students? Yes
Are academic scholarships available? Yes
Assistance programs available to students: Federal Stafford
Loan, Federal Perkins Loan, Federal Plus Loan, Federal
Pell Grant, Federal Work-Study Program, in-state
student aid programs

Central Michigan University

College of Extended Learning
Distance/Distributed Learning
Central Michigan University
Mt. Pleasant, MI 48859
Contact: William Rugg, Director
Department e-mail: celinfo@mail.cel.cmich.edu
Department Web address: www.ddl.cmich.edu
School Web address: www.cmich.edu
Institutional accreditation: North Central Association of
Colleges and Schools

Subjects Offered

Accounting, journalism, astronomy, management,
computer science, marketing, economics, math, English,
music, finance, physics, geography, political science,
human environmental studies, psychology, health
promotions rehabilitation, religion, sociology, Spanish,
statistics

Admissions Requirements

Is a minimum high school GPA required? No
Is provisional admission available? Yes
Is an admissions interview required? No
Can pre-requisite course work be waived? No
Are international students eligible to apply? Yes
Is the TOEFL required for international students? Yes
What is the minimum TOEFL score required? 550

Program Delivery

Primary method of program delivery: Text
One-way pre-recorded video: Yes
Audio: Yes
Hardware requirements: Pentium-class computer (or
equivalent Macintosh) 28.8KBPS or higher modem or
other Internet connection, 256-color display
Software requirements: Java-compatible browser (Internet
Explorer or Netscape 4 or higher), Internet access and an
e-mail address
Is the library accessible to students? Yes
Are computers accessible to students? Yes

Remote Sites

Other branches of the institution: Yes
Other college campuses: Yes
Students' homes: Yes
Work sites: Yes
Libraries: Yes
Elementary/Secondary schools: Yes
Correctional institutions: Yes

On-Campus Requirements

Is an on-campus component required? No

Tuition & Fees

In-state tuition per credit: $173
Out-of-state tuition per credit: $173
Average yearly cost of books: $50

Financial Aid

Is financial aid available to full-time students? Yes
Is financial aid available to part-time students? Yes
Are academic scholarships available? No
Assistance programs available to students: Federal Stafford
Loan, Federal Pell Grant, veterans' assistance

Central Piedmont Community College

PO Box 35009
Charlotte, NC 28235
Contact: David Flanagan, Director
Department e-mail: cww@cpcc.cc.nc.us
Department Web address: www.cww.cpcc.cc.nc.us
School Web address: www.cpcc.cc.nc.us
Institutional accreditation: Southern Association of
Colleges and Schools

Admissions Requirements

Is a minimum high school GPA required? No
Is an admissions interview required? No
Can pre-requisite course work be waived? Yes
Are international students eligible to apply? Yes
Is the TOEFL required for international students? Yes

Program Delivery

Two-way interactive video: Yes
Two-way audio, one-way video: No
One-way live video: Yes
One-way pre-recorded video: Yes

Audio graphics: No
Audio: No
Hardware requirements: 486 or higher, 28.8KBPS modem or higher
Software requirements: Browser, e-mail, word processing
Is the library accessible to students? Yes
Are computers accessible to students? Yes

Remote Sites

Other branches of the institution: Yes
Other college campuses: No
Students' homes: Yes
Work sites: No
Libraries: Yes
Elementary/Secondary schools: No
Community-based organizations: No
Correctional institutions: No

On-Campus Requirements

Is an on-campus component required? No

Tuition & Fees

In-state tuition per credit: $28
Out-of-state tuition per credit: $170
Average yearly cost of books: $500

Financial Aid

Is financial aid available to full-time students? Yes
Is financial aid available to part-time students? Yes
Are academic scholarships available? Yes
Assistance programs available to students: Federal Perkins Loan, Federal Pell Grant, Federal Work-Study Program, veterans' assistance

Central Virginia Community College

Learning Resources
3506 Wards Road
Lynchburg, VA 24502
Contact: Susan S. Beasley, Audiovisual Supervisor
School Web address: www.cv.cc.va.us
Institutional accreditation: Southern Association of Colleges and Schools

Subjects Offered

Biology, economics, business, health, administration of justice, math, office systems technology, chemistry, English, information systems technology, history, marketing, psychology, sociology

Admissions Requirements

Is a minimum high school GPA required? No
Is provisional admission available? Yes
Is an admissions interview required? No
Can pre-requisite course work be waived? Yes
Are international students eligible to apply? Yes
Is the TOEFL required for international students? Yes
What is the minimum TOEFL score required? 500

Program Delivery

Primary method of program delivery: Text
Two-way interactive video: Yes
Hardware requirements: Web access/Internet
Is the library accessible to students? Yes

Remote Sites

Other branches of the institution: Yes
Students' homes: Yes
Work sites: Yes

On-Campus Requirements

Is an on-campus component required? Yes
On-campus course work: Yes
On-campus program orientation: Yes
On-campus exams: Yes

Tuition & Fees

In-state tuition per credit: $37
Out-of-state tuition per credit: $165
Average yearly cost of books: $300

Financial Aid

Is financial aid available to full-time students? Yes
Is financial aid available to part-time students? Yes
Are academic scholarships available? Yes
Assistance programs available to students: Federal Pell Grant, Federal Work-Study Program, in-state student aid programs, veterans' assistance

Central Washington University

Office of the Provost
Academic Computing
400 East 8th Avenue
Ellensburg, WA 98926
Contact: David Kaufman, Assistant to the Provost
Department e-mail: kaufman@cwv.edu
Department Web address: www.cwu.edu/media
School Web address: www.cwu.edu
Institutional accreditation: Northwest Association of Schools and Colleges

Subjects Offered

Administrative management and business education, art, biological sciences, chemistry, curriculum and supervision, engineering, English, family and consumer sciences, geology, history, mathematics, music, organization development, physical education, psychology, resource management, teacher education, theater arts

Admissions Requirements

Is provisional admission available? Yes
Can pre-requisite course work be waived? Yes
Are international students eligible to apply? Yes
Is the TOEFL required for international students? Yes

Program Delivery

Primary method of program delivery: Remote site
Two-way interactive video: Yes
Is the library accessible to students? Yes
Are computers accessible to students? Yes

Remote Sites

Other branches of the institution: Yes

On-Campus Requirements

Is an on-campus component required? Yes
On-campus course work: Yes
On-campus exams: Yes

Tuition & Fees

In-state tuition per credit: $84
Out-of-state tuition per credit: $325
Average yearly cost of books: $672

Financial Aid

Is financial aid available to full-time students? Yes
Is financial aid available to part-time students? Yes
Are academic scholarships available? Yes
Assistance programs available to students: Federal Stafford Loan, Federal Perkins Loan, Federal Plus Loan, Federal Pell Grant, Federal Work-Study Program, in-state student aid programs, veterans' assistance

Central Wyoming College

2600 Peck Avenue
Riverton, WY 82501
Contact: Dr. Jan McCoy, Director, Distance Education
Department e-mail: jmccoy@cwc.cc.wy.us
School Web address: www.cwc.whecn.edu
Institutional accreditation: North Central Association of Colleges and Schools

Subjects Offered

Art, biology, computer info services, cooperative work experience, English, humanities, Spanish, math, nursing, philosophy, wellness, political science, psychology, surgical technician, theater, orientation to college, nursing assistant

Admissions Requirements

Is a minimum high school GPA required? No
Is provisional admission available? No
Is an admissions interview required? Yes
Can pre-requisite course work be waived? Yes
Are international students eligible to apply? Yes
Is the TOEFL required for international students? Yes

Program Delivery

Primary method of program delivery: Remote site
Two-way interactive video: Yes
Two-way audio, one-way video: No
One-way live video: No
One-way pre-recorded video: Yes
Audio graphics: No
Audio: Yes
Is the library accessible to students? Yes
Are computers accessible to students? Yes

Remote Sites

Other branches of the institution: Yes
Other college campuses: No
Students' homes: Yes
Work sites: No
Libraries: No
Elementary/Secondary schools: Yes
Community-based organizations: No
Correctional institutions: Yes

On-Campus Requirements

Is an on-campus component required? Yes

Tuition & Fees

In-state tuition per credit: $46
Out-of-state tuition per credit: $138
Average yearly cost of books: $600

Financial Aid

Is financial aid available to full-time students? Yes
Is financial aid available to part-time students? Yes
Are academic scholarships available? Yes
Assistance programs available to students: Federal Stafford Loan, Federal Plus Loan, Federal Pell Grant, Federal Work-Study Program

Cerritos Community College

Distance Education Program
Technology Training and Distance Education
1110 Alondra Drive
Norwalk, CA 90650
Contact: M.L. Bettino, Dean, Technology Training and
    Distance Education
Department e-mail: de-info@cerritos.edu
Department Web address: www.cerritos.edu/de
School Web address: www.cerritos.edu
Institutional accreditation: Accrediting Commission for
    Community and Junior Colleges of the Western
    Association of Schools and Colleges

Subjects Offered

Business, computer information systems, educational
    technology, earth science, health education, anthropol-
    ogy, economics, philosophy, political science, sociology,
    history, journalism, theater, English, reading

Admissions Requirements

Is a minimum high school GPA required? No
Is provisional admission available? Yes
Is an admissions interview required? No
Can pre-requisite course work be waived? No
Are international students eligible to apply? Yes
Is the TOEFL required for international students? Yes
What is the minimum TOEFL score required? 450

Program Delivery

Primary method of program delivery: Web
Two-way interactive video: Yes
Two-way audio, one-way video: No
One-way live video: Yes
One-way pre-recorded video: Yes
Audio graphics: No
Audio: Yes
Hardware requirements: PC or Macintosh with Internet
    access, modem or network card
Software requirements: Access to Internet and e-mail, some
    classes require Microsoft Office
Is the library accessible to students? Yes
Are computers accessible to students? Yes

Remote Sites

Other branches of the institution: Yes
Other college campuses: Yes
Students' homes: Yes
Work sites: Yes
Libraries: Yes
Elementary/Secondary schools: Yes
Community-based organizations: Yes
Correctional institutions: No

On-Campus Requirements

On-campus course work: No

Tuition & Fees

In-state tuition per credit: $11
Out-of-state tuition per credit: $131
Average yearly cost of books: $100

Financial Aid

Is financial aid available to full-time students? Yes
Is financial aid available to part-time students? Yes
Are academic scholarships available? Yes
Assistance programs available to students: Federal Stafford
    Loan, Federal Pell Grant, Federal Work-Study Program,
    in-state student aid programs, veterans' assistance

Chadron State College

Extended Campus Programs
1000 Main Street
Chadron, NE 69337
Contact: Steven Taylor, Assistant Vice President for
    Extended Campus Program
Department e-mail: alangford@csc.edu
School Web address: www.csc.edu/ecamous.htm
Institutional accreditation: North Central Association of
    Colleges and Schools

Subjects Offered

Accounting, management, business administration/
    education, marketing, counseling, mathematics, criminal
    justice, philosophy, education, political science, English,
    psychology, earth science, real estate, family and
    consumer science, sociology, health/physical education/
    recreation, social work, history, vocational education,
    industrial technology, information management systems

Admissions Requirements

Is a minimum high school GPA required? No
Is an admissions interview required? No
Are international students eligible to apply? Yes
Is the TOEFL required for international students? Yes
What is the minimum TOEFL score required? 550

Program Delivery

Primary method of program delivery: Remote site
Two-way interactive video: Yes

Tuition & Fees

In-state tuition per credit: $109
Out-of-state tuition per credit: $175
Average yearly cost of books: $600

Financial Aid

Is financial aid available to full-time students? Yes
Assistance programs available to students: Federal Stafford
Loan, Federal Perkins Loan, Federal Plus Loan, Federal
Pell Grant, Federal Work-Study Program, in-state
student aid programs, veterans' assistance

Champlain College

Distance Learning Program
Champlain College Online
163 South Williard Street
Burlington, VT 05401
Contact: John Lavallee, Director
Department e-mail: online@champlain.edu
School Web address: champlain.edu
Institutional accreditation: New England Association of
Schools and Colleges

Subjects Offered

Accounting, business, e-business and commerce, hotel and
restaurant management, international business,
management, software development, telecommunications, website development and management, computer
and information systems, professional studies

Admissions Requirements

Is provisional admission available? Yes
Is an admissions interview required? Yes
Is the TOEFL required for international students? Yes

Program Delivery

Is the library accessible to students? Yes
Are computers accessible to students? No

On-Campus Requirements

Is an on-campus component required? Yes
On-campus course work: Yes

Tuition & Fees

In-state tuition per credit: $330
Out-of-state tuition per credit: $330
Average yearly cost of books: $30

Financial Aid

Is financial aid available to full-time students? Yes
Is financial aid available to part-time students? Yes

Are academic scholarships available? Yes
Assistance programs available to students: Federal Stafford
Loan

Charles Stewart Mott Community College

Educational Systems
Distance Learning Office
1401 East Court Street
Flint, MI 48503
Contact: Lori France, Distance Learning Coordinator
Department e-mail: lfrance@mcc.edu
Department Web address: cwp.mcc.edu
School Web address: mcc.edu
Institutional accreditation: North Central Association of
Colleges and Schools

Subjects Offered

Math, geometric dimensioning and tolerancing, literature,
business management, geology, art appreciation,
psychology, music appreciation, sociology, English
composition, business, technical writing, economics,
computer programming, history, computer software
application, political science, quality assurance, blueprint
reading

Program Delivery

Hardware requirements: 486DX 66MHz PC or better,
8MB or RAM or higher, 14.4KBPS modem or higher,
Windows
Software requirements: Software appropriate to course (i.e.,
Microsoft Excel 2000 for PC
Is the library accessible to students? Yes
Are computers accessible to students? Yes

On-Campus Requirements

Is an on-campus component required? Yes
On-campus program orientation: Yes
On-campus exams: Yes

Tuition & Fees

In-state tuition per credit: $61
Out-of-state tuition per credit: $118
Average yearly additional fees: $44

Financial Aid

Is financial aid available to full-time students? Yes
Is financial aid available to part-time students? Yes
Are academic scholarships available? Yes
Assistance programs available to students: Federal Stafford
Loan, Federal Plus Loan, Federal Pell Grant, Federal
Work-Study Program, veterans' assistance

Charter Oak State College

Distance Learning Program
55 Paul Manafort Drive
New Britain, CT 06053
Contact: Susan Israel, Coordinator of Academic Program
Department e-mail: mintravia@mail.cosc.edu
School Web address: www.cosc.edu
Institutional accreditation: New England Association of Schools and Colleges

Subjects Offered

Anthroplogy, history, biology, interdisciplinary studies, art, mathematics, adult learning, philosophy, business, political science, communication, Latin America, film, economics, sociology, English, astronomy, geography

Admissions Requirements

Is a minimum high school GPA required? No
Is provisional admission available? No
Is an admissions interview required? No
Can pre-requisite course work be waived? Yes
Are international students eligible to apply? No

Program Delivery

Primary method of program delivery: Text
Two-way interactive video: No
Two-way audio, one-way video: No
One-way live video: No
One-way pre-recorded video: Yes
Audio graphics: No
Audio: No
Software requirements: Mac, Windows, or NT computers, 32MB of RAM, 100MB hard disk storage, 28.8KBPS modem, Netscape 4.0 or Internet Explorer, and Internet service provider

Remote Sites

Other branches of the institution: No
Other college campuses: No
Students' homes: Yes
Work sites: Yes

Tuition & Fees

In-state tuition per credit: $106
Out-of-state tuition per credit: $140
Average yearly cost of books: $15

Financial Aid

Is financial aid available to full-time students? Yes
Is financial aid available to part-time students? Yes
Are academic scholarships available? Yes
Assistance programs available to students: Federal Stafford Loan, Federal Plus Loan, Federal Pell Grant, in-state student aid programs

Citrus Community College

Distance Education
1000 West Foothill Boulevard
Glendora, CA 91741
Contact: Dr. Bruce Solheim and Main Greenwell-Cunnigham, Distance Education Coordinators
Department e-mail: online@citrus.cc.ca.us
School Web address: citruscollege.com

Subjects Offered

Anthrolpogy, psychology, business, sociology, art, speech, biology, supervision, communication, English, history, math, nursing, philosophy, political science

Admissions Requirements

Is a minimum high school GPA required? No
Is an admissions interview required? No
Can pre-requisite course work be waived? Yes
Are international students eligible to apply? Yes
Is the TOEFL required for international students? Yes

Program Delivery

Audio graphics: Yes
Audio: Yes
Hardware requirements: modem, Internet access, computer able to receive e-mail
Software requirements: Microsoft Word 95 or higher
Is the library accessible to students? Yes
Are computers accessible to students? Yes

Remote Sites

Students' homes: Yes
Work sites: Yes

On-Campus Requirements

Is an on-campus component required? Yes
On-campus course work: Yes
On-campus program orientation: Yes
On-campus exams: Yes

Tuition & Fees

In-state tuition per credit: $11
Out-of-state tuition per credit: $161
Average yearly cost of books: $400

Financial Aid

Is financial aid available to full-time students? Yes
Is financial aid available to part-time students? No
Are academic scholarships available? Yes

Assistance programs available to students: Federal Stafford
Loan, Federal Perkins Loan, Federal Plus Loan, Federal
Pell Grant, in-state student aid programs, veterans'
assistance

Clackamus Community College

Distance Learning
19600 South Molalla Avenue
Oregon City, OR 97004
Contact: Cynthia R. Andrew, Director, Learning Resource
Department e-mail: cyndia@clackamus.cc.us
Department Web address: www.dl.clackamus.cc.or.us
School Web address: www.clackamus.cc.or.us
Institutional accreditation: Northwest Association of
Schools and Colleges

Subjects Offered

Business, reading, career planning, science, college success,
sociology, computer science, cooperative work experience, criminal justice, drafting technology, English,
family studies, high school diploma, health

Admissions Requirements

Is a minimum high school GPA required? No
Is provisional admission available? Yes
Is an admissions interview required? No
Are international students eligible to apply? Yes
Is the TOEFL required for international students? Yes
What is the minimum TOEFL score required? 523

Program Delivery

Primary method of program delivery: Remote site
Two-way interactive video: Yes
Two-way audio, one-way video: Yes
One-way live video: Yes
One-way pre-recorded video: Yes
Is the library accessible to students? Yes
Are computers accessible to students? Yes

Remote Sites

Other branches of the institution: Yes
Students' homes: Yes
Work sites: Yes
Libraries: Yes
Elementary/Secondary schools: Yes

On-Campus Requirements

On-campus course work: Yes
On-campus program orientation: Yes
On-campus exams: Yes

Tuition & Fees

In-state tuition per credit: $37
Out-of-state tuition per credit: $131
Average yearly cost of books: $300

Financial Aid

Is financial aid available to full-time students? Yes
Is financial aid available to part-time students? Yes
Are academic scholarships available? Yes
Assistance programs available to students: Federal Stafford
Loan, Federal Perkins Loan, Federal Plus Loan, Federal
Pell Grant, Federal Work-Study Program, veterans'
assistance

Clarkson College

Undergraduate Nursing
Distance Learning
101 South 42nd Street
Omaha, NE 68131
Contact: Ellen Piskac, Director, Undergraduate Nursing
School Web address: www.clarksoncollege.edu
Institutional accreditation: North Central Association of
Colleges and Schools

Subjects Offered

Nursing, health-related business, medical imaging

Admissions Requirements

Is a minimum high school GPA required? Yes
Is provisional admission available? Yes
Is an admissions interview required? No
Can pre-requisite course work be waived? No
Are international students eligible to apply? Yes
Is the TOEFL required for international students? Yes
What is the minimum TOEFL score required? 600

Program Delivery

Primary method of program delivery: Web
Two-way interactive video: No
Two-way audio, one-way video: No
One-way live video: Yes
One-way pre-recorded video: Yes
Audio graphics: Yes
Audio: Yes
Is the library accessible to students? Yes
Are computers accessible to students? Yes

Remote Sites

Other branches of the institution: No
Other college campuses: No
Students' homes: Yes

Work sites: Yes
Libraries: No
Elementary/Secondary schools: No
Community-based organizations: No
Correctional institutions: No

On-Campus Requirements

Is an on-campus component required? No

Tuition & Fees

In-state tuition per credit: $289
Out-of-state tuition per credit: $289
Average yearly cost of books: $600

Financial Aid

Is financial aid available to full-time students? Yes
Is financial aid available to part-time students? Yes
Are academic scholarships available? Yes
Assistance programs available to students: Federal Stafford Loan, Federal Plus Loan, Federal Pell Grant, Federal Work-Study Program, in-state student aid programs, veterans' assistance

Clayton College & State University

Office of Distance Learning
5900 North Lee Street
Morrow, GA 30260-0285
Contact: C. Blaine Carpenter, PhD, Academic Director of Distance Learning
Department Web address: distancelearning.clayton.edu
School Web address: www.clayton.edu
Institutional accreditation: Southern Association of Colleges and Schools

Subjects Offered

Business, math, social science, humanities, health science, technology, natural science, integrative studies, information technology

Admissions Requirements

Is provisional admission available? Yes
Can pre-requisite course work be waived? Yes
Are international students eligible to apply? Yes
Is the TOEFL required for international students? Yes
What is the minimum TOEFL score required? 550

Program Delivery

Primary method of program delivery: Web
Two-way interactive video: No
Two-way audio, one-way video: No

One-way live video: No
One-way pre-recorded video: Yes
Audio graphics: No
Audio: No
Hardware requirements: 166 MHz Pentium (MMX) 32MB of RAM, 1.5 GB hard drive, 2x CD-ROM, 56KBPS modem, Ethernet card
Software requirements: MS Windows 95, MS Office 97, MSN Internet Explorer 4.0
Is the library accessible to students? Yes
Are computers accessible to students? Yes

Remote Sites

Other branches of the institution: No
Other college campuses: No
Students' homes: Yes
Work sites: Yes
Libraries: No
Elementary/Secondary schools: No
Community-based organizations: No
Correctional institutions: No

On-Campus Requirements

Is an on-campus component required? Yes
On-campus course work: Yes
On-campus admissions interview: No
On-campus program orientation: Yes
On-campus exams: Yes

Tuition & Fees

In-state tuition per credit: $681
Out-of-state tuition per credit: $1,386
Average yearly cost of books: $200
Average yearly additional fees: $20

Financial Aid

Is financial aid available to full-time students? Yes
Is financial aid available to part-time students? Yes
Are academic scholarships available? Yes
Assistance programs available to students: Federal Stafford Loan, Federal Plus Loan, Federal Pell Grant, Federal Work-Study Program, in-state student aid programs, veterans' assistance

Clovis Community College

Educational Services
417 Schepps Boulevard
Clovis, NM 88135
Contact: Becky Rowley, Vice President of Educational Services
School Web address: www.clovis.cc.nm.us

Institutional accreditation: North Central Association of Colleges and Schools

Subjects Offered

Accounting, English, history, health and physical education, math, psychology, sociology, special topics

Admissions Requirements

Is a minimum high school GPA required? No
Is an admissions interview required? No
Can pre-requisite course work be waived? Yes
Are international students eligible to apply? Yes
Is the TOEFL required for international students? No

Program Delivery

Primary method of program delivery: Text
Two-way interactive video: Yes
Two-way audio, one-way video: No
One-way live video: No
One-way pre-recorded video: No
Audio graphics: No
Audio: No
Is the library accessible to students? Yes
Are computers accessible to students? Yes

Remote Sites

Other branches of the institution: No
Other college campuses: No
Students' homes: No
Work sites: No
Libraries: No
Elementary/Secondary schools: Yes
Community-based organizations: No
Correctional institutions: No

On-Campus Requirements

Is an on-campus component required? No

Tuition & Fees

In-state tuition per credit: $32
Out-of-state tuition per credit: $40

Financial Aid

Is financial aid available to full-time students? Yes
Is financial aid available to part-time students? No
Are academic scholarships available? Yes
Assistance programs available to students: Federal Stafford Loan, Federal Pell Grant, Federal Work-Study Program, veterans' assistance

College of DuPage

Center for Independent Learning
COD Online
425 22nd Street
Glen Ellyn, IL 60137
Contact: Annette Haggray, Associate Dean
Department e-mail: schiesz@cdnet.cod.edu
Department Web address: www.cod.edu/online
School Web address: www.cod.edu
Institutional accreditation: North Central Association of Colleges and Schools

Subjects Offered

English, management, computer information systems, marketing, office technology, biology, Spanish, earth science, economics, chemistry, journalism, humanities, personal health, history, mathematics, accounting, political science, allied health, psychology, automotive technology

Admissions Requirements

Is a minimum high school GPA required? No
Is provisional admission available? No
Is an admissions interview required? No
Can pre-requisite course work be waived? No
Are international students eligible to apply? Yes

Program Delivery

Primary method of program delivery: Web
Two-way interactive video: No
Two-way audio, one-way video: No
One-way live video: No
One-way pre-recorded video: No
Audio graphics: No
Audio: No
Hardware requirements: 28.8KBPS modem, Mac or PC, 32MB RAM or better
Software requirements: Netscape 4.0 or higher and MS Explorer 4.0 or higher
Is the library accessible to students? Yes
Are computers accessible to students? Yes

Remote Sites

Other branches of the institution: Yes
Other college campuses: Yes
Students' homes: Yes
Work sites: Yes
Libraries: No
Elementary/Secondary schools: No
Community-based organizations: No
Correctional institutions: No

On-Campus Requirements

Is an on-campus component required? No

Tuition & Fees

In-state tuition per credit: $35
Out-of-state tuition per credit: $35
Average yearly cost of books: $300

Financial Aid

Is financial aid available to full-time students? Yes
Is financial aid available to part-time students? Yes
Are academic scholarships available? Yes
Assistance programs available to students: Federal Stafford Loan, Federal Perkins Loan, Federal Plus Loan, Federal Pell Grant, Federal Work-Study Program, in-state student aid programs, veterans' assistance

College of Health Sciences

Distance Learning
920 South Jefferson Street
Roanoke, VA 24301
Contact: Bridget Franklin, Director of Distance Learning
Department e-mail: bfranklin@health.chs.edu
School Web address: www.chs.edu
Institutional accreditation: Southern Association of Colleges and Schools

Subjects Offered

English, nutrition, statistics, philosophy, sociology, nursing, radiologic science, respiratory care, health organization management, business, occupational therapy, medical terminology

Admissions Requirements

Is provisional admission available? Yes
Is an admissions interview required? Yes
Can pre-requisite course work be waived? Yes
Are international students eligible to apply? Yes
Is the TOEFL required for international students? Yes
What is the minimum TOEFL score required? 500

Program Delivery

Primary method of program delivery: Web
Two-way interactive video: No
Two-way audio, one-way video: No
One-way live video: No
One-way pre-recorded video: Yes
Audio graphics: No
Audio: No
Hardware requirements: 486 or higher
Software requirements: Netscape or Internet Explorer
Is the library accessible to students? Yes

Remote Sites

Other branches of the institution: No
Other college campuses: No
Students' homes: Yes
Work sites: Yes
Libraries: No
Elementary/Secondary schools: No
Community-based organizations: No
Correctional institutions: No

On-Campus Requirements

Is an on-campus component required? Yes

Tuition & Fees

In-state tuition per credit: $370
Out-of-state tuition per credit: $370

Financial Aid

Is financial aid available to full-time students? Yes
Is financial aid available to part-time students? Yes
Are academic scholarships available? Yes
Assistance programs available to students: Federal Stafford Loan, Federal Plus Loan, Federal Pell Grant, Federal Work-Study Program, in-state student aid programs, veterans' assistance

College of Southern Maryland

Learning Technologies
Distance Learning
8730 Mitchell Road
PO Box 910
La Plata, MD 20646
Contact: Paul Toscano, Distance Learning Coordinator
Department e-mail: pault@csm.cc.md.us
Department Web address: www.csm.cc.md.us/distance/index.htm
School Web address: www.csm.cc.md.us
Institutional accreditation: Middle States Association of Colleges and Schools

Subjects Offered

Accounting, art appreciation, astronomy, biology, business, business and technical writing, communications, economics, education, elementary Spanish, English, environmental science, film/cinema, geography, geology, health, history, information technology, mathematics, office technology, philosophy, political science, psychology, sociology, wellness

Admissions Requirements

Is a minimum high school GPA required? No
Is an admissions interview required? No
Can pre-requisite course work be waived? Yes
Are international students eligible to apply? Yes
Is the TOEFL required for international students? Yes
What is the minimum TOEFL score required? 400

Program Delivery

Two-way interactive video: Yes
Two-way audio, one-way video: No
One-way live video: No
One-way pre-recorded video: Yes
Audio graphics: No
Audio: Yes
Hardware requirements: Internet access
Software requirements: Web browser
Is the library accessible to students? Yes

Remote Sites

Other branches of the institution: Yes

On-Campus Requirements

Is an on-campus component required? No

Tuition & Fees

In-state tuition per credit; $73
Out-of-state tuition per credit: $190
Average yearly cost of books: $600

Financial Aid

Is financial aid available to full-time students? Yes
Is financial aid available to part-time students? Yes
Are academic scholarships available? Yes
Assistance programs available to students: Federal Stafford
    Loan, Federal Plus Loan, Federal Pell Grant, Federal
    Work-Study Program, in-state student aid programs,
    veterans' assistance

College of West Virginia

School of Extended and Distance Learning
PO Box AG
Beckly, WV 25802-2830
Contact: Dr. Mark Miller, Assistant Vice President of
    Academic Affairs
Department e-mail: saeil@cwv.edu
Department Web address: www.cwv.edu/saeil
School Web address: www.cwv.edu
Institutional accreditation: North Central Association of
    Colleges and Schools

Subjects Offered

Accounting, art, astronomy, banking, biology, business law,
    chemistry, computer information systems, communica-
    tion, criminal justice, economics, English, environmen-
    tal science, entrepreneurship, finance, geography,
    geology, health care administration, health care medical
    information, history, health science, international
    business

Admissions Requirements

Is provisional admission available? No
Is an admissions interview required? No
Can pre-requisite course work be waived? Yes
Are international students eligible to apply? Yes
Is the TOEFL required for international students? Yes
What is the minimum TOEFL score required? 500

Program Delivery

Primary method of program delivery: Text
Two-way interactive video: No
Two-way audio, one-way video: No
One-way live video: No
One-way pre-recorded video: No
Audio graphics: Yes
Audio: No
Software requirements: Varies by program, Windows-
    compliant hardware and software
Is the library accessible to students? Yes
Are computers accessible to students? No

Remote Sites

Other branches of the institution: Yes
Other college campuses: No
Students' homes: Yes
Work sites: Yes
Libraries: Yes
Elementary/Secondary schools: Yes
Community-based organizations: Yes
Correctional institutions: Yes

Tuition & Fees

In-state tuition per credit: $170
Out-of-state tuition per credit: $170
Average yearly cost of books: $750

Financial Aid

Is financial aid available to full-time students? Yes
Is financial aid available to part-time students? Yes
Are academic scholarships available? Yes
Assistance programs available to students: Federal Stafford
    Loan, Federal Plus Loan, Federal Pell Grant, Federal
    Work-Study Program, in-state student aid programs,
    veterans' assistance

Colorado Mountain College

Admissions
PO Box 10001
Glenwood Springs, CO 81602
Department e-mail: joinus@coloradomtn.edu
School Web address: www.coloradomtn.edu
Institutional accreditation: North Central Association of
Colleges and Schools

Subjects Offered

Accounting, business, chemistry, economics, early
childhood education, education, electricity and wiring,
English composition, geology, heating, ventilation and
air conditioning, literature, management, marketing,
mathematics, physics, plumbing, political science,
sociology, theater, anthropology, art, astronomy, biology,
history, humanities, health and fitness, psychology,
philosophy, ethics, geography, music

Admissions Requirements

Is a minimum high school GPA required? No
Is provisional admission available? No
Is an admissions interview required? No
Can pre-requisite course work be waived? No
Are international students eligible to apply? Yes
Is the TOEFL required for international students? Yes

Program Delivery

Primary method of program delivery: Remote site
Two-way interactive video: Yes
Hardware requirements: Mac: Power PC or faster
processor, 16MB of RAM or more, 28.8KBPS modem
or more; PC: 75 MHz or faster processor, 16MB of
RAM or more
Software requirements: Mac: MacOS 7.55 or later; PC:
Windows 95, 98, or NT
Is the library accessible to students? Yes
Are computers accessible to students? Yes

Remote Sites

Other branches of the institution: Yes
Other college campuses: Yes
Students' homes: Yes
Libraries: Yes
Elementary/Secondary schools: Yes
Correctional institutions: Yes

On-Campus Requirements

Is an on-campus component required? Yes
On-campus exams: Yes

Tuition & Fees

In-state tuition per credit: $66
Out-of-state tuition per credit: $215
Average yearly cost of books: $550

Financial Aid

Is financial aid available to full-time students? Yes
Is financial aid available to part-time students? Yes
Are academic scholarships available? Yes
Assistance programs available to students: Federal Stafford
Loan, Federal Perkins Loan, Federal Plus Loan, Federal
Pell Grant, Federal Work-Study Program, in-state
student aid programs, veterans' assistance

Colorado State University

Division of Educational Outreach
Distance Degree Program—CSON
Spruce Hall
Fort Collins, CO 80523-1040
Contact: Arietta Wiedmann, PhD, Director of External
Studies
Department e-mail: info@learn.colostate.edu
Department Web address: www.csu2learn.colostate.edu
School Web address: www.colostate.edu
Institutional accreditation: North Central Association of
Colleges and Schools

Subjects Offered

Agriculture, animal science, anthropology, arts, astronomy,
biology, business, chemistry, civil engineering, communication, communication disorders, computer-assisted
design, computer science, criminal justice, earth
sciences, economics, education, engineering, English,
environmental studies, finance, fine arts, fishery and
wildlife biology, foreign language, geography, geology,
gerontology, grant writing, health and nutrition, history,
horticulture, human development and family studies,
human rehabilitative services, journalism

Admissions Requirements

Is provisional admission available? No
Is an admissions interview required? No
Are international students eligible to apply? Yes
Is the TOEFL required for international students? No

Program Delivery

Primary method of program delivery: Web
One-way pre-recorded video: Yes
Software requirements: Depends on course, computer-
related courses require Pentium, Internet, and e-mail
access

Is the library accessible to students? Yes
Are computers accessible to students? No

Remote Sites

Other branches of the institution: Yes
Other college campuses: Yes
Students' homes: Yes
Work sites: Yes
Libraries: Yes

On-Campus Requirements

Is an on-campus component required? No

Tuition & Fees

Application fee: $30
Can it be waived? No

Financial Aid

Is financial aid available to full-time students? Yes
Is financial aid available to part-time students? Yes
Are academic scholarships available? No
Assistance programs available to students: Federal Stafford
    Loan, Federal Perkins Loan, Federal Plus Loan, Federal
    Pell Grant, veterans' assistance

Community College of Southern Nevada

Rural Continuing and Distance Education
6375 West Charleston Boulevard
Las Vegas, NV 89146
Contact: Bradley Bleck, Associate Dean of Distance
    Education
Department e-mail: distanceed@ccsn.nevada.edu
Department Web address: www.ccsn.nevada.edu/
    distanceed
School Web address: www.ccsn.nevada.edu
Institutional accreditation: Northwest Association of
    Schools and Colleges

Subjects Offered

Accounting, art, business, astronomy, biology, computing,
    cardiorespiratory therapy, education, English, fire
    science, history, reading, health information technology,
    health and wellness, research on Internet, mathematics,
    music, medical assisting, philosophy, political science,
    psychology, reading, sociology, Spanish, phlebotomy,
    veterinary technology, study skills

Admissions Requirements

Is a minimum high school GPA required? No
Is provisional admission available? No

Is an admissions interview required? No
Can pre-requisite course work be waived? Yes
Are international students eligible to apply? Yes
Is the TOEFL required for international students? Yes
What is the minimum TOEFL score required? 450

Program Delivery

Primary method of program delivery: Web
Two-way interactive video: Yes
Two-way audio, one-way video: No
One-way live video: No
One-way pre-recorded video: Yes
Audio graphics: No
Audio: No
Hardware requirements: Computer capable of running
    Windows 95
Software requirements: Netscape or Internet Explorer
    version 4.0 or better, Windows 95
Is the library accessible to students? Yes
Are computers accessible to students? Yes

Remote Sites

Other branches of the institution: Yes
Other college campuses: Yes
Students' homes: Yes
Work sites: Yes
Libraries: Yes
Elementary/Secondary schools: Yes
Community-based organizations: Yes
Correctional institutions: No

On-Campus Requirements

Is an on-campus component required? No

Tuition & Fees

In-state tuition per credit: $43
Out-of-state tuition per credit: $64
Average yearly cost of books: $96

Financial Aid

Is financial aid available to full-time students? Yes
Is financial aid available to part-time students? Yes
Are academic scholarships available? Yes
Assistance programs available to students: Federal Stafford
    Loan, Federal Perkins Loan, Federal Plus Loan, Federal
    Pell Grant, Federal Work-Study Program, in-state
    student aid programs, veterans' assistance

Concordia College

171 White Plains Road
Bronxville, NY 10708
School Web address: www.concordia-ny.edu

Institutional accreditation: Middle States Association of
Colleges and Schools; New York State Education
Department

Subjects Offered

Business, English, psychology

Program Delivery

Primary method of program delivery: Remote site
Two-way interactive video: Yes
Two-way audio, one-way video: No
One-way live video: No
One-way pre-recorded video: No
Audio graphics: No
Audio: No
Is the library accessible to students? No
Are computers accessible to students? No

Remote Sites

Other branches of the institution: No
Other college campuses: Yes
Students' homes: No
Work sites: No
Libraries: No
Elementary/Secondary schools: Yes
Community-based organizations: No
Correctional institutions: No

Concordia University

School of Human Services
275 North Syndicate Street
St. Paul, MN 55104
Contact: Jim Ollhoff, Associate Dean
Department e-mail: cshs@csp.edu
Department Web address: www.cshs.csp.edu
School Web address: www.csp.edu
Institutional accreditation: North Central Association of
Colleges and Schools

Admissions Requirements

Is a minimum high school GPA required? Yes
Is provisional admission available? Yes
Can pre-requisite course work be waived? No
Are international students eligible to apply? Yes
Is the TOEFL required for international students? Yes
What is the minimum TOEFL score required? 550

Program Delivery

Primary method of program delivery: Web
Two-way interactive video: No
Two-way audio, one-way video: No
One-way live video: No

One-way pre-recorded video: No
Audio graphics: No
Audio: No
Is the library accessible to students? Yes
Are computers accessible to students? No

Remote Sites

Other branches of the institution: No
Other college campuses: Yes
Students' homes: Yes
Work sites: Yes
Libraries: Yes
Elementary/Secondary schools: No
Community-based organizations: No
Correctional institutions: No

On-Campus Requirements

Is an on-campus component required? Yes
On-campus course work: Yes
On-campus admissions interview: No
On-campus program orientation: Yes
On-campus exams: No

Tuition & Fees

In-state tuition per credit: $215
Out-of-state tuition per credit: $215
Average yearly cost of books: $500

Financial Aid

Is financial aid available to full-time students? Yes
Is financial aid available to part-time students? Yes
Are academic scholarships available? No
Assistance programs available to students: Federal Stafford
Loan, Federal Perkins Loan, Federal Pell Grant, veterans'
assistance

Connecticut State University System

Online CSU
39 Woodland Street
Hartford, CT 06118-2337
Contact: Robin Worley, Executive Office, Online CSU
Department e-mail: worleyr@sysoff.ctstateu.edu
School Web address: www.onlinecsu.ctstate.edu
Institutional accreditation: New England Association of
Schools and Colleges

Subjects Offered

Anthropology, chemistry, technology, statistics, business,
economics, nursing, mathematics, psychology, education, accounting, computer science

Admissions Requirements

Is a minimum high school GPA required? No
Are international students eligible to apply? Yes

Program Delivery

Primary method of program delivery: Web
Two-way interactive video: No
Two-way audio, one-way video: No
One-way live video: No
One-way pre-recorded video: Yes
Audio graphics: Yes
Audio: Yes
Hardware requirements: 90 MHz Pentium processor (604 Power PC Mac), 32MB of RAM, 28.8KBPS modem, sound card
Software requirements: Windows 95, 98, or NT, RealPlayer

Remote Sites

Other branches of the institution: Yes
Other college campuses: Yes
Students' homes: Yes
Work sites: Yes
Libraries: Yes
Elementary/Secondary schools: Yes
Community-based organizations: Yes
Correctional institutions: Yes

On-Campus Requirements

Is an on-campus component required? No

Tuition & Fees

In-state tuition per credit: $215
Out-of-state tuition per credit: $215

Financial Aid

Is financial aid available to full-time students? Yes
Is financial aid available to part-time students? Yes
Are academic scholarships available? Yes
Assistance programs available to students: Federal Stafford Loan, Federal Perkins Loan, Federal Plus Loan, Federal Pell Grant, Federal Work-Study Program, in-state student aid programs, veterans' assistance

Connors State College

Distance Education
RT 1 Box 1000
Warner, OK 74469
Contact: Dr. Ronald Ramming, Director of Distance Education
Department e-mail: rramming@connors.cc.ok.us
Department Web address: www.connors.cc.ok.us/disted

School Web address: www.connors.cc.ok.us
Institutional accreditation: North Central Association of Colleges and Schools

Subjects Offered

Agriculture, business, history, humanities, mathematics, geography, political science, psychology

Admissions Requirements

Is a minimum high school GPA required? No
Is provisional admission available? Yes
Is an admissions interview required? No
Can pre-requisite course work be waived? No
Are international students eligible to apply? Yes
Is the TOEFL required for international students? Yes

Program Delivery

Two-way interactive video: Yes
Two-way audio, one-way video: No
One-way live video: No
One-way pre-recorded video: No
Audio graphics: No
Audio: No
Is the library accessible to students? Yes
Are computers accessible to students? Yes

Remote Sites

Other branches of the institution: Yes
Other college campuses: Yes
Students' homes: Yes
Work sites: No
Libraries: Yes
Elementary/Secondary schools: Yes
Community-based organizations: No
Correctional institutions: Yes

On-Campus Requirements

Is an on-campus component required? Yes
On-campus admissions interview: No
On-campus program orientation: No
On-campus exams: Yes

Tuition & Fees

In-state tuition per credit: $44
Out-of-state tuition per credit: $111

Financial Aid

Is financial aid available to full-time students? Yes
Are academic scholarships available? Yes
Assistance programs available to students: Federal Stafford Loan, Federal Perkins Loan, Federal Plus Loan, Federal Pell Grant, Federal Work-Study Program, in-state student aid programs, veterans' assistance

Cossatot Technical College

Division of Distance Education
PO Box 960
DeQueen, AR 71832
Contact: Donald W. Park, Division Chair
Department e-mail: dpark@ctc.tec.ar.us
School Web address: ctc.tec.ar.us
Institutional accreditation: North Central Association of
    Colleges and Schools

Subjects Offered

General education, general studies

Admissions Requirements

Is a minimum high school GPA required? No
Is provisional admission available? Yes
Is an admissions interview required? No
Can pre-requisite course work be waived? Yes
Is the TOEFL required for international students? Yes
What is the minimum TOEFL score required? 500

Program Delivery

Primary method of program delivery: Web
Two-way interactive video: No
Two-way audio, one-way video: No
One-way live video: No
One-way pre-recorded video: Yes
Audio graphics: No
Audio: No
Hardware requirements: Pentium Processor 90 MHz using
    Windows 95, 98, or NT; 16MB of RAM, 28.8KBPS
    modem
Software requirements: Word processing software
Is the library accessible to students? Yes
Are computers accessible to students? No

Remote Sites

Other branches of the institution: Yes
Other college campuses: Yes
Students' homes: Yes
Work sites: Yes
Libraries: Yes
Elementary/Secondary schools: Yes
Community-based organizations: Yes
Correctional institutions: Yes

On-Campus Requirements

Is an on-campus component required? No

Tuition & Fees

In-state tuition per credit: $40
Out-of-state tuition per credit: $120
Average yearly cost of books: $100

Financial Aid

Is financial aid available to full-time students? Yes
Is financial aid available to part-time students? Yes
Are academic scholarships available? Yes
Assistance programs available to students: Federal Pell
    Grant, Federal Work-Study Program, in-state student aid
    programs, veterans' assistance

County College of Morris

Professional Programs: Distance Education
214 Center Grove Road
Randolph, NJ 07869
Contact: Mary Ann McGowan, Coordinator of Distance
    Learning
Department e-mail: mmcgowan@ccm.edu
Department Web address: www.ccm.edu/vclassrooms
School Web address: www.ccm.edu
Institutional accreditation: Middle States Association of
    Colleges and Schools

Subjects Offered

English, business, history, marketing, media, computers,
    economics, sociology, biology, psychology, office
    systems, immunology

Admissions Requirements

Is a minimum high school GPA required? No
Is an admissions interview required? No
Can pre-requisite course work be waived? Yes
Are international students eligible to apply? Yes
Is the TOEFL required for international students? Yes

Program Delivery

Two-way interactive video: Yes
One-way pre-recorded video: Yes
Audio: No
Software requirements: Internet, e-mail
Is the library accessible to students? Yes
Are computers accessible to students? Yes

Remote Sites

Other branches of the institution: Yes
Other college campuses: Yes
Students' homes: Yes
Work sites: Yes
Libraries: Yes
Elementary/Secondary schools: Yes
Community-based organizations: Yes

On-Campus Requirements

Is an on-campus component required? Yes
On-campus course work: Yes

Tuition & Fees

In-state tuition per credit: $144
Out-of-state tuition per credit: $194

Financial Aid

Is financial aid available to full-time students? Yes
Is financial aid available to part-time students? Yes
Are academic scholarships available? Yes
Assistance programs available to students: Federal Stafford Loan, Federal Perkins Loan, Federal Plus Loan, Federal Pell Grant, Federal Work-Study Program, veterans' assistance

Crown College

Crown Adult Programs (CAP)
6425 County 30
St. Bonifacius, MN 55375
Contact: Carl Polding, Director-CAP
Department e-mail: cap@crown.edu
Department Web address: www.crown.edu/cap
School Web address: www.crown.edu
Institutional accreditation: North Central Association of Colleges and Schools

Subjects Offered

Church leadership, biblical studies, ministry studies, missiology

Admissions Requirements

Is a minimum high school GPA required? Yes
Is provisional admission available? Yes
Is an admissions interview required? Yes
Can pre-requisite course work be waived? No
Are international students eligible to apply? Yes
Is the TOEFL required for international students? Yes

Program Delivery

Primary method of program delivery: Web
One-way pre-recorded video: Yes
Audio graphics: Yes
Audio: Yes
Hardware requirements: 90 MHz, 32 RAM, 28.8KBPS modem, 604 Power PC
Software requirements: Windows PC or Mac
Is the library accessible to students? Yes
Are computers accessible to students? Yes

Remote Sites

Students' homes: Yes

On-Campus Requirements

Is an on-campus component required? No

Tuition & Fees

In-state tuition per credit: $273
Out-of-state tuition per credit: $273
Average yearly cost of books: $20

Financial Aid

Is financial aid available to full-time students? Yes
Is financial aid available to part-time students? Yes
Are academic scholarships available? No
Assistance programs available to students: Federal Stafford Loan, Federal Perkins Loan, Federal Plus Loan, Federal Pell Grant, veterans' assistance

Dakota State University

Office of Distance Education
201 A Mundt Library
Madison, SD 57042
Contact: Deb Gearhart, Director of Distance Education
Department e-mail: dsuinfo@pluto.dsu.edu
Department Web address: www.courses.dsu.edu/disted/
School Web address: www.dsu.edu
Institutional accreditation: North Central Association of Colleges and Schools

Subjects Offered

Computer programming, English, mathematics, psychology, music, health information administration, sociology, business

Admissions Requirements

Is a minimum high school GPA required? No
Can pre-requisite course work be waived? Yes
Are international students eligible to apply? Yes
Is the TOEFL required for international students? Yes
What is the minimum TOEFL score required? 500

Program Delivery

Primary method of program delivery: Web
Two-way interactive video: Yes
Is the library accessible to students? Yes
Are computers accessible to students? No

On-Campus Requirements

Is an on-campus component required? No

Tuition & Fees

In-state tuition per credit: $132
Out-of-state tuition per credit: $132

Financial Aid

Is financial aid available to full-time students? Yes
Is financial aid available to part-time students? No

Dalhousie University

Office of Instructional Development and Technology
Distributed Education
Halifax, NS, Canada B3H 3J5
Contact: Alan Wright, Executive Director
Department e-mail: de@dal.ca
Department Web address: www.dal.ca/de
School Web address: www.dal.ca

Subjects Offered

Anatomy, continuing medical education, disability
management, employee benefit specialist, fire service,
health service administration, local government
administration, management, nursing, physiology, social
work, software management and development

Admissions Requirements

Is provisional admission available? No
Is an admissions interview required? No
Can pre-requisite course work be waived? No
Are international students eligible to apply? Yes
Is the TOEFL required for international students? Yes
What is the minimum TOEFL score required? 580

Program Delivery

Primary method of program delivery: Web
Audio graphics: Yes
Audio: Yes

Remote Sites

Other branches of the institution: Yes
Other college campuses: Yes
Students' homes: Yes
Work sites: Yes

On-Campus Requirements

Is an on-campus component required? Yes

Financial Aid

Is financial aid available to full-time students? Yes
Are academic scholarships available? Yes

Dallas Baptist University

Online Education
3000 Mountain Creek Parkway
Dallas, TX 75211
Contact: Kaye Shelton, Faculty Systems Coordinator
Department e-mail: online@dbu.edu
Department Web address: www.dbuonline.org
School Web address: www.dbu.edu

Institutional accreditation: Southern Association of
Colleges and Schools

Subjects Offered

Accounting, fine arts, experiential learning, introduction to
computers, macroeconomics, microeconomics, English,
finance, management, mathematics, management
information systems, marketing, psychology, religion,
sociology

Admissions Requirements

Is a minimum high school GPA required? Yes
Is provisional admission available? Yes
Can pre-requisite course work be waived? Yes
Are international students eligible to apply? No

Program Delivery

Primary method of program delivery: Web
Two-way interactive video: No
Two-way audio, one-way video: No
One-way live video: No
One-way pre-recorded video: Yes
Audio graphics: Yes
Audio: Yes
Hardware requirements: 90 MHz Pentium processor of
faster, 32MB of RAM, 28.8KBPS modem or faster,
sound card/speakers
Software requirements: Windows 95, 98, or NT (for PC
users); Mac OS 8.1 or later (for Mac users); JAVA-
capable browser; RealPlayer
Is the library accessible to students? Yes
Are computers accessible to students? Yes

Remote Sites

Other branches of the institution: No
Other college campuses: No
Students' homes: Yes
Work sites: Yes
Libraries: Yes
Elementary/Secondary schools: No
Community-based organizations: No
Correctional institutions: No

On-Campus Requirements

Is an on-campus component required? No

Tuition & Fees

In-state tuition per credit: $345
Out-of-state tuition per credit: $345
Average yearly cost of books: $250

Financial Aid

Is financial aid available to full-time students? Yes
Is financial aid available to part-time students? Yes
Are academic scholarships available? Yes
Assistance programs available to students: Federal Stafford Loan, Federal Perkins Loan, Federal Plus Loan, Federal Pell Grant, Federal Work-Study Program, in-state student aid programs, veterans' assistance

Dallas Community Colleges

Dallas TeleCollege
Instructional Services
9596 Walnut Street
Dallas, TX 75243-2112
Contact: Jim Picquet, Executive Dean of Distance Education
Department e-mail: lkn8852@dcccd.edu
School Web address: telecollege.dcccd.edu
Institutional accreditation: Southern Association of Colleges and Schools

Subjects Offered

General education, computer programming, computer-aided drafting and design, veterinary technology, business administration, child development, computer information systems, medical staff services, multimedia technology, office technology

Admissions Requirements

Is a minimum high school GPA required? No
Is provisional admission available? Yes
Is an admissions interview required? No
Can pre-requisite course work be waived? Yes
Are international students eligible to apply? Yes
Is the TOEFL required for international students? Yes
What is the minimum TOEFL score required? 530

Program Delivery

One-way pre-recorded video: Yes
Audio graphics: No
Audio: Yes
Hardware requirements: Multimedia computer with reliable Internet access and an e-mail account
Software requirements: Netscape 4.0 or higher, or Internet Explorer 4.0 or higher
Is the library accessible to students? Yes
Are computers accessible to students? Yes

On-Campus Requirements

Is an on-campus component required? No

Tuition & Fees

In-state tuition per credit: $58
Out-of-state tuition per credit: $370

Financial Aid

Is financial aid available to full-time students? Yes
Is financial aid available to part-time students? Yes
Are academic scholarships available? Yes
Assistance programs available to students: Federal Stafford Loan, Federal Pell Grant, in-state student aid programs, veterans' assistance

Davenport University

Learning Network
415 East Fulton Street
Grand Rapids, MI 49503
Contact: Frank Monervini, Executive Director
Department e-mail: admissionsln@davenport.edu
School Web address: www.learningnetwork.davenport.edu
Institutional accreditation: North Central Association of Colleges and Schools

Subjects Offered

Management, math, accounting, English, marketing, humanities, social science, general education, psychology, computer information systems, finance, economics, communications

Admissions Requirements

Is a minimum high school GPA required? No
Is provisional admission available? No
Is an admissions interview required? No
Are international students eligible to apply? Yes
Is the TOEFL required for international students? Yes
What is the minimum TOEFL score required? 550

Program Delivery

Primary method of program delivery: Web
Hardware requirements: Pentium 100, 32MB of RAM, 28.8KBPS modem, Internet and e-mail provider
Software requirements: Depends on class; Internet Explorer 5.0, word processing software
Is the library accessible to students? Yes
Are computers accessible to students? Yes

Remote Sites

Other branches of the institution: No
Other college campuses: No
Students' homes: No
Work sites: No
Libraries: No

Elementary/Secondary schools: No
Community-based organizations: No
Correctional institutions: No

On-Campus Requirements

Is an on-campus component required? No

Tuition & Fees

Application fee: $25
Can it be waived? No

Financial Aid

Is financial aid available to full-time students? Yes
Is financial aid available to part-time students? Yes
Are academic scholarships available? Yes
Assistance programs available to students: Federal Stafford Loan, Federal Perkins Loan, Federal Plus Loan, Federal Pell Grant, Federal Work-Study Program, veterans' assistance

Dawson Community College

Instructional Services
PO Box 421
300 College Drive
Glendale, MT 59330
Contact: Dr. Consuelo G. Lopez, Dean of Instructional Services
Department e-mail: lopez@dawson.cc.mt.us
School Web address: www.webmaster@dawson.cc.mt.us
Institutional accreditation: Northwest Association of Schools and Colleges

Subjects Offered

Agriculture, art, biology, business, early childhood education, chemical dependency, economics, education, English, history, health, human services, humanities, interdisciplinary studies, law enforcement, mathematics, Native American studies, political science, psychology, sociology

Admissions Requirements

Is a minimum high school GPA required? No
Is provisional admission available? No
Is an admissions interview required? No
Are international students eligible to apply? Yes
Is the TOEFL required for international students? Yes
What is the minimum TOEFL score required? 500

Program Delivery

Two-way interactive video: Yes
Two-way audio, one-way video: Yes
One-way live video: No
One-way pre-recorded video: Yes
Audio graphics: No
Audio: Yes
Hardware requirements: PC capable of running software requirements and Internet connection
Software requirements: Current version of Microsoft Office, current version of Internet Explorer or Netscape Navigator
Is the library accessible to students? Yes
Are computers accessible to students? Yes

Remote Sites

Other branches of the institution: Yes
Other college campuses: Yes
Students' homes: Yes
Work sites: No
Libraries: No
Elementary/Secondary schools: Yes
Community-based organizations: No
Correctional institutions: No

On-Campus Requirements

Is an on-campus component required? Yes
On-campus course work: Yes
On-campus admissions interview: No
On-campus program orientation: Yes
On-campus exams: Yes

Tuition & Fees

In-state tuition per credit: $79
Out-of-state tuition per credit: $179
Average yearly cost of books: $28

Financial Aid

Is financial aid available to full-time students? Yes
Is financial aid available to part-time students? Yes
Are academic scholarships available? Yes
Assistance programs available to students: Federal Stafford Loan, Federal Perkins Loan, Federal Plus Loan, Federal Pell Grant, Federal Work-Study Program, in-state student aid programs, veterans' assistance

Delaware County Community College

Community & Corporate Education
Distance Education
901 South Media Line Road
Media, PA 19063
Contact: Eric R. Wellington, Director of Distance Learning
Department e-mail: ewelling@dcccnet.dccc.edu
School Web address: www.dccc.edu
Institutional accreditation: Middle States Association of
  Colleges and Schools

Subjects Offered

Biology, business, business math, computer information
  systems, economics, English, health administration,
  history, humanities, interactive multimedia, office
  administration, philosophy, physical science, political
  science, psychology, sociology, Spanish

Admissions Requirements

Is a minimum high school GPA required? No
Is provisional admission available? Yes
Is an admissions interview required? No
Can pre-requisite course work be waived? Yes
Are international students eligible to apply? Yes
Is the TOEFL required for international students? No

Program Delivery

Primary method of program delivery: Remote site
Two-way interactive video: Yes
Two-way audio, one-way video: Yes
One-way live video: No
One-way pre-recorded video: Yes
Audio graphics: Yes
Audio: Yes
Hardware requirements: PC: Pentium 133 MHz with
  32MB of RAM. Mac: OS 8.5 or higher, 32MB of RAM,
  28.8KBPS modem
Software requirements: Windows 95; Internet Explorer 4.0,
  Netscape 4.0, or America Online 4.0 or above
Is the library accessible to students? Yes
Are computers accessible to students? Yes

Remote Sites

Other branches of the institution: Yes
Other college campuses: No
Students' homes: Yes
Work sites: Yes
Libraries: No
Elementary/Secondary schools: No
Community-based organizations: Yes
Correctional institutions: Yes

Tuition & Fees

In-state tuition per credit: $131
Out-of-state tuition per credit: $197
Average yearly cost of books: $20

Financial Aid

Is financial aid available to full-time students? Yes
Is financial aid available to part-time students? Yes
Are academic scholarships available? Yes
Assistance programs available to students: Federal Stafford
  Loan, Federal Plus Loan, Federal Pell Grant, Federal
  Work-Study Program, in-state student aid programs,
  veterans' assistance

Delgado Community College

Center for Advancement in Teaching, Media Services,
  Community Outreach
615 City Park Avenue
New Orleans, LA 70119
Contact: Dr. Jim Mazoue, Director
Department e-mail: jmazou@dcc.edu
School Web address: www.dcc.edu
Institutional accreditation: Southern Association of
  Colleges and Schools

Subjects Offered

Business, history, management, philosophy, psychology,
  pharmacy technician, English

Admissions Requirements

Is a minimum high school GPA required? No
Is provisional admission available? Yes
Is an admissions interview required? No
Can pre-requisite course work be waived? Yes
Are international students eligible to apply? Yes
Is the TOEFL required for international students? No

Program Delivery

Primary method of program delivery: Web
Two-way interactive video: Yes
Two-way audio, one-way video: No
One-way live video: Yes
One-way pre-recorded video: Yes
Audio graphics: No
Audio: No
Hardware requirements: Pentium or Power Mac equivalent
Software requirements: Internet browser
Is the library accessible to students? Yes
Are computers accessible to students? Yes

Remote Sites

Other branches of the institution: Yes
Other college campuses: Yes
Students' homes: Yes
Work sites: Yes
Libraries: Yes
Elementary/Secondary schools: Yes
Community-based organizations: Yes
Correctional institutions: No

On-Campus Requirements

Is an on-campus component required? Yes
On-campus course work: No
On-campus admissions interview: Yes
On-campus program orientation: Yes
On-campus exams: Yes

Tuition & Fees

Application fee: $15
Can it be waived? No
Average yearly additional fees: $320

Delta College

Distance Learning Office
1961 Delta Road, Office A-11a
University Center, MI 48710
Contact: Barry Baker, Executive Director, Communications Technology
Department e-mail: bgbaker@alpha.delta.edu
Department Web address: www.delta.edu/~telelrn
School Web address: www.delta.edu
Institutional accreditation: North Central Association of
  Colleges and Schools

Subjects Offered

Biology, chemistry, computer science, economics,
  education, English and composition, general business,
  history, humanities, literature, lifelong wellness, math,
  philosophy, political science, psychology, office assistant
  technology, sociology, speech, quality assurance

Admissions Requirements

Is a minimum high school GPA required? No
Is provisional admission available? Yes
Can pre-requisite course work be waived? Yes
Are international students eligible to apply? Yes
Is the TOEFL required for international students? No

Program Delivery

Primary method of program delivery: Web
Two-way interactive video: No

Two-way audio, one-way video: No
One-way live video: Yes
One-way pre-recorded video: Yes
Audio graphics: Yes
Audio: Yes
Hardware requirements: Pentium-based or better (Mac 040
  or better), 32MB of RAM, 28.8KBPS modem, Suga
  monitor
Software requirements: JAVA-enabled browser, word
  processing software
Is the library accessible to students? Yes
Are computers accessible to students? Yes

Remote Sites

Other branches of the institution: Yes
Other college campuses: Yes
Students' homes: Yes
Work sites: Yes
Libraries: Yes
Elementary/Secondary schools: Yes
Community-based organizations: Yes
Correctional institutions: Yes

On-Campus Requirements

Is an on-campus component required? No

Tuition & Fees

In-state tuition per credit: $90
Average yearly cost of books: $400

Financial Aid

Is financial aid available to full-time students? Yes
Is financial aid available to part-time students? Yes
Are academic scholarships available? Yes
Assistance programs available to students: Federal Stafford
  Loan, Federal Perkins Loan, Federal Plus Loan, Federal
  Pell Grant, Federal Work-Study Program, in-state
  student aid programs, veterans' assistance

East Carolina University—Business, Vocational, and Technical Information

General Classroom Building
Greenville, NC 27858
Contact: Dr. Ivan Wallace, Department Chair
Department e-mail: wallacei@mail.edu.edu
Department Web address: www.bvte.edu.edu
School Web address: www.ecu.edu

Admissions Requirements

Is a minimum high school GPA required? Yes
Is provisional admission available? No
Can pre-requisite course work be waived? No
Are international students eligible to apply? Yes

Tuition & Fees

In-state tuition per credit: $40
Out-of-state tuition per credit: $127

Financial Aid

Is financial aid available to full-time students? Yes
Is financial aid available to part-time students? Yes

East Carolina University— Department of Industrial Technology

Flanagan Building, Room 105
Greenville, NC 27858
Contact: Amy R. Frank, Director of Undergraduate
Distance Education & Transfer Programs
Department e-mail: itdept@mail.ecu.edu
Department Web address: www.sit.ecu.edu
School Web address: www.ecu.edu
Institutional accreditation: Southern Association of
Colleges and Schools

Subjects Offered

Industrial technology, manufacturing

Admissions Requirements

Is provisional admission available? Yes
Can pre-requisite course work be waived? Yes
Are international students eligible to apply? No

Program Delivery

Two-way interactive video: No
Two-way audio, one-way video: No
One-way live video: No
One-way pre-recorded video: No
Audio graphics: No
Audio: No
Hardware requirements: Pentium-class machine, 300 MHz
(500 with new system), 64MB of RAM (128 with new
system), 2 GB available hard-drive space (4 with new
system), 56KBPS modem
Software requirements: Must be able to install software on
their computer: Windows 95, 98, 2000, NT, or 2000,
98/2000 preferred, Microsoft Office
Is the library accessible to students? Yes

Remote Sites

Other college campuses: Yes
Students' homes: Yes
Work sites: Yes
Libraries: Yes

On-Campus Requirements

Is an on-campus component required? No

Tuition & Fees

In-state tuition per credit: $43
Out-of-state tuition per credit: $131

Financial Aid

Assistance programs available to students: Veterans'
assistance

East Carolina University— Physician Assistant Studies

Office of Admissions
Greenville, NC 27858
Contact: Edward D. Huechtker, Chair
Department e-mail: winnf@mail.ecu.edu
Department Web address: www.ecu.edu/pa
School Web address: www.ecu.edu
Institutional accreditation: Southern Association of
Colleges and Schools

Admissions Requirements

Is a minimum high school GPA required? Yes
Is provisional admission available? No
Is an admissions interview required? Yes
Can pre-requisite course work be waived? No
Are international students eligible to apply? No

Program Delivery

Two-way interactive video: Yes
One-way pre-recorded video: Yes
Hardware requirements: Laptop computer with the brand
and specifications designated by the department
Software requirements: RealPlayer, MS Word, MS Browser,
ICQ, Net Meeting, Net2Phone
Is the library accessible to students? Yes

Remote Sites

Students' homes: Yes

On-Campus Requirements

Is an on-campus component required? Yes
On-campus course work: Yes

Tuition & Fees

In-state tuition per credit: $40
Out-of-state tuition per credit: $127
Average yearly cost of books: $1,200
Average yearly additional fees: $700

Financial Aid

Is financial aid available to full-time students? Yes
Is financial aid available to part-time students? Yes
Are academic scholarships available? Yes
Assistance programs available to students: Federal Stafford Loan, Federal Pell Grant, veterans' assistance

East Carolina University— School of Human Environmental Sciences

Nutrition and Hospitality Management
Rivers Building
Greenville, NC 27858
Contact: Dr. Evelyn Farrior, Distance Education Coordinator
Department e-mail: farriore@mail.ecu.edu
Department Web address: www.ecu.edu/hes/home.htm
School Web address: www.ecu.edu

Subjects Offered

Hospitality management

Admissions Requirements

Is a minimum high school GPA required? Yes
Is provisional admission available? No
Can pre-requisite course work be waived? No
Are international students eligible to apply? Yes
Is the TOEFL required for international students? Yes

Tuition & Fees

In-state tuition per credit: $40
Out-of-state tuition per credit: $381

Financial Aid

Is financial aid available to full-time students? Yes
Is financial aid available to part-time students? Yes

East Carolina University— School of Nursing

Rivers Building
Greenville, NC
Contact: Karen Krupa, Director, RN/BSN Studies

Department e-mail: krupak@mail.ecu.edu
Department Web address: www.ecu.edu/nursing
School Web address: www.ecu.edu

Tuition & Fees

In-state tuition per credit: $40
Out-of-state tuition per credit: $127

Financial Aid

Is financial aid available to full-time students? Yes
Is financial aid available to part-time students? Yes

Eastern Kentucky University

Office of Extended Programs
521 Lancaster Avenue
Richmond, KY 40475
Contact: Dr. Kenneth R. Nelson, Director of Extended Programs
Department Web address: www.extendedprograms.eku.edu
School Web address: www.eku.edu
Institutional accreditation: Southern Association of Colleges and Schools

Subjects Offered

Connections, child and family studies, business, occupational therapy, special education, nutrition, real estate, technology, computer science, emergency medical care

Admissions Requirements

Is a minimum high school GPA required? Yes
Is provisional admission available? Yes
Is an admissions interview required? No
Can pre-requisite course work be waived? Yes
Are international students eligible to apply? Yes
Is the TOEFL required for international students? Yes
What is the minimum TOEFL score required? 500

Program Delivery

Two-way interactive video: Yes
Two-way audio, one-way video: Yes
One-way live video: No
One-way pre-recorded video: No
Audio graphics: No
Audio: No
Is the library accessible to students? Yes
Are computers accessible to students? Yes

Remote Sites

Other branches of the institution: Yes
Other college campuses: Yes

Students' homes: Yes
Work sites: No
Libraries: No
Elementary/Secondary schools: Yes
Community-based organizations: No
Correctional institutions: No

On-Campus Requirements

On-campus admissions interview: No

Tuition & Fees

In-state tuition per credit: $106
Out-of-state tuition per credit: $287
Average yearly cost of books: $700

Financial Aid

Is financial aid available to full-time students? Yes
Is financial aid available to part-time students? Yes
Are academic scholarships available? Yes
Assistance programs available to students: Federal Stafford Loan, Federal Perkins Loan, Federal Plus Loan, Federal Pell Grant, Federal Work-Study Program, in-state student aid programs, veterans' assistance

Eastern Oregon University

Division of Distance Education
One University Boulevard
La Grande, OR 97850-2899
Contact: Dr. Joseph Hart, Director, Distance Education
Department e-mail: dde@eou.edu
Department Web address: www.eou.edu/dde
School Web address: www.eou.edu
Institutional accreditation: Northwest Association of Schools and Colleges

Subjects Offered

Anthropology, agricultural economics, art, business, biology, botany, chemistry, computer science, crop and soil science, economics, English, gender studies, geography, geology, history, library studies, liberal studies, mathematics, multimedia studies, modern languages, music, physical education/health, philosophy, physics, science, sociology, statistics, theater, writing

Admissions Requirements

Is a minimum high school GPA required? Yes
Is provisional admission available? Yes
Is an admissions interview required? No
Can pre-requisite course work be waived? No
Are international students eligible to apply? Yes
Is the TOEFL required for international students? Yes
What is the minimum TOEFL score required? 500

Program Delivery

Primary method of program delivery: Text
Two-way interactive video: Yes
One-way pre-recorded video: Yes
Software requirements: E-mail and Web-browsing capabilities
Is the library accessible to students? Yes
Are computers accessible to students? No

Remote Sites

Other branches of the institution: Yes
Other college campuses: Yes
Students' homes: Yes
Work sites: Yes

On-Campus Requirements

Is an on-campus component required? No

Tuition & Fees

In-state tuition per credit: $95
Out-of-state tuition per credit: $95
Average yearly cost of books: $50

Financial Aid

Is financial aid available to full-time students? Yes
Is financial aid available to part-time students? Yes
Are academic scholarships available? Yes
Assistance programs available to students: Federal Stafford Loan, Federal Perkins Loan, Federal Plus Loan, Federal Pell Grant, Federal Work-Study Program, in-state student aid programs, veterans' assistance

Eastern Wyoming College, Outreach

3200 West C
Torrington, WY 82240
Contact: Dee Ludwig, Associate Dean of Instruction
Department e-mail: dludwig@ewc.cc.wy.us
Institutional accreditation: North Central Association of Colleges and Schools

Subjects Offered

English, political science, history, college studies, computer applications, business, science, mathematics

Admissions Requirements

Is a minimum high school GPA required? No
Is an admissions interview required? No
Can pre-requisite course work be waived? Yes
Are international students eligible to apply? Yes
Is the TOEFL required for international students? Yes

Program Delivery

Primary method of program delivery: Text
Two-way interactive video: No
Two-way audio, one-way video: No
One-way live video: No
One-way pre-recorded video: Yes
Audio graphics: No
Audio: No
Is the library accessible to students? Yes
Are computers accessible to students? Yes

Remote Sites

Other branches of the institution: Yes
Other college campuses: Yes
Students' homes: Yes
Work sites: No
Libraries: No
Elementary/Secondary schools: Yes
Community-based organizations: No
Correctional institutions: Yes

On-Campus Requirements

Is an on-campus component required? No

Tuition & Fees

In-state tuition per credit: $47
Out-of-state tuition per credit: $141
Average yearly cost of books: $600

Financial Aid

Is financial aid available to full-time students? Yes
Is financial aid available to part-time students? Yes
Are academic scholarships available? Yes
Assistance programs available to students: Federal Stafford Loan, Federal Perkins Loan, Federal Plus Loan, Federal Pell Grant, Federal Work-Study Program, in-state student aid programs, veterans' assistance

Eastern Wyoming College, Learning Information Systems

1973 Edison Drive
Piqua, OH 45356
Contact: Mary Beth Aust-Keefer, Associate Dean of Learning Information Systems
Department e-mail: austkeefer@edison.cc.oh.us
Department Web address: www.edison.cc.oh.us/online/newmenu.htm
School Web address: www.edison.cc.oh.us
Institutional accreditation: North Central Association of Colleges and Schools

Subjects Offered

Accounting, archeology, art history, business, computer applications, economics, English, humanities, Internet, psychology, religions, sociology

Admissions Requirements

Is a minimum high school GPA required? No
Is provisional admission available? Yes
Is an admissions interview required? No
Can pre-requisite course work be waived? Yes
Are international students eligible to apply? Yes
Is the TOEFL required for international students? Yes
What is the minimum TOEFL score required? 500

Program Delivery

Primary method of program delivery: Web
Two-way interactive video: No
Two-way audio, one-way video: Yes
One-way live video: Yes
One-way pre-recorded video: Yes
Audio graphics: No
Audio: No
Hardware requirements: Computer with access to Internet
Software requirements: Netscape or Internet Explorer versions 4 or higher, Adobe Acrobat, e-mail
Is the library accessible to students? Yes
Are computers accessible to students? Yes

Remote Sites

Other branches of the institution: Yes
Other college campuses: Yes
Students' homes: Yes
Work sites: Yes
Libraries: Yes
Elementary/Secondary schools: Yes
Community-based organizations: No
Correctional institutions: No

Financial Aid

Is financial aid available to full-time students? Yes
Is financial aid available to part-time students? Yes
Are academic scholarships available? Yes
Assistance programs available to students: Federal Stafford Loan, Federal Plus Loan, Federal Pell Grant, Federal Work-Study Program, in-state student aid programs, veterans' assistance

Embry-Riddle Aeronautical University

Department of Distance Learning
600 South Clyde Morris Boulevard
Daytona Beach, FL 32114-3900
Contact: Wm. Francis Herlehy III, Chair
Department Web address: www.ec.erau.edu/ddl
School Web address: www.erau.edu
Institutional accreditation: Southern Association of
Colleges and Schools

Subjects Offered

General education, aeronautics, management

Admissions Requirements

Is a minimum high school GPA required? No
Is provisional admission available? Yes
Is an admissions interview required? No
Can pre-requisite course work be waived? No
Are international students eligible to apply? Yes
Is the TOEFL required for international students? Yes
What is the minimum TOEFL score required? 500

Program Delivery

Primary method of program delivery: Web
Two-way interactive video: No
Two-way audio, one-way video: No
One-way live video: No
One-way pre-recorded video: Yes
Audio graphics: No
Audio: No
Hardware requirements: Any computer with capability of
accessing the Internet
Software requirements: Windows 95 or better
Is the library accessible to students? Yes
Are computers accessible to students? Yes

Tuition & Fees

In-state tuition per credit: $145
Out-of-state tuition per credit: $145

Financial Aid

Is financial aid available to full-time students? Yes
Is financial aid available to part-time students? Yes
Are academic scholarships available? No
Assistance programs available to students: Federal Stafford
Loan, Federal Pell Grant, veterans' assistance

Excelsior College

7 Columbia Circle
Albany, NY 12203
Contact: C. Wayne Williams, President
School Web address: www.excelsior.edu
Institutional accreditation: Middle States Association of
Colleges and Schools

Subjects Offered

Biology, management of human resources, psychology,
sociology, chemistry, communications, economics,
geography, geology, history, literature in English,
mathematics, music, philosophy, physics, political
science, psychology, sociology, world language and
literature, chemical technologies, computer technologies,
electromechanical technologies, electronic/instrumenta-
tion technologies, nuclear technologies, manufacturing
technologies, mechanical/welding technologies, nuclear
technologies, optical technologies

Admissions Requirements

Is a minimum high school GPA required? No
Are international students eligible to apply? Yes
Is the TOEFL required for international students? No

Program Delivery

Primary method of program delivery: Web
Is the library accessible to students? Yes

Remote Sites

Students' homes: Yes

On-Campus Requirements

Is an on-campus component required? No

Financial Aid

Is financial aid available to full-time students? Yes
Is financial aid available to part-time students? Yes
Assistance programs available to students: In-state student
aid programs, veterans' assistance

Flathead Valley Community College

777 Grandview Drive
Kalispell, MT 59901
School Web address: www.fvcc.cc.mt.us
Institutional accreditation: Northwest Association of
Schools and Colleges

Subjects Offered

Geography, computer applications

Admissions Requirements

Is a minimum high school GPA required? No
Is an admissions interview required? No
Are international students eligible to apply? Yes
Is the TOEFL required for international students? Yes
What is the minimum TOEFL score required? 500

Program Delivery

Primary method of program delivery: Web
Is the library accessible to students? Yes
Are computers accessible to students? Yes

Tuition & Fees

In-state tuition per credit: $65
Out-of-state tuition per credit: $196
Average yearly cost of books: $500

Financial Aid

Is financial aid available to full-time students? Yes
Is financial aid available to part-time students? Yes
Are academic scholarships available? Yes
Assistance programs available to students: Federal Stafford Loan, Federal Perkins Loan, Federal Plus Loan, Federal Pell Grant, Federal Work-Study Program, in-state student aid programs, veterans' assistance

Florida State University

Office of Distributed and Distance Learning
Suite C3500 University Center
Tallahassee, FL 32306-2550
Contact: Dr. Alan Mabe
Department e-mail: 2+2@mail.oddl.fsu.edu
Department Web address: www.fsu.edu/~distance
School Web address: www.fsu.edu
Institutional accreditation: Southern Association of Colleges and Schools

Subjects Offered •

Computer science, software engineering, information studies, geography, economics, nursing

Admissions Requirements

Is a minimum high school GPA required? Yes
Is provisional admission available? No
Is an admissions interview required? No
Can pre-requisite course work be waived? No
Are international students eligible to apply? Yes
Is the TOEFL required for international students? Yes

Program Delivery

Primary method of program delivery: Web

Hardware requirements: Telephone, television/VCR, computer with video card, sound card, CD-ROM, modem and printer
Software requirements: Internet service provider, Netscape or Internet Explorer
Is the library accessible to students? Yes
Are computers accessible to students? Yes

Remote Sites

Students' homes: Yes

On-Campus Requirements

Is an on-campus component required? No

Tuition & Fees

In-state tuition per credit: $97
Out-of-state tuition per credit: $261
Application fee: $20
Can it be waived? No
Average yearly cost of books: $120

Financial Aid

Is financial aid available to part-time students? Yes
Are academic scholarships available? Yes
Assistance programs available to students: Federal Stafford Loan, Federal Perkins Loan, Federal Plus Loan, Federal Pell Grant

Floyd College

Extended Learning
PO Box 1864, 3175 Highway 27 S
Rome, GA 30165
Contact: Carla Patterson, Extended Learning
Department e-mail: carla_patterson@fc.peachnet.edu
School Web address: www.fc.peachnet.edu/extendedlearning/
Institutional accreditation: Southern Association of Colleges and Schools

Subjects Offered

Sociology, history, political science, economics, business, psychology, English composition, world literature, physical education, biology, mathematics, allied health-medical terminology, geology, chemistry, American sign language, clinical calculations

Admissions Requirements

Is a minimum high school GPA required? Yes
Is provisional admission available? Yes
Is an admissions interview required? No
Can pre-requisite course work be waived? No
Are international students eligible to apply? Yes

Is the TOEFL required for international students? Yes
What is the minimum TOEFL score required? 550

Program Delivery

Two-way interactive video: Yes
Two-way audio, one-way video: No
One-way live video: Yes
One-way pre-recorded video: Yes
Hardware requirements: Pentium-class 166 MHz laptop
(or more advanced), compatible 10/100 Base T Ethernet
network hardware, compatible 28.8KBPS or greater
modem
Software requirements: Windows 95, Windows 98,
Windows NT 4.0 Workstation, or Windows 2000
Is the library accessible to students? Yes
Are computers accessible to students? Yes

Remote Sites

Other branches of the institution: Yes
Other college campuses: Yes
Students' homes: Yes
Work sites: Yes
Libraries: No
Elementary/Secondary schools: Yes
Community-based organizations: No
Correctional institutions: No

On-Campus Requirements

Is an on-campus component required? Yes
On-campus course work: Yes
On-campus admissions interview: No
On-campus program orientation: Yes
On-campus exams: Yes

Tuition & Fees

In-state tuition per credit: $56
Out-of-state tuition per credit: $216
Average yearly cost of books: $700

Financial Aid

Is financial aid available to full-time students? Yes
Is financial aid available to part-time students? Yes
Are academic scholarships available? Yes
Assistance programs available to students: Federal Stafford
Loan, Federal Perkins Loan, Federal Plus Loan, Federal
Pell Grant, Federal Work-Study Program, in-state
student aid programs, veterans' assistance

Foothill Community College

Distance Learning
Foothill Global Access
12345 El Monte Road
Los Altos Hills, CA 94022
Contact: Vivian Sinou, Dean, Distance and Mediated
Learning
Department e-mail: sinou@fhda.edu
School Web address: www.foothill.fhda.edu

Subjects Offered

Economics, geography, history, psychology, radio,
sociology, accounting, anthropology, art, computer
information systems, computer networks, drama,
English, mathematics, music, philosophy, political
science, speech, women's movement

Admissions Requirements

Is an admissions interview required? No
Are international students eligible to apply? Yes
Is the TOEFL required for international students? Yes

Program Delivery

Two-way interactive video: No
Two-way audio, one-way video: Yes
One-way live video: Yes
One-way pre-recorded video: Yes
Audio: Yes

Remote Sites

Other branches of the institution: Yes
Other college campuses: Yes
Students' homes: Yes
Work sites: Yes

Tuition & Fees

In-state tuition per credit: $7
Out-of-state tuition per credit: $85

Financial Aid

Is financial aid available to full-time students? Yes
Is financial aid available to part-time students? Yes
Are academic scholarships available? Yes
Assistance programs available to students: Federal Stafford
Loan, Federal Pell Grant, Federal Work-Study Program,
in-state student aid programs, veterans' assistance

Franciscan University of Steubenville

Distance Learning
1235 University Boulevard
Steubenville, OH 43952
Contact: Rev. Mr. Dominic Cerrato, Director of Distance Learning
Department e-mail: distance@franuniv.edu
School Web address: franuniv.edu
Institutional accreditation: North Central Association of Colleges and Schools

Subjects Offered

Theology

Admissions Requirements

Is a minimum high school GPA required? Yes
Is provisional admission available? Yes
Is an admissions interview required? No
Can pre-requisite course work be waived? No
Are international students eligible to apply? Yes
Is the TOEFL required for international students? Yes
What is the minimum TOEFL score required? 550

Program Delivery

Audio: Yes
Is the library accessible to students? No
Are computers accessible to students? No

On-Campus Requirements

Is an on-campus component required? Yes
On-campus course work: Yes
On-campus admissions interview: No
On-campus program orientation: No
On-campus exams: No

Tuition & Fees

In-state tuition per credit: $175
Out-of-state tuition per credit: $175
Average yearly cost of books: $640

Financial Aid

Is financial aid available to full-time students? No
Is financial aid available to part-time students? No
Are academic scholarships available? No
Assistance programs available to students: Federal Stafford Loan

Franklin Pierce Law Center

Educational Law Institute
2 White Street
Concord, NH 03301
Contact: Sarah E. Redfield, Professor
Department e-mail: sredfield@fplc.edu
Department Web address: www.edlaw.fplc.edu
School Web address: www.fplc.edu
Institutional accreditation: ABA

Subjects Offered

Education law

Admissions Requirements

Is a minimum high school GPA required? No
Is provisional admission available? Yes
Is an admissions interview required? Yes
Can pre-requisite course work be waived? Yes
Are international students eligible to apply? Yes
Is the TOEFL required for international students? Yes
What is the minimum TOEFL score required? 550

Program Delivery

Primary method of program delivery: Web
Two-way interactive video: No
Two-way audio, one-way video: No
One-way live video: No
One-way pre-recorded video: Yes
Audio graphics: Yes
Audio: Yes
Software requirements: No specific software needed other than current Internet browser
Is the library accessible to students? Yes
Are computers accessible to students? Yes

Remote Sites

Other branches of the institution: No
Other college campuses: No
Students' homes: Yes
Work sites: Yes
Libraries: No
Elementary/Secondary schools: No
Community-based organizations: No
Correctional institutions: No

On-Campus Requirements

Is an on-campus component required? Yes
On-campus course work: Yes
On-campus admissions interview: No
On-campus program orientation: No
On-campus exams: No

Tuition & Fees

In-state tuition per credit: $375
Out-of-state tuition per credit: $375
Average yearly cost of books: $100

Financial Aid

Is financial aid available to full-time students? Yes
Is financial aid available to part-time students? Yes
Are academic scholarships available? Yes
Assistance programs available to students: Federal Stafford
Loan, Federal Perkins Loan, Federal Pell Grant

Frostburg State University

Office of the Provost
101 Braddock Road
Frostburg, MD 21532
School Web address: www.frostburg.edu

Subjects Offered

Computer science, mathematics, chemistry, economics

Program Delivery

Primary method of program delivery: Web
Two-way interactive video: Yes

Remote Sites

Other branches of the institution: Yes
Students' homes: Yes

Gadsden State Community College

Lifelong Learning Center
1001 George Wallace Drive
PO Box 227
Gadsden, AL 35902-0227
Contact: Jane Radcliffe, Director of Lifelong Learning
Department e-mail: jradcliffe@gadsdenst.cc.al.us
School Web address: www.gadsdenst.cc.al.us
Institutional accreditation: Southern Association of
Colleges and Schools

Subjects Offered

English, business law, math, psychology, sociology, history,
literature, economics, ethics, nutrition

Admissions Requirements

Is a minimum high school GPA required? No
Is provisional admission available? Yes
Is an admissions interview required? No
Can pre-requisite course work be waived? No

Are international students eligible to apply? Yes
Is the TOEFL required for international students? Yes
What is the minimum TOEFL score required? 500

Program Delivery

Primary method of program delivery: Remote site
Two-way interactive video: No
Two-way audio, one-way video: No
One-way live video: No
One-way pre-recorded video: Yes
Audio graphics: No
Audio: Yes
Is the library accessible to students? Yes
Are computers accessible to students? Yes

Remote Sites

Other branches of the institution: Yes
Other college campuses: Yes
Students' homes: No
Work sites: Yes
Libraries: No
Elementary/Secondary schools: Yes
Community-based organizations: Yes
Correctional institutions: Yes

On-Campus Requirements

Is an on-campus component required? No

Tuition & Fees

In-state tuition per credit: $56
Out-of-state tuition per credit: $108

Financial Aid

Is financial aid available to full-time students? Yes
Is financial aid available to part-time students? Yes
Are academic scholarships available? Yes
Assistance programs available to students: Federal Pell
Grant, Federal Work-Study Program, in-state student aid
programs, veterans' assistance

Genesee Community College

Assessment and Instructional Research
Information Technology and Distance Learning
One College Road
Batavia, NY 14020
Contact: Robert Knipe, Dean
School Web address: www.genesee.suny.edu
Institutional accreditation: Middle States Association of
Colleges and Schools

Subjects Offered

Accounting, anthropology, art, business, economics, English, history, human services, literature, office technology, math, music, paralegal, retailing, psychology, education, biology, health, humanities, sociology

Admissions Requirements

Is a minimum high school GPA required? No
Is provisional admission available? Yes
Is an admissions interview required? No
Can pre-requisite course work be waived? No
Are international students eligible to apply? Yes
Is the TOEFL required for international students? Yes
What is the minimum TOEFL score required? 460

Program Delivery

Two-way interactive video: Yes
Two-way audio, one-way video: No
One-way live video: No
One-way pre-recorded video: Yes
Audio graphics: No
Audio: Yes
Is the library accessible to students? Yes
Are computers accessible to students? Yes

Remote Sites

Other branches of the institution: Yes
Other college campuses: Yes
Students' homes: Yes
Work sites: Yes
Libraries: Yes
Elementary/Secondary schools: Yes
Community-based organizations: No
Correctional institutions: Yes

On-Campus Requirements

Is an on-campus component required? Yes
On-campus course work: No
On-campus admissions interview: No
On-campus program orientation: Yes
On-campus exams: Yes

Tuition & Fees

In-state tuition per credit: $97
Out-of-state tuition per credit: $106
Average yearly cost of books: $700

Financial Aid

Is financial aid available to full-time students? Yes
Is financial aid available to part-time students? Yes
Are academic scholarships available? Yes
Assistance programs available to students: Federal Stafford Loan, Federal Plus Loan, Federal Pell Grant, Federal Work-Study Program, in-state student aid programs, veterans' assistance

George Washington University—Center for Career Education

2029 K Street, NW
Washington, DC 20052
Department e-mail: drevent@gwu.edu
Department Web address: www.gwu.edu/~emp
School Web address: www.gwu.edu
Institutional accreditation: Middle States Association of Colleges and Schools

Subjects Offered

Best practices, Internet event marketing, coordination, weddings, marketing, starting and maintaining event business, fundraising, career advancement, catering design, corporate events, information systems, exposition/trade show, government, civic events

Admissions Requirements

Are international students eligible to apply? Yes
Is the TOEFL required for international students? No

Program Delivery

Primary method of program delivery: Text
One-way pre-recorded video: Yes

On-Campus Requirements

Is an on-campus component required? No

Financial Aid

Is financial aid available to full-time students? Yes
Is financial aid available to part-time students? Yes
Are academic scholarships available? Yes
Assistance programs available to students: Veterans' assistance

George Washington University—School of Medicine and Health Science

Office of Recruitment
2300 K Street, NW
Washington, DC 20052

Department Web address: learn.gwumc.edu/hscidist
School Web address: www.gwu.edu
Institutional accreditation: Middle States Association of
Colleges and Schools

Program Delivery

Primary method of program delivery: Web

On-Campus Requirements

Is an on-campus component required? No

Financial Aid

Is financial aid available to full-time students? Yes
Is financial aid available to part-time students? Yes
Assistance programs available to students: Veterans'
assistance

George Washington University—School of Public Health & Health Sciences

2300 K Street
Washington, DC 20052
Department Web address: learn.gwumc.edu/hscidist
School Web address: www.gwu.edu
Institutional accreditation: Middle States Association of
Colleges and Schools

Admissions Requirements

Are international students eligible to apply? Yes
Is the TOEFL required for international students? Yes

Program Delivery

Primary method of program delivery: Web
One-way pre-recorded video: Yes
Audio: Yes

On-Campus Requirements

Is an on-campus component required? Yes

Tuition & Fees

Application fee: $55

Georgia Center for Continuing Education

University System of Georgia Independent Study
1197 South Lumpkin Street, Suite 193
Athens, GA 30602

Contact: Dr. Nancy Thompson, Department Head
Department e-mail: usgise@arches.uga.edu
Department Web address: www.gactr.uga.edu/usgis
School Web address: www.gactr.uga.edu
Institutional accreditation: Southern Association of
Colleges and Schools

Subjects Offered

Agriculture, crop and soil sciences, horticulture, anthropology, art, astronomy, biology, classics, drama, ecology, English, French, German, geography, geology, history, Italian, Latin, mathematics, philosophy, political science, psychology, religion, sociology, Spanish, speech communications, women's studies, educational psychology, recreation and leisure studies, child and family development, food and nutrition, forest resources

Admissions Requirements

Is a minimum high school GPA required? No
Is provisional admission available? No
Is an admissions interview required? No
Can pre-requisite course work be waived? Yes
Are international students eligible to apply? Yes

Program Delivery

Primary method of program delivery: Text
Two-way interactive video: No
Two-way audio, one-way video: Yes
One-way live video: No
One-way pre-recorded video: Yes
Audio graphics: No
Audio: Yes
Is the library accessible to students? Yes
Are computers accessible to students? No

Remote Sites

Students' homes: Yes
Work sites: Yes
Libraries: Yes
Correctional institutions: Yes

On-Campus Requirements

Is an on-campus component required? No

Tuition & Fees

In-state tuition per credit: $104

Financial Aid

Is financial aid available to part-time students? No
Are academic scholarships available? No

Golden Gate University

Cyber Campus
536 Mission Street
San Francisco, CA 94121
Contact: John Fyfe, Cyber Dean
Department e-mail: cybercampus@ggu.edu
School Web address: cybercampus.ggu.edu
Institutional accreditation: Western Association of Schools and Colleges

Subjects Offered

Accounting, arts administration, finance, economics, information systems, math, English, hotel/restaurant management, marketing, management, public administration, healthcare administration, humanities, operations management, philosophy, telecommunications, psychology

Admissions Requirements

Is a minimum high school GPA required? Yes
Is the TOEFL required for international students? Yes
What is the minimum TOEFL score required? 525

Program Delivery

Primary method of program delivery: Web
Is the library accessible to students? Yes
Are computers accessible to students? Yes

On-Campus Requirements

Is an on-campus component required? No

Financial Aid

Is financial aid available to full-time students? Yes
Are academic scholarships available? Yes
Assistance programs available to students: Federal Stafford Loan, Federal Perkins Loan, Federal Pell Grant, veterans' assistance

Graceland University— Addiction Studies

Division of Healthcare Professions
1 University Place
Lamoni, IA 50140
Contact: Susan M. Kirkpatrick, PhD, Provost
Department e-mail: iec@graceland.edu
Institutional accreditation: Northern Central Association of Colleges and Schools

Subjects Offered

Psychology, biology, chemistry, mathematics, sociology, speech, theatre, history, English, religion, physical education, science, economics, accounting, marketing, business, humanities, computer science

Admissions Requirements

Is provisional admission available? Yes
Can pre-requisite course work be waived? No
Are international students eligible to apply? Yes
Is the TOEFL required for international students? Yes
What is the minimum TOEFL score required? 550

Program Delivery

Primary method of program delivery: Text
Two-way interactive video: No
Two-way audio, one-way video: No
One-way live video: No
One-way pre-recorded video: Yes
Audio graphics: Yes
Audio: Yes
Is the library accessible to students? Yes
Are computers accessible to students? No

Remote Sites

Other branches of the institution: Yes
Other college campuses: No
Students' homes: No
Work sites: No
Libraries: No
Elementary/Secondary schools: No
Community-based organizations: No
Correctional institutions: No

On-Campus Requirements

Is an on-campus component required? Yes
On-campus course work: Yes
On-campus admissions interview: No
On-campus program orientation: No
On-campus exams: Yes

Tuition & Fees

In-state tuition per credit: $218
Out-of-state tuition per credit: $218
Average yearly cost of books: $960

Financial Aid

Is financial aid available to full-time students? No
Is financial aid available to part-time students? No
Are academic scholarships available? No

Graceland University— Liberal Studies Program

Division of Healthcare Professions
1 University Place
Lamoni, IA 50140
Contact: Sharon M. Kirkpatrick, PhD, Provost
Department e-mail: iec@graceland.edu
Institutional accreditation: North Central Association of Colleges and Schools

Subjects Offered

Psychology, biology, chemistry, mathematics, sociology, speech, theatre, history, English, religion, physical education, science, economics, accounting, marketing, business, humanities, computer science

Admissions Requirements

Is a minimum high school GPA required? No
Is provisional admission available? Yes
Is an admissions interview required? No
Can pre-requisite course work be waived? No
Are international students eligible to apply? Yes
Is the TOEFL required for international students? Yes
What is the minimum TOEFL score required? 550

Program Delivery

Primary method of program delivery: Text
Two-way interactive video: No
Two-way audio, one-way video: No
One-way live video: No
One-way pre-recorded video: Yes
Audio graphics: Yes
Audio: No
Is the library accessible to students? Yes
Are computers accessible to students? No

Remote Sites

Other branches of the institution: Yes
Other college campuses: Yes
Students' homes: No
Work sites: No
Libraries: No
Elementary/Secondary schools: No
Community-based organizations: No
Correctional institutions: No

On-Campus Requirements

Is an on-campus component required? Yes
On-campus course work: Yes
On-campus admissions interview: No
On-campus program orientation: No
On-campus exams: Yes

Tuition & Fees

In-state tuition per credit: $275
Out-of-state tuition per credit: $275
Average yearly cost of books: $800

Financial Aid

Is financial aid available to full-time students? No
Is financial aid available to part-time students? No
Are academic scholarships available? No

Graceland University— Nursing Program

Division of Healthcare Professions
1 University Place
Lamoni, IA 50140
Contact: Sharon M. Kirkpatrick, PhD, Provost
Department e-mail: iec@graceland.edu
Institutional accreditation: North Central Association of Colleges and Schools

Subjects Offered

Psychology, biology, chemistry, mathematics, sociology, speech, theatre, history, English, religion, physical education, science, economics, accounting, marketing, business, humanities, computer science

Admissions Requirements

Is a minimum high school GPA required? No
Is provisional admission available? Yes
Can pre-requisite course work be waived? Yes
Are international students eligible to apply? Yes
Is the TOEFL required for international students? Yes
What is the minimum TOEFL score required? 550

Program Delivery

Primary method of program delivery: Text
Two-way interactive video: No
Two-way audio, one-way video: No
One-way live video: No
One-way pre-recorded video: Yes
Audio graphics: Yes
Audio: No
Is the library accessible to students? Yes
Are computers accessible to students? No

Remote Sites

Other branches of the institution: No
Other college campuses: No
Students' homes: No
Work sites: No

Libraries: No
Elementary/Secondary schools: Yes
Community-based organizations: Yes
Correctional institutions: Yes

On-Campus Requirements

Is an on-campus component required? Yes
On-campus course work: Yes
On-campus admissions interview: No
On-campus program orientation: No
On-campus exams: Yes

Tuition & Fees

In-state tuition per credit: $275
Out-of-state tuition per credit: $275
Average yearly cost of books: $800

Financial Aid

Is financial aid available to full-time students? No
Is financial aid available to part-time students? No
Are academic scholarships available? No

Graceland University— Partnership Program

1 University Place
Lamoni, IA 50140
Contact: Michael Casey, PhD, Vice Provost and Dean of
    Partnership Program
Department e-mail: robb@graceland.edu
Department Web address: www.graceland.edu/partnership/
    index.htm
School Web address: www.graceland.edu
Institutional accreditation: North Central Association of
    Colleges and Schools

Subjects Offered

Theatre, music, science, computer science, mathematics,
    English, speech communication, philosophy, religion,
    accounting, business administration, economics,
    sociology, criminal justice, information technology,
    history, education, psychology, liberal studies

Admissions Requirements

Is a minimum high school GPA required? Yes
Is provisional admission available? Yes
Can pre-requisite course work be waived? Yes
Are international students eligible to apply? Yes
Is the TOEFL required for international students? Yes
What is the minimum TOEFL score required? 450

Program Delivery

Primary method of program delivery: Remote site
Two-way interactive video: Yes
Two-way audio, one-way video: No
One-way live video: Yes
One-way pre-recorded video: Yes
Audio graphics: No
Audio: No
Software requirements: Ability to access the Internet
Is the library accessible to students? Yes
Are computers accessible to students? Yes

Remote Sites

Other branches of the institution: No
Other college campuses: Yes
Students' homes: No
Work sites: Yes
Libraries: No
Elementary/Secondary schools: Yes
Community-based organizations: No
Correctional institutions: No

On-Campus Requirements

Is an on-campus component required? No

Tuition & Fees

In-state tuition per credit: $180
Out-of-state tuition per credit: $180
Average yearly cost of books: $1,250

Financial Aid

Is financial aid available to full-time students? Yes
Is financial aid available to part-time students? Yes
Are academic scholarships available? No
Assistance programs available to students: Federal Stafford
    Loan, Federal Perkins Loan, Federal Plus Loan, Federal
    Pell Grant, in-state student aid programs, veterans'
    assistance

Greenville Technical College

Distance Education/Weekend College
PO Box 5616
Greenville, SC 29606-5616
Contact: Jerry Sams
Department Web address: www.college-online.com
School Web address: www.greenvilletech.com
Institutional accreditation: Southern Association of
    Colleges and Schools

Subjects Offered

Humanities, foreign language, biology, computer technol-
    ogy, office systems, math

Admissions Requirements

Is a minimum high school GPA required? No
Is provisional admission available? Yes
Can pre-requisite course work be waived? Yes
Are international students eligible to apply? Yes
Is the TOEFL required for international students? Yes

Program Delivery

Two-way audio, one-way video: Yes
One-way pre-recorded video: Yes
Is the library accessible to students? Yes
Are computers accessible to students? Yes

Remote Sites

Other branches of the institution: Yes
Other college campuses: Yes
Students' homes: Yes
Work sites: No
Libraries: No
Elementary/Secondary schools: No
Community-based organizations: No
Correctional institutions: No

On-Campus Requirements

Is an on-campus component required? Yes
On-campus course work: No
On-campus admissions interview: Yes
On-campus program orientation: Yes
On-campus exams: Yes

Tuition & Fees

In-state tuition per credit: $57
Out-of-state tuition per credit: $134
Average yearly cost of books: $550

Financial Aid

Is financial aid available to full-time students? Yes
Is financial aid available to part-time students? Yes
Are academic scholarships available? Yes
Assistance programs available to students: Federal Stafford
    Loan, Federal Plus Loan, Federal Pell Grant, Federal
    Work-Study Program, in-state student aid programs,
    veterans' assistance

Halifax Community College

PO Drawer 809
Weldon, NC 27890
Contact: Joan G. Gilstrap, Director of Distance Learning
Department e-mail: gilstrapj@halifax.hcc.cc.nc.us
Department Web address: www.online.hcc.cc.nc.us
School Web address: www.hcc.cc.nc.us

Institutional accreditation: Southern Association of
    Colleges and Schools

Subjects Offered

English, psychology, communications, art, graphic design,
    economics, electronics engineering technology

Admissions Requirements

Is a minimum high school GPA required? No
Is provisional admission available? No
Is an admissions interview required? No
Can pre-requisite course work be waived? No
Are international students eligible to apply? Yes
Is the TOEFL required for international students? No

Program Delivery

Primary method of program delivery: Remote site
Two-way interactive video: Yes
Two-way audio, one-way video: No
One-way live video: No
One-way pre-recorded video: No
Audio graphics: No
Audio: No
Hardware requirements: Min. 133 MHz microprocessor,
    33.6KBPS or faster modem, 32MB of RAM, 100MB
    free hard disk space
Software requirements: Windows 95 or higher, MS Word
    or comparable word processing program, browser
    (Netscape or Internet Explorer) 4.0 or higher
Is the library accessible to students? Yes
Are computers accessible to students? Yes

Remote Sites

Other branches of the institution: No
Other college campuses: No
Students' homes: Yes
Work sites: No
Libraries: Yes
Elementary/Secondary schools: No
Community-based organizations: No
Correctional institutions: No

On-Campus Requirements

Is an on-campus component required? No

Tuition & Fees

In-state tuition per credit: $27
Out-of-state tuition per credit: $170
Average yearly cost of books: $11

Financial Aid

Is financial aid available to full-time students? Yes
Is financial aid available to part-time students? Yes

Are academic scholarships available? Yes

Assistance programs available to students: Federal Stafford Loan, Federal Pell Grant, Federal Work-Study Program, in-state student aid programs, veterans' assistance

Harcourt Learning Direct Center for Degree Studies

925 Oak Street
Scranton, PA 18515
Contact: Connie C. Dempsey, Director, Compliance and Academic Affairs
School Web address: www.harcourt-learning.com
Institutional accreditation: Distance Education and Training Council

Subjects Offered

Business management, accounting, business management with marketing option, accounting with finance option, hospitality management, applied computer science, civil engineering technology, electrical engineering technology, electronics technology, mechanical engineering technology, industrial engineering technology

Admissions Requirements

Is a minimum high school GPA required? No
Is provisional admission available? No
Is an admissions interview required? No
Can pre-requisite course work be waived? No
Are international students eligible to apply? Yes
Is the TOEFL required for international students? No

Program Delivery

Primary method of program delivery: Text
Hardware requirements: All students need to have access to a PC

Remote Sites

Other college campuses: Yes

On-Campus Requirements

Is an on-campus component required? Yes

Harold Washington College

Center for Distance Learning
30 East Lake Street
Chicago, IL 60601
Contact: Pamela C. Lattimore, Dean
Department e-mail: cdl@ccc.edu
School Web address: www.ccc.edu

Institutional accreditation: North Central Association of Colleges and Schools

Subjects Offered

Anthropology, art appreciation, astronomy, biology, child development, computer information systems, counseling, English, humanities, geography, geology, health, history, literature, math, music, philosophy, physical science, psychology, sociology, Spanish, business

Admissions Requirements

Is a minimum high school GPA required? No
Is an admissions interview required? No
Are international students eligible to apply? Yes

Program Delivery

Primary method of program delivery: Remote site
Two-way interactive video: Yes
One-way pre-recorded video: Yes
Hardware requirements: Connection to the Internet of 28.8KBPS or faster
Software requirements: Windows 95, 98, NT or MacOS 7.5 or later, Netscape 4.0 or later (version 4.5 highly recommended) or Internet Explorer 4.0 or later
Are computers accessible to students? Yes

Remote Sites

Other branches of the institution: Yes
Other college campuses: Yes

On-Campus Requirements

On-campus exams: Yes

Tuition & Fees

In-state tuition per credit: $48
Application fee: $25

Financial Aid

Is financial aid available to full-time students? Yes
Is financial aid available to part-time students? Yes
Are academic scholarships available? Yes
Assistance programs available to students: Federal Stafford Loan, Federal Perkins Loan, Federal Pell Grant, Federal Work-Study Program, veterans' assistance

Harrisburg Area Community College

Distance Education
One HACC Drive
Harrisburg, PA 17110
Contact: Elaine Stoneroad, Manager, Distance Education

Department e-mail: distance@hacc.edu

Department Web address: www.hacc.edu/programs/disted/disted.htm

School Web address: www.hacc.edu

Institutional accreditation: Middle States Association of Colleges and Schools

Subjects Offered

Accounting, anthropology, business, general technology, management, marketing, economics, English, geography, government and politics, history, humanities, philosophy, psychology, sociology, biology, computer science, computer information systems, geology, mathematics, physical science, nutrition

Admissions Requirements

Is a minimum high school GPA required? No

Is provisional admission available? Yes

Is an admissions interview required? Yes

Can pre-requisite course work be waived? Yes

Are international students eligible to apply? Yes

Is the TOEFL required for international students? Yes

What is the minimum TOEFL score required? 500

Program Delivery

Primary method of program delivery: Web

Two-way interactive video: Yes

One-way pre-recorded video: Yes

Audio: Yes

Is the library accessible to students? Yes

Are computers accessible to students? Yes

Remote Sites

Other branches of the institution: Yes

Students' homes: Yes

Work sites: Yes

Correctional institutions: Yes

On-Campus Requirements

Is an on-campus component required? No

Tuition & Fees

In-state tuition per credit: $131

Out-of-state tuition per credit: $197

Average yearly cost of books: $25

Financial Aid

Is financial aid available to full-time students? Yes

Is financial aid available to part-time students? Yes

Are academic scholarships available? Yes

Assistance programs available to students: Federal Stafford Loan, Federal Perkins Loan, Federal Pell Grant, Federal Work-Study Program, veterans' assistance

Hawkeye Community College

Distance Learning

1501 East Orange Road

Waterloo, IA 50704

Contact: Dr. Roger Rezabek, Director of Distance Learning

Department e-mail: distance@hawkeye.cc.ia.us

Department Web address: www.hawkeye.cc.ia.us/academic/distance/distance.htm

School Web address: www.hawkeye.cc.ia.us

Institutional accreditation: North Central Association of Colleges and Schools

Subjects Offered

Business, accounting, mathematics, psychology, sociology, composition, science

Admissions Requirements

Is a minimum high school GPA required? No

Is provisional admission available? Yes

Is an admissions interview required? No

Can pre-requisite course work be waived? Yes

Are international students eligible to apply? Yes

Program Delivery

Primary method of program delivery: Remote site

Two-way interactive video: Yes

One-way pre-recorded video: Yes

Software requirements: Computer literacy

Is the library accessible to students? Yes

Are computers accessible to students? Yes

Remote Sites

Other branches of the institution: Yes

Students' homes: Yes

Work sites: Yes

Libraries: Yes

Elementary/Secondary schools: Yes

Correctional institutions: Yes

On-Campus Requirements

Is an on-campus component required? No

Tuition & Fees

In-state tuition per credit: $70

Out-of-state tuition per credit: $140

Financial Aid

Is financial aid available to full-time students? Yes

Is financial aid available to part-time students? Yes

Are academic scholarships available? Yes

Assistance programs available to students: Federal Stafford Loan, Federal Plus Loan, Federal Pell Grant, Federal Work-Study Program, in-state student aid programs, veterans' assistance

Hillsborough Community College

eCampus
39 Columbia Drive
Tampa, FL 33606
Contact: Michael Comins, Director of Academic Technology
Department e-mail: mcomins@hcc.cc.fl.us
Department Web address: www.hcc.cc.fl.us/ecampus
School Web address: www.hcc.cc.fl.us
Institutional accreditation: Southern Association of Colleges and Schools

Subjects Offered

Computer science, astronomy, biology, earth science, American history, economics, marketing, management, English, political science, geology, psychology, art, algebra, calculus, sociology, finance, business, child development, opticianry

Admissions Requirements

Is a minimum high school GPA required? No
Is provisional admission available? Yes
Is an admissions interview required? Yes
Can pre-requisite course work be waived? Yes
Are international students eligible to apply? Yes
Is the TOEFL required for international students? Yes
What is the minimum TOEFL score required? 500

Program Delivery

Two-way interactive video: Yes
One-way pre-recorded video: Yes
Audio: Yes
Is the library accessible to students? Yes
Are computers accessible to students? Yes

Remote Sites

Other branches of the institution: Yes
Other college campuses: Yes
Students' homes: Yes
Work sites: Yes
Libraries: Yes
Elementary/Secondary schools: No
Correctional institutions: No

On-Campus Requirements

Is an on-campus component required? No

Tuition & Fees

In-state tuition per credit: $48
Out-of-state tuition per credit: $118
Application fee: $20
Can it be waived? No
Average yearly cost of books: $600

Financial Aid

Is financial aid available to full-time students? Yes
Is financial aid available to part-time students? Yes
Are academic scholarships available? Yes
Assistance programs available to students: Federal Stafford Loan, Federal Plus Loan, Federal Pell Grant, Federal Work-Study Program, in-state student aid programs, veterans' assistance

Horry-Georgetown Technical College

Department of Distance Learning
PO Box 261566
Conway, SC 29528-6066
Contact: Janey Oliphint, Director of Distance Learning
Department e-mail: oliphint@hor.tec.sc.us
Department Web address: www.hor.tec.sc.us/distancelearning/
School Web address: www.hor.tec.sc.us
Institutional accreditation: Southern Association of Colleges and Schools

Subjects Offered

Astronomy, business, management, supervision, American government, human relations, psychology, English composition, business communications, Internet communications

Admissions Requirements

Is a minimum high school GPA required? No
Is provisional admission available? Yes
Is an admissions interview required? No
Can pre-requisite course work be waived? Yes
Are international students eligible to apply? Yes
Is the TOEFL required for international students? Yes
What is the minimum TOEFL score required? 500

Program Delivery

Two-way interactive video: Yes
Two-way audio, one-way video: Yes
One-way live video: Yes

One-way pre-recorded video: Yes
Hardware requirements: Pentium
Software requirements: Windows 95, Microsoft Office or
    Works, Internet
Is the library accessible to students? Yes
Are computers accessible to students? Yes

Remote Sites

Other branches of the institution: Yes
Other college campuses: Yes
Students' homes: Yes
Work sites: Yes
Libraries: Yes
Elementary/Secondary schools: Yes
Community-based organizations: Yes
Correctional institutions: No

On-Campus Requirements

Is an on-campus component required? Yes
On-campus course work: No
On-campus admissions interview: No
On-campus program orientation: Yes
On-campus exams: Yes

Tuition & Fees

In-state tuition per credit: $55
Out-of-state tuition per credit: $140
Average yearly cost of books: $85

Financial Aid

Is financial aid available to full-time students? Yes
Is financial aid available to part-time students? Yes
Are academic scholarships available? Yes
Assistance programs available to students: Federal Stafford
    Loan, Federal Pell Grant, Federal Work-Study Program,
    in-state student aid programs, veterans' assistance

Independence Community College

Instruction Office
Box 708
Brookside Drive and College Avenue
Independence, KS 67301
Contact: Ray Rothgeb, Dean of Instruction
Department e-mail: rothgeb@ind.cc.ks.us
School Web address: www.indy.cc.ks.us
Institutional accreditation: North Central Association of
    Colleges and Schools

Admissions Requirements

Is a minimum high school GPA required? No

Is provisional admission available? Yes
Is an admissions interview required? No
Can pre-requisite course work be waived? No
Are international students eligible to apply? Yes
Is the TOEFL required for international students? Yes
What is the minimum TOEFL score required? 400

Program Delivery

One-way pre-recorded video: Yes
Is the library accessible to students? No
Are computers accessible to students? No

Remote Sites

Other branches of the institution: Yes
Students' homes: Yes
Elementary/Secondary schools: Yes

On-Campus Requirements

Is an on-campus component required? No

Tuition & Fees

In-state tuition per credit: $41
Out-of-state tuition per credit: $66
Average yearly cost of books: $500

Financial Aid

Is financial aid available to full-time students? Yes
Is financial aid available to part-time students? Yes
Are academic scholarships available? Yes
Assistance programs available to students: Federal Stafford
    Loan, Federal Pell Grant, Federal Work-Study Program,
    veterans' assistance

Indiana College Network

714 North Senate Avenue
Indianapolis, IN 46202
Department e-mail: info@icn.org
School Web address: www.icn.org
Institutional accreditation: North Central Association of
    Colleges and Schools

Admissions Requirements

Is an admissions interview required? No
Are international students eligible to apply? Yes

Program Delivery

Primary method of program delivery: Web
Two-way interactive video: Yes
Two-way audio, one-way video: Yes
One-way pre-recorded video: Yes
Is the library accessible to students? Yes

Remote Sites

Other branches of the institution: Yes
Students' homes: Yes
Work sites: Yes
Libraries: Yes
Elementary/Secondary schools: Yes
Community-based organizations: Yes
Correctional institutions: Yes

On-Campus Requirements

On-campus course work: Yes

Financial Aid

Is financial aid available to full-time students? Yes
Are academic scholarships available? Yes

Indiana State University

Lifelong Learning
Distance Education
Office of Student Services—Lifelong Learning
Erickson Hall, Room 210-211
Terre Haute, IN 47809
Contact: Harry K. Barnes, Director
Department e-mail: studentservices@indstate.edu
Department Web address: indstate.edu/distance
School Web address: web.indstate.edu
Institutional accreditation: North Central Association for
    Colleges and Schools

Subjects Offered

Art, criminology, photojournalism, life science, human
    communication, parliament proceedings, industrial and
    retail security, crime prevention/correction, law
    enforcement/criminal justice, criminal law proceedings/
    juvenile delinquency, economics, English, geography,
    geology, history, advertising, electronics/computer
    technology, industrial/mechanical technology, industrial
    technology education, manufacturing and construction
    technology, mathematics, public administration,
    psychology, sociology, business report writing, account-
    ing, business statistics/business finance, insurance,
    organization behavior, international business, human
    resources, marketing and management, science,
    curriculum instruction and media technology

Admissions Requirements

Is a minimum high school GPA required? No
Is provisional admission available? Yes
Is an admissions interview required? No
Can pre-requisite course work be waived? Yes
Are international students eligible to apply? Yes

Is the TOEFL required for international students? Yes
What is the minimum TOEFL score required? 500

Program Delivery

Primary method of program delivery: Web
Two-way interactive video: Yes
Two-way audio, one-way video: Yes
One-way live video: Yes
One-way pre-recorded video: Yes
Audio graphics: Yes
Audio: Yes
Hardware requirements: For Windows 95–98, Pentium I,
    II, III, 32MB of RAM, 56KBPS V-90 modem, 100MB
    free disk space: for Macintosh System 8 or above
Software requirements: Netscape or Internet Explorer
    browser (4.0 or higher), word processor (MS Word
    preferred)
Is the library accessible to students? Yes
Are computers accessible to students? Yes

Remote Sites

Other branches of the institution: No
Other college campuses: Yes
Students' homes: Yes
Work sites: Yes
Libraries: Yes
Elementary/Secondary schools: Yes
Community-based organizations: Yes
Correctional institutions: Yes

On-Campus Requirements

On-campus course work: Yes
On-campus admissions interview: No
On-campus program orientation: No
On-campus exams: No

Tuition & Fees

In-state tuition per credit: $128
Out-of-state tuition per credit: $128
Average yearly cost of books: $25

Financial Aid

Is financial aid available to full-time students? Yes
Is financial aid available to part-time students? Yes
Are academic scholarships available? Yes
Assistance programs available to students: Federal Stafford
    Loan, Federal Perkins Loan, Federal Plus Loan, Federal
    Pell Grant, Federal Work-Study Program, veterans'
    assistance

Indiana University

Indiana University System
Office of Distributed Education
902 West New York Street
Indianapolis, IN 46202-5157
Contact: Erwin Boschmann, ES 2129
Department e-mail: scs@indiana.edu
Department Web address: www.indiana.edu/~iude/
School Web address: www.indiana.edu
Institutional accreditation: North Central Association of
    Colleges and Schools

Subjects Offered

Accounting, liberal arts/general studies/general humanities,
    mathematics, American studies, anatomy, anthropology,
    area, ethnic, cultural studies, art history/criticism,
    astronomy, astrophysics, biology, business/international
    business, business administration/management,
    chemistry, classical languages/literatures, communica-
    tions, computer information, computer science,
    conservation, logic, criminal justice, natural resources,
    labor relations/labor studies, developmental and child
    psychology, economics, education, English, European
    languages and literature, French, geology, health and
    physical education, physical fitness, health professions,
    history

Admissions Requirements

Is a minimum high school GPA required? No
Is provisional admission available? Yes
Is an admissions interview required? No
Can pre-requisite course work be waived? No
Are international students eligible to apply? Yes

Program Delivery

Primary method of program delivery: Text
Two-way interactive video: Yes
Two-way audio, one-way video: Yes
One-way live video: Yes
One-way pre-recorded video: Yes
Audio graphics: Yes
Audio: Yes
Is the library accessible to students? Yes
Are computers accessible to students? Yes

Remote Sites

Other branches of the institution: Yes
Other college campuses: Yes
Students' homes: Yes
Work sites: Yes
Libraries: Yes
Elementary/Secondary schools: Yes

Community-based organizations: Yes
Correctional institutions: Yes

On-Campus Requirements

Is an on-campus component required? No

Tuition & Fees

In-state tuition per credit: $100
Out-of-state tuition per credit: $100

Financial Aid

Is financial aid available to full-time students? Yes
Is financial aid available to part-time students? Yes
Are academic scholarships available? Yes
Assistance programs available to students: Federal Stafford
    Loan, Federal Perkins Loan, Federal Plus Loan, Federal
    Pell Grant, Federal Work-Study Program, in-state
    student aid programs, veterans' assistance

International Bible College

Distance Learning Department
3625 Helton Drive
Florence, AL 35630
Contact: Frank Foust, Director of Distance Learning
Department e-mail: ffoust@i-b-c.edu
School Web address: i-b-c.edu
Institutional accreditation: AABC

Subjects Offered

Bible and doctrine, general education, professional studies,
    counseling

Admissions Requirements

Is a minimum high school GPA required? No
Is provisional admission available? Yes
Can pre-requisite course work be waived? No
Are international students eligible to apply? Yes
Is the TOEFL required for international students? No

Program Delivery

Primary method of program delivery: Text
Two-way interactive video: No
Two-way audio, one-way video: No
One-way live video: No
One-way pre-recorded video: Yes
Audio graphics: No
Audio: No

Remote Sites

Other branches of the institution: No
Other college campuses: No
Students' homes: No

Work sites: No
Libraries: No
Elementary/Secondary schools: No
Community-based organizations: No
Correctional institutions: No

On-Campus Requirements

Is an on-campus component required? Yes
On-campus course work: Yes

Tuition & Fees

In-state tuition per credit: $188
Out-of-state tuition per credit: $188
Average yearly cost of books: $600

Financial Aid

Is financial aid available to full-time students? Yes
Is financial aid available to part-time students? Yes
Are academic scholarships available? Yes
Assistance programs available to students: Federal Stafford
    Loan, Federal Plus Loan, Federal Pell Grant, Federal
    Work-Study Program, veterans' assistance

Iowa State University

Extended and Continuing Education (ECE)
102 Scheman
Ames, IA 50011-1112
Contact: Ann Hill Duin, Associate Provost and Director of
    ECE
Department e-mail: conted@iastate.edu
Department Web address: www.iastate.edu

Subjects Offered

Agriculture, family and consumer science, liberal arts and
    sciences

Admissions Requirements

Is provisional admission available? Yes
Is an admissions interview required? No
Can pre-requisite course work be waived? Yes
Are international students eligible to apply? Yes

Program Delivery

Two-way interactive video: Yes
Two-way audio, one-way video: No
One-way live video: No
One-way pre-recorded video: Yes
Audio graphics: No
Audio: No

Remote Sites

Other branches of the institution: No

Other college campuses: Yes
Students' homes: Yes
Work sites: Yes
Libraries: Yes
Elementary/Secondary schools: Yes
Community-based organizations: Yes
Correctional institutions: No

Tuition & Fees

In-state tuition per credit: $122

Iowa Western Community College

2700 College Road
Council Bluffs, IA 51502
Contact: Barb Vredeveld
Institutional accreditation: North Central Association of
    Colleges and Schools

Subjects Offered

Intro to sociology, coaching authorization, human growth
    and development, personality and adjustment, tech
    math I, II, III, IV, electronic engineering technology,
    fiberoptics courses

Admissions Requirements

Is a minimum high school GPA required? No
Is an admissions interview required? No
Can pre-requisite course work be waived? Yes
Are international students eligible to apply? Yes
Is the TOEFL required for international students? Yes

Program Delivery

Primary method of program delivery: Web
Two-way interactive video: Yes
Hardware requirements: Pentium 400's—128MB
Software requirements: CAD Auto CD, 3D Studio VIZ
Is the library accessible to students? Yes
Are computers accessible to students? Yes

Remote Sites

Other branches of the institution: Yes
Students' homes: Yes
Work sites: Yes
Elementary/Secondary schools: Yes
Correctional institutions: Yes

Tuition & Fees

In-state tuition per credit: $70
Out-of-state tuition per credit: $105
Average yearly cost of books: $800

Financial Aid

Is financial aid available to full-time students? Yes
Is financial aid available to part-time students? Yes
Are academic scholarships available? Yes
Assistance programs available to students: Federal Stafford Loan, Federal Perkins Loan, Federal Plus Loan, Federal Pell Grant, Federal Work-Study Program, in-state student aid programs, veterans' assistance

Jacksonville State University

Distance Learning Program
700 Pelham Road North
Jacksonville, AL 36265
Contact: Franklin King, Interim Director of Distance Learning
Department e-mail: fking@j5ucc.jsu.edu
Department Web address: www.jsu.edu/depart/distance
School Web address: www.jsu.edu
Institutional accreditation: Commission of Colleges of the Southern Association of Colleges and Schools

Subjects Offered

History, special education, physical education, anthropology, elementary education, nursing, accounting, psychology, computer science, social work, economics, algebra, English, political science

Admissions Requirements

Is a minimum high school GPA required? No
Is provisional admission available? Yes
Is an admissions interview required? No
Can pre-requisite course work be waived? No
Are international students eligible to apply? Yes
Is the TOEFL required for international students? Yes
What is the minimum TOEFL score required? 500

Program Delivery

Primary method of program delivery: Web
Two-way interactive video: Yes
Two-way audio, one-way video: No
One-way live video: Yes
One-way pre-recorded video: Yes
Audio graphics: No
Audio: Yes
Hardware requirements: Minimum 28.8KBPS modem, 150 MHz processor, minimum 16MB RAM, monitor capable of at least 800 x 600 resolution
Software requirements: Netscape Communicator 4.0 or Higher, or Microsoft Internet Explorer 4.0 or Higher or an Equivalent Browser.

Is the library accessible to students? Yes
Are computers accessible to students? Yes

Remote Sites

Other branches of the institution: Yes
Other college campuses: Yes
Students' homes: Yes
Work sites: Yes
Libraries: Yes
Elementary/Secondary schools: Yes
Community-based organizations: No
Correctional institutions: No

On-Campus Requirements

Is an on-campus component required? No

Tuition & Fees

In-state tuition per credit: $110
Out-of-state tuition per credit: $220
Average yearly cost of books: $650

Financial Aid

Is financial aid available to full-time students? Yes
Is financial aid available to part-time students? Yes
Are academic scholarships available? Yes
Assistance programs available to students: Federal Stafford Loan, Federal Plus Loan, Federal Pell Grant, Federal Work-Study Program, in-state student aid programs, veterans' assistance

James Madison University

Office of Continuing Education
James Madison University, MSC 2502
Harrisonburg, VA 22807
Contact: Dr. Charles Curry
Department e-mail: continuing-ed@jmu.edu
Department Web address: www.imu.edu/continuingeducation
School Web address: www.imu.edu
Institutional accreditation: Commission on Colleges of the Southern Associate of Colleges and Schools

Subjects Offered

Communication sciences and disorders, MBA program, SOL workshops, adult degree program classes, INFOSEC

Admissions Requirements

Is a minimum high school GPA required? No
Can pre-requisite course work be waived? Yes
Are international students eligible to apply? Yes
Is the TOEFL required for international students? Yes

Program Delivery

Primary method of program delivery: Remote site
Two-way interactive video: Yes
Two-way audio, one-way video: No
One-way live video: No
One-way pre-recorded video: No
Audio graphics: No
Audio: No
Is the library accessible to students? Yes
Are computers accessible to students? Yes

Remote Sites

Other branches of the institution: No
Other college campuses: Yes
Students' homes: Yes
Work sites: No
Libraries: No
Elementary/Secondary schools: Yes
Community-based organizations: Yes
Correctional institutions: No

Tuition & Fees

In-state tuition per credit: $396
Out-of-state tuition per credit: $978
Average yearly cost of books: $30

Financial Aid

Is financial aid available to full-time students? Yes
Is financial aid available to part-time students? Yes
Are academic scholarships available? Yes
Assistance programs available to students: Federal Stafford Loan, Federal Perkins Loan, Federal Plus Loan, Federal Pell Grant, in-state student aid programs, veterans' assistance

Jamestown Community College

Academic Affairs
525 Falconer Street
Jamestown, NY 14701
Contact: Gary Porter, Dean of Academic Affairs
Department e-mail: garyporter@mail.sunyjcc.edu
Institutional accreditation: New York State Education Department

Subjects Offered

Biology, computer science, English, history, library, math, sociology, student success seminar

Admissions Requirements

Is a minimum high school GPA required? No
Is provisional admission available? Yes
Is an admissions interview required? Yes
Can pre-requisite course work be waived? Yes
Are international students eligible to apply? Yes
Is the TOEFL required for international students? No

Program Delivery

Primary method of program delivery: Web
Two-way interactive video: Yes
Is the library accessible to students? Yes

Remote Sites

Other branches of the institution: Yes
Other college campuses: Yes
Students' homes: Yes
Elementary/Secondary schools: Yes

On-Campus Requirements

Is an on-campus component required? No

Tuition & Fees

In-state tuition per credit: $92
Out-of-state tuition per credit: $162
Average yearly cost of books: $600

Financial Aid

Is financial aid available to full-time students? Yes
Is financial aid available to part-time students? Yes
Are academic scholarships available? Yes
Assistance programs available to students: Federal Stafford Loan, Federal Perkins Loan, Federal Plus Loan, Federal Pell Grant, Federal Work-Study Program, in-state student aid programs, veterans' assistance

Jones International University

9697 East Mineral Avenue
Englewood, CO 80112
Contact: Dr. Pamela Pease, President
Department e-mail: info@jonesinternational.edu
School Web address: jonesinternational.edu
Institutional accreditation: North Central Association of Colleges and Schools

Subjects Offered

Business communication

Admissions Requirements

Is a minimum high school GPA required? No
Is provisional admission available? Yes
Is an admissions interview required? No
Can pre-requisite course work be waived? No
Are international students eligible to apply? Yes
Is the TOEFL required for international students? Yes
What is the minimum TOEFL score required? 550

Program Delivery

Hardware requirements: Pentium processor with at least
    1.33 MHz, 16 MB of RAM, 13–15 inch 256-color
    monitor, 28.8KBPS modem
Software requirements: Internet browser, Netscape 3 or 4
    or Internet Explorer 4.01, chat, Adobe Acrobat Reader,
    and RealPlayer
Is the library accessible to students? Yes
Are computers accessible to students? No

Remote Sites

Other branches of the institution: No
Other college campuses: No
Students' homes: Yes
Work sites: Yes
Libraries: Yes
Elementary/Secondary schools: No
Community-based organizations: No
Correctional institutions: No

On-Campus Requirements

Is an on-campus component required? No

Tuition & Fees

In-state tuition per credit: $200
Out-of-state tuition per credit: $200
Average yearly cost of books: $500

Financial Aid

Is financial aid available to full-time students? Yes
Is financial aid available to part-time students? Yes
Are academic scholarships available? No
Assistance programs available to students: Veterans'
    assistance

Juniata College

1700 Moore Street
Huntingdon, PA 16652
Department e-mail: bichela@juniata.edu
School Web address: juniata.edu
Institutional accreditation: Middle States Association of
    Colleges and Schools

Subjects Offered

Information technology

Admissions Requirements

Is a minimum high school GPA required? No
Is an admissions interview required? No
Is the TOEFL required for international students? No

Program Delivery

Primary method of program delivery: Remote site
Two-way interactive video: Yes
Is the library accessible to students? Yes

Remote Sites

Elementary/Secondary schools: Yes

On-Campus Requirements

Is an on-campus component required? No

Kansas State University

Division of Continuing Education
Manhattan, KS 66506-6001
Contact: Dr. Elizabeth Unger
Department e-mail: info@dce.ksu.edu
Department Web address: www.dce.ksu.edu
School Web address: www.dce.ksu.edu
Institutional accreditation: North Central Association of
    Colleges and Schools

Subjects Offered

Animal science and industry, general business, food science
    and industry, social science, engineering, agriculture,
    education, human ecology

Admissions Requirements

Is a minimum high school GPA required? No
Are international students eligible to apply? No

Program Delivery

Two-way interactive video: Yes
Two-way audio, one-way video: Yes
One-way live video: Yes
One-way pre-recorded video: Yes
Audio: Yes

Remote Sites

Other branches of the institution: Yes
Other college campuses: Yes
Work sites: Yes
Libraries: Yes
Elementary/Secondary schools: Yes
Community-based organizations: Yes

On-Campus Requirements

Is an on-campus component required? No

Tuition & Fees

In-state tuition per credit: $100
Average yearly cost of books: $1,000
Average yearly additional fees: $30

Financial Aid

Is financial aid available to full-time students? Yes
Is financial aid available to part-time students? Yes
Are academic scholarships available? Yes
Assistance programs available to students: Federal Stafford Loan, Federal Perkins Loan, Federal Plus Loan, Federal Pell Grant, Federal Work-Study Program, in-state student aid programs, veterans' assistance

Kaskaskia College

27210 College Road
Centralia, IL 62801
School Web address: www.kc.cc.il.us
Institutional accreditation: North Central Association of Colleges and Schools

Subjects Offered

Child care, marine biology, administration of justice, environmental biology, math, business management, philosophy, chemistry, political science, economics, psychology, world geography, accounting, health, anthropology, history, art, literature, astronomy, computer applications

Admissions Requirements

Is a minimum high school GPA required? No
Is provisional admission available? Yes
Is an admissions interview required? No
Can pre-requisite course work be waived? No
Are international students eligible to apply? Yes
Is the TOEFL required for international students? Yes
What is the minimum TOEFL score required? 500

Program Delivery

Two-way interactive video: Yes
Two-way audio, one-way video: Yes
One-way live video: No
One-way pre-recorded video: Yes
Audio graphics: No
Audio: No
Software requirements: For online courses only, students need a computer and usually Microsoft Office
Is the library accessible to students? Yes
Are computers accessible to students? Yes

Remote Sites

Other branches of the institution: Yes
Other college campuses: No
Students' homes: Yes
Work sites: Yes
Libraries: Yes
Elementary/Secondary schools: Yes
Community-based organizations: No
Correctional institutions: Yes

On-Campus Requirements

Is an on-campus component required? Yes
On-campus course work: Yes
On-campus admissions interview: No
On-campus program orientation: Yes
On-campus exams: Yes

Tuition & Fees

In-state tuition per credit: $107
Out-of-state tuition per credit: $194
Average yearly cost of books: $540
Average yearly additional fees: $10

Financial Aid

Is financial aid available to full-time students? Yes
Is financial aid available to part-time students? Yes
Are academic scholarships available? Yes
Assistance programs available to students: Federal Pell Grant, Federal Work-Study Program, in-state student aid programs, veterans' assistance

Kentucky State University

Institutional Research and Planning
400 East Main Street
Frankfort, KY 40601
School Web address: www.kysu.edu

Subjects Offered

Health education, psychology, sociology, social work, accounting, criminal law, English, math, art, religion, Spanish

Program Delivery

Two-way interactive video: Yes

Remote Sites

Elementary/Secondary schools: Yes
Community-based organizations: Yes

Knowledge Systems Institute

Computer & Information Sciences
3420 Main Street
Skokie, IL 60076
Contact: Judy Pan, Executive Director
Department e-mail: office@ksi.edu
School Web address: ksi.edu
Institutional accreditation: Illinois State Board of Education

Subjects Offered

Visual Basic programming, computer systems, data structures, object-oriented program (C++), operating systems, database programming, computer networks, computer languages

Admissions Requirements

Is a minimum high school GPA required? No
Is provisional admission available? Yes
Is an admissions interview required? Yes
Can pre-requisite course work be waived? Yes
Are international students eligible to apply? Yes
Is the TOEFL required for international students? Yes
What is the minimum TOEFL score required? 550

Program Delivery

Primary method of program delivery: Web
Two-way interactive video: Yes
Audio: Yes
Hardware requirements: PC
Software requirements: Windows 95 or higher (98, 2000, NT) Internet connection with Netscape Navigator 2.0 or higher
Is the library accessible to students? Yes
Are computers accessible to students? Yes

Remote Sites

Other branches of the institution: No
Other college campuses: No
Students' homes: Yes
Work sites: No
Libraries: No
Elementary/Secondary schools: No
Community-based organizations: No
Correctional institutions: No

On-Campus Requirements

Is an on-campus component required? Yes
On-campus course work: No
On-campus admissions interview: Yes
On-campus program orientation: No
On-campus exams: Yes

Tuition & Fees

In-state tuition per credit: $295
Out-of-state tuition per credit: $295
Average yearly cost of books: $500
Average yearly additional fees: $40

Financial Aid

Is financial aid available to full-time students? Yes
Is financial aid available to part-time students? Yes
Are academic scholarships available? No
Assistance programs available to students: Federal Stafford Loan, Federal Plus Loan, Federal Work-Study Program, veterans' assistance

Lackawanna Junior College

Office of Distance Learning
501 Vine Street
Scranton, PA 18509
Contact: Griffith R. Lewis, Senior Director, MIS
Department e-mail: lewisg@ljc.edu
School Web address: www.ljc.edu
Institutional accreditation: Middle States Association of Colleges and Schools

Admissions Requirements

Is a minimum high school GPA required? No
Is provisional admission available? Yes
Is an admissions interview required? Yes
Can pre-requisite course work be waived? Yes
Are international students eligible to apply? Yes
Is the TOEFL required for international students? Yes

Program Delivery

Primary method of program delivery: Remote site
Two-way interactive video: Yes
Two-way audio, one-way video: No
One-way live video: No
One-way pre-recorded video: No
Audio graphics: No
Audio: No
Is the library accessible to students? No
Are computers accessible to students? No

Remote Sites

Other branches of the institution: Yes
Other college campuses: No
Students' homes: No
Work sites: No

Libraries: No
Elementary/Secondary schools: Yes
Community-based organizations: No
Correctional institutions: No

Tuition & Fees

In-state tuition per credit: $260
Out-of-state tuition per credit: $260
Average yearly cost of books: $50

Financial Aid

Is financial aid available to full-time students? Yes
Is financial aid available to part-time students? Yes
Are academic scholarships available? Yes
Assistance programs available to students: Federal Stafford
   Loan, Federal Perkins Loan, Federal Plus Loan, Federal
   Pell Grant, Federal Work-Study Program, in-state
   student aid programs, veterans' assistance

Lake Shore Community College

Instructional Design and Technology
1290 North Avenue
Cleveland, WI 53015
Contact: Dr. Douglas G. Gosses, Director, Instruction
   Design & Technology
School Web address: gotoltc.com
Institutional accreditation: North Central Association of
   Colleges and Schools

Subjects Offered

Computer applications, paralegal, logistics, field study,
   pharmacology for allied health, calculations and
   statistics, introduction to nuclear technology and
   regulations, nuclear systems and sources, radiation
   physics and biology, radioactive material disposal and
   management, English, advanced medical terminology,
   medical terminology, paralegal professional

Admissions Requirements

Is a minimum high school GPA required? No
Is provisional admission available? Yes
Is an admissions interview required? No
Can pre-requisite course work be waived? Yes
Are international students eligible to apply? Yes
Is the TOEFL required for international students? No

Program Delivery

Two-way interactive video: Yes
Two-way audio, one-way video: No
One-way live video: No

One-way pre-recorded video: Yes
Audio graphics: No
Audio: No
Hardware requirements: Varies by program
Software requirements: Microsoft Office 2000/97

Remote Sites

Other branches of the institution: Yes
Other college campuses: Yes
Students' homes: Yes
Work sites: Yes
Libraries: Yes
Elementary/Secondary schools: No
Community-based organizations: No
Correctional institutions: Yes

On-Campus Requirements

Is an on-campus component required? No

Tuition & Fees

In-state tuition per credit: $57
Out-of-state tuition per credit: $77
Average yearly cost of books: $200

Financial Aid

Is financial aid available to full-time students? Yes
Is financial aid available to part-time students? No
Are academic scholarships available? Yes
Assistance programs available to students: Federal Stafford
   Loan, Federal Perkins Loan, Federal Plus Loan, Federal
   Pell Grant, Federal Work-Study Program, in-state
   student aid programs, veterans' assistance

Lake Michigan College

2755 Napier Ave
Benton Harbor, MI 49022
School Web address: lmc.cc.mi.us

Subjects Offered

Biology, chemistry, business, history, political science,
   foreign language, sociology, psychology, humanities,
   philosophy

Admissions Requirements

Is a minimum high school GPA required? No
Is provisional admission available? Yes
Is an admissions interview required? No
Are international students eligible to apply? Yes
Is the TOEFL required for international students? Yes
What is the minimum TOEFL score required? 500

Program Delivery

Primary method of program delivery: Remote site
Two-way interactive video: Yes
Two-way audio, one-way video: No
One-way live video: No
One-way pre-recorded video: Yes
Audio graphics: No
Audio: No
Is the library accessible to students? Yes

Remote Sites

Other branches of the institution: Yes
Students' homes: Yes
Work sites: Yes
Elementary/Secondary schools: Yes
Community-based organizations: Yes

On-Campus Requirements

On-campus course work: Yes
On-campus program orientation: Yes
On-campus exams: Yes

Financial Aid

Is financial aid available to full-time students? Yes
Is financial aid available to part-time students? Yes
Are academic scholarships available? Yes
Assistance programs available to students: Federal Pell
    Grant, Federal Work-Study Program, in-state student aid
    programs, veterans' assistance

Lake Sumter Community College

Institutional Research
Education Services
9501 U.S. Highway 441
Leesburg, FL 34788
School Web address: www.lscc.cc.fl.us

Subjects Offered

Natural sciences, psychology, business, government,
    nursing

Admissions Requirements

Is a minimum high school GPA required? No
Is provisional admission available? No
Is an admissions interview required? No
Can pre-requisite course work be waived? Yes
Are international students eligible to apply? Yes
Is the TOEFL required for international students? Yes
What is the minimum TOEFL score required? 550

Program Delivery

Primary method of program delivery: Remote site
Two-way interactive video: Yes
One-way pre-recorded video: Yes

Remote Sites

Other branches of the institution: Yes
Students' homes: Yes

Financial Aid

Is financial aid available to full-time students? Yes
Is financial aid available to part-time students? Yes
Are academic scholarships available? Yes
Assistance programs available to students: Federal Stafford
    Loan, Federal Plus Loan

Lakehead University

Part-time and Distance Education
Regional Centre 0009, 955 Oliver Road
Thunder Bay, ON, Canada P7B 5E1
Contact: Gwen Wojda, Director
Department e-mail: parttime@lakeheadu.ca
School Web address: www.lakeheadu.ca
Institutional accreditation: Council of Ontario Universities

Subjects Offered

Anthropology, biology, chemistry, English, environmental
    studies, geography, gerontology, history, indigenous
    learning, kinesiology, library and information studies,
    mathematics, nursing, philosophy, political science,
    psychology, religious studies, social work, sociology,
    women's studies

Admissions Requirements

Is a minimum high school GPA required? Yes
Is provisional admission available? No
Is an admissions interview required? No
Can pre-requisite course work be waived? No
Are international students eligible to apply? Yes
Is the TOEFL required for international students? Yes
What is the minimum TOEFL score required? 550

Program Delivery

Primary method of program delivery: Text
Two-way interactive video: Yes
Two-way audio, one-way video: Yes
One-way live video: Yes
One-way pre-recorded video: Yes
Audio graphics: Yes
Audio: Yes

Hardware requirements: For online courses: access to PC with Windows 95/98 or PowerMac, connection to Internet, Netscape/Internet Explorer 4.0 or higher

Is the library accessible to students? Yes

Are computers accessible to students? Yes

Remote Sites

Other branches of the institution: Yes
Other college campuses: Yes
Students' homes: Yes
Work sites: Yes
Libraries: Yes
Elementary/Secondary schools: Yes
Community-based organizations: Yes
Correctional institutions: Yes

On-Campus Requirements

Is an on-campus component required? No

Tuition & Fees

In-state tuition per credit: $782
Out-of-state tuition per credit: $1,768

Financial Aid

Is financial aid available to full-time students? Yes
Is financial aid available to part-time students? Yes
Are academic scholarships available? Yes
Assistance programs available to students: Federal Stafford Loan, Federal Pell Grant, Federal Work-Study Program, in-state student aid programs

Lakeland College

Lakeland Online
PO Box 359
Sheboygan, WI 53082-0359
Contact: R. Wiverstad, Director of Lakeland Online (Interim)
School Web address: www.lakeland.edu
Institutional accreditation: North Central Association of Colleges and Schools

Subjects Offered

Business, computers, humanities, writing, history, mathematics

Admissions Requirements

Is a minimum high school GPA required? Yes
Is provisional admission available? Yes
Can pre-requisite course work be waived? No
Are international students eligible to apply? Yes
Is the TOEFL required for international students? Yes
What is the minimum TOEFL score required? 500

Program Delivery

Primary method of program delivery: Web
Is the library accessible to students? Yes
Are computers accessible to students? Yes

Remote Sites

Students' homes: Yes
Work sites: Yes

On-Campus Requirements

Is an on-campus component required? No

Tuition & Fees

In-state tuition per credit: $140
Out-of-state tuition per credit: $140

Financial Aid

Is financial aid available to full-time students? Yes
Is financial aid available to part-time students? Yes
Are academic scholarships available? Yes
Assistance programs available to students: Federal Stafford Loan, Federal Perkins Loan, Federal Plus Loan, veterans' assistance

Lansing Community College

Distance Learning/Educational Technology
8123 Distance Learning
PO Box 400100
Lansing, MI 48901-7210
Contact: Tim Brannan, Director of Distance Learning Education Technology
Department e-mail: icottrell@lansing.cc.mi.us
Department Web address: vcollege.lansing.cc.mi.us
School Web address: lansing.cc.mi.us
Institutional accreditation: North Central Association of Colleges and Schools

Subjects Offered

Accounting, history, astronomy, humanities, business, legal assistant, chemistry, math, computer information, physical fitness, computer applications, philosophy, criminal justice, political science, court reporting, psychology, computer science, sociology, economics, speech, electrical technology, theatre

Admissions Requirements

Is a minimum high school GPA required? No
Is an admissions interview required? No
Can pre-requisite course work be waived? Yes
Are international students eligible to apply? Yes

Is the TOEFL required for international students? Yes
What is the minimum TOEFL score required? 500

Program Delivery

Primary method of program delivery: Web
Two-way interactive video: Yes
Two-way audio, one-way video: No
One-way live video: No
One-way pre-recorded video: Yes
Audio graphics: No
Audio: No
Hardware requirements: 486 PC or Mac 040 with 16MB
  of RAM, 150MB of hard disk free space, and a
  14.4KBPS modem
Software requirements: Varies by course
Are computers accessible to students? Yes

Remote Sites

Other branches of the institution: Yes
Other college campuses: Yes
Students' homes: No
Work sites: No
Libraries: No
Elementary/Secondary schools: No
Community-based organizations: No
Correctional institutions: No

On-Campus Requirements

Is an on-campus component required? No

Tuition & Fees

In-state tuition per credit: $78
Out-of-state tuition per credit: $107
Average yearly cost of books: $200

Financial Aid

Is financial aid available to full-time students? Yes
Is financial aid available to part-time students? Yes
Are academic scholarships available? Yes
Assistance programs available to students: Federal Stafford
  Loan, Federal Perkins Loan, Federal Plus Loan, Federal
  Pell Grant, Federal Work-Study Program, in-state
  student aid programs, veterans' assistance

Lee University

Department of External Studies
100 Eight Street NE
Contact: Dr. Henry J. Smith, Chairman
Department e-mail: externalstudy@leeuniversity.edu
School Web address: leeuniversity.edu
Institutional accreditation: Commission on Colleges of the
  Southern Association of Colleges and Schools

Subjects Offered

Art, church history, biology, Christian education, English,
  urban ministry, humanities, pastoral ministry, history,
  theology, mathematics, music, physical science,
  sociology, speech, bible

Admissions Requirements

Is a minimum high school GPA required? Yes
Is provisional admission available? Yes
Can pre-requisite course work be waived? Yes
Are international students eligible to apply? Yes
Is the TOEFL required for international students? Yes

Program Delivery

Primary method of program delivery: Text
Two-way interactive video: No
Two-way audio, one-way video: No
One-way live video: No
One-way pre-recorded video: No
Audio graphics: No
Audio: No
Hardware requirements: Pentium II Class, 75 MHz
Software requirements: Word processor, e-mail, Internet
  Explorer v.5.0
Is the library accessible to students? Yes
Are computers accessible to students? Yes

Remote Sites

Other branches of the institution: Yes
Other college campuses: No
Students' homes: Yes
Work sites: No
Libraries: Yes
Elementary/Secondary schools: No
Community-based organizations: No
Correctional institutions: No

On-Campus Requirements

Is an on-campus component required? Yes
On-campus admissions interview: No
On-campus program orientation: No
On-campus exams: No

Tuition & Fees

In-state tuition per credit: $90
Out-of-state tuition per credit: $90
Average yearly cost of books: $15

Financial Aid

Is financial aid available to full-time students? Yes
Is financial aid available to part-time students? Yes
Are academic scholarships available? No

Assistance programs available to students: Federal Pell Grant, veterans' assistance

Lenoir Community College

Distance Education
231 High Way 58 South, PO Box 188
Kinston, NC 28502-0188
Contact: Duane Leith, Coordinator of Distance Learning
Department e-mail: dal500@e-mail.lenoir.cc.nc.us
Department Web address: www.disted.lenoir.cc.nc.us
School Web address: www.lenoir.cc.nc.us
Institutional accreditation: Southern Association of Colleges and Schools

Subjects Offered

Art, college preparation, history, foreign languages, English, psychology, computers, business, early childhood education, nutrition, medical, industrial engineering technology, office systems technology

Admissions Requirements

Is a minimum high school GPA required? No
Is provisional admission available? No
Is an admissions interview required? No
Can pre-requisite course work be waived? No
Are international students eligible to apply? Yes
Is the TOEFL required for international students? No

Program Delivery

Primary method of program delivery: Remote site
Two-way interactive video: Yes
Software requirements: Netscape 4.0 or Internet Explorer 4.1 or above
Is the library accessible to students? Yes
Are computers accessible to students? No

Remote Sites

Other college campuses: Yes

On-Campus Requirements

Is an on-campus component required? No

Tuition & Fees

In-state tuition per credit: $27
Out-of-state tuition per credit: $170
Average yearly cost of books: $400

Financial Aid

Is financial aid available to full-time students? Yes
Is financial aid available to part-time students? Yes
Are academic scholarships available? Yes
Assistance programs available to students: Federal Stafford

Loan, Federal Perkins Loan, Federal Plus Loan, Federal Pell Grant, Federal Work-Study Program, veterans' assistance

Lewis-Clark College

Extended Programs
Distance learning Technologies
500 8th Avenue
Lewiston, ID 83501
Contact: Kathy L. Martin, Director of Distance Learning Technologies
Department e-mail: kmartin@lcsc.edu
Department Web address: www.lcsc.edu/dlt
School Web address: www.lcsc.edu
Institutional accreditation: Northwest Association of Schools and Colleges

Subjects Offered

Literature, fine and performing arts, English, history, math, nursing, communications, business, office and business technology, social science, justice studies, psychology, education, natural science

Admissions Requirements

Is a minimum high school GPA required? Yes
Is provisional admission available? Yes
Can pre-requisite course work be waived? No
Are international students eligible to apply? Yes
Is the TOEFL required for international students? Yes

Program Delivery

Primary method of program delivery: Web
Two-way interactive video: Yes
Two-way audio, one-way video: No
One-way live video: No
One-way pre-recorded video: Yes
Audio graphics: No
Audio: No
Hardware requirements: Windows 95 or Mac 68040, 16MB RAM
Is the library accessible to students? Yes
Are computers accessible to students? Yes

Remote Sites

Other branches of the institution: Yes
Other college campuses: Yes
Students' homes: No
Work sites: No
Libraries: Yes
Elementary/Secondary schools: Yes
Community-based organizations: Yes
Correctional institutions: No

On-Campus Requirements

Is an on-campus component required? Yes
On-campus course work: Yes
On-campus admissions interview: No
On-campus program orientation: No
On-campus exams: Yes

Tuition & Fees

In-state tuition per credit: $110
Out-of-state tuition per credit: $110
Average yearly cost of books: $600

Financial Aid

Is financial aid available to full-time students? Yes
Is financial aid available to part-time students? Yes
Are academic scholarships available? Yes
Assistance programs available to students: Federal Stafford
 Loan, Federal Perkins Loan, Federal Pell Grant, Federal
 Work-Study Program, veterans' assistance

Life Bible College

School of Distance Learning
1100 Covina Boulevard
San Dimas, CA 91773
Contact: Brian Tomhave, Director, School of Distance
 Learning
Department e-mail: sdl@lifeBible.edu
School Web address: lifeBible.edu
Institutional accreditation: Accrediting Association of Bible
 Colleges

Subjects Offered

Bible, theology, general ministry, general education

Admissions Requirements

Is a minimum high school GPA required? Yes
Is provisional admission available? Yes
Is an admissions interview required? No
Can pre-requisite course work be waived? No
Are international students eligible to apply? Yes
Is the TOEFL required for international students? No

Program Delivery

Primary method of program delivery: Text
Audio: Yes
Is the library accessible to students? Yes
Are computers accessible to students? No

Remote Sites

Students' homes: Yes

On-Campus Requirements

Is an on-campus component required? No

Tuition & Fees

In-state tuition per credit: $65
Out-of-state tuition per credit: $65
Average yearly cost of books: $750

Financial Aid

Is financial aid available to full-time students? No
Is financial aid available to part-time students? No
Are academic scholarships available? No

Longview Community College

PACE
500 SW Longview Road
Lee Summit, MO 64030
Contact: Margaret Boyd, PACE Director
Department e-mail: boydme@longview.cc.mo.us
School Web address: www.kcmetro.mo.us
Institutional accreditation: North Central Association of
 Colleges and Schools

Subjects Offered

English, mathematics, humanities, sciences-biological-
 physical, psychology, sociology, philosophy, literature,
 mythology, history

Admissions Requirements

Is a minimum high school GPA required? No
Is an admissions interview required? No
Can pre-requisite course work be waived? No
Are international students eligible to apply? Yes
Is the TOEFL required for international students? Yes

Program Delivery

Two-way interactive video: Yes
Two-way audio, one-way video: Yes
One-way live video: Yes
One-way pre-recorded video: Yes
Is the library accessible to students? Yes
Are computers accessible to students? Yes

Remote Sites

Other branches of the institution: Yes
Other college campuses: Yes
Students' homes: Yes
Work sites: Yes
Elementary/Secondary schools: Yes

On-Campus Requirements

On-campus course work: Yes
On-campus exams: Yes

Tuition & Fees

Average yearly cost of books: $1,000

Financial Aid

Is financial aid available to full-time students? Yes
Is financial aid available to part-time students? Yes
Are academic scholarships available? Yes
Assistance programs available to students: Federal Stafford Loan, Federal Perkins Loan, Federal Pell Grant, Federal Work-Study Program, veterans' assistance

Loyola University Chicago

Mundelein College
Skyscraper Building, Room 204
6525 North Sheridan Road
Chicago, IL 60626
Contact: Hilary Ward Schnadt, PhD, Associate Dean for Curricular Affairs
Department e-mail: mundelein@luc.edu
Department Web address: www.luc.edu/schools/mundelein
School Web address: www.luc.edu
Institutional accreditation: North Central Association of Colleges and Schools

Subjects Offered

Computer science, physics, biology, philosophy, accounting

Admissions Requirements

Is a minimum high school GPA required? No
Is provisional admission available? No
Is an admissions interview required? No
Can pre-requisite course work be waived? Yes
Are international students eligible to apply? Yes
Is the TOEFL required for international students? No

Program Delivery

Primary method of program delivery: Web
Hardware requirements: PC: 90 MHz Pentium processor, 32MB of RAM, 28.8KBPS modem, sound card, speakers. Mac: Power PC Processor (604 Power PC minimum), modem, speaker
Software requirements: Varies by course—Internet Explorer 5.0, Windows 95/98 NT or MacOS 8.1 or later, RealPlayer
Is the library accessible to students? Yes
Are computers accessible to students? Yes

Remote Sites

Other college campuses: Yes

On-Campus Requirements

Is an on-campus component required? No

Tuition & Fees

In-state tuition per credit: $360
Out-of-state tuition per credit: $360
Average yearly cost of books: $700

Financial Aid

Is financial aid available to full-time students? Yes
Is financial aid available to part-time students? Yes
Are academic scholarships available? Yes
Assistance programs available to students: Federal Stafford Loan, Federal Perkins Loan, Federal Plus Loan, Federal Pell Grant, Federal Work-Study Program, in-state student aid programs, veterans' assistance

Loyola University New Orleans

City College
Off Campus Learning Program
6363 St. Charles Avenue, Box 14
New Orleans, LA 70118
Contact: Kristel Scheuermann, Off-Campus Learning Program Coordinator
Department e-mail: scheuer@loyno.edu
Department Web address: www.loyno.edu/citycollege
School Web address: www.loyno.edu
Institutional accreditation: Southern Association of Colleges and Schools

Subjects Offered

Nursing, criminal justice

Admissions Requirements

Is a minimum high school GPA required? Yes
Is provisional admission available? Yes
Is an admissions interview required? No
Are international students eligible to apply? No

Program Delivery

Two-way interactive video: No
Two-way audio, one-way video: No
One-way live video: No
One-way pre-recorded video: Yes
Audio graphics: No

Remote Sites

Work sites: Yes

On-Campus Requirements

Is an on-campus component required? Yes

Tuition & Fees

In-state tuition per credit: $220
Out-of-state tuition per credit: $220

Financial Aid

Is financial aid available to full-time students? Yes
Is financial aid available to part-time students? No
Are academic scholarships available? No

Madison Area Technical College

Educational Technology and Learning Applications
Distance Learning Department
3550 Anderson Street
Madison, WI 53704
Contact: Lew Terpstra, Director of Educational Technology
   and Learning Applications
Department Web address: www.madison.tec.wi.us/catalog/
   dislearn/dislearn.html
School Web address: www.madison.tec.wi.us
Institutional accreditation: North Central Association of
   Colleges and Schools

Subjects Offered

English composition, communications skills, computer
   programs/computer skills, sanitation, ocular anatomy,
   optical dispensary, system analysis design, algebra,
   psychology, sociology, business statistics, economics,
   small business management, accounting, speech,
   management techniques

Admissions Requirements

Is provisional admission available? No
Can pre-requisite course work be waived? Yes
Are international students eligible to apply? Yes
Is the TOEFL required for international students? No

Program Delivery

Primary method of program delivery: Remote site
Two-way interactive video: Yes
One-way pre-recorded video: Yes
Audio: Yes
Software requirements: Pentium II processor, 28.8KBPS
   modem, 1GB hard drive, 16MB of RAM, VGA, 16 bit

soundcard, 2x CDROM, Windows 95, Netscape or
   Internet Explorer 4.0
Is the library accessible to students? Yes
Are computers accessible to students? Yes

Remote Sites

Other branches of the institution: Yes
Other college campuses: Yes
Students' homes: Yes
Work sites: Yes
Libraries: Yes
Elementary/Secondary schools: Yes
Community-based organizations: Yes
Correctional institutions: Yes

On-Campus Requirements

Is an on-campus component required? Yes
On-campus program orientation: Yes
On-campus exams: Yes

Tuition & Fees

In-state tuition per credit: $67
Out-of-state tuition per credit: $120
Average yearly cost of books: $500

Financial Aid

Is financial aid available to full-time students? Yes
Are academic scholarships available? Yes
Assistance programs available to students: Federal Plus
   Loan, Federal Work-Study Program, in-state student aid
   programs, veterans' assistance

Mansfield University of Pennsylvania

Center for Lifelong Learning
Mansfield, PA 16933
Contact: Karen Norton, Director of Credit Programs
Department e-mail: knorton@mnsfld.edu
Department Web address: www.mnsfld.edu/depts/
   conteduc/index.html
School Web address: www.mnsfld.edu
Institutional accreditation: Middle States Association of
   Colleges and Schools

Subjects Offered

Nursing, criminal justice, psychology, English, dietetics,
   geology, biology, art, social work

Admissions Requirements

Is a minimum high school GPA required? Yes
Is provisional admission available? Yes

Can pre-requisite course work be waived? Yes
Are international students eligible to apply? Yes
Is the TOEFL required for international students? Yes
What is the minimum TOEFL score required? 550

Program Delivery

Primary method of program delivery: Remote site
Two-way interactive video: Yes
Hardware requirements: Pentium processor or G-3 preferred, modem
Software requirements: Anti-virus software, Netscape or Internet Explorer
Is the library accessible to students? Yes
Are computers accessible to students? Yes

Remote Sites

Other branches of the institution: Yes
Other college campuses: Yes
Students' homes: Yes
Work sites: Yes
Libraries: No
Elementary/Secondary schools: Yes
Community-based organizations: Yes
Correctional institutions: No

On-Campus Requirements

Is an on-campus component required? No

Tuition & Fees

In-state tuition per credit: $158
Out-of-state tuition per credit: $395
Average yearly cost of books: $25

Financial Aid

Is financial aid available to full-time students? Yes
Is financial aid available to part-time students? Yes
Are academic scholarships available? Yes
Assistance programs available to students: Federal Stafford Loan, Federal Perkins Loan, Federal Plus Loan, Federal Pell Grant, Federal Work-Study Program, in-state student aid programs, veterans' assistance

Maryland Institute College of Art

Office of Continuing Studies
MICA Online
1300 Mount Royal Avenue
Baltimore, MD 21217-4191
Department e-mail: cs@mica.edu
School Web address: www.mica.edu/cs/cs-main.html
School Web address: www.mica.edu

Institutional accreditation: Middle States Association of Colleges and Schools; National Association of Schools of Art and Design

Subjects Offered

Web design, fine arts

Admissions Requirements

Is a minimum high school GPA required? No
Can pre-requisite course work be waived? Yes
Are international students eligible to apply? Yes
Is the TOEFL required for international students? Yes
What is the minimum TOEFL score required? 550

Program Delivery

Primary method of program delivery: Web
Hardware requirements: Pentium PC or Power PC; Mac, 64MB RAM or higher, free hard disk space 200–300MB.
Software requirements: Netscape 4.0 or above or Explorer 4.0, software specific to the courses
Is the library accessible to students? No
Are computers accessible to students? No

On-Campus Requirements

Is an on-campus component required? No

Tuition & Fees

In-state tuition per credit: $225
Out-of-state tuition per credit: $225
Average yearly cost of books: $30

Financial Aid

Is financial aid available to part-time students? No
Are academic scholarships available? Yes

Marywood University

School of Continuing Education
OFF Campus Degree Program
2300 Adams Avenue
Scranton, PA 18509
Contact: Meg Cullen-Brown, Director, OFF Campus Degree Program
Department e-mail: ocdp@ac.marywood.edu
Department Web address: www.marywood.edu/disted/
School Web address: www.marywood.edu
Institutional accreditation: Middle States Association of Colleges and Schools

Subjects Offered

Business, art, history, philosophy, physical education, communications, accounting, management, mathematics, sociology, management information systems, ecology, English, religious studies, human resources, marketing, Spanish, psychology, economics, fine arts

Admissions Requirements

Is a minimum high school GPA required? Yes
Is provisional admission available? Yes
Are international students eligible to apply? Yes
Is the TOEFL required for international students? Yes

Program Delivery

Primary method of program delivery: Text
Two-way interactive video: Yes
Two-way audio, one-way video: No
Is the library accessible to students? Yes
Are computers accessible to students? Yes

Remote Sites

Other branches of the institution: Yes
Other college campuses: No
Students' homes: Yes
Work sites: Yes
Libraries: Yes
Elementary/Secondary schools: No
Community-based organizations: No
Correctional institutions: Yes

On-Campus Requirements

Is an on-campus component required? Yes
On-campus course work: Yes

Tuition & Fees

In-state tuition per credit: $297
Application fee: $40
Can it be waived? Yes
Average yearly cost of books: $85

Financial Aid

Is financial aid available to full-time students? Yes
Is financial aid available to part-time students? Yes
Are academic scholarships available? Yes
Assistance programs available to students: Federal Stafford Loan, Federal Pell Grant, veterans' assistance

Maui Community College

310 Kaahumanu Avenue
Kahului, HI 96732
Contact: Flo Wiger, Dean of Instruction
Department e-mail: flo.wiger@mauicc.hawaii.edu
School Web address: www.mauicc.hawaii.edu
Institutional accreditation: Western Association of Schools and Colleges

Subjects Offered

Accounting, agriculture, administrative justice, biology, economics, English, electronics, fire hydraulics, sanitation, nutrition, Hawaiian studies, history, linguistics, mathematics, nursing, physics, psychology, sociology, physiology

Admissions Requirements

Is a minimum high school GPA required? No
Is provisional admission available? Yes
Is an admissions interview required? No
Can pre-requisite course work be waived? Yes
Are international students eligible to apply? Yes
Is the TOEFL required for international students? Yes
What is the minimum TOEFL score required? 450

Program Delivery

Primary method of program delivery: Remote site
Two-way interactive video: Yes
Two-way audio, one-way video: Yes
One-way live video: Yes
One-way pre-recorded video: Yes
Audio graphics: No
Audio: No
Is the library accessible to students? Yes
Are computers accessible to students? Yes

Remote Sites

Other branches of the institution: Yes
Other college campuses: Yes
Students' homes: No
Work sites: No
Libraries: No
Elementary/Secondary schools: No
Community-based organizations: No
Correctional institutions: No

On-Campus Requirements

Is an on-campus component required? No

Tuition & Fees

In-state tuition per credit: $86
Out-of-state tuition per credit: $494
Average yearly cost of books: $736

Financial Aid

Is financial aid available to full-time students? Yes
Is financial aid available to part-time students? Yes
Are academic scholarships available? Yes
Assistance programs available to students: Federal Stafford Loan, Federal Perkins Loan, Federal Plus Loan, Federal Pell Grant, Federal Work-Study Program, in-state student aid programs

Memorial University of Newfoundland

School of Continuing Education
St. Johns, Newfoundland, Canada AIB BX8
Contact: Mr. Harvey Weir, Director
Department e-mail: hweir@mun.ca
Department Web address: www.ce.mun.ca
School Web address: www.mun.ca
Institutional accreditation: Government of Newfoundland and Labrador

Subjects Offered

Anthroplogy, library studies, biology, mathematics, business, medicine, classics, municipal administration, criminology, nursing, economics, philosophy, education, political science, English, psychology, folklore, religious studies, geography, social work, history, sociology, statistics technology, women's studies

Admissions Requirements

Is a minimum high school GPA required? Yes
Is provisional admission available? Yes
Is an admissions interview required? No
Can pre-requisite course work be waived? Yes
Are international students eligible to apply? Yes
Is the TOEFL required for international students? Yes
What is the minimum TOEFL score required? 550

Program Delivery

Primary method of program delivery: Text
Two-way interactive video: No
Two-way audio, one-way video: No
One-way live video: No
One-way pre-recorded video: Yes
Audio graphics: Yes
Audio: Yes
Hardware requirements: Pentium-class PC or higher or Power PC-based Mac or higher, sufficient RAM and hard drive space
Software requirements: Netscape Navigator 4.5, Internet Explorer 4.0 28.8KBPS modem, e-mail, ICP/IP protocol, Internet service provider
Is the library accessible to students? Yes
Are computers accessible to students? Yes

Remote Sites

Other branches of the institution: Yes
Other college campuses: Yes
Students' homes: Yes
Work sites: Yes
Libraries: Yes

Elementary/Secondary schools: Yes
Community-based organizations: Yes
Correctional institutions: No

On-Campus Requirements

Is an on-campus component required? Yes

Tuition & Fees

In-state tuition per credit: $110
Out-of-state tuition per credit: $220
Average yearly cost of books: $400

Financial Aid

Is financial aid available to full-time students? Yes
Is financial aid available to part-time students? Yes
Are academic scholarships available? Yes

Middle Tennessee State University

Continuing Studies
Academic Outreach and Distance Learning
1301 East Main Street
Murfreesboro, TN 37132
Contact: Dianna Zeh, Director, Academic Outreach
Department e-mail: dzeh@mtsu.edu
Department Web address: www.mtsu.edu/~contstud
School Web address: www.mtsu.edu
Institutional accreditation: Southern Association of Colleges and Schools

Subjects Offered

Criminal justice, economics, English, human sciences, health, mathematics, management and marketing, political science, philosophy, astronomy, sociology, recording industry, aerospace, women's studies, education, journalism, nursing, radio/television, social work

Admissions Requirements

Is a minimum high school GPA required? Yes
Is provisional admission available? Yes
Is an admissions interview required? No
Can pre-requisite course work be waived? Yes
Are international students eligible to apply? Yes
Is the TOEFL required for international students? Yes

Program Delivery

Primary method of program delivery: Web
Two-way interactive video: Yes
One-way pre-recorded video: Yes
Hardware requirements: Computer for online courses

Software requirements: Internet service provider for online courses
Is the library accessible to students? Yes

Remote Sites

Other college campuses: Yes
Work sites: Yes
Elementary/Secondary schools: Yes

On-Campus Requirements

Is an on-campus component required? No

Tuition & Fees

In-state tuition per credit: $97
Out-of-state tuition per credit: $340
Average yearly cost of books: $320

Financial Aid

Is financial aid available to full-time students? Yes
Is financial aid available to part-time students? Yes
Are academic scholarships available? Yes
Assistance programs available to students: Federal Stafford Loan, Federal Perkins Loan, Federal Plus Loan, Federal Pell Grant, Federal Work-Study Program, in-state student aid programs, veterans' assistance

Minnesota West Community and Technical College

Distributed Education
1450 College Way
Worthington, MN 56187
Contact: Gary L. Phelps, Associate Vice President, Distributed Learning
Department e-mail: gphelps@wr.mnwest.mnsw.edu
School Web address: www.mnwest.mnsw.edu
Institutional accreditation: North Central Association of Colleges and Schools

Subjects Offered

Accounting, physical education, sociology, lamb/wool, mathematics, hydraulics, small business management, C++, medical terminology

Admissions Requirements

Is a minimum high school GPA required? No
Is an admissions interview required? No
Can pre-requisite course work be waived? Yes
Are international students eligible to apply? Yes
Is the TOEFL required for international students? Yes

Program Delivery

Primary method of program delivery: Web
Two-way interactive video: Yes
Two-way audio, one-way video: No
One-way live video: No
One-way pre-recorded video: No
Audio graphics: No
Audio: No
Hardware requirements: Pentium; 56KBPS modem, monitor
Software requirements: Internet Explorer 5.0; Windows 95
Is the library accessible to students? Yes
Are computers accessible to students? Yes

Remote Sites

Other branches of the institution: Yes
Other college campuses: Yes
Students' homes: Yes
Work sites: Yes
Libraries: Yes
Elementary/Secondary schools: Yes
Community-based organizations: Yes
Correctional institutions: No

On-Campus Requirements

Is an on-campus component required? No

Tuition & Fees

In-state tuition per credit: $75
Out-of-state tuition per credit: $150
Average yearly cost of books: $750

Financial Aid

Is financial aid available to full-time students? Yes
Is financial aid available to part-time students? Yes
Are academic scholarships available? Yes
Assistance programs available to students: Federal Stafford Loan, Federal Perkins Loan, Federal Plus Loan, Federal Pell Grant, Federal Work-Study Program, in-state student aid programs, veterans' assistance

Minot State University

Continuing Education
500 University Avenue West
Minot, ND 58703
Contact: Teresa Loftesnes, Director, Continuing Education
Department e-mail: online@misu.nodak.edu
School Web address: www.minotstateu.edu/conted
Institutional accreditation: North Central Association of Colleges and Schools

Subjects Offered

Art and theatre, business, management, information technology, drivers education, education, nursing, special education, psychology, general education, criminal justice, accounting

Admissions Requirements

Is a minimum high school GPA required? No
Is provisional admission available? No
Is an admissions interview required? No
Can pre-requisite course work be waived? Yes
Are international students eligible to apply? Yes
Is the TOEFL required for international students? Yes

Program Delivery

Primary method of program delivery: Web
Two-way interactive video: Yes
Two-way audio, one-way video: No
One-way live video: No
One-way pre-recorded video: No
Audio graphics: No
Audio: No
Software requirements: Netscape 3.0 or Internet Explorer 4.0, 28.8KBPS modem, Windows 97 preferred
Is the library accessible to students? Yes
Are computers accessible to students? Yes

Remote Sites

Other branches of the institution: No
Other college campuses: Yes
Students' homes: Yes
Work sites: Yes
Libraries: Yes
Elementary/Secondary schools: Yes
Community-based organizations: No
Correctional institutions: No

On-Campus Requirements

Is an on-campus component required? No

Tuition & Fees

In-state tuition per credit: $139
Out-of-state tuition per credit: $139
Average yearly cost of books: $700

Financial Aid

Is financial aid available to full-time students? Yes
Is financial aid available to part-time students? Yes
Are academic scholarships available? Yes
Assistance programs available to students: Federal Stafford Loan, Federal Perkins Loan, Federal Plus Loan, Federal Pell Grant, Federal Work-Study Program, in-state student aid programs, veterans' assistance

Mira Costa Community College District

Academic Information Services
Knowledge Base
One Barnard Drive
Oceanside, CA 92056
Contact: Joseph Moreau, Dean of Academic Information Services
School Web address: www.miracosta.cc.ca.us
Institutional accreditation: Western Association of Schools and Colleges

Subjects Offered

Business, computer information systems, economics, English, film, geology, history, Internet and multimedia technology, music, oceanography, philosophy, real estate, sociology

Admissions Requirements

Is a minimum high school GPA required? No
Is provisional admission available? Yes
Is an admissions interview required? No
Can pre-requisite course work be waived? No
Are international students eligible to apply? Yes
Is the TOEFL required for international students? Yes
What is the minimum TOEFL score required? 450

Program Delivery

Primary method of program delivery: Web
Two-way interactive video: No
Two-way audio, one-way video: No
One-way live video: No
One-way pre-recorded video: No
Audio graphics: No
Audio: No
Hardware requirements: Pentium-class machine or Mac equivalent
Software requirements: Recent-version browser and operating system
Is the library accessible to students? Yes
Are computers accessible to students? Yes

Remote Sites

Other branches of the institution: Yes
Other college campuses: No
Students' homes: Yes
Work sites: Yes
Libraries: Yes
Elementary/Secondary schools: No
Community-based organizations: No
Correctional institutions: No

On-Campus Requirements

Is an on-campus component required? No

Tuition & Fees

In-state tuition per credit: $11
Out-of-state tuition per credit: $130
Average yearly cost of books: $750

Financial Aid

Is financial aid available to full-time students? Yes
Is financial aid available to part-time students? Yes
Are academic scholarships available? Yes
Assistance programs available to students: Federal Stafford
Loan, Federal Pell Grant, Federal Work-Study Program,
in-state student aid programs, veterans' assistance

Mississippi State University—Division of Continuing Education

PO Box 5247
Mississippi State, MS 39762
Contact: Duke West, Manager of Distance Education
Department e-mail: dwest@ce.msstate.edu
Department Web address: www.msstate.edu/dept/ced
School Web address: www.msstate.edu
Institutional accreditation: Southern Association of
Colleges and Schools

Subjects Offered

Teacher certification courses, telecommunication applications, technology laboratory management, elements of
desktop publishing, hypermedia for instruction, Internet
in the classroom, microcomputer in education, records
management

Admissions Requirements

Is a minimum high school GPA required? Yes
Is provisional admission available? Yes
Is an admissions interview required? No
Can pre-requisite course work be waived? Yes
Are international students eligible to apply? Yes
Is the TOEFL required for international students? Yes
What is the minimum TOEFL score required? 525

Program Delivery

Primary method of program delivery: Remote site
Two-way interactive video: Yes
Two-way audio, one-way video: No
One-way live video: No
One-way pre-recorded video: Yes

Audio graphics: No
Audio: No
Is the library accessible to students? Yes
Are computers accessible to students? Yes

Remote Sites

Other branches of the institution: Yes
Other college campuses: Yes
Students' homes: Yes
Work sites: Yes
Libraries: Yes
Elementary/Secondary schools: Yes
Community-based organizations: Yes
Correctional institutions: No

On-Campus Requirements

Is an on-campus component required? Yes
On-campus course work: Yes
On-campus admissions interview: No
On-campus program orientation: No
On-campus exams: No

Tuition & Fees

In-state tuition per credit: $126
Out-of-state tuition per credit: $129
Average yearly cost of books: $500

Financial Aid

Is financial aid available to full-time students? Yes
Is financial aid available to part-time students? Yes
Are academic scholarships available? Yes
Assistance programs available to students: Federal Stafford
Loan, Federal Perkins Loan, Federal Plus Loan, Federal
Pell Grant, Federal Work-Study Program, in-state
student aid programs, veterans' assistance

Mississippi State University—Geosciences

108 Hilbun Hall, PO Box 5448
Mississippi State, MS 39762
Contact: Dr. Mark Binkley, Professor
Department e-mail: bailey@geosci.msstate.edu
Department Web address: www.msstate.edu/dept/
geosciences/distance.html
School Web address: www.msstate.edu
Institutional accreditation: Southern Association of
Colleges and Schools

Subjects Offered

Meteorology, geography, oceanography, hydrology

Admissions Requirements

Is a minimum high school GPA required? Yes
Is provisional admission available? Yes
Is an admissions interview required? No
Can pre-requisite course work be waived? Yes
Are international students eligible to apply? Yes
Is the TOEFL required for international students? No

Program Delivery

Primary method of program delivery: Web
Two-way interactive video: No
Two-way audio, one-way video: No
One-way live video: No
One-way pre-recorded video: Yes
Audio graphics: No
Audio: No
Hardware requirements: Computer with 64MB RAM and 56KBPS modem
Software requirements: Internet browser
Is the library accessible to students? Yes
Are computers accessible to students? No

Remote Sites

Other branches of the institution: No
Other college campuses: No
Students' homes: No
Work sites: No
Libraries: No
Elementary/Secondary schools: No
Community-based organizations: No
Correctional institutions: No

Tuition & Fees

In-state tuition per credit: $130
Application fee: $25
Can it be waived? Yes
Average yearly cost of books: $2,400

Financial Aid

Is financial aid available to full-time students? Yes
Is financial aid available to part-time students? Yes
Are academic scholarships available? No
Assistance programs available to students: Federal Stafford Loan, Federal Perkins Loan, Federal Plus Loan, Federal Pell Grant, veterans' assistance

Missouri Southern State College

Lifelong Learning
3550 East Newman Road
Joplin, MD 64836

Contact: Jerry Williams, Director of Continuing Education/Distance Learning
Department e-mail: williams-r@mail.mssc.edu
Department Web address: www.mssc.edu/lifelonglearning
School Web address: www.mssc.edu
Institutional accreditation: North Central Association of Colleges and Schools

Subjects Offered

Criminal justice administration, law enforcement, computer information science, communications, economics, theatre, biology, history, psychology, Spanish, music, English, government, mathematics, computer-aided drafting, physical science, nursing, respiratory, business, art, kinesiology

Admissions Requirements

Is a minimum high school GPA required? No
Is provisional admission available? Yes
Is an admissions interview required? No
Can pre-requisite course work be waived? Yes
Are international students eligible to apply? Yes
Is the TOEFL required for international students? Yes

Program Delivery

Primary method of program delivery: Web
Two-way interactive video: Yes
Two-way audio, one-way video: Yes
One-way live video: Yes
One-way pre-recorded video: Yes
Audio: Yes
Hardware requirements: 28.8KBPS modem, Pentium 100MHz processor, 16MB RAM
Software requirements: Depends on course
Is the library accessible to students? Yes
Are computers accessible to students? Yes

Remote Sites

Other branches of the institution: No
Other college campuses: Yes
Students' homes: Yes
Work sites: Yes
Libraries: No
Elementary/Secondary schools: No
Community-based organizations: Yes
Correctional institutions: No

On-Campus Requirements

Is an on-campus component required? No

Tuition & Fees

In-state tuition per credit: $79
Out-of-state tuition per credit: $79

Financial Aid

Is financial aid available to full-time students? Yes
Is financial aid available to part-time students? Yes
Are academic scholarships available? Yes
Assistance programs available to students: Federal Stafford Loan, Federal Perkins Loan, Federal Plus Loan, Federal Pell Grant, Federal Work-Study Program, in-state student aid programs, veterans' assistance

Mohawk Valley Community College

Information Technology
Distance Education
1101 Sherman Drive
Utica, NY 13501
Contact: Jeff Kimball, Coordinator for Distance Education
Department e-mail: jkimball@mvcc.edu
Department Web address: www.mvcc.edu/mvcconline
School Web address: www.mvcc.edu
Institutional accreditation: Middle States Association of Colleges and Schools

Subjects Offered

Business/computers, computer science, psychology, sociology, food service, mathematics, technologies, humanities, human services

Admissions Requirements

Is a minimum high school GPA required? No
Is provisional admission available? Yes
Is an admissions interview required? No
Can pre-requisite course work be waived? Yes
Are international students eligible to apply? Yes
Is the TOEFL required for international students? Yes

Program Delivery

Primary method of program delivery: Web
Two-way interactive video: Yes
Two-way audio, one-way video: No
One-way live video: No
One-way pre-recorded video: No
Audio graphics: No
Audio: No
Hardware requirements: 200 MHz, at least 28.8KBPS modem
Software requirements: Course-dependent
Is the library accessible to students? Yes
Are computers accessible to students? Yes

Remote Sites

Other branches of the institution: Yes
Other college campuses: Yes
Students' homes: No
Work sites: Yes
Libraries: No
Elementary/Secondary schools: No
Community-based organizations: No
Correctional institutions: No

On-Campus Requirements

On-campus course work: No
On-campus admissions interview: No
On-campus program orientation: No
On-campus exams: Yes

Tuition & Fees

In-state tuition per credit: $95
Out-of-state tuition per credit: $143
Average yearly cost of books: $50

Financial Aid

Is financial aid available to full-time students? Yes
Is financial aid available to part-time students? Yes
Are academic scholarships available? Yes
Assistance programs available to students: Federal Stafford Loan, Federal Perkins Loan, Federal Plus Loan, Federal Pell Grant, Federal Work-Study Program, in-state student aid programs, veterans' assistance

Montana Tech of the University of Montana

Safety, Health, and Industrial Hygiene
OSH Extended Studies Program
1300 West Park Street
Butte, MT 59701-8997
Contact: Roger Jensen, Program Director
Department e-mail: rjensen@mtech.edu
School Web address: www.mtech.edu
Institutional accreditation: Northwest Association of Schools and Colleges

Subjects Offered

Environmental engineering, occupational safety and health, industrial hygiene, project engineering and management, microcomputer software, business and professional writing, executive function

Admissions Requirements

Is an admissions interview required? No
Can pre-requisite course work be waived? No

Are international students eligible to apply? Yes
Is the TOEFL required for international students? Yes

Program Delivery

Primary method of program delivery: Text
Hardware requirements: Pentium II, 64MB of RAM, 28.8KBPS modem
Software requirements: Windows 98, MS Internet Explorer 4.0
Is the library accessible to students? Yes
Are computers accessible to students? Yes

Remote Sites

Students' homes: Yes

On-Campus Requirements

Is an on-campus component required? Yes
On-campus course work: Yes
On-campus admissions interview: No
On-campus program orientation: No
On-campus exams: No

Tuition & Fees

In-state tuition per credit: $283
Out-of-state tuition per credit: $283
Application fee: $30
Can it be waived? No

Financial Aid

Is financial aid available to full-time students? Yes
Is financial aid available to part-time students? Yes
Are academic scholarships available? Yes
Assistance programs available to students: Federal Stafford Loan, Federal Perkins Loan, Federal Plus Loan, Federal Pell Grant, Federal Work-Study Program, in-state student aid programs, veterans' assistance

Montgomery County Community College

Institutional Research
Distance Learning
340 Dekalb Pike, PO Box
Blue Bell, PA 19422
Contact: John Mantroni, Director of Distance Learning
School Web address: www.mc3.edu
Institutional accreditation: Middle States Commission on Higher Education

Subjects Offered

Accounting, anthropology, biology, computer and information systems, Internet, criminal justice, English, economics, education, electronics, nursing, philosophy, psychology, geology, history, mathematics, sociology

Admissions Requirements

Is a minimum high school GPA required? No
Is provisional admission available? No
Is an admissions interview required? No
Can pre-requisite course work be waived? Yes
Are international students eligible to apply? Yes
Is the TOEFL required for international students? Yes

Program Delivery

Primary method of program delivery: Web
Two-way interactive video: Yes
Two-way audio, one-way video: No
One-way live video: No
One-way pre-recorded video: Yes
Audio graphics: Yes
Audio: No
Hardware requirements: Windows 95, Mac
Software requirements: HTML 4, Internet service provider connection
Is the library accessible to students? Yes
Are computers accessible to students? Yes

Remote Sites

Other branches of the institution: Yes
Other college campuses: Yes
Students' homes: Yes
Work sites: Yes
Libraries: Yes
Elementary/Secondary schools: No
Community-based organizations: Yes
Correctional institutions: No

On-Campus Requirements

Is an on-campus component required? No

Tuition & Fees

In-state tuition per credit: $72
Out-of-state tuition per credit: $236
Average yearly cost of books: $590

Financial Aid

Is financial aid available to full-time students? Yes
Is financial aid available to part-time students? Yes
Are academic scholarships available? Yes
Assistance programs available to students: Federal Stafford Loan, Federal Perkins Loan, Federal Plus Loan, Federal Pell Grant, Federal Work-Study Program, in-state student aid programs, veterans' assistance

Moody Bible Institute

Division of External Studies
820 North LaSalle Boulevard
Chicago, IL 60610
Contact: Stephen Kemp, Vice President and Dean of
External Studies
Department e-mail: xstudies@moody.edu
School Web address: www.moody.edu
Institutional accreditation: North Central Association of
Colleges and Schools

Subjects Offered

Bible, theology, ministry, religion, missions, education,
pastoral training

Admissions Requirements

Is a minimum high school GPA required? No
Is provisional admission available? Yes
Is an admissions interview required? No
Can pre-requisite course work be waived? Yes
Are international students eligible to apply? Yes

Program Delivery

Two-way interactive video: No
Two-way audio, one-way video: No
One-way live video: No
One-way pre-recorded video: No
Audio graphics: No
Audio: No
Software requirements: Web access
Is the library accessible to students? Yes
Are computers accessible to students? No

Remote Sites

Other branches of the institution: No
Other college campuses: No
Students' homes: Yes
Work sites: Yes
Libraries: No
Elementary/Secondary schools: Yes
Community-based organizations: Yes
Correctional institutions: Yes

On-Campus Requirements

Is an on-campus component required? No

Tuition & Fees

In-state tuition per credit: $120
Out-of-state tuition per credit: $120
Average yearly cost of books: $400

Financial Aid

Is financial aid available to full-time students? Yes
Is financial aid available to part-time students? Yes
Are academic scholarships available? No
Assistance programs available to students: Veterans'
assistance

Motlow State Community College

Institutional Research, Planning and Effectiveness
Center for Information Systems
PO Box 8500
Lynchburg, TN 37352-8500
Contact: Will Holt, Director of the Center for Information
Systems
Department e-mail: cholt@mscc.cctn.us
Department Web address: www.mscc.cc.tn.us
School Web address: www.mscc.cctn.us
Institutional accreditation: Southern Association of
Colleges and Schools

Subjects Offered

Business technology, chemistry, economics, education,
mathematics, medical terminology

Admissions Requirements

Is a minimum high school GPA required? No
Is provisional admission available? No
Is an admissions interview required? No
Can pre-requisite course work be waived? Yes
Are international students eligible to apply? Yes
Is the TOEFL required for international students? Yes
What is the minimum TOEFL score required? 500

Program Delivery

Primary method of program delivery: Text
Two-way interactive video: Yes
Hardware requirements: Personal computer, a dial-up
connection to an Internet service provider
Software requirements: For Internet courses—a PC with
Internet access. Some courses require Microsoft Office
2000, e-mail, Windows 95/98
Is the library accessible to students? Yes
Are computers accessible to students? Yes

Remote Sites

Other branches of the institution: Yes
Students' homes: Yes
Work sites: Yes

On-Campus Requirements

Is an on-campus component required? Yes
On-campus course work: Yes

Tuition & Fees

In-state tuition per credit: $56
Out-of-state tuition per credit: $224
Average yearly cost of books: $1,200

Financial Aid

Is financial aid available to full-time students? Yes
Is financial aid available to part-time students? Yes
Are academic scholarships available? Yes
Assistance programs available to students: Federal Pell
    Grant, Federal Work-Study Program, in-state student aid
    programs, veterans' assistance

Mount Allsion University

Continuing Education
65 York Street
Sackville, NB, Canada E4L 1E4
Contact: Marilyn McCullough, Director of Continuing
    and Distance Education
Department e-mail: mmccullough@mta.ca
School Web address: www.mta.ca

Subjects Offered

Canadian studies, computer science, English, geography,
    history, political science, mathematics, psychology,
    religious studies

Admissions Requirements

Is a minimum high school GPA required? Yes
Is provisional admission available? No
Is an admissions interview required? No
Can pre-requisite course work be waived? Yes
Are international students eligible to apply? Yes
Is the TOEFL required for international students? Yes
What is the minimum TOEFL score required? 550

Program Delivery

Audio: Yes
Is the library accessible to students? Yes
Are computers accessible to students? Yes

Remote Sites

Other college campuses: Yes
Students' homes: Yes

On-Campus Requirements

Is an on-campus component required? No

Tuition & Fees

In-state tuition per credit: $439
Out-of-state tuition per credit: $878
Average yearly cost of books: $20

Financial Aid

Is financial aid available to full-time students? Yes
Is financial aid available to part-time students? Yes
Are academic scholarships available? No

Mount Saint Vincent University

Distance Learning and Continuing Education
166 Bedford Highway
Halifax, NS, Canada B3M 2J6
Contact: Peggy Watts, Director, Distance Learning and
    Continuing Education
Department e-mail: distance@msvu.ca
School Web address: www.msvu.ca

Subjects Offered

English, French, mathematics, biology, history, information
    technology, business, gerontology, sociology, psychology,
    women's studies, economics, nutrition, family studies,
    religious studies

Admissions Requirements

Is a minimum high school GPA required? No
Is provisional admission available? Yes
Is an admissions interview required? No
Can pre-requisite course work be waived? Yes
Are international students eligible to apply? Yes
Is the TOEFL required for international students? Yes

Program Delivery

Two-way interactive video: Yes
One-way live video: Yes
Software requirements: CP/Windows
Is the library accessible to students? Yes
Are computers accessible to students? Yes

Remote Sites

Students' homes: Yes
Work sites: Yes

On-Campus Requirements

Is an on-campus component required? No

Tuition & Fees

Application fee: $30
Can it be waived? No

Financial Aid

Is financial aid available to full-time students? Yes
Is financial aid available to part-time students? Yes
Are academic scholarships available? Yes

Mount Wachusett Community College

Division of Continuing Education
444 Green Street
Gardner, MA 01440
Contact: John T. Fielding, PhD, Director Special Programs
Department e-mail: j_fielding@mwcc.mass.edu
School Web address: www.mwcc.mass.edu
Institutional accreditation: New England Association of
Schools and Colleges

Subjects Offered

Business administration, criminal justice, human services

Admissions Requirements

Is a minimum high school GPA required? No
Is provisional admission available? No
Can pre-requisite course work be waived? Yes
Are international students eligible to apply? Yes
Is the TOEFL required for international students? No

Program Delivery

Hardware requirements: An Internet browser
Is the library accessible to students? Yes
Are computers accessible to students? No

On-Campus Requirements

Is an on-campus component required? No

Tuition & Fees

In-state tuition per credit: $83
Out-of-state tuition per credit: $288
Average yearly cost of books: $800

Financial Aid

Is financial aid available to full-time students? Yes
Is financial aid available to part-time students? Yes
Are academic scholarships available? Yes
Assistance programs available to students: Federal Stafford
Loan, Federal Perkins Loan, Federal Plus Loan, Federal
Pell Grant, Federal Work-Study Program, in-state
student aid programs, veterans' assistance

Mountain Empire Community College

Continuing and Distance Education
US Route 23 South, Drawer 700
Big Stone Gap, VA 24219
Contact: Sue Ella Boatright-Wells, Director of Continuing
and Distance Education
Department e-mail: sboatright@me.cc.va.us
School Web address: www.me.cc.va.us
Institutional accreditation: Southern Association of
Colleges and Schools

Subjects Offered

Mathematics, English, science, psychology, sociology, child
development, information systems technology, accounting, art, environmental, health, Spanish, history, legal
administration, natural science, music, speech, orientation

Admissions Requirements

Is a minimum high school GPA required? No
Is provisional admission available? Yes
Is an admissions interview required? No
Can pre-requisite course work be waived? Yes
Are international students eligible to apply? Yes
Is the TOEFL required for international students? No

Program Delivery

Two-way interactive video: Yes
One-way pre-recorded video: Yes
Is the library accessible to students? Yes
Are computers accessible to students? Yes

Remote Sites

Other college campuses: Yes
Students' homes: Yes
Work sites: Yes
Libraries: Yes
Elementary/Secondary schools: Yes

On-Campus Requirements

Is an on-campus component required? No

Tuition & Fees

In-state tuition per credit: $42
Out-of-state tuition per credit: $174

Financial Aid

Is financial aid available to full-time students? Yes
Is financial aid available to part-time students? Yes
Are academic scholarships available? Yes

Assistance programs available to students: Federal Pell Grant, Federal Work-Study Program, in-state student aid programs, veterans' assistance

Mt. San Antonio College

Learning Resources
Distance Learning
1100 North Grand Avenue
Walnut, CA 91789
Contact: Kerry Stern, Dean, Learning Resources
Department e-mail: kstern@mtsac.edu
Department Web address: vclass.mtsac.edu/distance
School Web address: www.mtsac.edu
Institutional accreditation: Western Association of Schools and Colleges

Subjects Offered

American language, astronomy, business: accounting, economics, management, business: real estate, child development, computer information systems, computer applications, English, journalism, learning assistance, mathematics, philosophy, sociology

Admissions Requirements

Is a minimum high school GPA required? No
Is provisional admission available? No
Is an admissions interview required? No
Can pre-requisite course work be waived? No
Are international students eligible to apply? Yes
Is the TOEFL required for international students? Yes

Program Delivery

Primary method of program delivery: Web
Two-way interactive video: No
Two-way audio, one-way video: No
One-way live video: No
One-way pre-recorded video: Yes
Audio graphics: No
Audio: No
Software requirements: Internet access and Netscape Navigator 3.0 or Internet Explorer and an e-mail address
Is the library accessible to students? Yes
Are computers accessible to students? Yes

Remote Sites

Other branches of the institution: No
Other college campuses: No
Students' homes: Yes
Work sites: No
Libraries: No
Elementary/Secondary schools: No

Community-based organizations: No
Correctional institutions: No

On-Campus Requirements

Is an on-campus component required? Yes
On-campus course work: No
On-campus admissions interview: No
On-campus program orientation: Yes
On-campus exams: Yes

Tuition & Fees

In-state tuition per credit: $11
Out-of-state tuition per credit: $130
Average yearly cost of books: $800

Financial Aid

Is financial aid available to full-time students? Yes
Is financial aid available to part-time students? No
Are academic scholarships available? Yes
Assistance programs available to students: Federal Perkins Loan, Federal Pell Grant, Federal Work-Study Program, in-state student aid programs, veterans' assistance

Nassau Community College

Distance and Distributed Learning
College of the Air
One Education Drive
Garden City, NY 11530-6793
Contact: Arthur L. Friedman, Professor and Coordinator
Department e-mail: friedma@sunynassau.edu
School Web address: www.sunynassau.edu
Institutional accreditation: Middle States Association of Colleges and Schools

Subjects Offered

Art history, business, communications, economics, English literature, foreign languages, history, law (business), mathematics, marketing, music, health education, physical science, sociology, social problems

Admissions Requirements

Is a minimum high school GPA required? No
Is an admissions interview required? No
Can pre-requisite course work be waived? No
Are international students eligible to apply? Yes
Is the TOEFL required for international students? Yes
What is the minimum TOEFL score required? 500

Program Delivery

Primary method of program delivery: Text
One-way pre-recorded video: Yes
Audio: Yes

Is the library accessible to students? Yes
Are computers accessible to students? Yes

On-Campus Requirements

Is an on-campus component required? No

Tuition & Fees

In-state tuition per credit: $98
Out-of-state tuition per credit: $199
Average yearly cost of books: $700

National American University

On-line Distance Learning
321 Kansas City Street
Rapid City, SD 57701
Contact: Tricia Torpey, Director of Distance Learning
  Operations
Department e-mail: ptorpey@national.edu
School Web address: www.national.edu
Institutional accreditation: North Central Association of
  Colleges and Schools

Subjects Offered

Business, management, accounting, management information systems, mcse, ccna, linux, science, mathematics,
  psychology

Admissions Requirements

Is a minimum high school GPA required? No
Is an admissions interview required? No
Can pre-requisite course work be waived? Yes
Are international students eligible to apply? Yes
Is the TOEFL required for international students? Yes

Program Delivery

Primary method of program delivery: Web
Two-way interactive video: No
Two-way audio, one-way video: No
One-way live video: No
One-way pre-recorded video: Yes
Audio graphics: Yes
Audio: Yes
Hardware requirements: Pentium 100 MHz or equivalent
Software requirements: Windows 95, 98 or NT, Internet
  Explorer or Netscape
Is the library accessible to students? Yes
Are computers accessible to students? Yes

Remote Sites

Other branches of the institution: Yes
Other college campuses: Yes
Students' homes: Yes
Work sites: Yes
Libraries: Yes
Elementary/Secondary schools: Yes

On-Campus Requirements

Is an on-campus component required? No

Tuition & Fees

In-state tuition per credit: $200
Application fee: $25
Can it be waived? No
Average yearly cost of books: $540
Average yearly additional fees: $50

Financial Aid

Is financial aid available to full-time students? Yes
Is financial aid available to part-time students? Yes
Are academic scholarships available? Yes
Assistance programs available to students: Federal Stafford
  Loan, Federal Perkins Loan, Federal Plus Loan, Federal
  Pell Grant, Federal Work-Study Program, in-state
  student aid programs, veterans' assistance

New Jersey Institute of Technology

Continuing Professional Education
University Heights
Newark, NJ 07102
Contact: Dr. Gale Spak, Associate Vice President
Department e-mail: dl@njit.edu
Department Web address: cpe.njit.edu
School Web address: www.njit.edu
Institutional accreditation: Middle States Association of
  Colleges and Schools

Admissions Requirements

Is a minimum high school GPA required? Yes
Is provisional admission available? Yes
Can pre-requisite course work be waived? Yes
Are international students eligible to apply? Yes
Is the TOEFL required for international students? Yes
What is the minimum TOEFL score required? 550

Program Delivery

Primary method of program delivery: Web
Two-way interactive video: Yes
Two-way audio, one-way video: No

One-way live video: No
One-way pre-recorded video: Yes
Audio graphics: No
Audio: No
Hardware requirements: Pentium II with Internet access and sound card
Is the library accessible to students? Yes
Are computers accessible to students? No

Remote Sites

Other branches of the institution: Yes
Other college campuses: Yes
Students' homes: No
Work sites: No
Libraries: No
Elementary/Secondary schools: No
Community-based organizations: No
Correctional institutions: No

Tuition & Fees

In-state tuition per credit: $216
Out-of-state tuition per credit: $434
Average yearly cost of books: $300

Financial Aid

Is financial aid available to full-time students? Yes
Is financial aid available to part-time students? Yes
Are academic scholarships available? Yes
Assistance programs available to students: Federal Stafford Loan, Federal Perkins Loan, Federal Plus Loan, Federal Pell Grant, Federal Work-Study Program, in-state student aid programs, veterans' assistance

Newberry College

Academic Affairs Office
2100 College Street
Newberry, SC 29108
Department e-mail: admissions@newberry.edu
School Web address: www.newberry.edu
Institutional accreditation: Southern Association of Colleges and Schools

Subjects Offered

Religion, philosophy

Admissions Requirements

Is a minimum high school GPA required? Yes
Are international students eligible to apply? Yes
Is the TOEFL required for international students? Yes
What is the minimum TOEFL score required? 525

Program Delivery

Primary method of program delivery: Web
Software requirements: IBM or Apple Computer with min. Pentium processor, Win 3.1, 28.8KBPS modem, Internet access, Web browser, e-mail
Is the library accessible to students? Yes
Are computers accessible to students? Yes

On-Campus Requirements

Is an on-campus component required? Yes
On-campus course work: No
On-campus admissions interview: No
On-campus program orientation: No
On-campus exams: Yes

Tuition & Fees

In-state tuition per credit: $195
Out-of-state tuition per credit: $195
Average yearly cost of books: $700

Financial Aid

Is financial aid available to full-time students? Yes
Is financial aid available to part-time students? Yes
Are academic scholarships available? Yes
Assistance programs available to students: Federal Stafford Loan, Federal Perkins Loan, Federal Plus Loan, Federal Pell Grant, Federal Work-Study Program, in-state student aid programs, veterans' assistance

North Central State College

Distance Education
Kenwood Circle
Mansfield, OH 44901
Contact: Daniel Kraska, Coordinator
School Web address: www.ncstate.tec.oh.us
Institutional accreditation: North Central Association of Colleges and Schools

Subjects Offered

Business administration, humanities

Admissions Requirements

Is a minimum high school GPA required? No
Is provisional admission available? No
Is an admissions interview required? No
Can pre-requisite course work be waived? No
Are international students eligible to apply? Yes
Is the TOEFL required for international students? No

Program Delivery

Two-way interactive video: No
Two-way audio, one-way video: No
One-way live video: No
One-way pre-recorded video: Yes
Audio graphics: No
Audio: No
Is the library accessible to students? Yes
Are computers accessible to students? No

Remote Sites

Other branches of the institution: No
Other college campuses: No
Students' homes: No
Work sites: No
Libraries: No
Elementary/Secondary schools: No
Community-based organizations: No
Correctional institutions: No

Tuition & Fees

In-state tuition per credit: $55
Out-of-state tuition per credit: $110
Average yearly cost of books: $1,000

Financial Aid

Is financial aid available to full-time students? Yes
Is financial aid available to part-time students? Yes
Are academic scholarships available? Yes
Assistance programs available to students: Federal Stafford Loan, Federal Perkins Loan, Federal Plus Loan, Federal Pell Grant, Federal Work-Study Program, veterans' assistance

North Central Technical College

Learning Resources
1000 West Campus Drive
Wausau, WI 54401
Contact: Barbara Cummings, Team Leader, Learning Resources
Department e-mail: cummings@northcentral.tec.wi.us
Department Web address: www.northcentral.tec.wi.us/distance
School Web address: www.northcentral.tec.wi.us
Institutional accreditation: North Central Association of Colleges and Schools

Subjects Offered

Legal terminology and formatting, modern office technology, introduction to laser, communications, marketing, business law, professional development, family care, medical terminology, math of finance, psychology, chemistry

Admissions Requirements

Is a minimum high school GPA required? No
Is provisional admission available? Yes
Can pre-requisite course work be waived? No
Are international students eligible to apply? Yes
Is the TOEFL required for international students? Yes
What is the minimum TOEFL score required? 500

Program Delivery

Primary method of program delivery: Remote site
Two-way interactive video: Yes
One-way pre-recorded video: Yes
Is the library accessible to students? Yes
Are computers accessible to students? Yes

Remote Sites

Other branches of the institution: Yes
Other college campuses: Yes
Students' homes: Yes
Elementary/Secondary schools: Yes

On-Campus Requirements

Is an on-campus component required? No

Tuition & Fees

In-state tuition per credit: $62
Out-of-state tuition per credit: $62
Average yearly cost of books: $30

Financial Aid

Is financial aid available to full-time students? Yes
Is financial aid available to part-time students? Yes
Are academic scholarships available? Yes
Assistance programs available to students: Federal Stafford Loan, Federal Perkins Loan, Federal Plus Loan, Federal Pell Grant, Federal Work-Study Program, in-state student aid programs, veterans' assistance

North Central University

G. Raymond Institute for Church Leadership
910 Elliot Avenue
Minneapolis, MN 55404
Contact: Monty Bell, Director
Department e-mail: carlinst@northcentral.edu
School Web address: www.northcentral.edu
Institutional accreditation: North Central Association of Colleges and Schools

Subjects Offered

Liberal arts, christian education, biblical languages, bible, cross-cultural ministries, psychology, practices, theology

Admissions Requirements

Is a minimum high school GPA required? Yes
Is provisional admission available? No
Is an admissions interview required? No
Can pre-requisite course work be waived? No
Are international students eligible to apply? Yes
Is the TOEFL required for international students? Yes
What is the minimum TOEFL score required? 500

Program Delivery

Primary method of program delivery: Text
Two-way interactive video: No
Two-way audio, one-way video: No
One-way live video: No
One-way pre-recorded video: Yes
Audio graphics: No
Audio: Yes
Is the library accessible to students? Yes
Are computers accessible to students? No

Remote Sites

Other branches of the institution: No
Other college campuses: No
Students' homes: Yes
Work sites: No
Libraries: No
Elementary/Secondary schools: No
Community-based organizations: No
Correctional institutions: Yes

On-Campus Requirements

Is an on-campus component required? No

Tuition & Fees

In-state tuition per credit: $99
Out-of-state tuition per credit: $99
Average yearly cost of books: $30

Financial Aid

Is financial aid available to full-time students? No
Is financial aid available to part-time students? No
Are academic scholarships available? No

North Florida Community College

1000 Turner Davis Drive
Madison, FL 32340

Contact: Sheila Hiss, Director of Library Services
Department e-mail: hisss@nflcc.cc.fl.us
Department Web address: edtech.nflcc.cc.fl.us/library
Institutional accreditation: Southern Association of Colleges and Schools

Subjects Offered

Sociology, criminal justice, library science, computer science

Admissions Requirements

Is a minimum high school GPA required? No
Is provisional admission available? No
Is an admissions interview required? No
Can pre-requisite course work be waived? No
Are international students eligible to apply? Yes
Is the TOEFL required for international students? Yes
What is the minimum TOEFL score required? 550

Program Delivery

Primary method of program delivery: Web
Two-way interactive video: No
Two-way audio, one-way video: No
One-way live video: No
One-way pre-recorded video: Yes
Audio graphics: No
Audio: No
Hardware requirements: The ability to run latest version or Netscape or Explorer
Software requirements: Netscape or Explorer browser, e-mail
Is the library accessible to students? Yes
Are computers accessible to students? Yes

Remote Sites

Other branches of the institution: No
Other college campuses: No
Students' homes: Yes
Work sites: Yes
Libraries: No
Elementary/Secondary schools: No
Community-based organizations: No
Correctional institutions: No

On-Campus Requirements

Is an on-campus component required? No

Tuition & Fees

In-state tuition per credit: $47
Out-of-state tuition per credit: $169
Average yearly cost of books: $1,000

Financial Aid

Is financial aid available to full-time students? Yes
Is financial aid available to part-time students? Yes
Are academic scholarships available? Yes
Assistance programs available to students: Federal Pell
Grant, Federal Work-Study Program, in-state student aid
programs, veterans' assistance

North Hampton Community College

Distance Learning
3835 Green Pond Road
Bethlehem, PA 18020-7599
Contact: Brenda Johhnson, Director of Distance Learning
Department e-mail: bjohnson@northhampton.edu
School Web address: www.northhampton.edu
Institutional accreditation: Middle States Association of
Colleges and Schools

Subjects Offered

Accounting, biology, business, chemistry, computer
science, early childhood development, economics,
English, geography, history, journalism, library,
mathematics, communications, physical education,
philosophy, plastics, political science, psychology,
sociology

Admissions Requirements

Is a minimum high school GPA required? No
Is provisional admission available? Yes
Is an admissions interview required? No
Can pre-requisite course work be waived? No
Are international students eligible to apply? Yes
Is the TOEFL required for international students? No

Program Delivery

Two-way interactive video: No
Two-way audio, one-way video: No
One-way live video: No
One-way pre-recorded video: Yes
Audio graphics: No
Audio: No
Hardware requirements: Access to a PC and a printer
Software requirements: Internet, Windows 95, e-mail,
Internet Explorer or Netscape Navigator
Is the library accessible to students? Yes
Are computers accessible to students? Yes

Remote Sites

Other branches of the institution: Yes
Other college campuses: No

Students' homes: Yes
Work sites: No
Libraries: No
Elementary/Secondary schools: No
Community-based organizations: No
Correctional institutions: No

On-Campus Requirements

Is an on-campus component required? No

Tuition & Fees

In-state tuition per credit: $167
Out-of-state tuition per credit: $254
Average yearly cost of books: $1,000

Financial Aid

Is financial aid available to full-time students? Yes
Is financial aid available to part-time students? Yes
Are academic scholarships available? Yes
Assistance programs available to students: Federal Stafford
Loan, Federal Perkins Loan, Federal Plus Loan, Federal
Pell Grant, Federal Work-Study Program, in-state
student aid programs, veterans' assistance

North Iowa Area Community College

Evening Credit
500 College Drive
Madison City, IA 50401
Contact: Don Kamps, Evening Dean
Department e-mail: kampsdon@niacc.cc.ia.us
School Web address: www.niacc.cc.ia.us
Institutional accreditation: North Central Association of
Colleges and Schools

Subjects Offered

Psychology, personal finance, American history, cultural
anthropology, English, computers, economics, mathematics, chemistry, geography, art, entrepreneurship,
medical technology, career decision-making

Admissions Requirements

Is a minimum high school GPA required? No
Is provisional admission available? No
Is an admissions interview required? No
Can pre-requisite course work be waived? Yes
Are international students eligible to apply? Yes
Is the TOEFL required for international students? Yes
What is the minimum TOEFL score required? 500

Program Delivery

Two-way interactive video: Yes
Two-way audio, one-way video: No
One-way live video: No
One-way pre-recorded video: Yes
Audio graphics: No
Audio: No
Is the library accessible to students? Yes
Are computers accessible to students? Yes

Remote Sites

Other branches of the institution: Yes
Other college campuses: No
Students' homes: Yes
Work sites: Yes
Libraries: Yes
Elementary/Secondary schools: Yes
Community-based organizations: Yes
Correctional institutions: Yes

On-Campus Requirements

Is an on-campus component required? No

Tuition & Fees

In-state tuition per credit: $65
Out-of-state tuition per credit: $97
Average yearly cost of books: $1,500
Average yearly additional fees: $11

Financial Aid

Is financial aid available to full-time students? Yes
Is financial aid available to part-time students? Yes
Are academic scholarships available? Yes
Assistance programs available to students: Federal Stafford
Loan, Federal Perkins Loan, Federal Plus Loan, Federal
Pell Grant, Federal Work-Study Program

Northwest Missouri State University

Admission Office
800 University Drive
Maryville, MO 64468
Contact: Roger Ough, Dean of Enrollment Management
Department e-mail: admission@mail.nwmissouri.edu
Department Web address: www.nwmissouri.edu/admission/ad_front.html
School Web address: www.northwestonline.edu
Institutional accreditation: North Central Association of
Colleges and Schools

Subjects Offered

Art, math, music, management, accounting, finance,
American history, humanities, earth science, geography,
philosophy, ethics, theatre, computer science, marketing

Admissions Requirements

Is a minimum high school GPA required? Yes
Is provisional admission available? Yes
Is an admissions interview required? No
Can pre-requisite course work be waived? Yes
Are international students eligible to apply? Yes
Is the TOEFL required for international students? Yes
What is the minimum TOEFL score required? 500

Program Delivery

Two-way interactive video: No
Two-way audio, one-way video: No
One-way live video: No
One-way pre-recorded video: Yes
Audio graphics: Yes
Audio: Yes
Hardware requirements: 90 MHz Pentium PC or 604
Power PC Mac, 32MB of RAM, 28.8KBPS modem,
speakers
Software requirements: Microsoft Office 97 and current
Internet web browser, RealPlayer
Is the library accessible to students? Yes
Are computers accessible to students? Yes

Remote Sites

Other branches of the institution: No
Other college campuses: No
Students' homes: No
Work sites: No
Libraries: No
Elementary/Secondary schools: No
Community-based organizations: No
Correctional institutions: No

On-Campus Requirements

Is an on-campus component required? No

Tuition & Fees

In-state tuition per credit: $180
Out-of-state tuition per credit: $180
Average yearly cost of books: $250

Financial Aid

Is financial aid available to full-time students? Yes
Is financial aid available to part-time students? Yes
Are academic scholarships available? Yes
Assistance programs available to students: Federal Stafford
Loan, Federal Perkins Loan, Federal Plus Loan, Federal

Pell Grant, Federal Work-Study Program, in-state student aid programs, veterans' assistance

Northern Kentucky University

Credit Continuing Education and Distance Learning
Nunn Drive
Highland Heights, KY 41099
Contact: Barbara Hedges, Director
Department e-mail: hedges@nku.edu
Department Web address: www.nku.edu/~cont-ed
School Web address: www.nku.edu
Institutional accreditation: Southern Association of Colleges and Schools

Subjects Offered

Anthropology, geography, history, psychology, social work, education, technology, music, nursing, speech, English, German, political science

Admissions Requirements

Is a minimum high school GPA required? No
Is provisional admission available? Yes
Is an admissions interview required? No
Can pre-requisite course work be waived? No
Are international students eligible to apply? Yes
Is the TOEFL required for international students? Yes
What is the minimum TOEFL score required? 500

Program Delivery

Primary method of program delivery: Remote site
Two-way interactive video: Yes
Two-way audio, one-way video: No
One-way live video: No
One-way pre-recorded video: Yes
Audio graphics: No
Audio: No
Software requirements: Internet access
Is the library accessible to students? Yes
Are computers accessible to students? Yes

Remote Sites

Other branches of the institution: Yes
Other college campuses: Yes
Students' homes: Yes
Work sites: Yes
Libraries: No
Elementary/Secondary schools: Yes
Community-based organizations: Yes
Correctional institutions: No

On-Campus Requirements

On-campus course work: Yes
On-campus exams: Yes

Tuition & Fees

In-state tuition per credit: $97
Out-of-state tuition per credit: $274
Average yearly cost of books: $200

Financial Aid

Is financial aid available to full-time students? Yes
Is financial aid available to part-time students? Yes
Are academic scholarships available? Yes
Assistance programs available to students: Federal Stafford Loan, Federal Perkins Loan, Federal Plus Loan, Federal Pell Grant, Federal Work-Study Program, in-state student aid programs, veterans' assistance

Northwestern College

The Center for Distance Education
3003 Snelling Avenue North
St. Paul, MN 55113
Contact: Dr. Timothy Tomlingon, Dean of Alternative Education
Department e-mail: distance@nwc.edu
Department Web address: distance.nwc.edu
School Web address: nwc.edu
Institutional accreditation: North Central Association of Colleges and Schools

Subjects Offered

Math, science, bible, history, psychology, Greek, theology

Admissions Requirements

Is a minimum high school GPA required? Yes
Is provisional admission available? Yes
Is an admissions interview required? No
Can pre-requisite course work be waived? Yes
Are international students eligible to apply? Yes
Is the TOEFL required for international students? Yes
What is the minimum TOEFL score required? 530

Program Delivery

Primary method of program delivery: Text
Two-way interactive video: No
Two-way audio, one-way video: No
One-way live video: No
One-way pre-recorded video: Yes
Audio graphics: No
Audio: Yes

Hardware requirements: Personal computer, modem
Software requirements: Internet Explorer 4.0 or Netscape 4.0 or higher
Is the library accessible to students? Yes
Are computers accessible to students? Yes

Remote Sites

Other branches of the institution: No
Other college campuses: No
Students' homes: Yes
Work sites: Yes
Libraries: No
Elementary/Secondary schools: No
Community-based organizations: No
Correctional institutions: Yes
Is an on-campus component required? No

Tuition & Fees

In-state tuition per credit: $200
Out-of-state tuition per credit: $200
Average yearly cost of books: $250

Financial Aid

Is financial aid available to full-time students? Yes
Is financial aid available to part-time students? Yes
Are academic scholarships available? No
Assistance programs available to students: Federal Stafford Loan, Federal Plus Loan, Federal Pell Grant, in-state student aid programs

Northwestern State University

Information Systems
Electronic Learning Systems
210 Boy Hall
Natchitoches, LA 71497
Contact: Darlene Williams, Electronic Learning Systems Coordinator
Department e-mail: e_learning@nsula.edu
Department Web address: www.nsula.edu
School Web address: www.nsula.edu
Institutional accreditation: Southern Association of Colleges and Schools

Subjects Offered

Business administration, health education, chemistry, journalism, computer information systems, library media, criminal justice, math, computer applications, nursing, child development, orientation, adult education, philosophy, education, psychology, English, radiologic technology, education technology, science, fine arts, special education, theatre

Admissions Requirements

Is a minimum high school GPA required? Yes
Is provisional admission available? Yes
Is an admissions interview required? No
Can pre-requisite course work be waived? Yes
Are international students eligible to apply? Yes
Is the TOEFL required for international students? Yes
What is the minimum TOEFL score required? 550

Program Delivery

Primary method of program delivery: Web
Two-way interactive video: Yes
Two-way audio, one-way video: No
One-way live video: No
One-way pre-recorded video: Yes
Audio graphics: No
Audio: No
Hardware requirements: Win 95, 98, NT; 16MB or better, 28.8KBPS modem or better
Software requirements: Internet Explorer v.4 or better, MS Word
Is the library accessible to students? Yes
Are computers accessible to students? Yes

Remote Sites

Other branches of the institution: Yes
Other college campuses: Yes
Students' homes: Yes
Work sites: Yes
Libraries: Yes
Elementary/Secondary schools: Yes
Community-based organizations: Yes
Correctional institutions: No

On-Campus Requirements

Is an on-campus component required? No

Tuition & Fees

In-state tuition per credit: $336
Out-of-state tuition per credit: $218
Average yearly cost of books: $500
Average yearly additional fees: $20

Financial Aid

Is financial aid available to full-time students? Yes
Is financial aid available to part-time students? Yes
Are academic scholarships available? Yes
Assistance programs available to students: Federal Stafford Loan, Federal Perkins Loan, Federal Plus Loan, Federal Pell Grant, Federal Work-Study Program, in-state student aid programs, veterans' assistance

Northwood University

University College
Distance Education Program
4000 Whitting Drive
Midland, MI 48640
Contact: Marcella A. Matzke, Program Manager
Department e-mail: ucde@northwood.edu
Department Web address: www.northwoodonline.edu
School Web address: www.northwood.edu
Institutional accreditation: North Central Association of
    Colleges and Schools

Subjects Offered

Management, economics, accounting, law, natural science,
    English, marketing, finance, sociology, philosophy,
    mathematics

Admissions Requirements

Is a minimum high school GPA required? No
Is provisional admission available? Yes
Is an admissions interview required? No
Can pre-requisite course work be waived? No
Are international students eligible to apply? Yes
Is the TOEFL required for international students? Yes

Program Delivery

Primary method of program delivery: Remote site
Hardware requirements: Windows 95, 98, or NT; 90 MHz
    Pentium processor, 32MB RAM, sound card
Software requirements: Microsoft Internet Explorer 5.0,
    RealPlayer, Internet service provider, e-mail account
Is the library accessible to students? Yes
Are computers accessible to students? Yes

Remote Sites

Other branches of the institution: Yes
Other college campuses: Yes
Students' homes: Yes
Work sites: Yes

On-Campus Requirements

Is an on-campus component required? Yes
On-campus course work: Yes
On-campus exams: Yes

Tuition & Fees

In-state tuition per credit: $100
Out-of-state tuition per credit: $100
Average yearly cost of books: $500

Financial Aid

Is financial aid available to full-time students? Yes
Is financial aid available to part-time students? Yes

Are academic scholarships available? Yes
Assistance programs available to students: Federal Stafford
    Loan, Federal Perkins Loan, Federal Plus Loan, Federal
    Pell Grant, Federal Work-Study Program, in-state
    student aid programs, veterans' assistance

Ohlone College

Learning Resources & Instructional Technology
Online Education Program
43600 Mission Boulevard
Fremont, CA 94539
Contact: Shirley Peck, Dean
Department e-mail: speck@ohlone.cc.ca.us
Department Web address: www.ohlone.cc.ca.us/org/library
School Web address: www.oholone.cc.ca.us
Institutional accreditation: Western Association of Schools
    and Colleges

Subjects Offered

Allied health, speech, anthropology, art, physical therapist
    assistant, business administrator, consumer family
    science, computer science, English, English as second
    language, library studies, music, physical education

Program Delivery

Primary method of program delivery: Web
Two-way interactive video: Yes
Is the library accessible to students? Yes
Are computers accessible to students? No

Remote Sites

Other branches of the institution: Yes

Tuition & Fees

In-state tuition per credit: $11
Out-of-state tuition per credit: $134
Average yearly cost of books: $405

Financial Aid

Is financial aid available to full-time students? Yes
Is financial aid available to part-time students? Yes
Are academic scholarships available? Yes
Assistance programs available to students: Federal Stafford
    Loan, Federal Pell Grant, Federal Work-Study Program,
    in-state student aid programs, veterans' assistance

Oral Roberts University

School of Life Long Education
7777 South Lewis Avenue
Tulsa, OK 74171
Contact: Dr. Jeff Ogle, Dean

Department e-mail: slle@oru.edu

School Web address: oru.edu

Institutional accreditation: North Central Association of Colleges and Schools

Subjects Offered

Business administration, christian counseling, church ministries, theology, education

Admissions Requirements

Is a minimum high school GPA required? Yes

Is provisional admission available? Yes

Is an admissions interview required? No

Can pre-requisite course work be waived? No

Are international students eligible to apply? Yes

Is the TOEFL required for international students? No

Program Delivery

Primary method of program delivery: Text

Two-way interactive video: No

Two-way audio, one-way video: No

One-way live video: No

One-way pre-recorded video: Yes

Audio graphics: No

Audio: Yes

Software requirements: Word processing software for assignment preparation

Is the library accessible to students? Yes

Are computers accessible to students? No

Remote Sites

Other branches of the institution: No

Other college campuses: No

Students' homes: Yes

Work sites: No

Libraries: No

Elementary/Secondary schools: No

Community-based organizations: Yes

Correctional institutions: No

On-Campus Requirements

Is an on-campus component required? Yes

On-campus course work: Yes

On-campus admissions interview: No

On-campus program orientation: Yes

On-campus exams: Yes

Tuition & Fees

In-state tuition per credit: $125

Out-of-state tuition per credit: $125

Average yearly cost of books: $800

Financial Aid

Is financial aid available to full-time students? Yes

Is financial aid available to part-time students? Yes

Are academic scholarships available? No

Assistance programs available to students: Federal Stafford Loan, Federal Pell Grant, veterans' assistance

Ottawa University

1001 South Cedar #43

Ottawa, KS 66067-3399

School Web address: www.ottawa.edu

Institutional accreditation: North Central Association of Colleges and Schools

Subjects Offered

Management of health care services, law enforcement administration, police science

Admissions Requirements

Is a minimum high school GPA required? No

Are international students eligible to apply? Yes

Is the TOEFL required for international students? Yes

Program Delivery

Primary method of program delivery: Web

Hardware requirements: Varies by program

Software requirements: Varies by program

Is the library accessible to students? Yes

Financial Aid

Is financial aid available to full-time students? Yes

Is financial aid available to part-time students? Yes

Are academic scholarships available? Yes

Assistance programs available to students: Federal Stafford Loan, Federal Pell Grant, veterans' assistance

Palm Beach Community College

Distance Learning

3000 St. Lucie Avenue

Boca Raton, FL 33431

Contact: Dr. R. Celeste Beck, Provost

Department e-mail: learn@pbcc.cc.fl.us

Department Web address: www.pbcc.cc.fl.us/dl

School Web address: www.pbcc.cc.fl.us

Institutional accreditation: Southern Association of Colleges and Schools

Subjects Offered

Mathematics, English, literature, science, history, health, economics, psychology, accounting, criminology, sociology, business, Internet research, computer programs

Admissions Requirements

Is a minimum high school GPA required? No
Is provisional admission available? Yes
Is an admissions interview required? No
Can pre-requisite course work be waived? Yes
Are international students eligible to apply? Yes
Is the TOEFL required for international students? Yes

Program Delivery

Primary method of program delivery: Web
Two-way interactive video: Yes
One-way pre-recorded video: Yes
Audio: Yes
Hardware requirements: 266 MHz processor, 2GB hard drive, 64 MB of RAM, Windows 95, 16x CD-ROM, modem
Software requirements: Encourage use of MS Word
Is the library accessible to students? Yes
Are computers accessible to students? Yes

Remote Sites

Other branches of the institution: Yes
Students' homes: Yes
Work sites: Yes

On-Campus Requirements

Is an on-campus component required? Yes
On-campus program orientation: Yes
On-campus exams: Yes

Tuition & Fees

In-state tuition per credit: $46
Out-of-state tuition per credit: $170
Average yearly cost of books: $500

Financial Aid

Is financial aid available to full-time students? Yes
Is financial aid available to part-time students? Yes
Are academic scholarships available? Yes
Assistance programs available to students: Federal Stafford Loan, Federal Perkins Loan, Federal Plus Loan, Federal Pell Grant, Federal Work-Study Program, in-state student aid programs, veterans' assistance

Palo Alto College

Extended Services and Community Outreach
1400 West Villaret Boulevard
San Antonio, TX 78224
Contact: Pamela B. Hill, EdD, Dean, Extended Services and Community Outreach
Department Web address: www.accd.edu/pac/distedu/disted.htm
School Web address: www.accd.edu/pac
Institutional accreditation: Southern Association of Colleges and Schools

Subjects Offered

Accounting, agribusiness management, art appreciation, biology, chemistry, communications, computer information systems, computer science, criminal justice, economics, English, government, history, humanities, library and information studies, music appreciation, orientation, philosophy, physical education, psychology, sociology

Admissions Requirements

Is provisional admission available? Yes
Is an admissions interview required? No
Can pre-requisite course work be waived? Yes
Are international students eligible to apply? Yes
Is the TOEFL required for international students? Yes
What is the minimum TOEFL score required? 450

Program Delivery

Primary method of program delivery: Web
Two-way interactive video: Yes
Two-way audio, one-way video: No
One-way live video: Yes
One-way pre-recorded video: Yes
Hardware requirements: Pentium processor 90 MHz, or Power PC 16MB of RAM, Internet service provider
Software requirements: Windows 95 or better, MacOS 7.55 or later, e-mail access, Internet browser: Netscape 3.01 or Internet Explorer 3.02 or higher
Is the library accessible to students? Yes
Are computers accessible to students? Yes

Remote Sites

Other college campuses: Yes
Students' homes: Yes
Elementary/Secondary schools: Yes

On-Campus Requirements

Is an on-campus component required? No

Tuition & Fees

In-state tuition per credit: $132
Out-of-state tuition per credit: $472
Average yearly cost of books: $550

Financial Aid

Is financial aid available to full-time students? Yes
Is financial aid available to part-time students? Yes
Are academic scholarships available? Yes
Assistance programs available to students: Federal Stafford
Loan, Federal Plus Loan, Federal Pell Grant, Federal
Work-Study Program, in-state student aid programs,
veterans' assistance

Park University

School of Extended Learning
Distance Learning
8700 NW River Front Park Drive
Parkville, MO 64152
Contact: Dr. Thomas W. Peterman, Vice President for
Distance Learning
Department e-mail: tomp@mail.park.edu
Department Web address: www.park.edu/dist/dist/htm
School Web address: www.park.edu
Institutional accreditation: North Central Association of
Colleges and Schools

Subjects Offered

Accounting, biology, chemistry, criminal justice, computer
science, economics, English, geography, geology, history,
human resources, humanities, management (business),
marketing, natural science, philosophy, public administration, psychology, sociology

Admissions Requirements

Is a minimum high school GPA required? No
Is provisional admission available? Yes
Is an admissions interview required? No
Can pre-requisite course work be waived? No
Are international students eligible to apply? Yes
Is the TOEFL required for international students? No

Program Delivery

Hardware requirements: Access to Internet, Pentium
processor
Software requirements: Internet access and browser
Is the library accessible to students? Yes
Are computers accessible to students? Yes

Remote Sites

Other branches of the institution: Yes
Other college campuses: Yes

Students' homes: Yes
Work sites: Yes
Libraries: Yes
Elementary/Secondary schools: Yes
Community-based organizations: Yes
Correctional institutions: Yes

On-Campus Requirements

Is an on-campus component required? No

Tuition & Fees

In-state tuition per credit: $123
Out-of-state tuition per credit: $123
Average yearly cost of books: $25

Financial Aid

Is financial aid available to full-time students? Yes
Is financial aid available to part-time students? Yes
Are academic scholarships available? Yes
Assistance programs available to students: Federal Stafford
Loan, Federal Perkins Loan, Federal Plus Loan, Federal
Pell Grant, Federal Work-Study Program, veterans'
assistance

Patrick Henry Community College

Learning Resource Center
PO Box 5311
Martinsville, VA 24112
Contact: Carolyn Byrd, Director of Instructional Support
Service
Department e-mail: phbyrdc@ph.cc.va.us
Department Web address: www.ph.cc.va.us/lrc
School Web address: www.ph.cc.va.us
Institutional accreditation: Southern Association of
Colleges and Schools

Subjects Offered

Information technology, English, mathematics, history,
religion, criminal justice, chemistry, music, health,
psychology, sociology, child development, child care

Admissions Requirements

Is a minimum high school GPA required? No
Can pre-requisite course work be waived? Yes
Are international students eligible to apply? No

Program Delivery

Primary method of program delivery: Web
Two-way interactive video: Yes
One-way live video: Yes

Hardware requirements: Pentium 64MB of RAM, 200 MB hard drive space, sound card, 24x CD-ROM, 28.8KBPS modem, Super VGA monitor, Internet
Software requirements: course-dependent
Is the library accessible to students? Yes
Are computers accessible to students? Yes

Remote Sites

Other branches of the institution: Yes
Other college campuses: Yes
Students' homes: Yes

On-Campus Requirements

Is an on-campus component required? No

Tuition & Fees

In-state tuition per credit: $37
Out-of-state tuition per credit: $169
Average yearly cost of books: $700

Financial Aid

Is financial aid available to full-time students? Yes
Is financial aid available to part-time students? Yes
Are academic scholarships available? Yes
Assistance programs available to students: Federal Pell Grant, Federal Work-Study Program, in-state student aid programs, veterans' assistance

Pellissippi State Technical Community College

Distance Learning Department
10915 Hardin Valley Road
PO Box 22990
Knoxville, TN 37933-0990
Contact: Lana Doncaster, Director
School Web address: www.pstcc.cc.tn.us
Institutional accreditation: Southern Association of Colleges and Schools

Admissions Requirements

Is a minimum high school GPA required? No
Is provisional admission available? Yes
Is an admissions interview required? Yes
Can pre-requisite course work be waived? Yes
Is the TOEFL required for international students? Yes
What is the minimum TOEFL score required? 450

Program Delivery

Primary method of program delivery: Web
Two-way interactive video: Yes
Two-way audio, one-way video: No

One-way live video: No
One-way pre-recorded video: No
Audio graphics: No
Audio: No
Hardware requirements: Internet service provider
Software requirements: Web browser, word processing package
Is the library accessible to students? Yes
Are computers accessible to students? No

Remote Sites

Other branches of the institution: Yes
Other college campuses: No
Students' homes: No
Work sites: No
Libraries: No
Elementary/Secondary schools: No
Community-based organizations: No
Correctional institutions: No

On-Campus Requirements

Is an on-campus component required? No

Financial Aid

Is financial aid available to full-time students? Yes
Is financial aid available to part-time students? Yes
Are academic scholarships available? Yes
Assistance programs available to students: Federal Stafford Loan, Federal Plus Loan, Federal Pell Grant, Federal Work-Study Program, in-state student aid programs, veterans' assistance

Piedmont College

Department of Institutional Research and Effectiveness
PO Box 10
165 Central Avenue
Demorest, GA 30535
School Web address: www.piedmont.edu
Institutional accreditation: Southern Association of Colleges and Schools

Subjects Offered

Elementary statistics, calculus with analytical geometry I, history, memory and the holocaust

Admissions Requirements

Is a minimum high school GPA required? No
Is provisional admission available? Yes
Is an admissions interview required? No
Can pre-requisite course work be waived? Yes
Are international students eligible to apply? Yes

Is the TOEFL required for international students? Yes
What is the minimum TOEFL score required? 500

Program Delivery

Is the library accessible to students? Yes
Are computers accessible to students? Yes

Remote Sites

Other branches of the institution: Yes
Other college campuses: Yes
Students' homes: Yes
Elementary/Secondary schools: Yes

Tuition & Fees

In-state tuition per credit: $363
Out-of-state tuition per credit: $363
Average yearly cost of books: $600

Financial Aid

Is financial aid available to full-time students? Yes
Is financial aid available to part-time students? Yes
Are academic scholarships available? Yes
Assistance programs available to students: Federal Stafford Loan, Federal Pell Grant, Federal Work-Study Program, in-state student aid programs

Piedmont Technical College

Instructional Technology
PO Box 1467
520 North Emerald Road
Greenwood, SC 29648
Contact: Dr. Daniel Koenig, Associate Vice President Instructional Support and Technology
Department e-mail: koenig.d@piedmont.tec.sc.us
Department Web address: www.piedmont.tec.sc.us/dl
School Web address: www.piedmont.tec.sc.us
Institutional accreditation: Southern Association of Colleges and Schools

Subjects Offered

Nutrition, art appreciation, business, history, biology, economics, philosophy, industrial electronics, psychology, sociology, Spanish language, funeral services, mathematics, English composition, literature

Admissions Requirements

Is a minimum high school GPA required? No
Is provisional admission available? Yes
Is an admissions interview required? No
Can pre-requisite course work be waived? Yes
Are international students eligible to apply? Yes

Is the TOEFL required for international students? Yes
What is the minimum TOEFL score required? 500

Program Delivery

Primary method of program delivery: Web
Two-way interactive video: Yes
Two-way audio, one-way video: Yes
One-way live video: No
One-way pre-recorded video: Yes
Audio graphics: No
Audio: No
Hardware requirements: Pentium 300 MHz, 56KBPS modem
Software requirements: Internet browser
Is the library accessible to students? Yes
Are computers accessible to students? Yes

Remote Sites

Other branches of the institution: Yes
Other college campuses: Yes
Students' homes: Yes
Work sites: Yes
Libraries: Yes
Elementary/Secondary schools: Yes
Community-based organizations: Yes
Correctional institutions: No

On-Campus Requirements

Is an on-campus component required? No

Tuition & Fees

In-state tuition per credit: $60
Out-of-state tuition per credit: $90
Average yearly cost of books: $200

Financial Aid

Is financial aid available to full-time students? Yes
Is financial aid available to part-time students? Yes
Are academic scholarships available? Yes
Assistance programs available to students: Federal Perkins Loan, Federal Plus Loan, Federal Pell Grant, Federal Work-Study Program, in-state student aid programs, veterans' assistance

Pikes Peak Community College

Educational Services
Office of Distance Education
5675 South Academy Boulevard
Colorado Springs, CO 80907

Contact: Julie Grabner Witherow, Director of Distance Education

Department e-mail: distance.ed@ppcc.cccoes.edu

Department Web address: www.ppcc.cccoes.edu/distanceed/default.htm

School Web address: www.ppcc.cccoes.edu

Institutional accreditation: National Central Association of Colleges and Schools

Subjects Offered

Accounting, business (including management), computer information systems, computer science, English (grammar and composition), geography, history, integrated circuit fabrication, literature, marketing, computer networking, math (including statistics), political science, psychology, space science, satellite communication, scriptwriting, theatre

Admissions Requirements

Is a minimum high school GPA required? No

Is provisional admission available? Yes

Is an admissions interview required? No

Can pre-requisite course work be waived? Yes

Are international students eligible to apply? Yes

Is the TOEFL required for international students? Yes

What is the minimum TOEFL score required? 450

Program Delivery

Primary method of program delivery: Web

Two-way interactive video: No

Two-way audio, one-way video: Yes

One-way live video: Yes

One-way pre-recorded video: Yes

Audio graphics: No

Audio: No

Hardware requirements: PC: 166 MHz Intel Pentium processor, 32 MB of RAM, 28.8KBPS modem, 16 bit soundcard/speakers. Mac: MacOS 8.5, 64MB of RAM, virtual memory set to 128MB

Software requirements: Windows 95, 98, NT 4.0 with service pack 6A, Internet connection, and Web browser

Is the library accessible to students? Yes

Are computers accessible to students? Yes

Remote Sites

Other branches of the institution: Yes

Other college campuses: No

Students' homes: Yes

Work sites: No

Libraries: No

Elementary/Secondary schools: Yes

Community-based organizations: No

Correctional institutions: Yes

On-Campus Requirements

Is an on-campus component required? No

Tuition & Fees

In-state tuition per credit: $56

Out-of-state tuition per credit: $267

Application fee: $9

Can it be waived? No

Financial Aid

Is financial aid available to full-time students? Yes

Is financial aid available to part-time students? Yes

Are academic scholarships available? Yes

Assistance programs available to students: Federal Stafford Loan, Federal Plus Loan, Federal Pell Grant, Federal Work-Study Program, in-state student aid programs, veterans' assistance

Plattsburgh State University

Center for Lifelong Learning

Distance Learning Office

101 Board Street, Sibley Hall 418 A

Plattsburgh, NY 12901

Contact: Cheryl A. Marshall, Coordinator, Distance Learning Office

Department e-mail: cheryl.marshall@plattsburgh.edu

School Web address: www.plattsburgh.edu

Institutional accreditation: Middle States Association of Colleges and Schools

Subjects Offered

Nursing, anthropology, Canadian studies, economics, Latin American studies, library research, business organization, business research, labor relations

Admissions Requirements

Is provisional admission available? No

Is an admissions interview required? No

Can pre-requisite course work be waived? No

Program Delivery

Primary method of program delivery: Remote site

Two-way interactive video: Yes

Hardware requirements: Pentium PC recommended

Is the library accessible to students? Yes

Are computers accessible to students? No

Remote Sites

Other branches of the institution: Yes

On-Campus Requirements

Is an on-campus component required? No

Tuition & Fees

In-state tuition per credit: $137
Out-of-state tuition per credit: $346
Average yearly cost of books: $35

Financial Aid

Is financial aid available to full-time students? Yes
Is financial aid available to part-time students? Yes
Are academic scholarships available? Yes
Assistance programs available to students: Federal Stafford
Loan, Federal Perkins Loan, Federal Plus Loan, Federal
Pell Grant, in-state student aid programs, veterans'
assistance

Prairie Bible College

Prairie Distance Education
PO Box 4000
Three Hills, AB, Canada T0M 2N0
Contact: Dr. Arnold L. Stauffer, Associate Dean
Department e-mail: distance.ed@pbi.ab.ca
Department Web address: www.pbi.ab.ca/distanceed
School Web address: www.pbi.ab.ca
Institutional accreditation: Accrediting Association of Bible
Colleges

Subjects Offered

Bible, theology, history, bible languages, arts and sciences,
practical training, intercultural studies, education,
pastoral ministry, humanities, social sciences, music,
field education, church development

Admissions Requirements

Is a minimum high school GPA required? No
Is provisional admission available? Yes
Is an admissions interview required? No
Can pre-requisite course work be waived? Yes
Are international students eligible to apply? Yes
Is the TOEFL required for international students? Yes

Program Delivery

Primary method of program delivery: Text
One-way pre-recorded video: Yes
Audio: Yes
Is the library accessible to students? Yes
Are computers accessible to students? No

Remote Sites

Students' homes: Yes
Community-based organizations: Yes
Correctional institutions: Yes

On-Campus Requirements

Is an on-campus component required? No

Tuition & Fees

In-state tuition per credit: $125
Out-of-state tuition per credit: $125
Average yearly cost of books: $480

Financial Aid

Is financial aid available to full-time students? No
Is financial aid available to part-time students? No
Are academic scholarships available? No

Prescott College

Admissions Office
Adult Degree Program
220 Grove Avenue
Prescott, AZ 86301
Contact: Steve Walters, Dean of Adult Degree Programs
Department e-mail: admissions@prescott.edu
School Web address: www.prescott.edu
Institutional accreditation: North Central Association of
Colleges and Schools

Subjects Offered

Arts and letters, community development, education,
environmental studies, integrative studies, liberal arts

Admissions Requirements

Is a minimum high school GPA required? No
Is provisional admission available? Yes
Is an admissions interview required? Yes
Can pre-requisite course work be waived? Yes
Are international students eligible to apply? Yes
Is the TOEFL required for international students? Yes
What is the minimum TOEFL score required? 550

Program Delivery

Primary method of program delivery: Text
Is the library accessible to students? Yes
Are computers accessible to students? Yes

Remote Sites

Other branches of the institution: Yes
Students' homes: Yes

Work sites: Yes
Libraries: Yes
Elementary/Secondary schools: Yes
Community-based organizations: Yes
Correctional institutions: Yes

On-Campus Requirements

Is an on-campus component required? Yes
On-campus course work: Yes
On-campus program orientation: Yes

Tuition & Fees

In-state tuition per credit: $208
Out-of-state tuition per credit: $208
Average yearly cost of books: $400

Financial Aid

Is financial aid available to full-time students? Yes
Is financial aid available to part-time students? No
Are academic scholarships available? Yes
Assistance programs available to students: Federal Stafford
    Loan, Federal Perkins Loan, Federal Plus Loan, Federal
    Pell Grant, Federal Work-Study Program, in-state
    student aid programs, veterans' assistance

Prince George's Community College

Office of Distance Learning
301 Largo Road
Largo, MD 20772
Contact: Mary Wells, Director of Distance Learning
Department Web address: www.pgweb/pgweb/pgdocs/
    distlern/index.htm
School Web address: www.pgweb.pg.cc.md.us
Institutional accreditation: Middle States Association of
    Colleges and Schools

Subjects Offered

Business administration, business management, psychology,
    sociology, marketing, pre-law, computer science,
    mathematics, English, criminal justice

Admissions Requirements

Is a minimum high school GPA required? No
Is an admissions interview required? No
Are international students eligible to apply? Yes
Is the TOEFL required for international students? Yes
What is the minimum TOEFL score required? 450

Program Delivery

Primary method of program delivery: Remote site
Two-way interactive video: Yes
One-way pre-recorded video: Yes
Software requirements: Internet access, Netscape 4.0,
    Internet Explorer 4.0
Is the library accessible to students? No
Are computers accessible to students? No

Remote Sites

Other college campuses: Yes

On-Campus Requirements

Is an on-campus component required? Yes
On-campus program orientation: Yes

Tuition & Fees

In-state tuition per credit: $75
Out-of-state tuition per credit: $140

Financial Aid

Is financial aid available to full-time students? Yes
Is financial aid available to part-time students? Yes
Are academic scholarships available? Yes
Assistance programs available to students: Federal Stafford
    Loan, Federal Plus Loan, Federal Pell Grant, Federal
    Work-Study Program, in-state student aid programs,
    veterans' assistance

Pueblo Community College

Title III/Distance Learning
900 West Orman Avenue
Pueblo, CO 81004
Contact: Jo-Ann Kipple, Coordinator of Title III and
    Distance Learning
Department e-mail: jo-ann.kipple@pcc.cccoes.edu
Department Web address: www.pcc.cccoes.edu
School Web address: www.pcc.ccoes.edu
Institutional accreditation: North Central Association of
    Colleges and Schools

Subjects Offered

Arts-general education, business, construction electrician,
    emergency management and planning, gerontology,
    occupational safety and health, accounting, agricultural
    business, networking, computer information systems,
    public administration, biology, chemistry, English,
    mathematics, Spanish, economics

Admissions Requirements

Is a minimum high school GPA required? No
Is an admissions interview required? No
Can pre-requisite course work be waived? Yes
Are international students eligible to apply? Yes
Is the TOEFL required for international students? Yes
What is the minimum TOEFL score required? 450

Program Delivery

Two-way interactive video: Yes
One-way live video: Yes
One-way pre-recorded video: Yes
Audio graphics: Yes
Audio: Yes
Is the library accessible to students? Yes
Are computers accessible to students? Yes

Remote Sites

Other branches of the institution: Yes
Other college campuses: Yes
Students' homes: Yes
Work sites: Yes
Libraries: Yes
Elementary/Secondary schools: Yes
Community-based organizations: Yes
Correctional institutions: Yes

On-Campus Requirements

Is an on-campus component required? No

Tuition & Fees

In-state tuition per credit: $73
Out-of-state tuition per credit: $284
Average yearly cost of books: $720
Average yearly additional fees: $208

Financial Aid

Is financial aid available to full-time students? Yes
Is financial aid available to part-time students? Yes
Are academic scholarships available? Yes
Assistance programs available to students: Federal Stafford Loan, Federal Plus Loan, Federal Pell Grant, Federal Work-Study Program, in-state student aid programs, veterans' assistance

Regis University

School of Professional Studies
Regis Online
3333 Regis Boulevard, L-12
Denver, CO 80221-1099
Contact: Cheryl Richards, Director, Marketing and Admissions

Department e-mail: muaic@regis.edu
Department Web address: www.regis.edu/spsundergrad
School Web address: www.regis.edu
Institutional accreditation: North Central Association of Colleges and Schools

Subjects Offered

Accounting, business, communication arts, computer science, economics, experiential learning, English, mathematics, psychology, religious studies

Admissions Requirements

Is a minimum high school GPA required? No
Is provisional admission available? No
Is an admissions interview required? No
Can pre-requisite course work be waived? Yes
Are international students eligible to apply? Yes
Is the TOEFL required for international students? Yes

Program Delivery

Primary method of program delivery: Web
Two-way interactive video: No
Two-way audio, one-way video: No
One-way live video: No
One-way pre-recorded video: No
Audio graphics: No
Audio: Yes
Hardware requirements: Pentium, sound card, 28.8KBPS modem or other Internet connectivity
Software requirements: Office 98 or higher, Excel, Word, either Netscape or Internet Explorer (latest version)
Is the library accessible to students? Yes
Are computers accessible to students? No

Remote Sites

Other branches of the institution: Yes
Other college campuses: No
Students' homes: No
Work sites: Yes
Libraries: No
Elementary/Secondary schools: No
Community-based organizations: No
Correctional institutions: No

On-Campus Requirements

Is an on-campus component required? No

Tuition & Fees

In-state tuition per credit: $245
Out-of-state tuition per credit: $245
Average yearly cost of books: $50

Financial Aid

Is financial aid available to full-time students? Yes
Is financial aid available to part-time students? Yes
Are academic scholarships available? Yes
Assistance programs available to students: Federal Stafford
Loan, Federal Perkins Loan, Federal Plus Loan, Federal
Pell Grant, veterans' assistance

Richard Stockton College of New Jersey

Center for Instructional Media and Technology
Distance Education
PO Box 195
Pomona, NJ 08240-0195
Contact: Mark R. Jackson, Director of Media Services and
Distance Education
Department Web address: www2.stockton.edu/html/media
School Web address: www.stockton.edu
Institutional accreditation: Middle States Association of
Colleges and Schools

Subjects Offered

General arts and humanities, marketing, sociology, general
studies, general integration and synthesis, natural
sciences and math, social and behavioral sciences,
management, nursing, political science, criminal justice,
psychology, anthropology, communications, literature

Admissions Requirements

Is a minimum high school GPA required? No
Is provisional admission available? Yes
Can pre-requisite course work be waived? No
Are international students eligible to apply? Yes
Is the TOEFL required for international students? Yes

Program Delivery

Primary method of program delivery: Remote site
Two-way interactive video: Yes
Two-way audio, one-way video: Yes
One-way live video: No
One-way pre-recorded video: Yes
Audio graphics: No
Audio: Yes
Hardware requirements: Pentium 90, 32MB of RAM, 2GB
hard drive, monitor, sound card, speakers. Mac: Power
PC with 32MB RAM, 2GB hard drive
Software requirements: Netscape browser 4.0 or higher,
Windows 95, Windows 98; Mac OS 7.0 or higher
Is the library accessible to students? Yes
Are computers accessible to students? Yes

Remote Sites

Other branches of the institution: No
Other college campuses: No
Students' homes: Yes
Work sites: Yes
Libraries: Yes
Correctional institutions: No

On-Campus Requirements

Is an on-campus component required? Yes
On-campus course work: Yes
On-campus program orientation: Yes
On-campus exams: Yes

Tuition & Fees

In-state tuition per credit: $150
Out-of-state tuition per credit: $220
Average yearly cost of books: $35

Financial Aid

Is financial aid available to full-time students? Yes
Is financial aid available to part-time students? Yes
Are academic scholarships available? Yes
Assistance programs available to students: Federal Stafford
Loan, Federal Perkins Loan, Federal Plus Loan, Federal
Pell Grant, Federal Work-Study Program, in-state
student aid programs, veterans' assistance

Rio Salado College

Academic Programs
223 West 14th Street
Tempe, AZ 85281-6950
Contact: Karen L. Mills Sr., Associate Dean for Instruction
Department e-mail: more.info@riomail.maricopa.edu
School Web address: www.rio.maricopa.edu

Subjects Offered

Accounting, anthropology, art humanities, astronomy,
biology, business, chemical dependency, chemistry,
child/family studies, communication, computers,
theater, total quality management, counseling and
personal development, economics, education, English,
English humanities, food and nutrition, French,
geography, geology, German, health related, small
business, Spanish, history, humanities, library skills,
management and supervision, mathematics, medical
terminology, office automation, philosophy

Admissions Requirements

Is a minimum high school GPA required? No
Is an admissions interview required? No

Can pre-requisite course work be waived? Yes
Are international students eligible to apply? Yes

Program Delivery

Is the library accessible to students? Yes
Are computers accessible to students? Yes

On-Campus Requirements

Is an on-campus component required? No

Tuition & Fees

In-state tuition per credit: $41
Out-of-state tuition per credit: $125
Average yearly cost of books: $30

Financial Aid

Is financial aid available to full-time students? Yes
Is financial aid available to part-time students? Yes
Are academic scholarships available? Yes
Assistance programs available to students: Federal Pell
    Grant, Federal Work-Study Program, in-state student aid
    programs, veterans' assistance

Riverside Community College District

Open Campus
4800 Magnolia
Riverside, CA 92506
Contact: Glen Brady, Director of Distance Education
Department e-mail: glbrady@rccd.cc.ca.us
School Web address: www.opencampus.com
Institutional accreditation: Western Association of Schools
    and Colleges

Subjects Offered

Art, history, math, music, computer science, economics,
    business, astronomy, anthropology, early childhood,
    oceanography, philosophy, political science, psychology,
    sociology, Spanish, reading

Admissions Requirements

Is a minimum high school GPA required? No
Is provisional admission available? No
Can pre-requisite course work be waived? Yes
Are international students eligible to apply? Yes
Is the TOEFL required for international students? Yes

Program Delivery

Two-way interactive video: No
Two-way audio, one-way video: No
One-way live video: No

One-way pre-recorded video: Yes
Audio graphics: Yes
Audio: Yes
Hardware requirements: 486 or better
Software requirements: Netscape or Explorer
Is the library accessible to students? Yes
Are computers accessible to students? Yes

Remote Sites

Other branches of the institution: Yes
Other college campuses: Yes
Students' homes: Yes
Work sites: Yes
Libraries: Yes
Elementary/Secondary schools: Yes
Community-based organizations: Yes
Correctional institutions: Yes

On-Campus Requirements

Is an on-campus component required? No

Tuition & Fees

In-state tuition per credit: $11
Out-of-state tuition per credit: $130

Financial Aid

Is financial aid available to full-time students? Yes
Is financial aid available to part-time students? Yes
Are academic scholarships available? Yes

Robert Morris College

Enrollment Services
Owesin of Adult and Continuing Education
600 Fifth Avenue
Pittsburgh, PA 15219
Contact: Darry B. Tannehill, Dean
Department e-mail: tannehill@robertmorrise.edu
School Web address: www.robert-morris.edu
Institutional accreditation: Middle States Association of
    Colleges and Schools

Subjects Offered

Accounting, psychology, sociology, communication,
    economics, nutrition, literature

Admissions Requirements

Is a minimum high school GPA required? Yes
Is provisional admission available? Yes
Is an admissions interview required? Yes
Can pre-requisite course work be waived? Yes
Are international students eligible to apply? Yes

Is the TOEFL required for international students? Yes
What is the minimum TOEFL score required? 550

Program Delivery

Primary method of program delivery: Web
One-way live video: Yes
Audio: Yes
Hardware requirements: 90 MHz Pentium processor,
    32MB RAM
Software requirements: Windows 95, 98, or NT
Is the library accessible to students? Yes
Are computers accessible to students? Yes

Remote Sites

Other branches of the institution: No
Other college campuses: No
Students' homes: Yes
Work sites: Yes
Libraries: Yes
Elementary/Secondary schools: No
Community-based organizations: No
Correctional institutions: No

On-Campus Requirements

Is an on-campus component required? Yes
On-campus course work: Yes
On-campus admissions interview: Yes
On-campus program orientation: Yes
On-campus exams: Yes

Tuition & Fees

In-state tuition per credit: $300
Average yearly cost of books: $850

Financial Aid

Is financial aid available to full-time students? Yes
Is financial aid available to part-time students? Yes
Are academic scholarships available? Yes
Assistance programs available to students: Federal Stafford
    Loan, Federal Perkins Loan, Federal Plus Loan, Federal
    Pell Grant, in-state student aid programs, veterans'
    assistance

Rochester Institute of Technology

Office Online Learning
58 Lomb Memorial Drive
Rochester, NY 14063
Contact: Joe Nairn, Director
Department e-mail: spages@rit.edu
Department Web address: www.rit.edu/parttime

School Web address: www.rit.edu
Institutional accreditation: Middle States Association of
    Colleges and Schools

Admissions Requirements

Is a minimum high school GPA required? Yes
Is provisional admission available? Yes
Can pre-requisite course work be waived? Yes
Are international students eligible to apply? Yes
Is the TOEFL required for international students? Yes
What is the minimum TOEFL score required? 550

Program Delivery

Primary method of program delivery: Web
Two-way interactive video: Yes
Two-way audio, one-way video: Yes
One-way live video: No
One-way pre-recorded video: Yes
Audio graphics: No
Audio: Yes
Software requirements: Netscape Navigator 4.0 or higher
    or Microsoft Explorer 4.0 or higher
Is the library accessible to students? Yes
Are computers accessible to students? Yes

Remote Sites

Other branches of the institution: No
Other college campuses: No
Students' homes: Yes
Work sites: Yes
Libraries: No
Elementary/Secondary schools: Yes
Community-based organizations: No
Correctional institutions: No

On-Campus Requirements

Is an on-campus component required? No

Tuition & Fees

In-state tuition per credit: $258
Out-of-state tuition per credit: $283

Financial Aid

Is financial aid available to full-time students? Yes
Is financial aid available to part-time students? Yes
Are academic scholarships available? Yes
Assistance programs available to students: Federal Stafford
    Loan, Federal Perkins Loan, Federal Plus Loan, Federal
    Pell Grant, Federal Work-Study Program, in-state
    student aid programs, veterans' assistance

Rockland Community College

Instructional Technology Center
Distance Learning Program
145 College Road
Suffern, NY 10901
Contact: Dr. Harry Nelsen, Director, ITC
Department e-mail: ikoplik@sunyrockland.edu
Department Web address: www.sunyrockland.edu/
virtualrcc
School Web address: www.sunyrockland.edu
Institutional accreditation: Middle States Association of
Colleges and Schools

Subjects Offered

Anthropolgy, medical terminology, art, political science,
business, psychology, economics, science, geography,
nursing, finance, pathophysiology, health, physical
education, marketing, philosophy

Admissions Requirements

Can pre-requisite course work be waived? Yes
Are international students eligible to apply? No

Program Delivery

Primary method of program delivery: Text
Two-way interactive video: No
Two-way audio, one-way video: No
One-way live video: No
One-way pre-recorded video: Yes
Audio graphics: No
Audio: Yes
Software requirements: Any browser (Netscape, Explorer)
Is the library accessible to students? Yes
Are computers accessible to students? Yes

Remote Sites

Other branches of the institution: Yes
Students' homes: Yes

On-Campus Requirements

Is an on-campus component required? Yes
On-campus course work: No
On-campus admissions interview: No
On-campus program orientation: Yes
On-campus exams: Yes

Tuition & Fees

In-state tuition per credit: $97
Out-of-state tuition per credit: $194
Average yearly cost of books: $2,000

Financial Aid

Is financial aid available to full-time students? Yes
Is financial aid available to part-time students? Yes
Are academic scholarships available? Yes
Assistance programs available to students: Federal Stafford
Loan, Federal Perkins Loan, Federal Plus Loan, Federal
Pell Grant, Federal Work-Study Program, in-state
student aid programs, veterans' assistance

Roger Williams University

Open College
150 Washington Street
Providence, RI 02903
Contact: John W. Stout, Dean
Department e-mail: jws@alpha.rwu.edu
Department Web address: www.rwu.edu/uvc
School Web address: www.rwu.edu
Institutional accreditation: New England Association of
Schools and Colleges

Subjects Offered

Business management, criminal justice, industrial
technology, public administration, social science

Admissions Requirements

Is provisional admission available? Yes
Can pre-requisite course work be waived? Yes
Are international students eligible to apply? Yes
Is the TOEFL required for international students? Yes
What is the minimum TOEFL score required? 550

Program Delivery

Primary method of program delivery: Text
Two-way interactive video: No
Two-way audio, one-way video: No
One-way live video: No
One-way pre-recorded video: Yes
Audio graphics: No
Audio: No
Is the library accessible to students? Yes
Are computers accessible to students? No

On-Campus Requirements

Is an on-campus component required? No

Tuition & Fees

In-state tuition per credit: $235
Application fee: $35
Can it be waived? Yes
Average yearly cost of books: $800

Financial Aid

Is financial aid available to full-time students? Yes
Is financial aid available to part-time students? Yes
Are academic scholarships available? Yes
Assistance programs available to students: Federal Stafford Loan, Federal Perkins Loan, Federal Plus Loan, Federal Pell Grant, in-state student aid programs, veterans' assistance

Rogers State University

RSU Online Global Campus—Enrollment Management
1701 West Will Rogers
Claremore, OK 74017
Contact: Kevin Cook, Director, RSU Online
Department e-mail: online@rsu.edu
School Web address: rsuonline.edu
Institutional accreditation: North Central Association of Colleges and Schools

Subjects Offered

Art, history, business, accounting, marketing, management, humanities, computer science, information technologies, business administration, math, broadcasting, music, biology, political science, chemistry, philosophy, economics, government, English, psychology, geography, sociology, astronomy, Spanish

Admissions Requirements

Is a minimum high school GPA required? No
Is provisional admission available? Yes
Is an admissions interview required? No
Can pre-requisite course work be waived? Yes
Are international students eligible to apply? Yes
Is the TOEFL required for international students? Yes
What is the minimum TOEFL score required? 500

Program Delivery

Primary method of program delivery: Web
Audio graphics: Yes
Audio: Yes
Is the library accessible to students? Yes
Are computers accessible to students? Yes

Remote Sites

Other branches of the institution: Yes
Other college campuses: Yes
Students' homes: Yes
Work sites: Yes
Elementary/Secondary schools: Yes

On-Campus Requirements

Is an on-campus component required? No

Tuition & Fees

In-state tuition per credit: $104
Out-of-state tuition per credit: $197
Average yearly cost of books: $750

Financial Aid

Is financial aid available to full-time students? Yes
Is financial aid available to part-time students? Yes
Are academic scholarships available? Yes
Assistance programs available to students: Federal Stafford Loan, Federal Perkins Loan, Federal Plus Loan, Federal Pell Grant, Federal Work-Study Program, in-state student aid programs, veterans' assistance

Rose State College

6420 Southeast 15th
Midwest, OK 733110
Contact: Jan Taylor, Coordinator of Distance Learning
Department e-mail: jtaylor@ms.rose.cc.ok.us
School Web address: www.rose.cc.ok.us
Institutional accreditation: Oklahoma State Regents

Subjects Offered

English, art, sociology, commuter information system, psychology, nutrition, nursing, music, court reporting, philosophy, political science, history, business, macro-economics, microeconomics

Admissions Requirements

Is a minimum high school GPA required? No
Is provisional admission available? Yes
Is an admissions interview required? No
Can pre-requisite course work be waived? Yes
Are international students eligible to apply? Yes
Is the TOEFL required for international students? Yes
What is the minimum TOEFL score required? 500

Program Delivery

Primary method of program delivery: Remote site
Two-way interactive video: Yes
Two-way audio, one-way video: No
One-way live video: No
One-way pre-recorded video: No
Audio graphics: No
Audio: No
Software requirements: Webct Blackboard
Is the library accessible to students? Yes
Are computers accessible to students? Yes

Remote Sites

Other branches of the institution: Yes
Other college campuses: Yes
Students' homes: Yes
Work sites: Yes
Libraries: Yes
Elementary/Secondary schools: Yes
Community-based organizations: Yes
Correctional institutions: Yes

On-Campus Requirements

Is an on-campus component required? Yes
On-campus course work: Yes
On-campus admissions interview: No
On-campus program orientation: Yes
On-campus exams: Yes

Tuition & Fees

In-state tuition per credit: $32
Out-of-state tuition per credit: $99
Average yearly cost of books: $250
Average yearly additional fees: $15

Financial Aid

Is financial aid available to full-time students? Yes
Is financial aid available to part-time students? Yes
Are academic scholarships available? Yes
Assistance programs available to students: Federal Stafford
    Loan, Federal Perkins Loan, Federal Plus Loan, Federal
    Pell Grant, Federal Work-Study Program, in-state
    student aid programs, veterans' assistance

Saddleback College

Office of Instruction
Distance Education
28000 Marguerite Parkway
Mission Viejo, CA 92692
Contact: Don Busche, Vice President, Instruction
Department e-mail: snelson@saddleback.cc.ca.us
Department Web address: www.iserver.saddleback.cc.ca.us/
    div/dl/fall00.html
School Web address: www.saddleback.cc.ca.us
Institutional accreditation: Western Association of Schools
    and Colleges

Subjects Offered

Accounting, business management, computer information
    systems, real estate, creative writing (English 3),
    journalism, anthropology, history of the U.S., library
    science, music appreciation, political science, psychology,
    sociology

Admissions Requirements

Is a minimum high school GPA required? No
Is provisional admission available? Yes
Is an admissions interview required? No
Can pre-requisite course work be waived? No
Are international students eligible to apply? Yes
Is the TOEFL required for international students? Yes
What is the minimum TOEFL score required? 470

Program Delivery

Primary method of program delivery: Web
One-way pre-recorded video: Yes
Audio: Yes
Is the library accessible to students? Yes
Are computers accessible to students? Yes

Remote Sites

Students' homes: Yes
Work sites: Yes
Libraries: Yes

On-Campus Requirements

Is an on-campus component required? Yes
On-campus program orientation: Yes
On-campus exams: Yes

Tuition & Fees

In-state tuition per credit: $11
Out-of-state tuition per credit: $143

Financial Aid

Is financial aid available to full-time students? Yes
Is financial aid available to part-time students? Yes
Are academic scholarships available? Yes
Assistance programs available to students: Federal Stafford
    Loan, Federal Perkins Loan, Federal Pell Grant, Federal
    Work-Study Program, in-state student aid programs,
    veterans' assistance

Saint Josephs College

Graduate and Professional Studies
278 Whites Bridge Road
Standard, ME 04084
Contact: Dr. Susan Nesbitt, Dean, Graduate and
    Professional Studies
School Web address: www.sjc.edu
Institutional accreditation: New England Association of
    Schools and Colleges

Subjects Offered

Criminal justice, health care, nursing, christian tradition,
    business, management

Admissions Requirements

Is a minimum high school GPA required? No
Is provisional admission available? Yes
Is an admissions interview required? No
Can pre-requisite course work be waived? Yes
Are international students eligible to apply? Yes
Is the TOEFL required for international students? Yes
What is the minimum TOEFL score required? 485

Program Delivery

Primary method of program delivery: Text
Audio: Yes
Hardware requirements: For online courses: personal
    computer w/486 processor, 16MB of RAM, 200MB
    hard drive, 28.8KBPS modem
Software requirements: Word 6.0; a current browser
    Internet browser for online courses
Is the library accessible to students? Yes
Are computers accessible to students? Yes

Remote Sites

Students' homes: Yes
Libraries: Yes

On-Campus Requirements

Is an on-campus component required? Yes
On-campus course work: Yes
On-campus admissions interview: No
On-campus program orientation: No
On-campus exams: No

Tuition & Fees

In-state tuition per credit: $195
Out-of-state tuition per credit: $195
Average yearly cost of books: $100

Financial Aid

Is financial aid available to full-time students? Yes
Is financial aid available to part-time students? Yes
Assistance programs available to students: Federal Stafford
    Loan, Federal Pell Grant, veterans' assistance

Saint Mary of the Woods

Office of Admission
Women's External Degree
Guerin Hall
St. Mary of the Woods, IN 47876
Contact: Gwen Hagemeyer, Director, WED Admission
School Web address: www.smwc.edu
Institutional accreditation: North Central Association of
    Colleges and Schools

Subjects Offered

Accounting, accounting information systems, business
    administration, computer information systems, digital
    media communications, English, education, gerontology,
    history/political science/pre-law, humanities, human
    services, human resource management, journalism,
    marketing, mathematics, occupation therapy applica-
    tions, paralegal studies, professional writing, psychology,
    social science/history, theology

Admissions Requirements

Is a minimum high school GPA required? Yes
Is provisional admission available? Yes
Is an admissions interview required? No
Can pre-requisite course work be waived? No
Are international students eligible to apply? Yes
Is the TOEFL required for international students? Yes
What is the minimum TOEFL score required? 500

Program Delivery

Primary method of program delivery: Text
Is the library accessible to students? Yes
Are computers accessible to students? Yes

On-Campus Requirements

Is an on-campus component required? Yes
On-campus program orientation: Yes

Tuition & Fees

In-state tuition per credit: $287
Out-of-state tuition per credit: $287
Average yearly cost of books: $1,000

Financial Aid

Is financial aid available to full-time students? Yes
Is financial aid available to part-time students? Yes
Are academic scholarships available? No
Assistance programs available to students: Federal Stafford
    Loan, Federal Perkins Loan, Federal Plus Loan, Federal
    Pell Grant, Federal Work-Study Program, in-state
    student aid programs

Salt Lake Community College

Distance Education
PO Box 30808
Salt Lake City, UT 84123
Contact: Shanna Schaefermeyer, Director, Distance
    Education
Department e-mail: schaefsh@slcc.edu
Department Web address: ecampus.slcc.edu

School Web address: www.slcc.edu

Institutional accreditation: Northwest Association of Schools and Colleges

Subjects Offered

Biology, American institutions, business, economics, management, communication, computer information systems, criminal justice, English, health sciences, human services, humanities, interdisciplinary studies, mathematics, non-destructive testing, philosophy, physics, physical therapy assistance, railroad operations, sociology, visual arts and design, paraeducation

Admissions Requirements

Is a minimum high school GPA required? No

Is provisional admission available? No

Is an admissions interview required? No

Can pre-requisite course work be waived? No

Are international students eligible to apply? Yes

Program Delivery

Primary method of program delivery: Web

Two-way interactive video: Yes

Two-way audio, one-way video: Yes

One-way live video: Yes

One-way pre-recorded video: Yes

Hardware requirements: Pentium, 200 MHz or Macintosh

Software requirements: Microsoft Word, Internet browser

Is the library accessible to students? Yes

Are computers accessible to students? Yes

Remote Sites

Other branches of the institution: Yes

Other college campuses: Yes

Students' homes: Yes

Work sites: Yes

Libraries: Yes

Elementary/Secondary schools: Yes

Correctional institutions: Yes

On-Campus Requirements

Is an on-campus component required? No

Tuition & Fees

In-state tuition per credit: $70

Out-of-state tuition per credit: $215

Average yearly cost of books: $25

Financial Aid

Is financial aid available to full-time students? Yes

Is financial aid available to part-time students? No

Are academic scholarships available? Yes

Assistance programs available to students: Federal Stafford Loan, Federal Perkins Loan, Federal Plus Loan, Federal Pell Grant, Federal Work-Study Program, in-state student aid programs, veterans' assistance

San Antonio College

Distance Education

1300 San Pedro Avenue

San Antonio, TX 78212

Contact: Helen Torres, Director of Distance Education

Department e-mail: disteduc@accd.edu

Department Web address: www.accd.edu/sac/distance/distance

School Web address: www.accd.edu

Institutional accreditation: Southern Association of Colleges and Schools

Subjects Offered

Arts, astronomy, biology, business management, banking, computer literacy, criminal justice, English as a second language, English composition I and II, geography, geology, government, history, humanities, human resources, international business, math, music, physics, psychology, college reading, sociology, Spanish I and II

Admissions Requirements

Is a minimum high school GPA required? No

Is provisional admission available? Yes

Is an admissions interview required? No

Can pre-requisite course work be waived? Yes

Are international students eligible to apply? Yes

Program Delivery

One-way pre-recorded video: Yes

Software requirements: Windows 3.1 or higher; Internet browser 5.0 or higher

Is the library accessible to students? Yes

Are computers accessible to students? Yes

On-Campus Requirements

Is an on-campus component required? Yes

On-campus course work: Yes

On-campus admissions interview: No

On-campus program orientation: Yes

On-campus exams: Yes

Tuition & Fees

In-state tuition per credit: $30

Out-of-state tuition per credit: $109

Average yearly cost of books: $0

Financial Aid

Is financial aid available to full-time students? Yes
Is financial aid available to part-time students? Yes
Are academic scholarships available? Yes
Assistance programs available to students: Federal Stafford Loan, Federal Perkins Loan, Federal Pell Grant, Federal Work-Study Program, in-state student aid programs, veterans' assistance

San Bernardino Community College District

Distance Education and Off-Campus Programs
701 South Mt. Vernon Avenue
San Bernardino, CA 92410
Department Web address: learnonline.sbccd.ca.us
School Web address: www.sbccd.cc.ca.us
Institutional accreditation: Western Association of Schools and Colleges

Subjects Offered

Anthropology, biology, child development, art, chemistry, geology, geography, history, philosophy, religious studies, sociology, psychology, communications, business, math, astronomy, physics, economics, politics, health education

Admissions Requirements

Is a minimum high school GPA required? No
Is an admissions interview required? No
Can pre-requisite course work be waived? Yes
Are international students eligible to apply? Yes
Is the TOEFL required for international students? No

Program Delivery

Primary method of program delivery: Web
One-way pre-recorded video: Yes
Is the library accessible to students? Yes
Are computers accessible to students? Yes

Remote Sites

Students' homes: Yes

Tuition & Fees

In-state tuition per credit: $11
Out-of-state tuition per credit: $130
Average yearly cost of books: $400
Average yearly additional fees: $21

Financial Aid

Is financial aid available to full-time students? Yes
Is financial aid available to part-time students? Yes

Are academic scholarships available? Yes
Assistance programs available to students: Federal Work-Study Program, in-state student aid programs, veterans' assistance

San Diego State University

Academic Affairs
Office of Distributed Learning
5500 Campanile Drive
San Diego, CA 92182-8010
Contact: Tracy Lau, Principal Coordinator for Distributed Learning
Department e-mail: dl@sdsu.edu
Department Web address: www.sdsu.edu/dl
School Web address: www.sdsu.edu
Institutional accreditation: Western Association of Schools and Colleges

Subjects Offered

Art, history, exercise and nutrition science, music, political science, recreation, women's studies

Program Delivery

Primary method of program delivery: Web
Two-way interactive video: No
Two-way audio, one-way video: No
One-way live video: No
One-way pre-recorded video: No
Audio graphics: No
Audio: No
Is the library accessible to students? Yes
Are computers accessible to students? Yes

Remote Sites

Other branches of the institution: No
Other college campuses: No
Students' homes: Yes
Work sites: Yes
Libraries: No
Elementary/Secondary schools: No
Community-based organizations: No
Correctional institutions: No

Tuition & Fees

In-state tuition per credit: $140
Out-of-state tuition per credit: $140

Financial Aid

Is financial aid available to full-time students? Yes
Is financial aid available to part-time students? Yes
Are academic scholarships available? Yes
Assistance programs available to students: Federal Stafford

Loan, Federal Perkins Loan, Federal Plus Loan, Federal Pell Grant, Federal Work-Study Program, in-state student aid programs, veterans' assistance

San Juan College

Vice President for Learning
Learning Technology
4601 College Boulevard
Farmington, NM 87402
Contact: Ms. Ann Degner, Director of Learning Technology
Department e-mail: degner@sjc.cc.nm.us
School Web address: www.sjc.cc.nm.us
Institutional accreditation: North Central Association of Colleges and Schools

Subjects Offered

Industrial water treatment

Admissions Requirements

Is a minimum high school GPA required? No
Is an admissions interview required? No
Can pre-requisite course work be waived? No
Are international students eligible to apply? Yes
Is the TOEFL required for international students? No

Program Delivery

Primary method of program delivery: Text
Two-way interactive video: No
Two-way audio, one-way video: No
One-way live video: No
One-way pre-recorded video: No
Audio graphics: No
Audio: No
Is the library accessible to students? Yes
Are computers accessible to students? No

Remote Sites

Other branches of the institution: No
Other college campuses: No
Students' homes: Yes
Work sites: Yes
Libraries: Yes
Elementary/Secondary schools: No
Community-based organizations: No
Correctional institutions: No

On-Campus Requirements

Is an on-campus component required? No

Tuition & Fees

In-state tuition per credit: $15
Out-of-state tuition per credit: $25
Average yearly cost of books: $2,500

Financial Aid

Is financial aid available to full-time students? No
Is financial aid available to part-time students? No
Are academic scholarships available? No

Seattle Central Community College

Distance Learning
1701 Broadway, BE1148
Seattle, WA 98122
Contact: Queenie Baker, Director
Department e-mail: dislrn@sccd.ctc.edu
Department Web address: distantlearning.net
School Web address: www.seattlecentral.org

Subjects Offered

Astronomy, anthropology, business statistics, composition-English, literature, poetry, environmental science, geography, history, chemistry, intermediate algebra, meteorology, humanities, journalism, philosophy, psychology, Spanish, economics, music, accounting, introduction to business, introduction to law, oceanography, nutrition, sociology

Admissions Requirements

Is a minimum high school GPA required? No
Is provisional admission available? Yes
Is an admissions interview required? No
Can pre-requisite course work be waived? Yes
Are international students eligible to apply? Yes
Is the TOEFL required for international students? Yes

Program Delivery

Primary method of program delivery: Web
Two-way interactive video: Yes
One-way live video: Yes
One-way pre-recorded video: Yes
Audio: Yes
Hardware requirements: 486 or higher, 28KBPS modem
Software requirements: Netscape or Internet Explorer 4.0 or higher
Is the library accessible to students? Yes
Are computers accessible to students? Yes

Remote Sites

Other branches of the institution: Yes
Other college campuses: Yes
Students' homes: Yes
Work sites: Yes
Libraries: Yes
Elementary/Secondary schools: Yes
Community-based organizations: Yes
Correctional institutions: Yes

On-Campus Requirements

Is an on-campus component required? No

Tuition & Fees

In-state tuition per credit: $54
Out-of-state tuition per credit: $64
Average yearly cost of books: $600

Financial Aid

Is financial aid available to full-time students? Yes
Is financial aid available to part-time students? Yes
Are academic scholarships available? Yes
Assistance programs available to students: Federal Pell
    Grant, Federal Work-Study Program, in-state student aid
    programs, veterans' assistance

Sinclair Community College

Distance Learning
444 West Third Street
Dayton, OH 45402
Contact: Peggy Falkenstein, Dean of Distance Learning
Department e-mail: lpahud@sinclair.edu
Institutional accreditation: North Central Association
    Colleges and Schools

Subjects Offered

Accounting, allied health, art, biology, business informa-
    tion systems, computer information systems, develop-
    ment, economics, English, finance, history, humanities,
    law, literature, management, marketing, music, physics,
    psychology, sociology, safety risk management

Admissions Requirements

Is a minimum high school GPA required? No
Is provisional admission available? No
Is an admissions interview required? No
Can pre-requisite course work be waived? Yes
Are international students eligible to apply? Yes
Is the TOEFL required for international students? Yes
What is the minimum TOEFL score required? 520

Program Delivery

Two-way interactive video: Yes
Two-way audio, one-way video: Yes
One-way live video: No
One-way pre-recorded video: No
Audio graphics: No
Audio: Yes
Hardware requirements: 486 computer (or higher) or
    Macintosh equivalent, 28.8KBPS modem (or higher),
    4.0 or higher browser, 8MB of RAM (or higher), 8MB
    free hard disk space
Software requirements: Windows 3.1 or higher, an Internet
    account with access to the Web
Is the library accessible to students? No
Are computers accessible to students? No

Remote Sites

Other branches of the institution: No
Other college campuses: No
Students' homes: No
Work sites: Yes
Libraries: No
Elementary/Secondary schools: Yes
Community-based organizations: No
Correctional institutions: Yes

On-Campus Requirements

Is an on-campus component required? No

Tuition & Fees

In-state tuition per credit: $48
Out-of-state tuition per credit: $81
Average yearly cost of books: $500

Financial Aid

Is financial aid available to full-time students? Yes
Is financial aid available to part-time students? Yes
Are academic scholarships available? Yes
Assistance programs available to students: Federal Pell
    Grant, Federal Work-Study Program, in-state student aid
    programs, veterans' assistance

Skagit Valley College

Distance Education
2405 East College Way
Mount Vernon, WA 98273
Contact: Mark Veljkov, Associate Dean
Department e-mail: veljkov@skagit.ctc.edu
School Web address: svc.ctc.edu

Subjects Offered

Business administration, natural science, computer information, nutrition, computer science, office technologies, earth science, philosophy, English, physical education, Spanish, psychology, history, social science, humanities, sociology, literature, speech, math, political science, multimedia

Admissions Requirements

Is provisional admission available? Yes
Is an admissions interview required? No
Can pre-requisite course work be waived? Yes

Program Delivery

Two-way interactive video: No
Two-way audio, one-way video: No
One-way live video: No
One-way pre-recorded video: No
Audio graphics: No
Audio: No

Remote Sites

Other branches of the institution: Yes
Other college campuses: Yes
Students' homes: Yes
Work sites: Yes
Libraries: Yes
Elementary/Secondary schools: Yes
Correctional institutions: Yes

On-Campus Requirements

Is an on-campus component required? No

Tuition & Fees

In-state tuition per credit: $56
Out-of-state tuition per credit: $217

Financial Aid

Is financial aid available to full-time students? Yes
Is financial aid available to part-time students? Yes
Are academic scholarships available? Yes
Assistance programs available to students: Federal Stafford Loan, Federal Perkins Loan, Federal Plus Loan, Federal Pell Grant, Federal Work-Study Program, in-state student aid programs, veterans' assistance

Skidmore College

University Without Walls
815 North Broadway
Saratoga Springs, NY 12866
Contact: Cornel J. Reinwart, Director

Department e-mail: uww@skidmore.edu
Department Web address: www.skidmore.edu/uww
School Web address: www.skidmore.edu

Subjects Offered

American studies, history, art/art history, management/business, biology, math/computer science, chemistry/physics, music, classics, philosophy/religion, economics, psychology, English, sociology/anthropology/human services, exercise science, theatre, foreign language/literature, environmental studies, geosciences, women's studies, government/international affairs

Admissions Requirements

Is a minimum high school GPA required? No
Is provisional admission available? No
Is an admissions interview required? Yes
Can pre-requisite course work be waived? Yes
Are international students eligible to apply? Yes
Is the TOEFL required for international students? No

Program Delivery

Primary method of program delivery: Web
Hardware requirements: Varies
Software requirements: Varies
Is the library accessible to students? Yes

Remote Sites

Other branches of the institution: No
Other college campuses: Yes
Students' homes: Yes
Work sites: Yes
Libraries: Yes
Elementary/Secondary schools: No
Community-based organizations: Yes
Correctional institutions: No

On-Campus Requirements

Is an on-campus component required? Yes
On-campus admissions interview: Yes

Tuition & Fees

In-state tuition per credit: $500
Out-of-state tuition per credit: $500
Average yearly cost of books: $900

Financial Aid

Is financial aid available to full-time students? Yes
Is financial aid available to part-time students? Yes
Are academic scholarships available? Yes
Assistance programs available to students: Federal Stafford Loan, Federal Plus Loan, Federal Pell Grant, in-state student aid programs, veterans' assistance

Sonoma State University

Extended Education
Liberal Studies Degree Completion Program
1801 East Cotati Avenue
Rohnert Park, CA 94928
Contact: Beth Warner, Administrative Coordinator
Department e-mail: beth.warner@sonoma.edu
Department Web address: sonoma.edu/exed/isdcp
School Web address: sonoma.edu

Subjects Offered

Interdisciplinary liberal studies

Admissions Requirements

Is a minimum high school GPA required? No
Is provisional admission available? Yes
Can pre-requisite course work be waived? No
Are international students eligible to apply? Yes
Is the TOEFL required for international students? No

Program Delivery

Primary method of program delivery: Web
Two-way interactive video: No
Two-way audio, one-way video: No
One-way live video: No
One-way pre-recorded video: Yes
Audio graphics: No
Audio: No
Hardware requirements: Computer, modem
Software requirements: Web browser
Is the library accessible to students? Yes
Are computers accessible to students? Yes

Remote Sites

Other branches of the institution: No
Other college campuses: No
Students' homes: Yes
Work sites: Yes
Libraries: Yes
Elementary/Secondary schools: Yes
Community-based organizations: Yes
Correctional institutions: No

On-Campus Requirements

Is an on-campus component required? Yes
On-campus course work: Yes

Tuition & Fees

In-state tuition per credit: $290
Out-of-state tuition per credit: $290
Average yearly cost of books: $300

Financial Aid

Is financial aid available to full-time students? Yes
Is financial aid available to part-time students? Yes
Are academic scholarships available? Yes
Assistance programs available to students: Federal Stafford
    Loan, Federal Perkins Loan, Federal Plus Loan, Federal
    Pell Grant, in-state student aid programs, veterans'
    assistance

Southeast Community College, Academic Education

8800 O Street
Lincoln, NE 68520
Contact: Randy Hiatt, Distance Learning Director
Department e-mail: rhiatt@sccm.cc.ne.us
School Web address: www.college.sccm.cc.ne.us
Institutional accreditation: North Central Association of
    Colleges and Schools

Subjects Offered

Business administration, humanities, science, math, social
    service, health, child care, food service

Admissions Requirements

Is a minimum high school GPA required? No
Is provisional admission available? Yes
Is an admissions interview required? No
Can pre-requisite course work be waived? Yes
Are international students eligible to apply? Yes

Program Delivery

Primary method of program delivery: Remote site
Two-way interactive video: Yes
Two-way audio, one-way video: Yes
One-way live video: Yes
One-way pre-recorded video: Yes
Is the library accessible to students? Yes
Are computers accessible to students? Yes

Remote Sites

Other branches of the institution: Yes
Other college campuses: Yes
Students' homes: Yes
Work sites: Yes
Libraries: Yes
Elementary/Secondary schools: Yes
Community-based organizations: No
Correctional institutions: No

On-Campus Requirements

Is an on-campus component required? No

Tuition & Fees

In-state tuition per credit: $29
Out-of-state tuition per credit: $34

Financial Aid

Is financial aid available to full-time students? Yes
Is financial aid available to part-time students? Yes
Are academic scholarships available? Yes
Assistance programs available to students: Federal Stafford
    Loan, Federal Perkins Loan, Federal Plus Loan, Federal
    Pell Grant, Federal Work-Study Program, in-state
    student aid programs, veterans' assistance

Southeast Community College, Distance Learning

4771 West Scott Road
Beatrice, NE 68310
Contact: Neal L. Henning, PhD, Director of Distance
    Learning
Department e-mail: nhenning@sccm.cc.ne.us
Department Web address: online.scc.cc.ne.us
School Web address: www.scc.cc.ne.us
Institutional accreditation: North Central Association of
    Colleges and Schools

Subjects Offered

Psychology, ethics, sociology, computer application,
    accounting, business law, composition, literature,
    communications, speech, math, health, child care

Admissions Requirements

Is a minimum high school GPA required? No
Is provisional admission available? Yes
Is an admissions interview required? No
Can pre-requisite course work be waived? Yes
Are international students eligible to apply? Yes

Program Delivery

Primary method of program delivery: Web
Two-way interactive video: Yes
Two-way audio, one-way video: Yes
One-way live video: Yes
One-way pre-recorded video: Yes
Hardware requirements: CR-ROM, Internet access
Software requirements: CR-ROM, Internet access
Is the library accessible to students? Yes
Are computers accessible to students? Yes

Remote Sites

Other branches of the institution: Yes
Other college campuses: Yes
Students' homes: Yes
Work sites: Yes
Elementary/Secondary schools: Yes

On-Campus Requirements

Is an on-campus component required? No

Tuition & Fees

In-state tuition per credit: $29
Out-of-state tuition per credit: $34
Average yearly cost of books: $50

Financial Aid

Is financial aid available to full-time students? Yes
Is financial aid available to part-time students? Yes
Are academic scholarships available? Yes
Assistance programs available to students: Federal Stafford
    Loan, Federal Perkins Loan, Federal Plus Loan, Federal
    Pell Grant, Federal Work-Study Program, in-state
    student aid programs, veterans' assistance

Southern Illinois University Carbondale

Division of Continuing Education
Office of Distance Education
Mailcode 4311
Carbondale, IL 62901
Contact: Worthen Hunsaker, Associate Vice Chancellor,
    Academic Affairs & Research
Department Web address: www.dce.siu.edu/
    siuconnected.html
School Web address: www.siu.edu
Institutional accreditation: North Central Association of
    Colleges and Schools

Subjects Offered

Foreign language, political science, administration of
    justice, recreation, art, Russian, biology, Spanish,
    agriculture, engineering, geography, finance, philosophy,
    management, marketing, mathematics

Admissions Requirements

Is a minimum high school GPA required? Yes
Is provisional admission available? Yes
Can pre-requisite course work be waived? Yes
Are international students eligible to apply? Yes
Is the TOEFL required for international students? Yes

Program Delivery

Two-way interactive video: Yes
One-way pre-recorded video: Yes
Audio: Yes
Hardware requirements: varies with course
Software requirements: varies with course
Is the library accessible to students? Yes
Are computers accessible to students? Yes

Remote Sites

Other branches of the institution: Yes
Other college campuses: Yes
Students' homes: Yes
Work sites: Yes
Libraries: Yes
Elementary/Secondary schools: Yes
Correctional institutions: No

On-Campus Requirements

Is an on-campus component required? No

Tuition & Fees

In-state tuition per credit: $142
Application fee: $30
Can it be waived? No
Average yearly cost of books: $200

Financial Aid

Is financial aid available to full-time students? Yes
Is financial aid available to part-time students? Yes
Are academic scholarships available? Yes
Assistance programs available to students: Federal Stafford Loan, Federal Perkins Loan, Federal Plus Loan, Federal Pell Grant, Federal Work-Study Program, in-state student aid programs, veterans' assistance

Southern Illinois University Edwardsville

Admissions
Edwardsville, IL 62026
Department e-mail: admis@siue.edu
Department Web address: www.admis.siue.edu
School Web address: www.siue.edu
Institutional accreditation: North Central Association of Colleges and Schools

Admissions Requirements

Is a minimum high school GPA required? No
Is provisional admission available? Yes
Is an admissions interview required? No
Can pre-requisite course work be waived? Yes

Are international students eligible to apply? Yes
Is the TOEFL required for international students? Yes
What is the minimum TOEFL score required? 550

Program Delivery

Primary method of program delivery: Remote site
Two-way interactive video: Yes
Hardware requirements: Varies
Software requirements: Varies
Is the library accessible to students? Yes
Are computers accessible to students? Yes

Remote Sites

Other college campuses: Yes

On-Campus Requirements

Is an on-campus component required? No

Tuition & Fees

Application fee: $0
Average yearly additional fees: $72

Financial Aid

Is financial aid available to full-time students? Yes
Is financial aid available to part-time students? Yes
Are academic scholarships available? Yes
Assistance programs available to students: Federal Stafford Loan, Federal Perkins Loan, Federal Plus Loan, Federal Pell Grant, Federal Work-Study Program, in-state student aid programs, veterans' assistance

Southwest Texas State University

Office of Correspondence and Extension Studies
302 Asbnorth
601 University Drive
San Marcus, TX 78666
Contact: James Andrews, Director
Department e-mail: corrstudy@lists.ideal.swt.edu
Department Web address: www.ideal.swt.edu/correspondence
School Web address: www.swt.edu
Institutional accreditation: Southern Association of Colleges and Schools

Subjects Offered

Art and design, art theory and practice, biology, career and technology education, criminal justice, dance, English, geography, health information management, history, long-term care administration, mathematics, music, music, philosophy, political science, psychology, sociology, Spanish, theater arts

Admissions Requirements

Are international students eligible to apply? Yes
Is the TOEFL required for international students? Yes
What is the minimum TOEFL score required? 550

Program Delivery

Two-way interactive video: No
Two-way audio, one-way video: No
One-way live video: No
One-way pre-recorded video: Yes
Audio graphics: No
Audio: Yes
Is the library accessible to students? No

Remote Sites

Other branches of the institution: Yes
Other college campuses: Yes
Students' homes: Yes
Work sites: No
Libraries: Yes
Elementary/Secondary schools: No
Community-based organizations: No
Correctional institutions: Yes

On-Campus Requirements

Is an on-campus component required? Yes
On-campus course work: Yes
On-campus admissions interview: No
On-campus program orientation: No
On-campus exams: No

Financial Aid

Is financial aid available to full-time students? No

Southwestern Michigan College

Community Services
58900 Cherry Grove Road
Dowapia, MI 49047
Contact: Ilene Sheffer
Department e-mail: isheffer@smc.cc.mi.us
School Web address: www.smc.cc.mi.us
Institutional accreditation: North Central Association of Colleges and Schools

Subjects Offered

Accounting and business courses, speech and psychology

Admissions Requirements

Is a minimum high school GPA required? No
Is provisional admission available? Yes

Is an admissions interview required? No
Can pre-requisite course work be waived? Yes
Are international students eligible to apply? Yes
Is the TOEFL required for international students? No

Program Delivery

Primary method of program delivery: Text
Two-way interactive video: Yes
Two-way audio, one-way video: Yes
One-way live video: Yes
One-way pre-recorded video: Yes
Audio graphics: No
Audio: Yes
Hardware requirements: Pentiums only
Software requirements: Students must use software installed by our microcomputer resource staff, Office 98
Is the library accessible to students? Yes
Are computers accessible to students? Yes

Remote Sites

Other branches of the institution: Yes
Other college campuses: Yes
Students' homes: No
Work sites: Yes
Libraries: Yes
Elementary/Secondary schools: Yes
Community-based organizations: Yes
Correctional institutions: No

On-Campus Requirements

Is an on-campus component required? No

Tuition & Fees

In-state tuition per credit: $48
Out-of-state tuition per credit: $73
Average yearly cost of books: $1,000

Financial Aid

Is financial aid available to full-time students? Yes
Is financial aid available to part-time students? Yes
Are academic scholarships available? Yes
Assistance programs available to students: Federal Stafford Loan, Federal Perkins Loan, Federal Plus Loan, Federal Pell Grant, Federal Work-Study Program, in-state student aid programs, veterans' assistance

State University of Georgia

Distance Education Center
Honor's House
Carrouton, GA 30117
Contact: Melanie Clay
Department e-mail: distance@westga.edu

Department Web address: www.westga.edu./distance

School Web address: www.westga.edu

Institutional accreditation: Southern Association of Colleges and Schools

Subjects Offered

Education, business, nursing, political science

Admissions Requirements

Is a minimum high school GPA required? Yes

Can pre-requisite course work be waived? Yes

Program Delivery

Primary method of program delivery: Web

Two-way interactive video: Yes

Two-way audio, one-way video: No

One-way live video: No

One-way pre-recorded video: Yes

Audio graphics: No

Audio: No

Hardware requirements: Access to computer

Is the library accessible to students? Yes

Are computers accessible to students? Yes

Remote Sites

Other branches of the institution: Yes

Other college campuses: Yes

Students' homes: Yes

Work sites: No

Libraries: No

Elementary/Secondary schools: Yes

Community-based organizations: No

Correctional institutions: No

On-Campus Requirements

Is an on-campus component required? No

Tuition & Fees

In-state tuition per credit: $130

Out-of-state tuition per credit: $365

Financial Aid

Is financial aid available to full-time students? Yes

Is financial aid available to part-time students? Yes

Are academic scholarships available? Yes

Assistance programs available to students: Federal Stafford Loan, Federal Perkins Loan, Federal Plus Loan, Federal Pell Grant, Federal Work-Study Program, in-state student aid programs, veterans' assistance

State University of New York at New Paltz

Continuing and Professional Education

Extension and Distance Learning

75 South Manheim Boulevard, Suite 9

New Paltz, NY 12561

Contact: Helise Winters, Coordinator, Extensions and Distance Learning

Department Web address: www.newpaltz.edu/continuing_ed

School Web address: www.newpaltz.edu

Institutional accreditation: Middle States Association of Colleges and Schools

Subjects Offered

Anthropology, astronomy, political science, English, sociology, communication, education

Admissions Requirements

Is a minimum high school GPA required? Yes

Can pre-requisite course work be waived? Yes

Are international students eligible to apply? Yes

Is the TOEFL required for international students? Yes

Program Delivery

Primary method of program delivery: Web

Two-way interactive video: Yes

Two-way audio, one-way video: No

One-way live video: No

One-way pre-recorded video: No

Audio graphics: No

Audio: No

Hardware requirements: Pentium processor, 32MB RAM (64MB or higher preferred) 28.8KBPS modem (56KBPS preferred)

Software requirements: Windows 98, 95 or NT, Macintosh System 8 or higher

Is the library accessible to students? Yes

Are computers accessible to students? Yes

Remote Sites

Students' homes: Yes

Tuition & Fees

In-state tuition per credit: $137

Out-of-state tuition per credit: $346

Application fee: $30

Can it be waived? Yes

Average yearly cost of books: $60

Average yearly additional fees: $21

Financial Aid

Is financial aid available to full-time students? Yes

Are academic scholarships available? Yes

Assistance programs available to students: Federal Stafford Loan, Federal Perkins Loan, Federal Pell Grant, Federal Work-Study Program, in-state student aid programs

State University of New York at Oswego

Department of Communication Studies

Division of Continuing Education

35 A Lanigan Hall

Oswego, NY 13126

Contact: Michael S. Ameigh, Coordinator

Department e-mail: ameigh@oswego.edu

Department Web address: www.oswego.edu/academics/ departments/communication

School Web address: www.oswego.edu

Institutional accreditation: Higher Education Commission

Subjects Offered

History, vocational teacher preparation, economics, communication, master of business admin, psychology

Admissions Requirements

Is a minimum high school GPA required? No

Is provisional admission available? No

Is an admissions interview required? No

Can pre-requisite course work be waived? Yes

Are international students eligible to apply? Yes

Is the TOEFL required for international students? No

Program Delivery

Two-way interactive video: Yes

Hardware requirements: PC or Mac with Learning Space software and Web access.

Software requirements: Lotus Learning Space (IBM), Web browser, and Internet access

Is the library accessible to students? Yes

Are computers accessible to students? Yes

Remote Sites

Other branches of the institution: Yes

Other college campuses: Yes

Students' homes: Yes

Work sites: Yes

Libraries: Yes

Elementary/Secondary schools: Yes

Correctional institutions: Yes

On-Campus Requirements

Is an on-campus component required? No

Tuition & Fees

In-state tuition per credit: $137

Out-of-state tuition per credit: $346

Average yearly cost of books: $200

Average yearly additional fees: $30

Financial Aid

Is financial aid available to full-time students? Yes

Is financial aid available to part-time students? No

Are academic scholarships available? Yes

Assistance programs available to students: Federal Stafford Loan, Federal Perkins Loan, Federal Plus Loan, Federal Pell Grant, Federal Work-Study Program, in-state student aid programs, veterans' assistance

Strayer University

Admission

Strayer Online

PO Box 487

Newington, VA 22122

Contact: Allen Durgin, Coordinator

Department e-mail: axd@strayer.edu

Department Web address: www.strayer.edu/online/frtr.html

School Web address: www.strayer.edu

Institutional accreditation: Middle States Association of Colleges and Schools

Admissions Requirements

Is a minimum high school GPA required? No

Is provisional admission available? No

Is an admissions interview required? No

Can pre-requisite course work be waived? Yes

Are international students eligible to apply? Yes

Is the TOEFL required for international students? Yes

What is the minimum TOEFL score required? 500

Program Delivery

Primary method of program delivery: Web

Audio: Yes

Hardware requirements: 300MHz, 64MB RAM, sound card, and speakers

Software requirements: All free downloads from website

Is the library accessible to students? Yes

Are computers accessible to students? No

Remote Sites

Students' homes: Yes

On-Campus Requirements

Is an on-campus component required? No

Tuition & Fees

In-state tuition per credit: $220
Out-of-state tuition per credit: $220
Average yearly cost of books: $800

Financial Aid

Is financial aid available to full-time students? Yes
Is financial aid available to part-time students? Yes
Are academic scholarships available? Yes
Assistance programs available to students: Federal Stafford Loan, Federal Perkins Loan, Federal Plus Loan, Federal Pell Grant, veterans' assistance

Suffolk County Community College

College Instructional Technology
533 College Road
Selden, NY 11784
Contact: Donald R. Coscia, Associate Dean For College Instructional Technology
Department e-mail: cosciad@sunysuffolk.edu
Department Web address: www.sunysuffolk.edu/web/virtualcampus/
School Web address: www.sunysuffolk.edu
Institutional accreditation: Middle States Association of Colleges and Schools

Subjects Offered

Accounting, art, astronomy, business, chemical dependency, computer information systems, electronics, English, film & cinema, geology, health & nutrition, history: American & western civilization, law, management, mathematics, nursing, ophthalmic dispensing, political science, psychology, sociology, women's studies

Admissions Requirements

Is a minimum high school GPA required? No
Is provisional admission available? No
Is an admissions interview required? No
Can pre-requisite course work be waived? Yes
Are international students eligible to apply? Yes
Is the TOEFL required for international students? No

Program Delivery

Primary method of program delivery: Web
Two-way interactive video: Yes
Two-way audio, one-way video: No
One-way live video: No
One-way pre-recorded video: Yes
Audio graphics: No
Audio: No

Hardware requirements: PC with Pentium processor; 32MB of RAM; 28.8KBPS modem; Internet connection; printer
Software requirements: Windows 95 or higher; Mac System 7 or higher; Internet Explorer 4.0 or higher; word processor able to save as MS Word 6.0
Is the library accessible to students? Yes
Are computers accessible to students? Yes

Remote Sites

Other branches of the institution: Yes
Other college campuses: Yes
Students' homes: Yes
Work sites: Yes
Libraries: Yes
Elementary/Secondary schools: Yes
Community-based organizations: No
Correctional institutions: No

On-Campus Requirements

Is an on-campus component required? Yes
On-campus course work: Yes
On-campus admissions interview: No
On-campus program orientation: Yes
On-campus exams: Yes

Tuition & Fees

In-state tuition per credit: $99
Out-of-state tuition per credit: $198
Application fee: $30
Can it be waived? No
Average yearly cost of books: $600
Average yearly additional fees: $138

Financial Aid

Is financial aid available to full-time students? Yes
Is financial aid available to part-time students? Yes
Are academic scholarships available? Yes
Assistance programs available to students: Federal Stafford Loan, Federal Perkins Loan, Federal Plus Loan, Federal Pell Grant, Federal Work-Study Program, in-state student aid programs, veterans' assistance

SUNY Ulster County Community College

Cottekill Road
Stone Ridge, NY 12484
Contact: Susan Weatherly, Admissions Recruiter
Department e-mail: admissions@sunyulster.edu
School Web address: www.sunyulster.edu
Institutional accreditation: Commission on Higher Education

Subjects Offered

Psychology, sociology, English, history, math, science/
biology/chemistry, human services, business, computer
information science, computer science, philosophy

Admissions Requirements

Is a minimum high school GPA required? No
Is provisional admission available? Yes
Is an admissions interview required? No
Can pre-requisite course work be waived? Yes
Are international students eligible to apply? Yes
Is the TOEFL required for international students? Yes

Program Delivery

Primary method of program delivery: Web
Hardware requirements: Netscape Navigator 3.0 or higher
or Internet Explorer 4.0 or browser
Software requirements: None
Is the library accessible to students? Yes

On-Campus Requirements

Is an on-campus component required? No

Tuition & Fees

In-state tuition per credit: $89
Out-of-state tuition per credit: $178
Average yearly cost of books: $30

Financial Aid

Is financial aid available to full-time students? Yes
Is financial aid available to part-time students? Yes
Are academic scholarships available? Yes
Assistance programs available to students: Federal Stafford
Loan, Federal Perkins Loan, Federal Plus Loan, Federal
Pell Grant, Federal Work-Study Program, in-state
student aid programs, veterans' assistance

Sussex County Community College

Academic Affairs
1 College Hill
Newton, NJ 07860
Contact: Dr. Thomas A. Isekenegbe, Associate Dean of
Academic Affairs
Department e-mail: academicaffairs@sussex.cc.nj.us
School Web address: www.sussex.cc.nj.us
Institutional accreditation: Middle States Association of
Colleges and Schools

Subjects Offered

English composition, psychology, sociology, computer
science, website development, art appreciation, music
appreciation, economics, history, journalism, chemistry,
mathematics, astronomy

Admissions Requirements

Is provisional admission available? Yes
Is an admissions interview required? No
Are international students eligible to apply? Yes
Is the TOEFL required for international students? No

Program Delivery

Primary method of program delivery: Web
Two-way interactive video: Yes
Two-way audio, one-way video: Yes
One-way pre-recorded video: Yes
Audio: Yes
Hardware requirements: Pentium with a modem
Is the library accessible to students? Yes
Are computers accessible to students? Yes

Remote Sites

Students' homes: Yes
Elementary/Secondary schools: Yes

On-Campus Requirements

Is an on-campus component required? Yes
On-campus program orientation: Yes

Tuition & Fees

In-state tuition per credit: $68
Out-of-state tuition per credit: $140
Average yearly cost of books: $350

Financial Aid

Is financial aid available to full-time students? Yes
Is financial aid available to part-time students? Yes
Are academic scholarships available? Yes
Assistance programs available to students: Federal Stafford
Loan, Federal Perkins Loan, Federal Plus Loan, Federal
Pell Grant, Federal Work-Study Program, in-state
student aid programs, veterans' assistance

Syracuse University

Continuing Education
Independent Study Degree Program
700 University Avenue, Suite 326
Syracuse, NY 13244
Contact: Robert M. Colley, Director—Distance Education
Department e-mail: suisdp@uc.syr.edu

Department Web address: www.suce.syr.edu/distanceed
School Web address: www.syr.edu
Institutional accreditation: Middle States Association of Colleges and Schools

Subjects Offered

Liberal arts

Admissions Requirements

Is a minimum high school GPA required? No
Is provisional admission available? No
Is an admissions interview required? No
Can pre-requisite course work be waived? No
Are international students eligible to apply? Yes
Is the TOEFL required for international students? Yes
What is the minimum TOEFL score required? 600

Program Delivery

Primary method of program delivery: Text
Hardware requirements: Pentium computer preferred, 56KBPS modem
Is the library accessible to students? Yes
Are computers accessible to students? Yes

Remote Sites

Students' homes: Yes
Work sites: Yes
Libraries: Yes

On-Campus Requirements

Is an on-campus component required? Yes
On-campus course work: Yes
On-campus admissions interview: No
On-campus program orientation: Yes
On-campus exams: Yes

Tuition & Fees

In-state tuition per credit: $371
Out-of-state tuition per credit: $371
Average yearly cost of books: $300

Financial Aid

Is financial aid available to full-time students? Yes
Is financial aid available to part-time students? Yes
Are academic scholarships available? Yes
Assistance programs available to students: Federal Stafford Loan, Federal Perkins Loan, Federal Plus Loan, Federal Pell Grant, in-state student aid programs, veterans' assistance

Taylor University

College of Adult and Lifelong Learning
World Wide Campus
1025 Rudisill Road
Fort Wayne, IN 46807
Contact: Terry Wise, Vice President for Adult and Continuing
Department e-mail: wwcampus@tayloru.edu
School Web address: www.wwcampus.tayloru.edu
Institutional accreditation: North Central Association of Colleges and Schools

Subjects Offered

African American studies, biblical languages, biblical studies, business, accounting and economics, Christian education, church history, communication arts, computing and science systems, conflict management, criminal justice, education, English, fine arts, history, humanities, inter-area studies, literature, mathematics, missions, natural science, pastoral studies, philosophy, political science, psychology, religion, social sciences, social work, theology, youth ministry

Admissions Requirements

Is provisional admission available? Yes
Is an admissions interview required? Yes
Can pre-requisite course work be waived? Yes
Are international students eligible to apply? Yes
Is the TOEFL required for international students? Yes

Program Delivery

Primary method of program delivery: Text
Two-way interactive video: No
Two-way audio, one-way video: No
One-way live video: No
One-way pre-recorded video: No
Audio graphics: No
Audio: No
Hardware requirements: Pentium 100 with 16MB of RAM, Windows 95, 98, or NT, 800 x 600 monitor, or Apple Power PC
Software requirements: MS Word 97 (highly recommended)
Is the library accessible to students? Yes
Are computers accessible to students? No

Remote Sites

Other branches of the institution: No
Other college campuses: No
Students' homes: Yes
Work sites: No
Libraries: Yes

Elementary/Secondary schools: No
Community-based organizations: No
Correctional institutions: Yes

On-Campus Requirements

Is an on-campus component required? No

Tuition & Fees

In-state tuition per credit: $129
Out-of-state tuition per credit: $129
Average yearly cost of books: $1,350

Financial Aid

Is financial aid available to full-time students? Yes
Is financial aid available to part-time students? Yes
Are academic scholarships available? No
Assistance programs available to students: Federal Stafford Loan, Federal Perkins Loan, Federal Plus Loan, Federal Pell Grant, Federal Work-Study Program, veterans' assistance

Terra State Community College

Institutional Research
Educational Catalyst Center
2830 Napoleon Road
Fremont, OH 43420
Contact: Kathleen McCabe, Dean, Business, Social Sciences, Mathematics, and Arts
Department e-mail: kmccabe@terra.cc.oh.us
School Web address: www.terra.cc.oh.us
Institutional accreditation: North Central Association of Colleges and Schools

Subjects Offered

Mathematics, sociology, computer science, computer-aided design, accounting, English composition, humanities, business law, psychology, economics, French, industrial safety, music technology

Admissions Requirements

Is a minimum high school GPA required? No
Is provisional admission available? No
Is an admissions interview required? No
Can pre-requisite course work be waived? Yes
Are international students eligible to apply? Yes
Is the TOEFL required for international students? Yes

Program Delivery

Hardware requirements: Computer that supports Internet access and e-mailing

Software requirements: Microsoft Office and compatible browser
Is the library accessible to students? Yes
Are computers accessible to students? Yes

On-Campus Requirements

Is an on-campus component required? No

Tuition & Fees

In-state tuition per credit: $54
Out-of-state tuition per credit: $134
Average yearly cost of books: $825

Financial Aid

Is financial aid available to full-time students? Yes
Is financial aid available to part-time students? Yes
Are academic scholarships available? Yes
Assistance programs available to students: Federal Stafford Loan, Federal Plus Loan, Federal Pell Grant, Federal Work-Study Program, in-state student aid programs, veterans' assistance

Texas A&M University— Corpus Christi

School of Nursing
6300 Ocean Drive
Corpus Christi, TX 78412
Contact: Rebecca Jones, PhD, Professor and Director
School Web address: www.tamucc.edu
Institutional accreditation: Southern Association of Colleges and Schools

Subjects Offered

RN to BSN

Admissions Requirements

Is a minimum high school GPA required? Yes
Is provisional admission available? Yes
Is an admissions interview required? No
Can pre-requisite course work be waived? No
Are international students eligible to apply? Yes

Program Delivery

Primary method of program delivery: Remote site
Two-way interactive video: Yes
Hardware requirements: Computer (PC)
Software requirements: MS Word, e-mail address
Is the library accessible to students? Yes
Are computers accessible to students? Yes

Remote Sites

Other branches of the institution: Yes
Other college campuses: Yes

On-Campus Requirements

Is an on-campus component required? No

Tuition & Fees

In-state tuition per credit: $230
Out-of-state tuition per credit: $365
Average yearly cost of books: $250

Financial Aid

Is financial aid available to full-time students? Yes
Is financial aid available to part-time students? Yes
Are academic scholarships available? Yes
Assistance programs available to students: Federal Stafford
  Loan, Federal Perkins Loan, Federal Plus Loan, Federal
  Pell Grant, Federal Work-Study Program, in-state
  student aid programs, veterans' assistance

Thomas Edison State College

Institutional Research and Outcomes Assessment
Distance Independent Adult Learning (Dial)
101 West State Street
Trenton, NJ 08608-1176
Contact: Mr. William Seaton, Associate Vice President
Department e-mail: info@tesc.edu
School Web address: www.tesc.edu
Institutional accreditation: Middle States Association of
  Colleges and Schools

Subjects Offered

Composition, geography, art history, history, communications, political science, English literature, psychology,
  American literature, sociology, humanities, biology,
  philosophy, chemistry, religion, computer science,
  Spanish, environmental science, earth science, geology,
  anthropology, math/statistics, economics, physics,
  accounting, radiation protection, business, management

Admissions Requirements

Is a minimum high school GPA required? Yes
Is provisional admission available? No
Is an admissions interview required? No
Can pre-requisite course work be waived? No
Are international students eligible to apply? Yes
Is the TOEFL required for international students? Yes
What is the minimum TOEFL score required? 500

Program Delivery

Primary method of program delivery: Text
Two-way interactive video: No
Two-way audio, one-way video: No
One-way live video: No
One-way pre-recorded video: Yes
Audio graphics: No
Audio: Yes
Is the library accessible to students? Yes

Remote Sites

Other branches of the institution: No
Other college campuses: No
Students' homes: Yes
Work sites: Yes
Libraries: Yes
Elementary/Secondary schools: No
Community-based organizations: No
Correctional institutions: No

On-Campus Requirements

Is an on-campus component required? No

Tuition & Fees

In-state tuition per credit: $75
Out-of-state tuition per credit: $99
Average yearly cost of books: $75

Financial Aid

Is financial aid available to part-time students? Yes
Are academic scholarships available? Yes
Assistance programs available to students: Federal Stafford
  Loan, Federal Plus Loan, Federal Pell Grant, in-state
  student aid programs, veterans' assistance

Tide Water Community College

1700 College Crescent
Virginia Beach, VA 23456
Department e-mail: tcjonef@tc.cc.va.us
Department Web address: tc.cc.va.us/dl
School Web address: tc.cc.va.us
Institutional accreditation: Southern Association of
  Colleges and Schools

Subjects Offered

English, meteorology, mathematics, student development,
  sociology, music appreciation, psychology, biology,
  medical terminology, economics, history, information
  systems technology, education, business

Admissions Requirements

Is a minimum high school GPA required? No
Can pre-requisite course work be waived? Yes
Are international students eligible to apply? Yes
Is the TOEFL required for international students? Yes
What is the minimum TOEFL score required? 450

Program Delivery

Primary method of program delivery: Remote site
Two-way interactive video: Yes
Two-way audio, one-way video: No
One-way live video: No
One-way pre-recorded video: No
Audio graphics: No
Audio: No
Hardware requirements: Pentium-class computer, 28KBPS modem or faster Internet connection
Software requirements: Windows 95, 98, or NT, Word 97, e-mail, Word Perfect, web browser
Is the library accessible to students? Yes
Are computers accessible to students? Yes

Remote Sites

Other branches of the institution: Yes
Other college campuses: Yes
Students' homes: No
Work sites: Yes
Libraries: No
Elementary/Secondary schools: Yes
Community-based organizations: Yes
Correctional institutions: No

On-Campus Requirements

On-campus course work: Yes
On-campus exams: Yes

Tuition & Fees

In-state tuition per credit: $37
Out-of-state tuition per credit: $169
Average yearly additional fees: $7

Financial Aid

Is financial aid available to full-time students? Yes
Is financial aid available to part-time students? Yes
Are academic scholarships available? Yes
Assistance programs available to students: Federal Stafford Loan, Federal Perkins Loan, Federal Pell Grant, Federal Work-Study Program, veterans' assistance

Tompkins Cortland Community College

Office of Academic Planning and Research
170 North Street
PO Box 139
Dryden, NY 13053-0139
Contact: Dr. John R. Conners, Dean of Academic Affairs
Department e-mail: hammonj@sunytccc.edu
School Web address: www.sunytccc.edu
Institutional accreditation: Middle States Association of Colleges and Schools

Subjects Offered

Accounting, art, business administration, chemical dependency studies, communications, computer applications, computer information systems, computer science, English, health, hotel and restaurant management, human sexuality, mathematics, paralegal, psychology, study skills, sociology

Admissions Requirements

Is a minimum high school GPA required? No
Is an admissions interview required? No
Can pre-requisite course work be waived? Yes
Are international students eligible to apply? Yes
Is the TOEFL required for international students? No

Program Delivery

Primary method of program delivery: Remote site
Two-way interactive video: Yes
Two-way audio, one-way video: No
One-way live video: No
One-way pre-recorded video: No
Audio graphics: No
Audio: No
Hardware requirements: Pentium processor, 32MB of RAM, 28.8KBPS modem, Mac System 7 or higher
Software requirements: Netscape Navigator or Internet Explorer 4.0 or higher, PPP/SLIP connection to Internet, MS Word 6.0 or higher
Is the library accessible to students? Yes
Are computers accessible to students? No

Remote Sites

Other branches of the institution: No
Other college campuses: Yes
Students' homes: Yes
Work sites: Yes
Libraries: No
Elementary/Secondary schools: Yes
Community-based organizations: No
Correctional institutions: No

On-Campus Requirements

Is an on-campus component required? No

Tuition & Fees

In-state tuition per credit: $100
Out-of-state tuition per credit: $200
Average yearly cost of books: $400
Average yearly additional fees: $15

Financial Aid

Is financial aid available to full-time students? Yes
Is financial aid available to part-time students? Yes
Are academic scholarships available? Yes
Assistance programs available to students: Federal Stafford
Loan, Federal Perkins Loan, Federal Plus Loan, Federal
Pell Grant, Federal Work-Study Program, in-state
student aid programs

Triton College

Distance Education
2000 Fifth Avenue
River Grove, IL 60171
Department Web address: www.triton.cc.il.us/
Internet_courses
School Web address: www.triton.cc.il.us
Institutional accreditation: North Central Association of
Colleges and Schools

Subjects Offered

Graphic design, education, humanities, biology, history,
philosophy, psychology, rhetoric, sociology, social
science, speech, Spanish, accounting, anthropology, art,
business, economics, health, marketing, math, music,
political science

Admissions Requirements

Is a minimum high school GPA required? No
Is an admissions interview required? No
Can pre-requisite course work be waived? Yes
Are international students eligible to apply? Yes
Is the TOEFL required for international students? Yes
What is the minimum TOEFL score required? 500

Program Delivery

Primary method of program delivery: Web
Two-way interactive video: No
Two-way audio, one-way video: No
One-way live video: No
One-way pre-recorded video: Yes
Audio graphics: No
Audio: Yes

Is the library accessible to students? Yes
Are computers accessible to students? Yes

Remote Sites

Other branches of the institution: No
Other college campuses: No
Students' homes: Yes
Work sites: No
Libraries: Yes
Elementary/Secondary schools: No
Community-based organizations: No
Correctional institutions: No

On-Campus Requirements

Is an on-campus component required? Yes
On-campus course work: Yes
On-campus admissions interview: No
On-campus program orientation: Yes
On-campus exams: Yes

Tuition & Fees

Average yearly additional fees: $164

Financial Aid

Is financial aid available to full-time students? Yes
Is financial aid available to part-time students? Yes
Are academic scholarships available? Yes
Assistance programs available to students: Federal Stafford
Loan, Federal Pell Grant, Federal Work-Study Program,
in-state student aid programs, veterans' assistance

Troy State University Florida Region

Special Programs
PO Box 2829
Fort Walton Beach, FL 32548
Contact: Kim Brooks, Special Programs Coordinator
Department e-mail: distlearn@tsufl.edu
School Web address: www.tsufl.edu/distancelearning/
Institutional accreditation: Southern Association of
Colleges and Schools

Subjects Offered

English, math, history, business, management, computer
science

Admissions Requirements

Is a minimum high school GPA required? Yes
Is provisional admission available? Yes
Is an admissions interview required? No
Can pre-requisite course work be waived? Yes
Are international students eligible to apply? Yes

Program Delivery

Primary method of program delivery: Web
Two-way interactive video: No
Two-way audio, one-way video: No
One-way live video: No
One-way pre-recorded video: Yes
Audio graphics: No
Audio: No
Hardware requirements: Must have Internet access
Software requirements: Word processing software, MS Office
Is the library accessible to students? Yes
Are computers accessible to students? Yes

Remote Sites

Other branches of the institution: No
Other college campuses: No
Students' homes: Yes
Work sites: Yes
Libraries: Yes
Elementary/Secondary schools: No
Community-based organizations: No
Correctional institutions: No

On-Campus Requirements

Is an on-campus component required? No

Tuition & Fees

In-state tuition per credit: $110
Average yearly cost of books: $480

Financial Aid

Is financial aid available to full-time students? Yes
Is financial aid available to part-time students? Yes
Are academic scholarships available? No
Assistance programs available to students: Federal Stafford Loan, Federal Plus Loan, Federal Pell Grant, Federal Work-Study Program, veterans' assistance

Troy State University Montgomery

Office of Institutional Research and Effectiveness
Distance Learning and Extended Academic Services
PO Drawer 4419
Montgomery, AL 36103-4419
Contact: Dr. Norman Wagner, Dean
Department e-mail: edp@tsum.edu
Department Web address: www.tsum.edu/dl/
School Web address: www.tsum.edu
Institutional accreditation: Southern Association of Colleges and Schools

Subjects Offered

Art, accounting, business, biology, economics, English, geography, history, business law, management, marketing, mathematics, political science, psychology, sociology, religions, science

Admissions Requirements

Is a minimum high school GPA required? Yes
Is provisional admission available? Yes
Is an admissions interview required? No
Can pre-requisite course work be waived? No
Are international students eligible to apply? No

Program Delivery

Two-way audio, one-way video: Yes
One-way live video: Yes
One-way pre-recorded video: Yes
Software requirements: For online interactive courses: Internet and e-mail access
Is the library accessible to students? Yes
Are computers accessible to students? No

Remote Sites

Students' homes: Yes

On-Campus Requirements

Is an on-campus component required? Yes

Tuition & Fees

In-state tuition per credit: $110
Out-of-state tuition per credit: $220
Average yearly cost of books: $20

Financial Aid

Is financial aid available to full-time students? Yes
Is financial aid available to part-time students? Yes
Are academic scholarships available? Yes
Assistance programs available to students: Federal Stafford Loan, Federal Plus Loan, Federal Pell Grant, Federal Work-Study Program, in-state student aid programs, veterans' assistance

The Union Institute

Center for Distance Learning
440 East McMillian Street
Cincinnati, OH 45206
Contact: Timothy Mott, Dean
Department e-mail: tmott@tui.edu
School Web address: tui.edu
Institutional accreditation: North Central Association of Colleges and Schools

Subjects Offered

Business, social science, computer info science, history, communications, arts, health care administration, humanities, counseling, biological sciences, education, physical sciences, literature, mathematics, psychology, criminal justice, social work, public administration

Admissions Requirements

Is a minimum high school GPA required? No
Is provisional admission available? No
Is an admissions interview required? Yes
Are international students eligible to apply? Yes
Is the TOEFL required for international students? No

Program Delivery

Primary method of program delivery: Web
Two-way audio, one-way video: Yes
Audio: Yes
Is the library accessible to students? Yes
Are computers accessible to students? No

Remote Sites

Other branches of the institution: Yes
Work sites: Yes

On-Campus Requirements

Is an on-campus component required? No

Tuition & Fees

In-state tuition per credit: $272
Out-of-state tuition per credit: $272
Average yearly cost of books: $1,050

Financial Aid

Is financial aid available to full-time students? Yes
Is financial aid available to part-time students? Yes
Are academic scholarships available? Yes
Assistance programs available to students: Federal Stafford Loan, Federal Perkins Loan, Federal Plus Loan, Federal Pell Grant, Federal Work-Study Program, in-state student aid programs

Universite Laval

Direction Generale De La Formation Continue
Bureau De La Formation A Distance
Contact: Jean-Benoit Caron
Department e-mail: dglc@dgfc.ulaval.edu
Department Web address: www.ulaval.ca/dgfc
School Web address: www.ulaval.ca

Subjects Offered

Anthropolgy, management, biochemistry, marketing, biology, nutrition, communications, philosophy, counseling, financial planning, ethnology, psychology, French grammar, sociology, geography, theology, computer science, journalism

Admissions Requirements

Is a minimum high school GPA required? Yes
Is an admissions interview required? No
Are international students eligible to apply? Yes
Is the TOEFL required for international students? No

Program Delivery

Primary method of program delivery: Text
Two-way interactive video: Yes
Two-way audio, one-way video: No
One-way live video: Yes
One-way pre-recorded video: Yes
Audio graphics: No
Audio: No
Is the library accessible to students? No
Are computers accessible to students? No

Remote Sites

Other branches of the institution: No
Other college campuses: No
Students' homes: Yes
Libraries: Yes

On-Campus Requirements

Is an on-campus component required? No

Tuition & Fees

In-state tuition per credit: $56
Application fee: $30
Can it be waived? No
Average yearly cost of books: $500

Financial Aid

Is financial aid available to full-time students? Yes
Is financial aid available to part-time students? No
Are academic scholarships available? Yes

University of Alaska— Fairbanks

Center for Distance Education and Independent Learning
4280 Geist Road
Fairbanks, AK 99709
Contact: Christopher Lott, Acting Director
Department e-mail: racde@uaf.edu

Department Web address: www.dist-ed.uaf.edu
School Web address: www.uaf.edu
Institutional accreditation: Northwest Association of
Schools and Colleges

Subjects Offered

Airframe and power plant, Alaska native politics, Alaska native studies, anthropology, applied business, art/music/theatre, aviation technology, biology, business administration, computer information and office systems, computer science, drafting, early childhood development, economics, education, English, geography, Greek, health science, history, journalism and broadcasting, Latin, linguistics, library science, mathematics, philosophy, political science, psychology, sociology, statistics, women's studies

Admissions Requirements

Is a minimum high school GPA required? Yes
Is provisional admission available? No
Is an admissions interview required? No
Can pre-requisite course work be waived? Yes
Are international students eligible to apply? Yes
Is the TOEFL required for international students? No

Program Delivery

Primary method of program delivery: Text
Two-way interactive video: No
Two-way audio, one-way video: Yes
One-way live video: Yes
One-way pre-recorded video: Yes
Audio graphics: No
Audio: Yes
Is the library accessible to students? Yes
Are computers accessible to students? Yes

Remote Sites

Other branches of the institution: Yes
Other college campuses: Yes
Students' homes: Yes
Work sites: No
Libraries: Yes
Elementary/Secondary schools: Yes
Community-based organizations: No
Correctional institutions: No

On-Campus Requirements

Is an on-campus component required? No

Tuition & Fees

In-state tuition per credit: $77
Application fee: $35
Can it be waived? No

Financial Aid

Is financial aid available to full-time students? Yes
Is financial aid available to part-time students? Yes
Are academic scholarships available? Yes
Assistance programs available to students: Federal Stafford Loan, Federal Perkins Loan, Federal Plus Loan, Federal Pell Grant, Federal Work-Study Program, in-state student aid programs, veterans' assistance

University of Alaska—Southeast

Sitka Campus
Distance Education
1332 Seward Avenue
Sitka, AK 99835
Contact: Denise Blankenship, Assistant to the Director
Department e-mail: denise.blankenship@uas.alaska.edu
School Web address: www.uas-sitka.net
Institutional accreditation: Northwest Association of
Schools and Colleges

Subjects Offered

Environmental technology, computer, information office systems, human service technician, early childhood education, health information technology, business, social work, liberal arts, health information management-coding, computer information office systems

Admissions Requirements

Is a minimum high school GPA required? No
Is provisional admission available? Yes
Is an admissions interview required? No
Can pre-requisite course work be waived? No
Are international students eligible to apply? Yes
Is the TOEFL required for international students? Yes

Program Delivery

Primary method of program delivery: Remote site
Two-way interactive video: No
Two-way audio, one-way video: No
One-way live video: No
One-way pre-recorded video: No
Audio graphics: No
Audio: Yes
Is the library accessible to students? Yes
Are computers accessible to students? Yes

Remote Sites

Other branches of the institution: Yes
Other college campuses: Yes
Students' homes: Yes

Work sites: Yes
Libraries: Yes
Elementary/Secondary schools: Yes
Community-based organizations: Yes
Correctional institutions: No

On-Campus Requirements

Is an on-campus component required? No

Tuition & Fees

Average yearly cost of books: $423

Financial Aid

Is financial aid available to full-time students? Yes
Is financial aid available to part-time students? Yes
Are academic scholarships available? Yes
Assistance programs available to students: Federal Stafford Loan, Federal Plus Loan, Federal Pell Grant, in-state student aid programs, veterans' assistance

University of Baltimore

Admission Office
1420 North Charles Street
Baltimore, MD 21201
Department e-mail: admissions@ubmail.ubalt.edu
Department Web address: ubonline.edu
School Web address: www.ubalt.edu

Subjects Offered

English, communications

Admissions Requirements

Is a minimum high school GPA required? No
Is provisional admission available? No
Is an admissions interview required? No
Can pre-requisite course work be waived? Yes
Are international students eligible to apply? Yes
Is the TOEFL required for international students? Yes

Program Delivery

Primary method of program delivery: Web

University of British Columbia

Distance Education and Technology, Continuing Studies
2329 West Mall, Room 1170
Vancouver, BC, Canada V6T 1Z4
Contact: Anthony W. Bates
Department e-mail: det@cstudies.ubc.ca
Department Web address: det.cstudies.ubc.ca

School Web address: www.ubc.ca
Institutional accreditation: British Columbia Provincial Legislation

Subjects Offered

Adult education, agricultural sciences, animal science, Canadian studies, civil engineering, computer science, dental hygiene: oral biological medical science, earth and ocean science, educational studies, English, film studies, food, nutrition and health, forestry, German, history, landscape architecture, language and literacy education, library, archival and information, music, nursing, pathology, pharmaceutical sciences, philosophy, plant science, psychology, resource management and environmental studies, social work, technology-based distributed learning, urban studies, women's studies and gender relations, wood products processing

Admissions Requirements

Is a minimum high school GPA required? Yes
Is provisional admission available? Yes
Can pre-requisite course work be waived? Yes
Are international students eligible to apply? Yes
Is the TOEFL required for international students? Yes

Program Delivery

Primary method of program delivery: Text
Two-way interactive video: Yes
Two-way audio, one-way video: Yes
One-way live video: No
One-way pre-recorded video: No
Audio graphics: Yes
Audio: Yes
Hardware requirements: Pentium PC or Power PC Macintosh
Software requirements: Netscape Navigator (version 4.72 minimum)
Is the library accessible to students? Yes
Are computers accessible to students? No

Remote Sites

Other branches of the institution: No
Other college campuses: No
Students' homes: Yes
Work sites: Yes
Libraries: Yes
Elementary/Secondary schools: No
Community-based organizations: Yes
Correctional institutions: No

On-Campus Requirements

Is an on-campus component required? Yes
On-campus course work: Yes

Tuition & Fees

In-state tuition per credit: $77
Out-of-state tuition per credit: $461

Financial Aid

Is financial aid available to full-time students? Yes
Is financial aid available to part-time students? No
Are academic scholarships available? Yes

University of California Extension Online

2000 Center Street, Suite 400
Berkeley, CA 94704
Contact: Mary Beth Almeda, Assistant Dean
Department e-mail: askcmil@uclink.berkeley.edu
School Web address: learn.berkeley.edu
Institutional accreditation: Western Association of Schools and Colleges

Subjects Offered

English, film studies, history, interdisciplinary studies, languages, music, philosophy and religion, computer information systems, accounting, finance, human resources development, management, marketing, computer science and engineering, e-commerce, education, health science, high school courses, mathematics and statistics

Admissions Requirements

Is a minimum high school GPA required? No
Are international students eligible to apply? Yes
Is the TOEFL required for international students? No

Program Delivery

Primary method of program delivery: Web
Two-way interactive video: No
Two-way audio, one-way video: No
One-way live video: No
One-way pre-recorded video: Yes
Audio: Yes
Hardware requirements: Minimum 486 CPU, 16MB RAM, PowerPC with 16MB RAM
Software requirements: Netscape Navigator 4.06, either Windows 95 or Mac System 8.1

Remote Sites

Other branches of the institution: No
Other college campuses: No
Students' homes: No
Work sites: No
Libraries: No

Elementary/Secondary schools: No
Community-based organizations: No
Correctional institutions: No

On-Campus Requirements

Is an on-campus component required? No

Tuition & Fees

In-state tuition per credit: $140
Out-of-state tuition per credit: $140

Financial Aid

Is financial aid available to full-time students? No
Is financial aid available to part-time students? No
Are academic scholarships available? No

University of California, Los Angeles

Distance Learning
10995 LeConte Avenue, Room 639
Los Angeles, CA 90024
Contact: Dr. Kathleen McGuire, Manager of Distance Learning Programs
Department e-mail: kmcguire@unex.ucla.edu
Department Web address: dstlrng.unex.ucla.edu
School Web address: unex.ucla.edu

Subjects Offered

Business, finance, human resources, computer, education, writing, management, journalism, investment and securities, public relations, foreign languages, health and physical education, American history, liberal arts, mathematics, philosophy, ethics, economics, visual and performing arts, design

Admissions Requirements

Is a minimum high school GPA required? No
Is provisional admission available? Yes
Is an admissions interview required? No
Are international students eligible to apply? Yes
Is the TOEFL required for international students? Yes
What is the minimum TOEFL score required? 600

Program Delivery

Primary method of program delivery: Remote site
Two-way interactive video: Yes
Audio: Yes
Hardware requirements: Navigator 4.0 or higher web browser, any Macintosh computer with reliable access to the Internet
Software requirements: Internet Explorer 4.0 or higher or Netscape Navigator

Is the library accessible to students? No
Are computers accessible to students? No

Remote Sites

Students' homes: Yes
Work sites: Yes
Libraries: Yes
Elementary/Secondary schools: Yes

On-Campus Requirements

Is an on-campus component required? No

Tuition & Fees

In-state tuition per credit: $475

Financial Aid

Is financial aid available to full-time students? Yes
Is financial aid available to part-time students? No
Assistance programs available to students: Federal Stafford
    Loan, Federal Perkins Loan, Federal Pell Grant, in-state
    student aid programs, veterans' assistance

University of Central Florida, Department of Engineering Technology

Engineering Technology at a Distance
4000 Central Florida Boulevard
Orlando, FL 32816
Contact: Dr. Lucy Morse, Director, Engineering Technol-
    ogy at a Distance
Department e-mail: morse@mail.ucf.edu
Department Web address: www-ent.engr.ucf.edu/classes/
    distance.htm
School Web address: www.ucf.edu
Institutional accreditation: Southern Association of
    Colleges and Schools

Admissions Requirements

Is a minimum high school GPA required? Yes
Is provisional admission available? No
Is an admissions interview required? Yes
Can pre-requisite course work be waived? No
Are international students eligible to apply? Yes
Is the TOEFL required for international students? Yes
What is the minimum TOEFL score required? 500

Program Delivery

Primary method of program delivery: Remote site
One-way pre-recorded video: Yes
Hardware requirements: Refer to website distrib.ucf.edu/
    studentinfo/home.html

Software requirements: Refer to website distrib.ucf.edu/
    studentinfo/home.html

Remote Sites

Other branches of the institution: Yes
Other college campuses: Yes
Work sites: Yes

On-Campus Requirements

Is an on-campus component required? No

Tuition & Fees

In-state tuition per credit: $76
Out-of-state tuition per credit: $321
Application fee: $20
Can it be waived? No
Average yearly cost of books: $600
Average yearly additional fees: $10

Financial Aid

Is financial aid available to full-time students? Yes
Is financial aid available to part-time students? Yes
Are academic scholarships available? Yes
Assistance programs available to students: Federal Stafford
    Loan, Federal Perkins Loan, Federal Plus Loan, Federal
    Pell Grant, Federal Work-Study Program, in-state
    student aid programs, veterans' assistance

University of Central Florida, Department of Health Professions

A.A./A.S. to Bachelor of Science in Health Services
    Administration
4000 Central Florida Boulevard
Orlando, FL 32816
Contact: Dr. Dawn Oetjen, Director of Undergraduate
    Studies
Department e-mail: doetjen@mail.ucf.edu
Department Web address: cohpa.ucf.edu/health.pro.has/
    undergraduate
School Web address: www.ucf.edu
Institutional accreditation: Southern Association of
    Colleges and Schools

Admissions Requirements

Is a minimum high school GPA required? Yes
Is provisional admission available? No
Is an admissions interview required? Yes
Can pre-requisite course work be waived? No
Are international students eligible to apply? Yes
Is the TOEFL required for international students? Yes
What is the minimum TOEFL score required? 550

Program Delivery

Primary method of program delivery: Web
Hardware requirements: Refer to website distrib.ucf.edu/
studentinfo/home.html
Software requirements: Refer to website distrib.ucf.edu/
studentinfo/home.html
Is the library accessible to students? Yes
Are computers accessible to students? Yes

Remote Sites

Students' homes: Yes
Work sites: Yes
Libraries: Yes

On-Campus Requirements

Is an on-campus component required? No

Tuition & Fees

In-state tuition per credit: $76
Out-of-state tuition per credit: $321
Average yearly cost of books: $600

Financial Aid

Is financial aid available to full-time students? Yes
Is financial aid available to part-time students? Yes
Are academic scholarships available? Yes
Assistance programs available to students: Federal Stafford
Loan, Federal Perkins Loan, Federal Plus Loan, Federal
Pell Grant, Federal Work-Study Program, in-state
student aid programs, veterans' assistance

University of Central Florida, Department of Instructional Programs

Vocational Education & Industry Training Bachelor of
Science Degree
4000 Central Florida Boulevard
Orlando, FL 32816
Contact: Dr. Larry Hudson, Bachelors Degree and Initial
Certification Coordinator
Department e-mail: lhudson@mail.ucf.edu
Department Web address: reach.ucf.edu/~voced
School Web address: www.ucf.edu
Institutional accreditation: Southern Association of
Colleges and Schools

Admissions Requirements

Is a minimum high school GPA required? Yes
Is provisional admission available? No
Is an admissions interview required? Yes

Can pre-requisite course work be waived? No
Are international students eligible to apply? Yes
Is the TOEFL required for international students? Yes
What is the minimum TOEFL score required? 550

Program Delivery

Primary method of program delivery: Web
Hardware requirements: refer to website distrib.ucf.edu/
studentinfo/home.html
Software requirements: refer to website distrib.ucf.edu/
studentinfo/home.html
Is the library accessible to students? Yes
Are computers accessible to students? Yes

Remote Sites

Students' homes: Yes
Work sites: Yes
Libraries: Yes
Correctional institutions: Yes

On-Campus Requirements

Is an on-campus component required? Yes
On-campus program orientation: Yes

Tuition & Fees

In-state tuition per credit: $76
Out-of-state tuition per credit: $321
Average yearly cost of books: $600

Financial Aid

Is financial aid available to full-time students? Yes
Is financial aid available to part-time students? Yes
Are academic scholarships available? Yes
Assistance programs available to students: Federal Stafford
Loan, Federal Perkins Loan, Federal Plus Loan, Federal
Pell Grant, Federal Work-Study Program, in-state
student aid programs, veterans' assistance

University of Central Florida, Liberal Studies Program

Liberal Studies Bachelor's Degree on the Web
4000 Central Florida Boulevard
Orlando, FL 32816
Contact: Dr. Donald E. Jones, Director, Liberal Studies
Department e-mail: ls@mail.ucf.edu
Department Web address: www.cas.ucf.edu/liberal_studies/
School Web address: www.ucf.edu
Institutional accreditation: Southern Association of
Colleges and Schools

Admissions Requirements

Is a minimum high school GPA required? Yes
Is provisional admission available? No
Is an admissions interview required? Yes
Can pre-requisite course work be waived? No
Are international students eligible to apply? Yes
Is the TOEFL required for international students? Yes
What is the minimum TOEFL score required? 550

Program Delivery

Primary method of program delivery: Web
Hardware requirements: refer to website distrib.ucf.edu/studentinfo/home.html
Software requirements: refer to website distrib.ucf.edu/studentinfo/home.html
Is the library accessible to students? Yes
Are computers accessible to students? Yes

Remote Sites

Students' homes: Yes
Work sites: Yes
Libraries: Yes

On-Campus Requirements

Is an on-campus component required? No

Tuition & Fees

In-state tuition per credit: $76
Out-of-state tuition per credit: $321
Average yearly cost of books: $600

Financial Aid

Is financial aid available to full-time students? Yes
Is financial aid available to part-time students? Yes
Are academic scholarships available? Yes
Assistance programs available to students: Federal Stafford Loan, Federal Perkins Loan, Federal Plus Loan, Federal Pell Grant, Federal Work-Study Program, in-state student aid programs, veterans' assistance

University of Central Florida, School of Nursing

Web-Based RN to BSN Program
4000 Central Florida Boulevard
Orlando, FL 32816
Contact: Dr. Linda Hennig, RN-BSN Program Coordinator
Department e-mail: lindah@mail.ucf.edu
Department Web address: cohpa.ucf.edu/nursing
School Web address: www.ucf.edu

Institutional accreditation: Southern Association of Colleges and Schools

Admissions Requirements

Is a minimum high school GPA required? Yes
Is provisional admission available? No
Is an admissions interview required? Yes
Can pre-requisite course work be waived? No
Are international students eligible to apply? Yes
Is the TOEFL required for international students? Yes
What is the minimum TOEFL score required? 550

Program Delivery

Primary method of program delivery: Web
Hardware requirements: refer to website distrib.ucf.edu/studentinfo/home.html
Software requirements: refer to website distrib.ucf.edu/studentinfo/home.html
Is the library accessible to students? Yes
Are computers accessible to students? Yes

Remote Sites

Students' homes: Yes
Work sites: Yes
Libraries: Yes

On-Campus Requirements

Is an on-campus component required? Yes
On-campus program orientation: Yes

Tuition & Fees

In-state tuition per credit: $76
Out-of-state tuition per credit: $321
Average yearly cost of books: $600

Financial Aid

Is financial aid available to full-time students? Yes
Is financial aid available to part-time students? Yes
Are academic scholarships available? Yes
Assistance programs available to students: Federal Stafford Loan, Federal Perkins Loan, Federal Plus Loan, Federal Pell Grant, Federal Work-Study Program, in-state student aid programs, veterans' assistance

University of Central Oklahoma

Distance Learning Technology
Information Technology
100 North University
Edmonds, OK 73034
Contact: Sandra Thomas, Stacey Meiser

Department e-mail: distance-education@ucok.edu
Department Web address: www.ucok.edu/cyber
School Web address: www.ucok.edu
Institutional accreditation: North Central Association of
Colleges and Schools

Subjects Offered

English as a second language, library materials, statistics,
secondary schools, instructional media, Asian American
literature, occupational and technology education, world
literature, psychology of grief, modern day drama,
African art, library materials for elementary schools,
multicultural art, reference bibliography, mythology,
careers in sociology, French culture, history of rhetoric,
German literature

Admissions Requirements

Is a minimum high school GPA required? Yes
Is provisional admission available? Yes
Is an admissions interview required? No
Can pre-requisite course work be waived? No
Are international students eligible to apply? Yes

Program Delivery

Primary method of program delivery: Web
Two-way interactive video: Yes
Two-way audio, one-way video: No
One-way live video: No
One-way pre-recorded video: No
Audio graphics: No
Audio: No
Is the library accessible to students? Yes
Are computers accessible to students? Yes

Remote Sites

Other branches of the institution: Yes
Other college campuses: Yes
Students' homes: No
Work sites: Yes
Libraries: Yes
Elementary/Secondary schools: Yes
Community-based organizations: Yes
Correctional institutions: No

On-Campus Requirements

Is an on-campus component required? No

Tuition & Fees

In-state tuition per credit: $50
Out-of-state tuition per credit: $200

Financial Aid

Is financial aid available to full-time students? Yes
Is financial aid available to part-time students? Yes
Are academic scholarships available? Yes
Assistance programs available to students: Federal Perkins
Loan, Federal Pell Grant, Federal Work-Study Program,
veterans' assistance

University of Charleston

Information Technology
2300 MacCorkle Avenue Southeast
Charleston, WV 25304
Contact: Alan Belcher, Professor
Department e-mail: abelcher@uchaswv.edu
Department Web address: www.uchaswv.edu/nexus/it
School Web address: www.uchaswv.edu

Subjects Offered

English, math, information technology, social science,
business, speech

Admissions Requirements

Is a minimum high school GPA required? Yes
Is provisional admission available? Yes
Is an admissions interview required? No
Can pre-requisite course work be waived? Yes
Are international students eligible to apply? Yes
Is the TOEFL required for international students? No

Program Delivery

Primary method of program delivery: Web
Hardware requirements: PC or Mac
Is the library accessible to students? Yes
Are computers accessible to students? No

On-Campus Requirements

Is an on-campus component required? No

Tuition & Fees

In-state tuition per credit: $200
Out-of-state tuition per credit: $200
Average yearly cost of books: $200

Financial Aid

Is financial aid available to full-time students? Yes
Is financial aid available to part-time students? Yes
Are academic scholarships available? No
Assistance programs available to students: Federal Stafford
Loan, Federal Perkins Loan, Federal Plus Loan, Federal
Pell Grant, Federal Work-Study Program, in-state
student aid programs, veterans' assistance

University of Cincinnati's Raymond Walters College

Outreach & Continuing Education
9555 Plainfield Road
Cincinnati, OH 45236-1096
Contact: Dr. Susan Kemper, Assistant Dean
Department e-mail: susan.kemper@uc.edu
Department Web address: www.rwc.uc.edu./admins/oce/oce.html
School Web address: www.rwc.uc.edu
Institutional accreditation: North Central Association of Colleges and Schools

Subjects Offered

Health and lifestyles, small business, sociology of family, nutrition pathways, American cinema, business enterprise, computer survey, ESL, photographic vision, modern world history, English, word processing, computer applications, office telecommunications

Admissions Requirements

Is a minimum high school GPA required? No
Is provisional admission available? Yes
Is an admissions interview required? No
Are international students eligible to apply? Yes
Is the TOEFL required for international students? Yes

Program Delivery

Is the library accessible to students? Yes
Are computers accessible to students? Yes

Remote Sites

Other branches of the institution: Yes

On-Campus Requirements

Is an on-campus component required? Yes
On-campus course work: Yes
On-campus program orientation: Yes
On-campus exams: Yes

Tuition & Fees

In-state tuition per credit: $99
Application fee: $30
Can it be waived? Yes
Average yearly additional fees: $50

Financial Aid

Is financial aid available to full-time students? Yes
Assistance programs available to students: Federal Stafford Loan, Federal Perkins Loan, Federal Plus Loan, Federal Pell Grant, Federal Work-Study Program, in-state student aid programs, veterans' assistance

University of Delaware

Division of Continuing Education
UD Online/Distance Learning
211 John M. Clayton Hall
Newark, DE 19716
Contact: Mary Pritchard, Director
Department e-mail: continuing-ed@udel.edu
Department Web address: udel.edu/cc
School Web address: udel.edu
Institutional accreditation: Middle States Association of Colleges and Schools

Subjects Offered

Animal science, English, biological science, history, business administration, hotel, restaurant and institution management, chemistry, individual family studies, communication, comparative literature, math, music, consumer studies, nursing, economics, nutrition, education, operations research, engineering, philosophy, engineering technology, sociology, statistics, urban affairs and public policy

Admissions Requirements

Is provisional admission available? Yes
Can pre-requisite course work be waived? Yes
Are international students eligible to apply? Yes
Is the TOEFL required for international students? Yes
What is the minimum TOEFL score required? 550

Program Delivery

Two-way interactive video: Yes
Two-way audio, one-way video: Yes
One-way live video: Yes
One-way pre-recorded video: Yes
Is the library accessible to students? Yes
Are computers accessible to students? No

Remote Sites

Other branches of the institution: Yes
Other college campuses: Yes
Students' homes: Yes
Work sites: Yes

On-Campus Requirements

Is an on-campus component required? Yes
On-campus course work: Yes

Tuition & Fees

In-state tuition per credit: $188
Out-of-state tuition per credit: $533
Average yearly cost of books: $900

Financial Aid

Is financial aid available to full-time students? Yes
Is financial aid available to part-time students? Yes
Are academic scholarships available? Yes
Assistance programs available to students: Federal Stafford
   Loan, Federal Perkins Loan, Federal Plus Loan, Federal
   Pell Grant, Federal Work-Study Program, in-state
   student aid programs, veterans' assistance

University of Houston

Division of Distance and Continuing Education
4242 South Mason Road
Houston, TX 77450
Contact: Marshall Schott, PhD, Associate Director of
   Distance Learning
Department e-mail: deadvisor@uh.edu
Department Web address: uh.edu/undistance/
School Web address: uh.edu

Admissions Requirements

Is provisional admission available? No
Is an admissions interview required? No
Can pre-requisite course work be waived? No
Are international students eligible to apply? Yes
Is the TOEFL required for international students? Yes

Program Delivery

Primary method of program delivery: Remote site
Two-way interactive video: Yes
Two-way audio, one-way video: Yes
One-way live video: Yes
One-way pre-recorded video: No
Audio graphics: No
Audio: No

Remote Sites

Other branches of the institution: Yes
Other college campuses: Yes
Students' homes: Yes
Work sites: Yes
Libraries: No
Elementary/Secondary schools: No
Community-based organizations: No
Correctional institutions: No

University of Iowa

Bachelor of Liberal Studies
Center for Credit
116 International Center
Iowa City, IA 52242-1802

Contact: Wayne Prophet, Assistant Dean
Department e-mail: credit-programs@uiowa.edu
Department Web address: www.uiowa.edu/ccp
School Web address: www.uiowa.edu
Institutional accreditation: North Central Association of
   Colleges and Schools

Subjects Offered

African American studies, English, African studies, French
   and Italian geography, aging studies, German global
   studies, American studies, journalism mass communication, anthropology, linguistics mathematics, art and art
   history, political science, Asian language, rhetoric, social
   work, sociology, center for the book, Spanish, statistics,
   theater arts, classics, women studies, nursing, communication studies, public health, dance, economics

Admissions Requirements

Is a minimum high school GPA required? No
Is provisional admission available? No
Is an admissions interview required? No
Can pre-requisite course work be waived? Yes
Are international students eligible to apply? No

Program Delivery

Primary method of program delivery: Text
Two-way interactive video: No
Two-way audio, one-way video: No
One-way live video: No
One-way pre-recorded video: Yes
Audio graphics: No
Audio: Yes
Is the library accessible to students? Yes
Are computers accessible to students? No

Remote Sites

Students' homes: Yes

On-Campus Requirements

Is an on-campus component required? No

Tuition & Fees

In-state tuition per credit: $92
Out-of-state tuition per credit: $92
Average yearly cost of books: $30

Financial Aid

Is financial aid available to full-time students? No
Is financial aid available to part-time students? No
Are academic scholarships available? Yes

University of London External Programme

Information Centre(OI/Prin)
Senate House Malet Street
London, WC1E 7HU
Department e-mail: enquiries@external.lon.ac.uk
Department Web address: www.lon.ac.uk./external
School Web address: www.lon.ac.uk./external

Subjects Offered

Accounting, Italian, banking, law, computing, management, divinity, mathematics, economics, philosophy, education, politics, English, sociology, French, Spanish, geography, German, information systems

Program Delivery

Primary method of program delivery: Text

Remote Sites

Students' homes: Yes

Financial Aid

Is financial aid available to full-time students? No
Is financial aid available to part-time students? No
Are academic scholarships available? No

University of Louisiana— Monroe

Continuing Education and Distance Learning
700 University Avenue
Monroe, LA 71209
Contact: Dr. Martha Upshaw, Director
Department e-mail: ceupshaw@ulm.edu
Department Web address: ulm.edu/ced/
School Web address: ulm.edu
Institutional accreditation: Southern Association of Colleges and Schools

Subjects Offered

Biology, health and human performance, computer science, history, chemistry, pharmacy, economics, philosophy, education, psychology, English, radio/TV/film, geography, sociology

Admissions Requirements

Is a minimum high school GPA required? No
Is provisional admission available? Yes
Is an admissions interview required? No
Can pre-requisite course work be waived? Yes

Are international students eligible to apply? Yes
Is the TOEFL required for international students? Yes

Program Delivery

Primary method of program delivery: Remote site
Two-way interactive video: Yes
One-way pre-recorded video: Yes
Hardware requirements: PC with a modem
Software requirements: Dial-up connection
Is the library accessible to students? Yes
Are computers accessible to students? Yes

Remote Sites

Students' homes: Yes
Libraries: Yes
Community-based organizations: Yes

Tuition & Fees

In-state tuition per credit: $69
Out-of-state tuition per credit: $97
Average yearly cost of books: $600
Average yearly additional fees: $15

Financial Aid

Is financial aid available to full-time students? Yes
Are academic scholarships available? Yes
Assistance programs available to students: Federal Stafford Loan, Federal Perkins Loan, Federal Plus Loan, Federal Pell Grant, Federal Work-Study Program, in-state student aid programs, veterans' assistance

University of Maine—Fort Kent

Vice President for Academic Affairs
25 Pleasant Street
Fort Kent, ME 04743
Contact: Carol Browne, Vice President for Academic Affairs
Department e-mail: csbrowne@maine.maine.edu
School Web address: www.umfk.maine.edu
Institutional accreditation: New England Association of Schools and Colleges

Subjects Offered

Psychology, government, anthropology, sociology, nursing

Admissions Requirements

Is a minimum high school GPA required? No
Is provisional admission available? No
Can pre-requisite course work be waived? Yes
Are international students eligible to apply? Yes

Is the TOEFL required for international students? Yes
What is the minimum TOEFL score required? 500

Program Delivery

Primary method of program delivery: Remote site
Two-way interactive video: Yes
Hardware requirements: PC, no Macs except for Internet access
Software requirements: Netscape 4.x or Internet Explorer 4.x, MS Office or Carol Suite
Is the library accessible to students? Yes
Are computers accessible to students? No

Remote Sites

Other college campuses: Yes
Elementary/Secondary schools: Yes

On-Campus Requirements

Is an on-campus component required? No

Tuition & Fees

In-state tuition per credit: $105
Application fee: $25
Can it be waived? No
Average yearly cost of books: $500

Financial Aid

Is financial aid available to full-time students? Yes
Is financial aid available to part-time students? Yes
Are academic scholarships available? Yes
Assistance programs available to students: Federal Stafford Loan, Federal Perkins Loan, Federal Plus Loan, Federal Pell Grant, Federal Work-Study Program, in-state student aid programs, veterans' assistance

University of Maine— Machias

Behavioral Science External Degree Program
9 O'Brien Avenue
Machias, ME 04654
Contact: Dr. James R. Lehman, BEX Faculty Coordinator
Department e-mail: bexhelp@acad.umm.maine.edu
Department Web address: www.umm.maine.edu/bex1
School Web address: www.umm.maine.edu
Institutional accreditation: New England Association of Schools and Colleges

Subjects Offered

Behavioral science, psychology, sociology, anthropology, research methods

Admissions Requirements

Is a minimum high school GPA required? Yes
Is provisional admission available? Yes
Is an admissions interview required? No
Can pre-requisite course work be waived? No
Are international students eligible to apply? Yes
Is the TOEFL required for international students? Yes
What is the minimum TOEFL score required? 500

Program Delivery

Primary method of program delivery: Web
Two-way interactive video: Yes
Two-way audio, one-way video: No
One-way live video: No
One-way pre-recorded video: Yes
Audio graphics: No
Audio: No
Hardware requirements: Mac or PC with connection to Internet
Software requirements: JAVA-enabled Web browser
Is the library accessible to students? Yes
Are computers accessible to students? Yes

Remote Sites

Other branches of the institution: Yes
Other college campuses: Yes
Students' homes: Yes
Work sites: Yes
Libraries: Yes
Elementary/Secondary schools: Yes
Community-based organizations: Yes
Correctional institutions: Yes

Tuition & Fees

In-state tuition per credit: $105
Out-of-state tuition per credit: $105
Average yearly cost of books: $6

Financial Aid

Is financial aid available to full-time students? Yes
Is financial aid available to part-time students? Yes
Are academic scholarships available? Yes
Assistance programs available to students: Federal Stafford Loan, Federal Perkins Loan, Federal Plus Loan, Federal Pell Grant, veterans' assistance

University of Maine— Augusta

46 University Drive
Augusta, ME 04330
School Web address: www.uma.maine.edu

Institutional accreditation: New England Association of Schools and Colleges

Subjects Offered

Marketing

Admissions Requirements

Is a minimum high school GPA required? Yes
Is an admissions interview required? No
Can pre-requisite course work be waived? Yes
Are international students eligible to apply? Yes
Is the TOEFL required for international students? Yes

Program Delivery

Primary method of program delivery: Remote site
Two-way audio, one-way video: Yes
Is the library accessible to students? Yes
Are computers accessible to students? Yes

Remote Sites

Other branches of the institution: Yes
Other college campuses: Yes
Students' homes: Yes
Work sites: Yes
Elementary/Secondary schools: Yes

On-Campus Requirements

Is an on-campus component required? No

Tuition & Fees

In-state tuition per credit: $105
Out-of-state tuition per credit: $257
Average yearly cost of books: $16

Financial Aid

Is financial aid available to full-time students? Yes
Is financial aid available to part-time students? Yes
Are academic scholarships available? Yes
Assistance programs available to students: Federal Stafford Loan, Federal Perkins Loan, Federal Plus Loan, Federal Pell Grant, Federal Work-Study Program, in-state student aid programs, veterans' assistance

University of Maine—Orono

Continuing Education Division
Distance Education
120 Chadbourne Hall
Orono, ME 04469-5713
Contact: James F. Toner, Associate Director
Department e-mail: ceds@umit.maine.edu
Department Web address: ume.maine.edu/ced/
School Web address: www.maine.edu

Subjects Offered

Anthropology, peace studies, art history, political science, animal and veterinary science, wildlife ecology, business administration, child development, education, philosophy, English, food science and nutrition, interdisciplinary studies, geography, new media, history, nursing, Latin, modern language classics, liberal studies

Admissions Requirements

Is a minimum high school GPA required? No
Is provisional admission available? No
Is an admissions interview required? No
Can pre-requisite course work be waived? No
Are international students eligible to apply? No

Program Delivery

Primary method of program delivery: Web
Two-way interactive video: Yes
Two-way audio, one-way video: Yes
One-way live video: Yes
One-way pre-recorded video: Yes
Audio graphics: Yes
Audio: Yes
Hardware requirements: 56KBPS modem, PC or Mac
Software requirements: Quicktime, RealPlayer, Flash and Shockwave Player, Netscape Navigator

Remote Sites

Other branches of the institution: Yes
Other college campuses: Yes
Students' homes: Yes
Work sites: Yes
Libraries: Yes
Elementary/Secondary schools: Yes
Community-based organizations: Yes
Correctional institutions: Yes

On-Campus Requirements

Is an on-campus component required? No

Tuition & Fees

In-state tuition per credit: $135
Out-of-state tuition per credit: $384

Financial Aid

Is financial aid available to full-time students? Yes
Is financial aid available to part-time students? Yes
Are academic scholarships available? Yes
Assistance programs available to students: Federal Stafford Loan, Federal Perkins Loan, Federal Plus Loan, Federal Pell Grant, Federal Work-Study Program, in-state student aid programs

University of Massachusetts—Lowell

Continuing Studies and Corporate Education
Cyber Ed Program
1 University Avenue
Lowell, MA 01854
Contact: Jacqueline F. Moloney, Dean of Continuing
    Studies and Corporate Education
Department e-mail: continuing_education@uml.edu
Department Web address: cybered.uml.edu
School Web address: continuinged.uml.edu
Institutional accreditation: New England Association of
    Schools and Colleges

Subjects Offered

Computers, information systems, programming, multimedia, Web development, liberal arts

Admissions Requirements

Is a minimum high school GPA required? No
Is provisional admission available? No
Is an admissions interview required? No
Can pre-requisite course work be waived? Yes
Are international students eligible to apply? Yes
Is the TOEFL required for international students? No

Program Delivery

Primary method of program delivery: Web
Two-way interactive video: No
Two-way audio, one-way video: No
One-way live video: No
One-way pre-recorded video: Yes
Audio graphics: Yes
Audio: Yes
Hardware requirements: Pentium PC or Macintosh with
    16MB of RAM and 28.8KBPS modem
Software requirements: Netscape Navigator 4.05 or higher,
    or Internet Explorer 4.0 or higher, or AOL 4.0 or higher
Is the library accessible to students? Yes
Are computers accessible to students? Yes

Remote Sites

Other branches of the institution: Yes
Libraries: Yes

On-Campus Requirements

Is an on-campus component required? No

Tuition & Fees

In-state tuition per credit: $205
Out-of-state tuition per credit: $205

Financial Aid

Is financial aid available to full-time students? Yes
Is financial aid available to part-time students? No
Are academic scholarships available? Yes
Assistance programs available to students: Federal Stafford
    Loan, Federal Perkins Loan, Federal Plus Loan, Federal
    Pell Grant, Federal Work-Study Program, in-state
    student aid programs, veterans' assistance

University of Mississippi— Institute for Continuing Studies

Department of Independent Studies
PO Box 729
University Avenue at Grove Loop
University, MS 38677-0729
Department e-mail: indstudy@olemiss.edu
School Web address: www.ics.olemiss.edu
Institutional accreditation: Southern Association of
    Colleges and Schools

Subjects Offered

Accounting, art, biology, career education, chemistry,
    economics and finance, education, educational
    psychology, elementary education, English, family and
    consumer science, foreign languages, health and safety
    education, history, journalism, leisure management,
    library science, marketing, mathematics, philosophy,
    political science, reading education, religion, special
    education, telecommunications, wellness education

Admissions Requirements

Is a minimum high school GPA required? No
Is provisional admission available? No
Is an admissions interview required? No
Can pre-requisite course work be waived? Yes
Are international students eligible to apply? Yes
Is the TOEFL required for international students? No

Program Delivery

Primary method of program delivery: Web
Is the library accessible to students? No
Are computers accessible to students? No

On-Campus Requirements

Is an on-campus component required? No

Tuition & Fees

In-state tuition per credit: $75
Out-of-state tuition per credit: $75

Financial Aid

Is financial aid available to full-time students? Yes
Is financial aid available to part-time students? No
Are academic scholarships available? No

University of Missouri—Center for Distance Education and Independent Study

136 Clark Hall
Columbia, MO 65211-4200
Contact: Dr. Evan Smith, University and Non-credit
  Coordinator
Department e-mail: cdis@missouri.edu
Department Web address: www.cdis.missouri.edu
School Web address: www.missouri.edu
Institutional accreditation: North Central Association of
  Colleges and Schools

Subjects Offered

Accountancy, animal sciences, anthropology, astronomy, atmospheric science, biological and agricultural science, biological sciences, black studies, classical studies, communication, computer science, consumer and family economics, criminology and criminal justice, economics, education, engineering, English, entomology, geography, geological sciences, German and Russian studies, health services management, history, human development and family studies, management and marketing, rural sociology/sociology, mathematics and statistics, military science, parks, recreation and tourism, pest management, philosophy, physical education, physics, plant pathology and plant science

Admissions Requirements

Can pre-requisite course work be waived? Yes
Are international students eligible to apply? Yes

Program Delivery

Primary method of program delivery: Text
Two-way interactive video: No
Two-way audio, one-way video: No
One-way live video: No
One-way pre-recorded video: No
Audio graphics: No
Audio: Yes
Is the library accessible to students? Yes
Are computers accessible to students? No

Remote Sites

Other branches of the institution: No
Other college campuses: No
Students' homes: No
Work sites: No
Libraries: No
Elementary/Secondary schools: No
Community-based organizations: No
Correctional institutions: No

Tuition & Fees

In-state tuition per credit: $137
Out-of-state tuition per credit: $137

Financial Aid

Is financial aid available to full-time students? No
Is financial aid available to part-time students? No
Are academic scholarships available? No

University of Missouri—Columbia

MU Direct: Continuing and Distance Education
102 Whitten Hall
Columbia, MO 65211
Contact: Linda Cupp, Director
Department e-mail: mudirect@missouri.edu
Department Web address: mudirect.missouri.edu
School Web address: www.missouri.edu
Institutional accreditation: North Central Association of
  Colleges and Schools

Subjects Offered

Nursing, radiography, respiratory therapy, household hazardous waste, medical terminology, radiologic pharmacology, labor studies, medial ethics, agricultural economics, philosophy, educational statistics, library science, health reporting

Admissions Requirements

Is an admissions interview required? No
Are international students eligible to apply? Yes
Is the TOEFL required for international students? Yes

Program Delivery

Primary method of program delivery: Web
Two-way interactive video: Yes
Two-way audio, one-way video: No
One-way live video: No
One-way pre-recorded video: No
Audio graphics: No
Audio: No

Hardware requirements: PC Pentium 166 MHz, 64MB of RAM, 2GB hard drive, 28.8KBPS modem, CD-ROM drive, Windows 98, Mac with comparable features

Software requirements: Netscape 4.05, Internet Explorer 4.0, Microsoft Office software or equivalent

Is the library accessible to students? Yes

Are computers accessible to students? Yes

Remote Sites

Other branches of the institution: Yes
Other college campuses: Yes
Students' homes: Yes
Work sites: Yes
Libraries: Yes
Elementary/Secondary schools: Yes
Community-based organizations: Yes
Correctional institutions: No

On-Campus Requirements

Is an on-campus component required? Yes
On-campus course work: Yes
On-campus admissions interview: No
On-campus program orientation: Yes
On-campus exams: No

Tuition & Fees

In-state tuition per credit: $137
Out-of-state tuition per credit: $137
Application fee: $25
Can it be waived? No

Financial Aid

Is financial aid available to full-time students? Yes
Is financial aid available to part-time students? Yes
Are academic scholarships available? Yes
Assistance programs available to students: Federal Stafford Loan, Federal Perkins Loan, Federal Plus Loan, Federal Pell Grant, in-state student aid programs, veterans' assistance

University of Nebraska— Lincoln

Division of Continuing Studies
Distance Education
336 NCCE 33rd and Holdrege
Lincoln, NE 68583-9800
Contact: James E. Sherwood, Associate Dean
Department e-mail: unldde2@unl.edu
Department Web address: dcs.unl.edu
School Web address: www.unl.edu

Institutional accreditation: North Central Association of Colleges and Schools

Subjects Offered

Accounting, agricultural economics, art and art history, biological sciences, broadcasting, classics, curriculum and instruction, economics, English, family and consumer science, finance, physics, political science, psychology, geography, health and human performance, history, industrial and management systems, journalism, management, marketing, mathematics, nursing, nutritional sciences, philosophy, real estate, sociology

Admissions Requirements

Is a minimum high school GPA required? Yes
Is provisional admission available? Yes
Is an admissions interview required? Yes
Can pre-requisite course work be waived? Yes
Are international students eligible to apply? Yes

Program Delivery

Two-way interactive video: Yes
Two-way audio, one-way video: Yes
One-way live video: Yes
One-way pre-recorded video: Yes
Audio graphics: Yes
Audio: Yes
Is the library accessible to students? Yes
Are computers accessible to students? Yes

Remote Sites

Other branches of the institution: Yes
Other college campuses: Yes
Students' homes: Yes
Work sites: Yes
Libraries: Yes
Elementary/Secondary schools: Yes
Community-based organizations: Yes
Correctional institutions: Yes

On-Campus Requirements

Is an on-campus component required? No

Tuition & Fees

In-state tuition per credit: $105
Average yearly cost of books: $500

Financial Aid

Is financial aid available to full-time students? Yes
Is financial aid available to part-time students? Yes
Are academic scholarships available? Yes
Assistance programs available to students: Federal Stafford

Loan, Federal Pell Grant, Federal Work-Study Program, in-state student aid programs, veterans' assistance

University of Nevada, Las Vegas

Distance Education and Creative Services
4505 Maryland Parkway, Box 451038
Las Vegas, NV 89154-1038
Contact: Charlotte Farr, Director
Department e-mail: distanceed@ccmail.nevada.edu
Department Web address: www.unlv.edu/infotech/distance_education
School Web address: www.unlv.edu
Institutional accreditation: Northwest Association of Schools and Colleges

Subjects Offered

African American studies, art, English, hotel management, nursing, psychology, theater, anthropology, education, environmental science, business, political science, social work, history

Admissions Requirements

Is a minimum high school GPA required? Yes
Is provisional admission available? Yes
Is an admissions interview required? No
Can pre-requisite course work be waived? Yes
Are international students eligible to apply? Yes
Is the TOEFL required for international students? Yes
What is the minimum TOEFL score required? 525

Program Delivery

Primary method of program delivery: Web
Two-way interactive video: Yes
One-way pre-recorded video: Yes
Hardware requirements: Internet access, Pentium PC
Software requirements: Word processor, Netscape browser
Is the library accessible to students? Yes
Are computers accessible to students? Yes

On-Campus Requirements

Is an on-campus component required? No

Tuition & Fees

In-state tuition per credit: $78
Out-of-state tuition per credit: $159
Average yearly cost of books: $700

Financial Aid

Is financial aid available to full-time students? Yes
Are academic scholarships available? Yes

Assistance programs available to students: Federal Stafford Loan, Federal Perkins Loan, Federal Pell Grant, Federal Work-Study Program, in-state student aid programs, veterans' assistance

University of Nevada, Reno

College of Extended Studies
Independent Learning Program
PO Box 14429
Reno, NV 89507
Contact: Mrs. Kerri Garcia, Director
Department e-mail: istudy@unr.nevada.edu
Department Web address: www.dce.unr.edu/istudy/
School Web address: www.unr.edu
Institutional accreditation: Northwest Association of Schools and Colleges

Subjects Offered

Accounting, anthropology, Basque, criminal justice, curriculum and instruction, economics, educational leadership, English, environment, French, gaming management, geography, health ecology, history, human development and family studies, Italian, journalism, managerial science, mathematics, music, nutrition, political science, psychology, sociology, Spanish, western traditions, women's studies, hotel administration

Admissions Requirements

Is a minimum high school GPA required? No
Can pre-requisite course work be waived? Yes
Are international students eligible to apply? Yes
Is the TOEFL required for international students? No

Program Delivery

Primary method of program delivery: Text
Two-way interactive video: No
Two-way audio, one-way video: No
One-way live video: No
One-way pre-recorded video: Yes
Audio graphics: Yes
Audio: Yes
Hardware requirements: Computer with modem or access to the Internet (for Internet courses)
Software requirements: some form of word processing software (Word Perfect, Word, etc.), Internet access and e-mail for online courses
Is the library accessible to students? No
Are computers accessible to students? No

On-Campus Requirements

Is an on-campus component required? Yes
On-campus course work: Yes

On-campus admissions interview: No

On-campus program orientation: No

On-campus exams: No

Tuition & Fees

In-state tuition per credit: $81

Out-of-state tuition per credit: $81

Average yearly cost of books: $1,200

Financial Aid

Is financial aid available to full-time students? Yes

Is financial aid available to part-time students? Yes

Are academic scholarships available? Yes

Assistance programs available to students: Federal Pell Grant, veterans' assistance

University of New Orleans

UNO—Metropolitan College

New Orleans, LA 70148

Contact: Carl E. Drichta, Associate Dean and Director

Department e-mail: metrocollege@uno.edu

Department Web address: metrocollege.uno.edu

School Web address: www.uno.edu

Institutional accreditation: Southern Association of Colleges and Schools

Subjects Offered

Business and urban society, health services, American studies

Admissions Requirements

Is a minimum high school GPA required? Yes

Is provisional admission available? Yes

Is an admissions interview required? No

Can pre-requisite course work be waived? No

Are international students eligible to apply? Yes

Is the TOEFL required for international students? Yes

What is the minimum TOEFL score required? 500

Program Delivery

Primary method of program delivery: Text

Two-way interactive video: Yes

One-way live video: Yes

One-way pre-recorded video: Yes

Is the library accessible to students? Yes

Are computers accessible to students? Yes

Remote Sites

Other branches of the institution: Yes

Other college campuses: Yes

Students' homes: Yes

Work sites: Yes

Libraries: Yes

Elementary/Secondary schools: Yes

Community-based organizations: Yes

Tuition & Fees

In-state tuition per credit: $413

Out-of-state tuition per credit: $1,751

Average yearly cost of books: $500

Average yearly additional fees: $20

Financial Aid

Is financial aid available to full-time students? Yes

Is financial aid available to part-time students? Yes

Are academic scholarships available? Yes

Assistance programs available to students: Federal Stafford Loan, Federal Perkins Loan, Federal Plus Loan, Federal Pell Grant, Federal Work-Study Program, in-state student aid programs, veterans' assistance

University of North Carolina at Chapel Hill

Friday Center for Continuing Education

Self-paced Study Online

CB #1020 The Friday Center

Chapel Hill, NC 27599-1020

Contact: Cheryl Kemp, Associate Director of Academic Programs and Services

Department e-mail: pubpro@unc.edu

Department Web address: www.fridaycenter.unc.edu

School Web address: www.unc.edu

Institutional accreditation: Southern Association of Colleges and Schools

Subjects Offered

History, physics, psychology, sociology, African and African American studies, art, business, dramatic art, English, geography, information and library science, journalism, philosophy, political science, religion

Admissions Requirements

Is a minimum high school GPA required? No

Is an admissions interview required? No

Can pre-requisite course work be waived? Yes

Are international students eligible to apply? Yes

Is the TOEFL required for international students? No

Program Delivery

Primary method of program delivery: Web

Two-way interactive video: No

Two-way audio, one-way video: No

One-way live video: No

One-way pre-recorded video: No
Audio graphics: No
Audio: No
Hardware requirements: Computer: 486 IBM-compatible or Mac equivalent, memory: 8MB of RAM, modem: 33.6KBPS
Software requirements: Access to Internet and e-mail, Web browser equivalent to Netscape 4.61 or higher, or Internet Explorer 4.01 or higher
Is the library accessible to students? Yes
Are computers accessible to students? No

Remote Sites

Other branches of the institution: No
Other college campuses: No
Students' homes: Yes
Work sites: No
Libraries: No
Elementary/Secondary schools: No
Community-based organizations: No
Correctional institutions: No

On-Campus Requirements

Is an on-campus component required? No

Tuition & Fees

In-state tuition per credit: $63
Out-of-state tuition per credit: $130

University of North Carolina at Chapel Hill— Independent Studies

Friday Center for Continuing Education
CB #1020 The Friday Center
Chapel Hill, NC 27599-1020
Contact: Cheryl Kemp, Associate Director for Academic Programs and Services
Department e-mail: pubpro@unc.edu
Department Web address: www.fridaycenter.unc.edu
School Web address: www.unc.edu
Institutional accreditation: Southern Association of Colleges and Schools

Subjects Offered

Accounting, African studies, anthropology, art, biology, business, chemistry, classics, communication studies, economics, education, English, environmental sciences, French, geography, health administration, history, hospitality management, interdisciplinary studies, Italian, Latin, library science, marine, earth and

atmospheric science, mathematics, music, nursing, nutrition, philosophy, physics, political science, psychology, recreation administration, religious studies, Russian

Admissions Requirements

Is a minimum high school GPA required? No
Is an admissions interview required? No
Can pre-requisite course work be waived? Yes
Are international students eligible to apply? Yes
Is the TOEFL required for international students? No

Program Delivery

Primary method of program delivery: Text
Two-way interactive video: No
Two-way audio, one-way video: No
One-way live video: No
One-way pre-recorded video: No
Audio graphics: No
Audio: No
Is the library accessible to students? Yes
Are computers accessible to students? No

Remote Sites

Other branches of the institution: No
Other college campuses: No
Students' homes: Yes
Work sites: No
Libraries: No
Elementary/Secondary schools: No
Community-based organizations: No
Correctional institutions: Yes

On-Campus Requirements

Is an on-campus component required? No

Tuition & Fees

In-state tuition per credit: $52
Out-of-state tuition per credit: $110

University of North Carolina at Wilmington

Institutional Research
601 South College Road
Wilmington, NC 28403-3297
Department e-mail: manningn@uncwil.edu
Department Web address: www.uncwil.edu/oir
School Web address: www.uncwil.edu
Institutional accreditation: Southern Association of Colleges and Schools

Admissions Requirements

Is a minimum high school GPA required? Yes
Is provisional admission available? No
Is an admissions interview required? No
Can pre-requisite course work be waived? No
Are international students eligible to apply? Yes
Is the TOEFL required for international students? Yes
What is the minimum TOEFL score required? 550

Program Delivery

Primary method of program delivery: Web
Two-way interactive video: No
Two-way audio, one-way video: No
One-way live video: No
Audio graphics: Yes
Audio: Yes
Hardware requirements: PC
Software requirements: PPTFront Page, Windows,
    Explorer, SPSS, Micrographics Draw
Is the library accessible to students? Yes
Are computers accessible to students? Yes

Remote Sites

Other branches of the institution: Yes
Other college campuses: No
Students' homes: Yes
Work sites: Yes
Libraries: Yes
Elementary/Secondary schools: No
Community-based organizations: No
Correctional institutions: No

On-Campus Requirements

Is an on-campus component required? Yes
On-campus course work: Yes
On-campus admissions interview: No
On-campus program orientation: Yes
On-campus exams: Yes

Tuition & Fees

In-state tuition per credit: $1,102
Out-of-state tuition per credit: $8,452
Average yearly cost of books: $750

Financial Aid

Is financial aid available to full-time students? Yes
Is financial aid available to part-time students? Yes
Are academic scholarships available? Yes
Assistance programs available to students: Federal Stafford
    Loan, Federal Perkins Loan, Federal Plus Loan, Federal
    Pell Grant, Federal Work-Study Program, in-state
    student aid programs, veterans' assistance

University of Northern Iowa

Continuing Education
Bachelor of Liberal Studies Program
132 SHC
Cedar Falls, IA 50614-0223
Contact: Michelle Clark, Coordinator/Advisor
Department e-mail: michelle.clark@uni.edu
Department Web address: www.edu/contined/cp/
    degreeprogs/ugraddegrees/blsdegree.html
School Web address: www.uni.edu
Institutional accreditation: North Central Association of
    Colleges and Schools

Subjects Offered

Accounting, communication studies, design, family and
    consumer sciences, economics, educational psychology,
    education, English, geography, health, history, humani-
    ties, management, marketing, mathematics, music,
    political science, psychology, religion, social science,
    social work, sociology

Admissions Requirements

Is a minimum high school GPA required? Yes
Is provisional admission available? No
Is an admissions interview required? No
Can pre-requisite course work be waived? No
Are international students eligible to apply? Yes
Is the TOEFL required for international students? Yes

Program Delivery

Primary method of program delivery: Text
Is the library accessible to students? Yes
Are computers accessible to students? Yes

Remote Sites

Students' homes: Yes

On-Campus Requirements

Is an on-campus component required? No

Tuition & Fees

In-state tuition per credit: $92
Out-of-state tuition per credit: $92

Financial Aid

Is financial aid available to full-time students? No
Is financial aid available to part-time students? No
Are academic scholarships available? No

University of Northwestern Ohio

College of Distance Learning
1441 North Cable Road
Lima, OH 45805
Contact: Cheryl Mueller, PhD, Vice President for
Academic Affairs
Department e-mail: jlmarkha@unoh.edu
Department Web address: www2.unoh.edu
School Web address: www.unoh.edu
Institutional accreditation: North Central Association of
Colleges and Schools

Subjects Offered

Accounting, business, office technology, health care

Admissions Requirements

Is a minimum high school GPA required? No
Is provisional admission available? Yes
Is an admissions interview required? No
Can pre-requisite course work be waived? Yes
Are international students eligible to apply? Yes
Is the TOEFL required for international students? Yes
What is the minimum TOEFL score required? 500

Program Delivery

Primary method of program delivery: Web
Two-way interactive video: No
Two-way audio, one-way video: No
One-way live video: Yes
One-way pre-recorded video: No
Audio graphics: No
Audio: Yes
Hardware requirements: Pentium or equivalent processor,
32MB of RAM, display capable of 640 x 480 pixels with
16 million colors, CD-ROM drive, sound card with
speakers, 28.8KBPS modem
Software requirements: Windows 3.1/MacOS (95/98/NT/
2000 recommended), recent browser-Netscape/Internet
Explorer 4.0 or later, Real Audio player, Microsoft Office
2000
Is the library accessible to students? Yes
Are computers accessible to students? Yes

Remote Sites

Other branches of the institution: No
Other college campuses: No
Students' homes: No
Work sites: No
Libraries: Yes
Elementary/Secondary schools: Yes

Community-based organizations: No
Correctional institutions: No

On-Campus Requirements

Is an on-campus component required? No

Tuition & Fees

In-state tuition per credit: $170
Out-of-state tuition per credit: $170
Average yearly cost of books: $50

Financial Aid

Is financial aid available to full-time students? Yes
Is financial aid available to part-time students? Yes
Are academic scholarships available? Yes
Assistance programs available to students: Federal Stafford
Loan, Federal Plus Loan, Federal Pell Grant, Federal
Work-Study Program, in-state student aid programs,
veterans' assistance

University of Oregon

Continuing Education
1277 University of Oregon
Eugene, OR 97403-1277
Contact: Sandra Gladney, Program Coordinator
Department e-mail: dasst@continue.uoregon.edu
Department Web address: de.uoregon.edu
School Web address: www.uoregon.edu
Institutional accreditation: Northwest Association of
Schools and Colleges

Subjects Offered

Astronomy, physics, geology, oceanography, art and gender,
art and human values, political science, economics,
linguistics

Financial Aid

Is financial aid available to full-time students? Yes
Is financial aid available to part-time students? No

University of Pennsylvania

College of General Studies
PennAdvance Program
3440 Market Street, Suite 100
Philadelphia, PA 19104-3335
Contact: Dr. Jean L. Scholz, Director of Distributed
Learning
Department e-mail: advance@sas.upenn.edu
Department Web address: www.advance.upenn.edu
School Web address: www.upenn.edu

Institutional accreditation: Middle States Association of Colleges and Schools

Subjects Offered

Anthroplogy, biology, economics, English, environmental studies, geology, mathematics, physics, psychology, sociology, statistics, theater arts

Admissions Requirements

Is a minimum high school GPA required? Yes
Is provisional admission available? No
Is an admissions interview required? No
Can pre-requisite course work be waived? No
Are international students eligible to apply? Yes
Is the TOEFL required for international students? No

Program Delivery

Two-way interactive video: No
Two-way audio, one-way video: No
One-way live video: Yes
One-way pre-recorded video: Yes
Audio graphics: No
Audio: Yes
Hardware requirements: Windows 95, 98, NT, MacOS 7.5.1, Pentium 120 MHz, 32MB of RAM, sound card and speakers
Software requirements: Internet Explorer or Netscape Navigator, RealPlayer, cookies, JAVA, JAVAscript, Shockwave Flash, modem
Is the library accessible to students? Yes
Are computers accessible to students? Yes

Remote Sites

Other branches of the institution: No
Other college campuses: No
Students' homes: Yes
Work sites: Yes
Libraries: Yes
Elementary/Secondary schools: No
Community-based organizations: No

On-Campus Requirements

Is an on-campus component required? No

Tuition & Fees

In-state tuition per credit: $1,100
Application fee: $55
Can it be waived? No
Average yearly cost of books: $100

Financial Aid

Is financial aid available to full-time students? No
Is financial aid available to part-time students? No
Are academic scholarships available? No

University of Phoenix Online

3157 East Elwood Street
Phoenix, AZ 85034
Contact: Michael Berkowitz, National Director of Enrollment
Department e-mail: online@gpollogrp.edu
School Web address: online.uophx.edu
Institutional accreditation: North Central Association of Colleges and Schools

Subjects Offered

Business, management, technology management, information systems, education, nursing, accounting, e-business, information technology

Admissions Requirements

Is a minimum high school GPA required? No
Is provisional admission available? Yes
Is an admissions interview required? No
Can pre-requisite course work be waived? Yes
Are international students eligible to apply? Yes
Is the TOEFL required for international students? Yes
What is the minimum TOEFL score required? 580

Program Delivery

Primary method of program delivery: Web
Hardware requirements: Pentium or better with at least 32MB of RAM, 1.5 GB or larger hard drive, SVGA monitor, Internet connection of 28.8KBPS or faster
Software requirements: Windows 95 or better, browser and e-mail software are provided by University of Phoenix Online
Is the library accessible to students? Yes
Are computers accessible to students? No

On-Campus Requirements

Is an on-campus component required? No

Tuition & Fees

In-state tuition per credit: $390
Application fee: $85
Can it be waived? No
Average yearly cost of books: $900

Financial Aid

Is financial aid available to full-time students? Yes
Is financial aid available to part-time students? No
Are academic scholarships available? Yes
Assistance programs available to students: Federal Stafford Loan, Federal Perkins Loan, Federal Plus Loan, Federal Pell Grant, veterans' assistance

University of Pittsburgh

University External Studies Program
4200 Fifth Avenue, Room 411
Pittsburgh, PA 15260
Contact: Laurie Petty, Manager, Extension Studies
Department e-mail: cgs@pitt.edu
Department Web address: www.pitt.edu/~cgs/
School Web address: www.pitt.edu
Institutional accreditation: Middle States Association of
Colleges and Schools

Subjects Offered

Administration of justice, anthropology, astronomy,
classics, communication, communicative science
disorders, dental hygiene, economics, English, statistics,
theatre arts, geology, German, history, legal studies,
mathematics, nursing, philosophy, political science,
psychology, public administration, religious studies

Admissions Requirements

Is a minimum high school GPA required? No
Is provisional admission available? Yes
Is an admissions interview required? No
Can pre-requisite course work be waived? Yes
Are international students eligible to apply? Yes
Is the TOEFL required for international students? Yes

Program Delivery

Primary method of program delivery: Text
Two-way interactive video: Yes
Is the library accessible to students? Yes
Are computers accessible to students? Yes

Remote Sites

Other branches of the institution: Yes
Other college campuses: Yes
Community-based organizations: Yes

On-Campus Requirements

Is an on-campus component required? Yes

Tuition & Fees

In-state tuition per credit: $222
Out-of-state tuition per credit: $481
Average yearly cost of books: $35

Financial Aid

Is financial aid available to full-time students? Yes
Is financial aid available to part-time students? Yes
Are academic scholarships available? Yes
Assistance programs available to students: Federal Stafford
Loan, Federal Perkins Loan, Federal Pell Grant, Federal
Work-Study Program, in-state student aid programs,
veterans' assistance

University of St. Francis

500 North Wilcox Street
Joliet, IL 60435
Department Web address: www.stfrancis.edu/online/
index.html
School Web address: www.stfrancis.edu
Institutional accreditation: North Central Association of
Colleges and Schools

Admissions Requirements

Is a minimum high school GPA required? Yes
Is provisional admission available? No
Is an admissions interview required? No
Can pre-requisite course work be waived? Yes
Are international students eligible to apply? Yes
Is the TOEFL required for international students? Yes
What is the minimum TOEFL score required? 550

Program Delivery

Primary method of program delivery: Web
Hardware requirements: IBM-compatible 100 MHz
processor, 56KBPS modem
Software requirements: Office 97
Is the library accessible to students? Yes
Are computers accessible to students? Yes

On-Campus Requirements

Is an on-campus component required? No

Tuition & Fees

In-state tuition per credit: $425
Out-of-state tuition per credit: $425
Average yearly cost of books: $850

Financial Aid

Is financial aid available to full-time students? Yes
Is financial aid available to part-time students? No
Are academic scholarships available? Yes
Assistance programs available to students: Federal Stafford
Loan, Federal Perkins Loan, Federal Plus Loan, Federal
Pell Grant, in-state student aid programs, veterans'
assistance

University of Southern Colorado

Division of Continuing Education
External Degree Department
2200 Bonforte Boulevard
Pueblo, CO 81001-4901
Contact: Roger E. Stubenrouch, Director, Continuing
 Education
Department e-mail: coned@uscolo.edu
Department Web address: www.uscolo.edu/coned
School Web address: www.uscolo.edu
Institutional accreditation: North Central Association of
 Colleges and Schools

Subjects Offered

Anthropology, biology, business administration, chemistry,
 art, psychology, sociology, management, history, political
 science, nursing, social work, economics, geography,
 geology, marketing, mathematics, English, education

Admissions Requirements

Is provisional admission available? No
Is an admissions interview required? No
Can pre-requisite course work be waived? No
Are international students eligible to apply? Yes
Is the TOEFL required for international students? Yes
What is the minimum TOEFL score required? 500

Program Delivery

Primary method of program delivery: Text
One-way pre-recorded video: Yes
Audio: No
Software requirements: MS Word, Excel, PowerPoint
 required of all students
Is the library accessible to students? Yes
Are computers accessible to students? No

Remote Sites

Other college campuses: Yes
Work sites: Yes

On-Campus Requirements

Is an on-campus component required? No

Tuition & Fees

In-state tuition per credit: $80
Out-of-state tuition per credit: $80
Average yearly cost of books: $650

Financial Aid

Is financial aid available to full-time students? No
Is financial aid available to part-time students? No
Are academic scholarships available? No

University of Southern Indiana

Distance Education
USI Learning Network
8600 University Boulevard
Evansville, IN 47712
Contact: Karen H. Bonnell, PhD, Manager of Instruc-
 tional Technology Services
Department Web address: www.usi.edu/distance
School Web address: www.usi.edu
Institutional accreditation: North Central Association of
 Colleges and Schools

Subjects Offered

Communication, business, psychology, political science,
 advertising, public relations, education, science
 (biology), nursing, health professions, English

Admissions Requirements

Is a minimum high school GPA required? Yes
Is provisional admission available? Yes
Is an admissions interview required? No
Can pre-requisite course work be waived? No
Are international students eligible to apply? Yes
Is the TOEFL required for international students? Yes

Program Delivery

Primary method of program delivery: Web
Two-way interactive video: Yes
Two-way audio, one-way video: Yes
One-way live video: No
One-way pre-recorded video: Yes
Audio graphics: No
Audio: No
Is the library accessible to students? Yes
Are computers accessible to students? Yes

Remote Sites

Other branches of the institution: No
Other college campuses: Yes
Students' homes: Yes
Work sites: Yes
Libraries: Yes
Elementary/Secondary schools: Yes
Community-based organizations: Yes
Correctional institutions: No

On-Campus Requirements

Is an on-campus component required? Yes
On-campus course work: Yes
On-campus admissions interview: Yes
On-campus program orientation: Yes
On-campus exams: Yes

Tuition & Fees

In-state tuition per credit: $97
Out-of-state tuition per credit: $238
Average yearly cost of books: $500

Financial Aid

Is financial aid available to full-time students? Yes
Is financial aid available to part-time students? Yes
Are academic scholarships available? Yes
Assistance programs available to students: Federal Stafford Loan, Federal Perkins Loan, Federal Plus Loan, Federal Pell Grant, Federal Work-Study Program, in-state student aid programs, veterans' assistance

University of Southern Mississippi

Continuing Education and Distance Learning
Box 5136
Hattiesburg, MS 39406-5136
Contact: Sue Pace, Director
Department e-mail: distance.learning@usm.edu
Department Web address: dl.cice.usm.edu
School Web address: www.usm.edu
Institutional accreditation: Southern Association of Colleges and Schools

Subjects Offered

Adult education, child development, community health, English, environmental science, family studies, geography, human performance and recreation, management, management information systems, nutrition and food science, nursing, philosophy, research and foundations, software engineering technology, speech and hearing sciences, special education, technical and occupational education

Admissions Requirements

Is provisional admission available? Yes
Is an admissions interview required? No
Can pre-requisite course work be waived? No
Are international students eligible to apply? Yes
Is the TOEFL required for international students? Yes
What is the minimum TOEFL score required? 525

Program Delivery

Primary method of program delivery: Web
Two-way interactive video: No
Two-way audio, one-way video: No
One-way live video: No
One-way pre-recorded video: No
Audio graphics: No
Audio: No
Hardware requirements: Pentium 90 MHz processor, 32 MB of RAM, 2 GHz hard drive, monitor, sound card, CD-ROM, speakers. Apple Mac: Power PC with 32 MB of RAM and 2GHz hard drive
Is the library accessible to students? Yes
Are computers accessible to students? Yes

Remote Sites

Other branches of the institution: Yes
Other college campuses: Yes
Students' homes: Yes
Work sites: Yes
Libraries: Yes
Elementary/Secondary schools: Yes
Community-based organizations: Yes
Correctional institutions: Yes

Tuition & Fees

In-state tuition per credit: $124
Out-of-state tuition per credit: $288

Financial Aid

Is financial aid available to full-time students? Yes
Is financial aid available to part-time students? Yes
Are academic scholarships available? Yes
Assistance programs available to students: Federal Stafford Loan, Federal Perkins Loan, Federal Plus Loan, Federal Pell Grant, Federal Work-Study Program, in-state student aid programs, veterans' assistance

University of Texas at Austin

Continuing and Extended Education
Distance Education Center
PO Box 7700
Austin, TX 78713-7700
Contact: Susan Toalson, Assistant Director
Department e-mail: dec@utexas.edu
Department Web address: www.utexas.edu/cee/dec
School Web address: www.utexas.edu

Subjects Offered

Anthropology, astronomy, biology, business, curriculum and instruction, Czech, economics, French, geography,

German, government, history, kinesiology and health education, Latin, mathematics, nutrition, philosophy, physics, psychology, religious studies, rhetoric and composition, social work, sociology, Spanish, statistics, women's studies

Admissions Requirements

Is a minimum high school GPA required? No
Is an admissions interview required? No
Are international students eligible to apply? Yes
Is the TOEFL required for international students? No

Program Delivery

Primary method of program delivery: Text
Audio: Yes

Remote Sites

Other branches of the institution: Yes
Students' homes: Yes
Community-based organizations: Yes
Correctional institutions: Yes

On-Campus Requirements

Is an on-campus component required? No

Tuition & Fees

In-state tuition per credit: $83

University of Toledo

Division of Distance Learning
2801 West Bancroft
Toledo, OH 43606
Contact: Dr. Karen Rhoda, Interim Director of Distance Learning
Department e-mail: utdl@utoledo.edu
Department Web address: www.ucollege.utoledo.edu/dislrn/htm
School Web address: www.utoledo.edu

Subjects Offered

Business technology, marketing, political science, psychology, nutrition, German, Spanish, history, African studies, engineering, computer science and engineering technology, geography, health education, humanities, legal assisting, mathematics, philosophy/religion, respiratory care, special education, computer applications, communication, economics, social work, physics, adult liberal studies, curriculum instruction, education technology, theory and social foundations

Admissions Requirements

Is provisional admission available? Yes
Is an admissions interview required? No
Are international students eligible to apply? Yes
Is the TOEFL required for international students? Yes

Program Delivery

Primary method of program delivery: Web
Two-way interactive video: Yes
Two-way audio, one-way video: No
One-way live video: No
One-way pre-recorded video: Yes
Audio graphics: No
Audio: No
Hardware requirements: 486 processor or better, 100 MHz processor, 16MB RAM, 28.8KBPS modem
Software requirements: Windows 95, 98, or NT, or Mac equivalent

Remote Sites

Other branches of the institution: Yes
Other college campuses: Yes
Students' homes: Yes
Work sites: Yes
Libraries: Yes
Elementary/Secondary schools: Yes
Community-based organizations: Yes
Correctional institutions: No

On-Campus Requirements

Is an on-campus component required? No

Tuition & Fees

In-state tuition per credit: $159
Out-of-state tuition per credit: $441
Application fee: $30

Financial Aid

Is financial aid available to full-time students? Yes
Is financial aid available to part-time students? Yes
Are academic scholarships available? Yes
Assistance programs available to students: Federal Stafford Loan, Federal Perkins Loan, Federal Plus Loan, Federal Pell Grant, Federal Work-Study Program, in-state student aid programs, veterans' assistance

University of Toronto School of Continuing Studies

Business and Professional Studies
158 St. George Street
Toronto, Ontario, Canada M5S 2V8
Contact: Hoa Trinh, Senior Coordinator
School Web address: www.learn.utoronto.ca

Subjects Offered

Accounting and finance, business management, business law and taxation, human resources management, marketing, risk management

Admissions Requirements

Is a minimum high school GPA required? No
Is an admissions interview required? No
Are international students eligible to apply? Yes
Is the TOEFL required for international students? No

Program Delivery

Primary method of program delivery: Text
Two-way interactive video: No
Two-way audio, one-way video: No
One-way live video: No
One-way pre-recorded video: No
Audio graphics: No
Audio: Yes
Is the library accessible to students? No
Are computers accessible to students? No

Remote Sites

Other branches of the institution: No
Other college campuses: No
Students' homes: No
Work sites: No
Libraries: No
Elementary/Secondary schools: No
Community-based organizations: No
Correctional institutions: No

On-Campus Requirements

Is an on-campus component required? Yes
On-campus course work: No
On-campus admissions interview: No
On-campus program orientation: No
On-campus exams: Yes

Tuition & Fees

In-state tuition per credit: $455
Out-of-state tuition per credit: $555

Financial Aid

Is financial aid available to full-time students? No
Is financial aid available to part-time students? No
Are academic scholarships available? No

University of Utah— Academic Outreach & Continuing Education

Distance Education
1905 East South Campus Drive
Salt Lake City, UT 84112-9359
Contact: Robert Merrills, Program Director
Department e-mail: industry@acoce.utah.edu
School Web address: www.utah.edu
Institutional accreditation: Northwest Association of Schools and Colleges

Subjects Offered

Anthropology, gerontology, art, history, biology, mathematics, chemistry, meteorology, communications, music, economics, physics, educational studies, political studies, English, psychology, finance, foods and nutrition, geography

Admissions Requirements

Is a minimum high school GPA required? No
Can pre-requisite course work be waived? No
Are international students eligible to apply? Yes
Is the TOEFL required for international students? No

Program Delivery

Primary method of program delivery: Text
Two-way interactive video: No
Two-way audio, one-way video: No
One-way live video: No
One-way pre-recorded video: No
Audio graphics: No
Audio: No
Software requirements: Microsoft Word or Word Perfect
Is the library accessible to students? Yes
Are computers accessible to students? Yes

Remote Sites

Other branches of the institution: Yes
Other college campuses: Yes

On-Campus Requirements

Is an on-campus component required? No

Tuition & Fees

In-state tuition per credit: $85
Out-of-state tuition per credit: $85

Financial Aid

Is financial aid available to full-time students? No
Is financial aid available to part-time students? No
Are academic scholarships available? No

University of Windsor

Student Information Resource Center
401 Sunset Avenue
Windsor, Ontario, N9B3P4
Department e-mail: askme@uwindsor.ca
Department Web address: uwindsor.ca/coned/depro.html
School Web address: uwindsor.ca
Institutional accreditation: Association of Universities and Colleges of Canada

Subjects Offered

English, chemistry, philosophy, computer science, social science, geology, economics, mathematics, political science, nursing, women's studies, statistics, psychology, accounting, social work, management and labor studies, sociology, finance, science, management and science, biology, marketing, business strategy and entrepreneurship

Admissions Requirements

Is a minimum high school GPA required? Yes
Is provisional admission available? No
Is an admissions interview required? No
Can pre-requisite course work be waived? Yes
Are international students eligible to apply? Yes
Is the TOEFL required for international students? Yes
What is the minimum TOEFL score required? 550

Program Delivery

Primary method of program delivery: Text
Two-way interactive video: Yes
One-way pre-recorded video: Yes
Audio: Yes
Hardware requirements: 486 or higher IBM compatible computer w/CD-ROM
Software requirements: Windows 95 or 98, e-mail programs, Netscape 4.x or Microsoft Internet Explorer 4.x
Is the library accessible to students? Yes

Remote Sites

Other branches of the institution: No
Other college campuses: Yes
Students' homes: Yes
Work sites: Yes
Libraries: Yes
Elementary/Secondary schools: No
Community-based organizations: Yes
Correctional institutions: Yes

Financial Aid

Is financial aid available to full-time students? Yes
Is financial aid available to part-time students? No
Are academic scholarships available? Yes
Assistance programs available to students: Federal Stafford Loan, veterans' assistance

University of Wisconsin— Milwaukee

Distance Learning & Instructional Support
PO Box 413
Milwaukee, WI 53201
Contact: Nancy Morris, Manager, Distance Learning & Instructional Support
Department Web address: www.uwm.edu/universityoutreach/deuwm
School Web address: www.uwm.edu

Subjects Offered

Nursing, education, information resources, architecture, allied health, communications, foreign languages, business and management

Admissions Requirements

Is a minimum high school GPA required? No
Is provisional admission available? Yes
Can pre-requisite course work be waived? Yes
Are international students eligible to apply? Yes
Is the TOEFL required for international students? Yes
What is the minimum TOEFL score required? 500

Program Delivery

Two-way interactive video: Yes
Two-way audio, one-way video: Yes
One-way live video: Yes
One-way pre-recorded video: Yes
Audio graphics: Yes
Audio: Yes
Hardware requirements: PC/Mac, 33.6KBPS modem, sound card
Software requirements: Depends on department/program generally MS Office, Netscape or Internet Explorer
Is the library accessible to students? Yes
Are computers accessible to students? No

Remote Sites

Other branches of the institution: Yes
Other college campuses: Yes
Students' homes: Yes
Work sites: Yes
Libraries: Yes
Elementary/Secondary schools: Yes
Community-based organizations: Yes

Tuition & Fees

Average yearly cost of books: $600

Financial Aid

Is financial aid available to full-time students? Yes
Is financial aid available to part-time students? Yes
Are academic scholarships available? Yes
Assistance programs available to students: Federal Stafford
Loan, Federal Perkins Loan, Federal Plus Loan, Federal
Pell Grant, Federal Work-Study Program, in-state
student aid programs, veterans' assistance

University of Wisconsin— Platteville

Distance Learning Center
B12 Karrmann Library
1 University Plaza
Platteville, WI 53818
Department e-mail: disted@uwplatt.edu
Department Web address: www.uwplatt.edu/~disted
School Web address: www.uwplatt.edu
Institutional accreditation: North Central Association of
Colleges and Schools

Subjects Offered

Accounting, art, business administration, computer
science, economics, geography, industrial studies,
marketing, mathematics, psychology, speech

Admissions Requirements

Is a minimum high school GPA required? Yes
Is provisional admission available? Yes
Is an admissions interview required? No
Can pre-requisite course work be waived? No
Are international students eligible to apply? Yes
Is the TOEFL required for international students? Yes
What is the minimum TOEFL score required? 500

Program Delivery

Primary method of program delivery: Text
Hardware requirements: see requirements at
www.uwplatt.edu/~disted

Software requirements: see requirements at
www.uwplatt.edu/~disted
Is the library accessible to students? Yes
Are computers accessible to students? No

Remote Sites

Students' homes: Yes
Work sites: Yes

On-Campus Requirements

Is an on-campus component required? No

Tuition & Fees

Application fee: $35
Can it be waived? No
Average yearly cost of books: $75
Average yearly additional fees: $100

Financial Aid

Is financial aid available to full-time students? Yes
Is financial aid available to part-time students? Yes
Are academic scholarships available? Yes
Assistance programs available to students: Federal Stafford
Loan, Federal Plus Loan, Federal Pell Grant, in-state
student aid programs, veterans' assistance

Upper Iowa University

External Degree
PO Box 1861
Fayette, IA 52142-1860
Contact: Barbara J. Schultz, Director of External Degree
Department e-mail: extdegree@uiu.edu
School Web address: www.uiu.edu
Institutional accreditation: North Central Association of
Colleges and Schools

Subjects Offered

Art, mathematics, biology, physical science, business
administration, political science, communications,
public administration, English, psychology, history,
sociology, management information systems

Admissions Requirements

Is a minimum high school GPA required? No
Is an admissions interview required? No
Are international students eligible to apply? Yes
Is the TOEFL required for international students? Yes
What is the minimum TOEFL score required? 500

Program Delivery

Primary method of program delivery: Text
Two-way interactive video: No

Two-way audio, one-way video: No
One-way live video: No
One-way pre-recorded video: Yes
Audio graphics: No
Audio: No
Is the library accessible to students? Yes
Are computers accessible to students? Yes

On-Campus Requirements

Is an on-campus component required? No

Tuition & Fees

In-state tuition per credit: $155
Out-of-state tuition per credit: $155
Average yearly cost of books: $900
Average yearly additional fees: $35

Financial Aid

Is financial aid available to full-time students? No
Is financial aid available to part-time students? Yes
Are academic scholarships available? No
Assistance programs available to students: Federal Stafford
   Loan, Federal Pell Grant, veterans' assistance

Utah State University

Independent & Distance Education
3080 Old Main Hill
Logan, UT 84322-3080
Contact: Vincent J. Lafferty, Director of Independent &
   Distance Education
Department e-mail: de-info@ext.usu.edu
Department Web address: www.ext.usu.edu/distance
School Web address: www.usu.edu

Admissions Requirements

Is a minimum high school GPA required? Yes
Is provisional admission available? Yes
Is an admissions interview required? No
Can pre-requisite course work be waived? Yes
Are international students eligible to apply? Yes
Is the TOEFL required for international students? Yes
What is the minimum TOEFL score required? 500

Program Delivery

Primary method of program delivery: Remote site
Two-way interactive video: Yes
Two-way audio, one-way video: Yes
One-way live video: Yes
Hardware requirements: Pentium II, 128MB RAM,
   speakers, sound card
Software requirements: Microsoft Office, Visual Basic,
   Windows 2000, Real Audio, Web browser

Is the library accessible to students? Yes
Are computers accessible to students? Yes

Remote Sites

Other branches of the institution: Yes
Other college campuses: Yes
Students' homes: Yes
Work sites: Yes
Libraries: Yes
Elementary/Secondary schools: Yes
Correctional institutions: Yes

On-Campus Requirements

Is an on-campus component required? No

Tuition & Fees

Average yearly cost of books: $500

Financial Aid

Is financial aid available to full-time students? Yes
Is financial aid available to part-time students? Yes
Are academic scholarships available? Yes
Assistance programs available to students: Federal Stafford
   Loan, Federal Perkins Loan, Federal Plus Loan, Federal
   Pell Grant, Federal Work-Study Program, in-state
   student aid programs, veterans' assistance

Utah Valley State College

Institutional Research
Distance Learning
800 West University Parkway
Orem, UT 84098
Contact: Monty Georgi, Director
Department e-mail: bakerel@uvsc.edu
Department Web address: www.uvsc.edu/ir/
School Web address: www.uvsc.edu

Utica College

Graduate & Continuing Education
1600 Burrstone Road
Utica, NY 13502
Contact: James S. Pula, Dean, Graduate & Continuing
   Education
Department e-mail: conteduc@utica.ucsu.edu
School Web address: www.utica.edu
Institutional accreditation: Middle States Association of
   Colleges and Schools

Subjects Offered

Graduate program in economic crime management

Admissions Requirements

Is a minimum high school GPA required? No
Is provisional admission available? Yes
Can pre-requisite course work be waived? Yes
Are international students eligible to apply? Yes
Is the TOEFL required for international students? Yes
What is the minimum TOEFL score required? 500

Program Delivery

Primary method of program delivery: Web
Two-way interactive video: No
Two-way audio, one-way video: Yes
One-way live video: Yes
One-way pre-recorded video: Yes
Audio graphics: Yes
Audio: Yes
Hardware requirements: See above
Software requirements: Pentium computer, 28.8 KBPS
   modem, e-mail, Internet access
Is the library accessible to students? Yes
Are computers accessible to students? Yes

Remote Sites

Other branches of the institution: No
Other college campuses: Yes
Students' homes: Yes
Work sites: Yes
Libraries: Yes
Elementary/Secondary schools: Yes
Community-based organizations: Yes
Correctional institutions: No

On-Campus Requirements

Is an on-campus component required? Yes
On-campus course work: Yes
On-campus admissions interview: No
On-campus program orientation: No
On-campus exams: Yes

Tuition & Fees

Application fee: $50

Financial Aid

Is financial aid available to full-time students? Yes
Is financial aid available to part-time students? Yes
Are academic scholarships available? Yes
Assistance programs available to students: Federal Stafford
   Loan, Federal Perkins Loan, Federal Plus Loan, Federal
   Pell Grant, Federal Work-Study Program, in-state
   student aid programs, veterans' assistance

Vincennes University

Continuing Studies
Distance Education
1002 North First Street
Vincennes, IN 47591
Contact: Vernon E. Houchins, Dean of Continuing
   Studies
Department e-mail: disted@indian.vinu.edu
Department Web address: www.vinu.edu/distance
School Web address: www.vinu.edu
Institutional accreditation: North Central Association of
   Colleges and Schools

Subjects Offered

Education, study skills, psychology, literature, sociology,
   history, computer information, recreation management,
   business, chemistry, English, math, speech, economics,
   law enforcement, government, corrections, portfolio
   development, health information management, fitness
   and wellness, surgical technology, earth science

Admissions Requirements

Is a minimum high school GPA required? No
Is provisional admission available? Yes
Is an admissions interview required? No
Can pre-requisite course work be waived? No
Are international students eligible to apply? Yes
Is the TOEFL required for international students? Yes

Program Delivery

Primary method of program delivery: Text
Two-way interactive video: Yes
Two-way audio, one-way video: Yes
One-way pre-recorded video: Yes
Hardware requirements: 486-66 MHz, 16MB of RAM,
   28.8KBPS modem
Software requirements: Windows 95, Word 6.0, Netscape
   4.0 or Internet Explorer 4.0 or above

Remote Sites

Other branches of the institution: Yes
Other college campuses: Yes
Students' homes: Yes
Work sites: Yes
Libraries: Yes
Elementary/Secondary schools: Yes
Community-based organizations: Yes
Correctional institutions: Yes

On-Campus Requirements

Is an on-campus component required? No

Tuition & Fees

In-state tuition per credit: $83
Out-of-state tuition per credit: $83
Application fee: $20
Average yearly cost of books: $700
Average yearly additional fees: $25

Financial Aid

Is financial aid available to full-time students? Yes
Is financial aid available to part-time students? Yes
Are academic scholarships available? Yes
Assistance programs available to students: Federal Stafford Loan, Federal Perkins Loan, Federal Plus Loan, Federal Pell Grant, Federal Work-Study Program, in-state student aid programs, veterans' assistance

Washington State University

Extended Degree Programs
Van Doren 202
PO Box 645220
Pullman, WA 99164-5220
Contact: Dr. Janet Ross Kendall, Director, Extended Degree Programs
Department e-mail: edp@wsu.edu
Department Web address: www.eus.wsu.edu/edp
School Web address: www.wsu.edu
Institutional accreditation: Northwest Association of Schools and Colleges

Subjects Offered

Accounting, agricultural economics/economics, American studies, animal science/zoology, anthropology, architecture, Asian studies, biology, business/business law, communication, criminal justice, electrical engineering, English, entomology, environmental science/soil science, finance, fine arts, food science and human nutrition, foreign languages and literatures, French/Spanish, genetics-cell biology, geology, history, horticulture, human development, humanities, insurance, interior design, management/management information systems, marketing, mathematics, natural resource sciences, philosophy, political science

Admissions Requirements

Is provisional admission available? No
Is an admissions interview required? No
Can pre-requisite course work be waived? No
Are international students eligible to apply? Yes
Is the TOEFL required for international students? Yes

Program Delivery

Two-way interactive video: Yes
Two-way audio, one-way video: No
One-way live video: Yes
One-way pre-recorded video: Yes
Audio graphics: Yes
Audio: Yes
Hardware requirements: a computer capable of supporting a browser of version 3.0 or above, with video/audio
Software requirements: Web access with e-mail
Is the library accessible to students? Yes

Remote Sites

Other branches of the institution: Yes
Other college campuses: Yes
Students' homes: Yes
Work sites: Yes
Libraries: Yes
Elementary/Secondary schools: No
Community-based organizations: No
Correctional institutions: No

On-Campus Requirements

Is an on-campus component required? No

Tuition & Fees

In-state tuition per credit: $183
Out-of-state tuition per credit: $275
Average yearly cost of books: $35

Financial Aid

Is financial aid available to full-time students? Yes
Is financial aid available to part-time students? Yes
Are academic scholarships available? Yes
Assistance programs available to students: Federal Stafford Loan, Federal Perkins Loan, Federal Plus Loan, Federal Pell Grant, Federal Work-Study Program, in-state student aid programs, veterans' assistance

Waukesha County Technical College

Instructional Resources
800 Main Street
Pewaukee, WI 53072
Contact: Dr. Randall Coorough, Director, Instructional Technology and Design
School Web address: www.waukesha.tec.wi.us
Institutional accreditation: North Central Association of Colleges and Schools

Subjects Offered

Community health, human services, allied health, finance, accounting, real estate, mortgage lending, general education, business, marketing, computer training

Admissions Requirements

Is a minimum high school GPA required? No
Is provisional admission available? Yes
Is an admissions interview required? No
Can pre-requisite course work be waived? No
Are international students eligible to apply? Yes

Program Delivery

Primary method of program delivery: Web
Two-way interactive video: Yes
Two-way audio, one-way video: No
One-way live video: No
One-way pre-recorded video: No
Audio graphics: No
Audio: No
Hardware requirements: Windows Pentium level with 28.8KBPS modem
Software requirements: Web browser and word processor (Word or Word Perfect)
Is the library accessible to students? Yes
Are computers accessible to students? Yes

Remote Sites

Other branches of the institution: Yes
Other college campuses: Yes
Students' homes: Yes
Work sites: Yes
Libraries: Yes
Elementary/Secondary schools: Yes
Community-based organizations: Yes
Correctional institutions: Yes

Tuition & Fees

In-state tuition per credit: $62
Out-of-state tuition per credit: $481
Application fee: $30
Can it be waived? No
Average yearly additional fees: $7

Financial Aid

Is financial aid available to full-time students? Yes
Is financial aid available to part-time students? Yes
Are academic scholarships available? Yes
Assistance programs available to students: Federal Stafford Loan, Federal Perkins Loan, Federal Plus Loan, Federal Pell Grant, Federal Work-Study Program, in-state student aid programs, veterans' assistance

Wayne County Community College District

Distance Learning
801 West Fort Street
Detroit, MI 48226
Contact: Deborah Fiedler, Associate Dean, Distance Learning
Department e-mail: dfiedler@mail.wccc.edu
School Web address: www.wccc.edu
Institutional accreditation: North Central Association of Colleges and Schools

Subjects Offered

Business, mathematics, geography, geology, humanities, English, political science, sociology, allied health, anthropology, economics, history, philosophy, marketing, management, accounting, psychology

Admissions Requirements

Is a minimum high school GPA required? No
Is an admissions interview required? No
Can pre-requisite course work be waived? Yes
Are international students eligible to apply? Yes
Is the TOEFL required for international students? Yes

Program Delivery

Two-way interactive video: Yes
One-way pre-recorded video: Yes
Audio: Yes
Software requirements: Netscape 4.0/Internet Explorer 4.0 or higher, HTML, JAVA and JAVAscript enabled
Is the library accessible to students? Yes
Are computers accessible to students? Yes

Remote Sites

Other branches of the institution: Yes
Students' homes: Yes
Work sites: Yes
Community-based organizations: Yes

On-Campus Requirements

Is an on-campus component required? Yes
On-campus course work: Yes
On-campus program orientation: Yes
On-campus exams: Yes

Tuition & Fees

In-state tuition per credit: $70
Out-of-state tuition per credit: $89
Average yearly cost of books: $72

Financial Aid

Is financial aid available to full-time students? Yes
Is financial aid available to part-time students? Yes
Are academic scholarships available? Yes
Assistance programs available to students: Federal Stafford
    Loan, Federal Pell Grant, Federal Work-Study Program,
    in-state student aid programs, veterans' assistance

West Valley College

Instructional Development Distance Learning
Distance Learning
1400 Fruitvale Avenue
Saratoga, CA 95070
Contact: Steve Peltz, Instructional Technology Distance
    Learning Coordinator
Department e-mail: steve-peltz@westvalley.dl
Department Web address: www.westvalley.edu/wvc.dl
School Web address: www.westvalley.edu
Institutional accreditation: The Accrediting Commission
    for Community

Subjects Offered

Cultural anthropology, physical geology, art appreciation,
    contemporary health issues, astronomy, music apprecia-
    tion, business law, human nutrition, function of
    management, oceanography, sales strategies, physical
    education, stretch and flex, introduction to business,
    introduction to sociology, small business start-up,
    conversational Spanish, culture, marketing principles,
    introduction to film

Admissions Requirements

Is a minimum high school GPA required? No
Is provisional admission available? No
Is an admissions interview required? No
Can pre-requisite course work be waived? Yes
Are international students eligible to apply? Yes
Is the TOEFL required for international students? No

Program Delivery

Primary method of program delivery: Web
Two-way interactive video: Yes
Two-way audio, one-way video: No
One-way live video: Yes
One-way pre-recorded video: Yes
Audio graphics: No
Audio: Yes
Hardware requirements: Anything that will run Netscape
Software requirements: Netscape
Is the library accessible to students? Yes
Are computers accessible to students? Yes

Remote Sites

Other branches of the institution: No
Other college campuses: No
Students' homes: Yes
Work sites: Yes
Libraries: Yes
Elementary/Secondary schools: No
Community-based organizations: Yes
Correctional institutions: Yes

On-Campus Requirements

Is an on-campus component required? Yes
On-campus course work: No
On-campus admissions interview: Yes
On-campus program orientation: Yes
On-campus exams: Yes

Tuition & Fees

In-state tuition per credit: $11
Out-of-state tuition per credit: $130

Financial Aid

Is financial aid available to full-time students? Yes
Is financial aid available to part-time students? Yes
Are academic scholarships available? Yes
Assistance programs available to students: Federal Stafford
    Loan, Federal Perkins Loan, Federal Pell Grant, Federal
    Work-Study Program, in-state student aid programs

West Virginia Wesleyan College

Distance Education
59 College Ave
Buckhannon, WV 26201
Contact: Judith M. Knorr, Distance Education
    Coordinator
Department e-mail: distanceed@wvwc.edu
Department Web address: www.wvwc.edu/aca/distance.edu
School Web address: www.wvwc.edu
Institutional accreditation: North Central Association of
    Colleges and Schools

Subjects Offered

Business, psychology, chemistry, religion, economics,
    sociology, English, history, interdisciplinary, mathemat-
    ics, physical education, philosophy, physical science,
    political science

Admissions Requirements

Is a minimum high school GPA required? No
Is provisional admission available? No

Is an admissions interview required? Yes
Can pre-requisite course work be waived? No
Are international students eligible to apply? Yes
Is the TOEFL required for international students? No

Program Delivery

Primary method of program delivery: Text
Two-way interactive video: No
Two-way audio, one-way video: No
One-way live video: No
Audio graphics: No
Audio: Yes
Hardware requirements: Windows 95 or better Mac 8.1 or later. Some courses utilize CD-ROMs
Software requirements: Best viewed with the Internet Explorer 5.0 or better or Netscape Communicator 4.5 or better
Is the library accessible to students? Yes
Are computers accessible to students? Yes

On-Campus Requirements

Is an on-campus component required? No

Tuition & Fees

In-state tuition per credit: $125
Out-of-state tuition per credit: $125

Financial Aid

Is financial aid available to full-time students? Yes
Is financial aid available to part-time students? Yes
Are academic scholarships available? No
Assistance programs available to students: Federal Stafford Loan, Federal Plus Loan, Federal Pell Grant, veterans' assistance

Western Illinois University

School of Extended and Continuing Education
Extended Learning
One University Circle
Macomb, IL 61455
Contact: Joyce E. Nielsen, PhD, Associate Dean
Department e-mail: joyce_nielsen@ccmail.wiu.edu
Department Web address: www.wiu.edu/users/sece
School Web address: www.wiu.edu
Institutional accreditation: North Central Association of Colleges and Schools

Subjects Offered

Accountancy, African American studies, agriculture, biological sciences, communication, computer science, curriculum and instruction, economics, educational administration, educational and interdisciplinary studies, engineering technology, English and journalism, family and consumer sciences, foreign language, geography, geology, health education and promotion, law enforcement and justice administration, management, marketing and finance, mathematics, philosophy and religious studies, political science, psychology, recreation, park, and tourism administration, sociology

Admissions Requirements

Is a minimum high school GPA required? No
Is provisional admission available? Yes
Is an admissions interview required? No
Can pre-requisite course work be waived? Yes
Are international students eligible to apply? No

Program Delivery

Primary method of program delivery: Remote site
Two-way interactive video: Yes
Two-way audio, one-way video: Yes
One-way live video: No
One-way pre-recorded video: Yes
Audio graphics: Yes
Audio: Yes
Hardware requirements: connection to the Internet
Software requirements: e-mail, word processing
Is the library accessible to students? Yes
Are computers accessible to students? Yes

Remote Sites

Other branches of the institution: Yes
Other college campuses: Yes
Students' homes: Yes
Work sites: Yes
Libraries: Yes
Elementary/Secondary schools: Yes
Community-based organizations: Yes
Correctional institutions: Yes

On-Campus Requirements

Is an on-campus component required? No

Tuition & Fees

In-state tuition per credit: $94
Out-of-state tuition per credit: $94

Financial Aid

Is financial aid available to full-time students? Yes
Is financial aid available to part-time students? Yes
Are academic scholarships available? Yes
Assistance programs available to students: Federal Stafford Loan, Federal Perkins Loan, Federal Plus Loan, Federal Pell Grant, Federal Work-Study Program, in-state student aid programs, veterans' assistance

Western Kansas Community College

Virtual Education Consortium
EDUKAN
245 NE 30th Road
Great Bend, KS 67530
Contact: Gillian M. Gabelmann, PhD, Executive Director, EDUKAN
Department e-mail: gabelmanng@barton.cc.ks.us
Department Web address: www.edukan.org

Subjects Offered

Mathematics, accounting, horse production, Native American culture, anthropology, art, biology, business, chemistry, computers, economics, social sciences, literature, English, writing, geography, history, ethics, music, health, physical sciences, government, speech

Admissions Requirements

Is a minimum high school GPA required? No
Can pre-requisite course work be waived? No

Program Delivery

Primary method of program delivery: Web
Is the library accessible to students? Yes
Are computers accessible to students? Yes

Remote Sites

Other branches of the institution: Yes
Other college campuses: Yes
Students' homes: Yes
Work sites: Yes
Libraries: Yes
Elementary/Secondary schools: Yes

On-Campus Requirements

Is an on-campus component required? No

Tuition & Fees

In-state tuition per credit: $115
Out-of-state tuition per credit: $115

Financial Aid

Is financial aid available to full-time students? Yes
Is financial aid available to part-time students? Yes
Are academic scholarships available? Yes
Assistance programs available to students: Federal Stafford Loan, Federal Perkins Loan, Federal Pell Grant, Federal Work-Study Program, in-state student aid programs, veterans' assistance

Western Montana College of The University of Montana

Outreach Division
710 South Atlantic Street
Dillon, MT 59725
Contact: Anneliese Ripley, Dean, Outreach and Research
Department e-mail: outreach@wmc.edu
School Web address: www.wmc.edu
Institutional accreditation: Northwest Association of Schools and Colleges

Subjects Offered

Education, business, computer science, psychology, English

Admissions Requirements

Is a minimum high school GPA required? Yes
Is provisional admission available? Yes
Is an admissions interview required? No
Can pre-requisite course work be waived? Yes
Are international students eligible to apply? Yes
Is the TOEFL required for international students? Yes

Program Delivery

Primary method of program delivery: Remote site
Hardware requirements: PC Windows 95, 98, or NT, 90 MHz Pentium processor, 32MB RAM, 28.8KBPS modem, sound card, speakers, RealPlayer. MacOS 8.1 or later, 604 PowerPC
Software requirements: Microsoft Internet Explorer 5.0 or higher (PC), 4.5 (Mac)
Is the library accessible to students? Yes
Are computers accessible to students? Yes

Remote Sites

Other college campuses: Yes

On-Campus Requirements

Is an on-campus component required? Yes

Tuition & Fees

In-state tuition per credit: $423
Out-of-state tuition per credit: $1,049
Average yearly cost of books: $400
Average yearly additional fees: $30

Financial Aid

Is financial aid available to full-time students? Yes
Is financial aid available to part-time students? Yes
Are academic scholarships available? Yes
Assistance programs available to students: Federal Stafford

Loan, Federal Perkins Loan, Federal Plus Loan, Federal Pell Grant, in-state student aid programs, veterans' assistance

Western Nebraska Community College

Educational Services
Information Technology
1601 East 27th Street
Scottsbluff, NE 69361
Contact: Don Estes, Distance Learning Coordinator
Department e-mail: destes@wncc.net
School Web address: www.wncc.net
Institutional accreditation: North Central Association of Colleges and Schools

Subjects Offered

Criminal justice, English, mathematics, humanities, practical nursing, health information management services, literature, accounting, railroad, history, foreign language, information technology

Admissions Requirements

Is a minimum high school GPA required? No
Is provisional admission available? Yes
Is an admissions interview required? No
Can pre-requisite course work be waived? Yes
Are international students eligible to apply? Yes
Is the TOEFL required for international students? Yes
What is the minimum TOEFL score required? 500

Program Delivery

Primary method of program delivery: Remote site
Two-way interactive video: Yes
Hardware requirements: Hardware that will support current software
Is the library accessible to students? Yes
Are computers accessible to students? Yes

Remote Sites

Other branches of the institution: Yes
Other college campuses: Yes
Elementary/Secondary schools: Yes

On-Campus Requirements

Is an on-campus component required? Yes
On-campus course work: Yes
On-campus admissions interview: No
On-campus program orientation: Yes

Tuition & Fees

In-state tuition per credit: $43
Out-of-state tuition per credit: $49
Average yearly cost of books: $600

Financial Aid

Is financial aid available to full-time students? Yes
Is financial aid available to part-time students? Yes
Are academic scholarships available? Yes
Assistance programs available to students: Federal Stafford Loan, Federal Plus Loan, Federal Pell Grant, Federal Work-Study Program, in-state student aid programs, veterans' assistance

Western Oregon University

Division of Extended Programs
345 North Monmouth Avenue
Monmouth, OR 97361
Department e-mail: extend@wou.edu
Department Web address: www.wou.edu/provost/extprogram
School Web address: www.wou.edu
Institutional accreditation: Northwest Association of Schools and Colleges

Subjects Offered

Fire service administration, criminal justice, political science, education, social science

Admissions Requirements

Is a minimum high school GPA required? No
Is provisional admission available? Yes
Is an admissions interview required? No
Can pre-requisite course work be waived? Yes
Are international students eligible to apply? Yes
Is the TOEFL required for international students? Yes

Program Delivery

Primary method of program delivery: Text
Hardware requirements: 486 processor or better
Software requirements: Access to Internet and e-mail
Is the library accessible to students? Yes
Are computers accessible to students? Yes

Remote Sites

Other college campuses: Yes
Work sites: Yes
Community-based organizations: Yes
Correctional institutions: Yes

On-Campus Requirements

Is an on-campus component required? No

Tuition & Fees

In-state tuition per credit: $95
Out-of-state tuition per credit: $95
Average yearly cost of books: $75

Financial Aid

Is financial aid available to full-time students? Yes
Is financial aid available to part-time students? Yes
Are academic scholarships available? Yes
Assistance programs available to students: Federal Stafford
    Loan, Federal Perkins Loan, Federal Plus Loan, Federal
    Pell Grant, Federal Work-Study Program, in-state
    student aid programs, veterans' assistance

Western Piedmont Community College

Business Technologies Division
1001 Burkemont Avenue
Morganton, NC 28655
Department e-mail: jcarswell@wp.cc.nc.us
Department Web address: www.wp.cc.nc.us/bustech
School Web address: www.wp.cc.nc.us
Institutional accreditation: Southern Association of
    Colleges and Schools

Subjects Offered

Accounting, business administration, information systems,
    Internet technology, marketing, paralegal, criminal
    justice, office systems, English, mathematics, psychology,
    economics, sociology

Admissions Requirements

Is provisional admission available? Yes
Can pre-requisite course work be waived? No
Are international students eligible to apply? Yes
Is the TOEFL required for international students? Yes

Program Delivery

Primary method of program delivery: Web
One-way pre-recorded video: Yes
Is the library accessible to students? Yes
Are computers accessible to students? Yes

Remote Sites

Other college campuses: Yes
Students' homes: Yes
Work sites: Yes
Libraries: Yes

On-Campus Requirements

Is an on-campus component required? Yes
On-campus course work: Yes
On-campus program orientation: Yes
On-campus exams: Yes

Tuition & Fees

In-state tuition per credit: $27
Out-of-state tuition per credit: $170
Average yearly cost of books: $400

Financial Aid

Is financial aid available to full-time students? Yes
Are academic scholarships available? Yes
Assistance programs available to students: Federal Stafford
    Loan, Federal Perkins Loan, Federal Plus Loan, Federal
    Pell Grant, Federal Work-Study Program, in-state
    student aid programs, veterans' assistance

Western Washington University

Woodring College of Education
Extension Services
Mail Stop 5241
Bellingham, WA 98225-5241
Contact: Larrene Shannon, ED, Director
Department e-mail: professional.development@wwu.edu
Department Web address: www.wce.wwu.edu
School Web address: www.wwu.edu

Subjects Offered

Education, human services, early childhood, emergency
    management, grant writing

Admissions Requirements

Is provisional admission available? Yes
Can pre-requisite course work be waived? Yes
Are international students eligible to apply? Yes

Program Delivery

Primary method of program delivery: Web

On-Campus Requirements

Is an on-campus component required? No

Tuition & Fees

In-state tuition per credit: $133
Out-of-state tuition per credit: $133

Westmoreland County Community College

Learning Resources Center
400 Armbrust Road
Youngwood, PA 15697-1895
Contact: Mary J. Stubbs, PhD, Director, Learning Resources/Special Projects
Department e-mail: stubbsms@westmoreland.cc.pa.us
School Web address: westmoreland.cc.pa.us
Institutional accreditation: Middle States Association of Colleges and Schools

Subjects Offered

Art, history, biology, human services, banking and finance, health and physical education, business, humanities, early childhood education, media technology, economics, mathematics, English, philosophy, earth and planetary science, physics, French, political science, food service, psychology, geography, sociology

Admissions Requirements

Is a minimum high school GPA required? No
Is an admissions interview required? No
Can pre-requisite course work be waived? Yes
Are international students eligible to apply? Yes
Is the TOEFL required for international students? Yes
What is the minimum TOEFL score required? 500

Program Delivery

Primary method of program delivery: Remote site
Two-way interactive video: Yes
Hardware requirements: Minimum of a Pentium (PC) or Power Mac (Macintosh) processor, a CD-ROM drive, access to a letter-quality printer
Software requirements: Internet access with a speed of at least 36.6KBPS, e-mail, Netscape Navigator 4.0 or higher, or Microsoft Internet Explorer 4.0 or higher
Is the library accessible to students? Yes
Are computers accessible to students? No

Remote Sites

Other branches of the institution: Yes
Work sites: Yes
Elementary/Secondary schools: Yes
Correctional institutions: Yes

On-Campus Requirements

Is an on-campus component required? No

Tuition & Fees

In-state tuition per credit: $100
Out-of-state tuition per credit: $150
Average yearly cost of books: $650

Financial Aid

Is financial aid available to full-time students? Yes
Is financial aid available to part-time students? Yes
Are academic scholarships available? Yes
Assistance programs available to students: Federal Stafford Loan, Federal Pell Grant, Federal Work-Study Program, in-state student aid programs, veterans' assistance

Wilfrid Laurier University

Office of Part-time, Distance, and Continuing Education
75 University Avenue West
Waterloo, Ontario, Canada N2L 3C5
Contact: Sandy Hughes, Manager, Part-time Distance and Continuing Education
Department e-mail: 22coned@wlu.ca
Department Web address: www.wlu.ca/~wwwconte/index.shtml
School Web address: www.wlu.ca

Subjects Offered

Anthropology, business, Canadian studies, economics, English, fine arts, French, geography, geology, German, history, philosophy, psychology, biology, science, Spanish, sociology

Admissions Requirements

Is an admissions interview required? No
Are international students eligible to apply? Yes

Program Delivery

Primary method of program delivery: Web
One-way pre-recorded video: Yes
Hardware requirements: VCR, JAVA-enabled PC-486
Is the library accessible to students? Yes
Are computers accessible to students? Yes

Remote Sites

Other branches of the institution: Yes
Other college campuses: Yes
Students' homes: Yes
Work sites: Yes

On-Campus Requirements

Is an on-campus component required? No

Tuition & Fees

Average yearly cost of books: $80
Average yearly additional fees: $30

Financial Aid

Is financial aid available to full-time students? Yes
Is financial aid available to part-time students? Yes
Are academic scholarships available? Yes

Wytheville Community College

1000 East Main Street
Wytheville, VA 24382
Contact: Gary Laing, Division Chair, Engineering, Technology/Mathematics
Department e-mail: wclaing@wc.cc.va.us
Department Web address: www.wc.cc.va.us/dl
School Web address: www.wc.cc.va.us
Institutional accreditation: Southern Association of Colleges and Schools

Subjects Offered

Web site design

Admissions Requirements

Is a minimum high school GPA required? No
Is provisional admission available? Yes
Is an admissions interview required? No
Can pre-requisite course work be waived? No
Are international students eligible to apply? Yes
Is the TOEFL required for international students? Yes
What is the minimum TOEFL score required? 500

Program Delivery

Primary method of program delivery: Web
Software requirements: Internet access only
Is the library accessible to students? Yes
Are computers accessible to students? Yes

Remote Sites

Students' homes: Yes
Work sites: Yes
Libraries: Yes

On-Campus Requirements

Is an on-campus component required? No

Tuition & Fees

In-state tuition per credit: $39
Out-of-state tuition per credit: $171

Financial Aid

Is financial aid available to full-time students? No
Is financial aid available to part-time students? No
Are academic scholarships available? Yes

York College of Pennsylvania

Administrative Services
Special Programs
One Country Club Road
York, PA 17405-7199
Contact: Leroy M. Keeney, Director, Special Programs
Department e-mail: special-programs@ycp.edu
School Web address: www.ycp.edu
Institutional accreditation: Middle States Association of Colleges and Schools

Subjects Offered

Nursing, computer software, computer-Web design, business skills, technical-computer, Microsoft certified systems engineering

Admissions Requirements

Is provisional admission available? Yes
Can pre-requisite course work be waived? Yes
Are international students eligible to apply? Yes

Program Delivery

Primary method of program delivery: Remote site
Two-way audio, one-way video: Yes
Hardware requirements: Pentium
Software requirements: Microsoft
Is the library accessible to students? Yes
Are computers accessible to students? Yes

Remote Sites

Work sites: Yes

On-Campus Requirements

Is an on-campus component required? No

Tuition & Fees

In-state tuition per credit: $205
Out-of-state tuition per credit: $205
Average yearly cost of books: $500

Financial Aid

Is financial aid available to full-time students? Yes
Is financial aid available to part-time students? Yes
Are academic scholarships available? Yes

Assistance programs available to students: Federal Stafford Loan, Federal Perkins Loan, Federal Plus Loan, Federal Pell Grant, Federal Work-Study Program, in-state student aid programs

York Technical College

Distance Learning
452 South Anderson Road
Rock Hill, SC 29730
Contact: Anita McBride, Department Manager
Department e-mail: mcbride@yorktech.com
Department Web address: academic.yorktech.com/
    department/distance/default.htm
School Web address: www.yorktech.com
Institutional accreditation: Southern Association of
    Colleges and Schools

Subjects Offered

Psychology, history, sociology, speech, English, mathematics, American government, business, digital circuits, accounting, office systems technology

Admissions Requirements

Is a minimum high school GPA required? No
Is provisional admission available? Yes
Can pre-requisite course work be waived? Yes
Are international students eligible to apply? Yes
Is the TOEFL required for international students? No

Program Delivery

Primary method of program delivery: Web
Two-way interactive video: Yes
Hardware requirements: At least a 486 computer
Software requirements: JAVA-enabled browser, Internet
    provider
Is the library accessible to students? Yes
Are computers accessible to students? Yes

Remote Sites

Other branches of the institution: Yes
Other college campuses: Yes
Students' homes: No
Work sites: No
Libraries: No
Elementary/Secondary schools: Yes
Community-based organizations: No
Correctional institutions: No

Tuition & Fees

In-state tuition per credit: $47
Out-of-state tuition per credit: $143
Average yearly cost of books: $700

Financial Aid

Is financial aid available to full-time students? Yes
Is financial aid available to part-time students? No
Are academic scholarships available? Yes
Assistance programs available to students: Federal Pell
    Grant, Federal Work-Study Program, veterans' assistance

Distance Learning Survey—Graduate Programs

American Graduate University

733 North Dodsworth Avenue
Covina, CA 91724
Contact: Marie Sirney, Director of Admissions
Department e-mail: info@agu.edu
School Web address: www.agu.edu
Institutional accreditation: Distance Education and
    Training Council

Subjects Offered

Theology ethics, church history, Bible

Admissions Requirements

Is a minimum undergraduate GPA required? No
Is provisional admission available? No
Is an admissions interview required? No
Can pre-requisite course work be waived? Yes
Are international students eligible to apply? Yes
Is the TOEFL required for international students? No

Program Delivery

Primary method of program delivery: Text
Two-way interactive video: No
Two-way audio, one-way video: No
One-way live video: No
One-way pre-recorded video: No
Audio graphics: No
Audio: No
Is the library accessible to students? Yes
Are computers accessible to students? No

Remote Sites

Other branches of the institution: No
Other college campuses: No
Students' homes: Yes
Work sites: Yes
Libraries: Yes
Elementary/Secondary schools: No
Community-based organizations: No
Correctional institutions: Yes

On-Campus Requirements

Is an on-campus component required? No

Financial Aid

Is financial aid available to full-time students? No
Is financial aid available to part-time students? No
Are academic scholarships available? No

American Military University

Operations
9104-P Manassas Drive
Manassas Park, VA 20111
Contact: James P. Etter, Chancellor
Department e-mail: jherhusky@amunet.edu
School Web address: www.amunet.edu
Institutional accreditation: Distance Education and
    Training Council

Subjects Offered

Transportation management, unconventional warfare,
    defense management, civil war studies, naval warfare,
    land warfare, management, air warfare, intelligence

Admissions Requirements

Is a minimum undergraduate GPA required? Yes
Is provisional admission available? Yes
Is an admissions interview required? No
Can pre-requisite course work be waived? Yes
Are international students eligible to apply? Yes
Is the TOEFL required for international students? Yes
What is the minimum TOEFL score required? 550

Program Delivery

Primary method of program delivery: Web
Hardware requirements: Ability to connect with Internet
Software requirements: Internet Explorer (or other
    browser)
Is the library accessible to students? Yes
Are computers accessible to students? Yes

On-Campus Requirements

Is an on-campus component required? No

Tuition & Fees

In-state tuition per credit: $250
Out-of-state tuition per credit: $250
Average yearly cost of books: $375

Financial Aid

Is financial aid available to full-time students? No
Is financial aid available to part-time students? No
Are academic scholarships available? No

Anderson University School of Theology

1100 East 5th Street
Anderson, IN 46012-3495
Contact: Dr. David Sebastion, Dean
Department e-mail: dlsebas@anderson.edu
School Web address: www.anderson.edu/sot
Institutional accreditation: Association of Theological Schools

Subjects Offered

Christian history, Christian stewardship, women in ministry, Christian relationship, leadership of management, Christian education, Church of God history, pastoral care, church growth/church planting

Admissions Requirements

Is a minimum undergraduate GPA required? No
Is provisional admission available? Yes
Is an admissions interview required? No
Can pre-requisite course work be waived? Yes
Are international students eligible to apply? Yes
Is the TOEFL required for international students? Yes

Program Delivery

Two-way interactive video: No
Two-way audio, one-way video: No
One-way live video: No
One-way pre-recorded video: Yes
Audio graphics: No
Audio: Yes
Hardware requirements: Screen resolution 800 x 600 pixels, 90 MHz processor; 32MB of RAM; 28.8KBPS modem
Software requirements: Microsoft Internet Explorer 5.0 (PC), 4.5 (Mac), Internet service provider, RealPlayer, Windows 95, Mac OS 8.1; e-mail
Is the library accessible to students? Yes
Are computers accessible to students? Yes

Remote Sites

Other branches of the institution: No
Other college campuses: No
Students' homes: No
Work sites: No
Libraries: No
Elementary/Secondary schools: No
Community-based organizations: No
Correctional institutions: No

On-Campus Requirements

Is an on-campus component required? No

Tuition & Fees

In-state tuition per credit: $327
Out-of-state tuition per credit: $327
Average yearly cost of books: $600

Financial Aid

Is financial aid available to full-time students? Yes
Is financial aid available to part-time students? Yes
Are academic scholarships available? Yes
Assistance programs available to students: Federal Stafford Loan

Andrew Jackson University

School of Business/School of Civil Sciences
10 Old Montgomery Highway
Birmingham, AL 35209
Contact: Robert Norris Jr./James E. Bridges Jr., Dean
Department e-mail: info@aju.edu
School Web address: www.aju.edu
Institutional accreditation: Distance Education and Training Council

Subjects Offered

Business administration, public administration, criminal justice

Admissions Requirements

Is a minimum undergraduate GPA required? Yes
Is provisional admission available? Yes
Is an admissions interview required? No
Can pre-requisite course work be waived? Yes
Are international students eligible to apply? Yes
Is the TOEFL required for international students? Yes
What is the minimum TOEFL score required? 550

Program Delivery

Two-way interactive video: No
Two-way audio, one-way video: No
One-way live video: No
One-way pre-recorded video: No
Audio graphics: No
Audio: No
Software requirements: Internet access, Microsoft Word or Word Perfect
Is the library accessible to students? No
Are computers accessible to students? No

Remote Sites

Other branches of the institution: No
Other college campuses: No
Students' homes: Yes
Work sites: No
Libraries: No
Elementary/Secondary schools: No
Community-based organizations: No
Correctional institutions: No

On-Campus Requirements

Is an on-campus component required? No

Tuition & Fees

In-state tuition per credit: $137
Out-of-state tuition per credit: $137
Average yearly cost of books: $1,200

Financial Aid

Is financial aid available to full-time students? No
Is financial aid available to part-time students? No
Are academic scholarships available? No

Antioch University, The McGregor School—Conflict Resolution

800 Livermore Street
Yellow Spring, OH 45387
Contact: Dr. Katherine Hale, Professor and Chair
Department e-mail: admiss@mcgregor.edu
School Web address: www.mcgregor.edu
Institutional accreditation: North Central Association of Colleges and Schools

Admissions Requirements

Is a minimum undergraduate GPA required? No
Is provisional admission available? No
Is an admissions interview required? Yes
Can pre-requisite course work be waived? No
Are international students eligible to apply? Yes
Is the TOEFL required for international students? No

Program Delivery

Two-way interactive video: No
Two-way audio, one-way video: No
One-way live video: No
One-way pre-recorded video: No
Audio graphics: No
Audio: No

Software requirements: Netscape 4.x and above or Internet Explorer 4.x and above, AOL 4.0 and above
Is the library accessible to students? Yes
Are computers accessible to students? Yes

Remote Sites

Other branches of the institution: No
Other college campuses: No
Students' homes: Yes
Work sites: Yes
Libraries: Yes
Elementary/Secondary schools: No
Community-based organizations: Yes
Correctional institutions: No

On-Campus Requirements

Is an on-campus component required? Yes
On-campus course work: Yes
On-campus admissions interview: No
On-campus program orientation: Yes
On-campus exams: No
On-campus thesis defense: No

Tuition & Fees

Application fee: $50
Can it be waived? No
Average yearly cost of books: $800

Financial Aid

Is financial aid available to full-time students? Yes
Is financial aid available to part-time students? No
Are academic scholarships available? No
Assistance programs available to students: Federal Stafford Loan, Federal Work-Study Program

Antioch University, The McGregor School—Liberal and Professional Studies

Individualized Master of Arts
800 Livermore Street
Yellow Springs, OH 45387
Contact: Dr. Iris Weisman, Associate Professor and Chair
Department e-mail: admiss@mcgregor.edu
School Web address: www.mcgregor.edu
Institutional accreditation: North Central Association of Colleges and Schools

Admissions Requirements

Is a minimum undergraduate GPA required? No
Is provisional admission available? Yes

Is an admissions interview required? Yes
Can pre-requisite course work be waived? No
Are international students eligible to apply? Yes
Is the TOEFL required for international students? No

Program Delivery

Two-way interactive video: No
Two-way audio, one-way video: No
One-way live video: No
One-way pre-recorded video: No
Audio graphics: No
Audio: No
Software requirements: Netscape 4.x and above or Internet
    Explorer 4.x and above, or AOL 4.0 and above
Is the library accessible to students? Yes
Are computers accessible to students? Yes

Remote Sites

Other branches of the institution: No
Other college campuses: Yes
Students' homes: Yes
Work sites: Yes
Libraries: Yes
Elementary/Secondary schools: Yes
Community-based organizations: Yes
Correctional institutions: No

On-Campus Requirements

Is an on-campus component required? Yes
On-campus course work: Yes
On-campus admissions interview: No
On-campus program orientation: Yes
On-campus exams: No
On-campus thesis defense: No

Tuition & Fees

Application fee: $50
Can it be waived? No

Financial Aid

Is financial aid available to full-time students? Yes
Is financial aid available to part-time students? No
Are academic scholarships available? No
Assistance programs available to students: Federal Stafford
    Loan, Federal Work-Study Program

Antioch University, The McGregor School— Intercultural Relations

Individualized Master of Arts
800 Livermore Street
Yellow Spring, OH 45387
Contact: Dr. Linda Ziegahn, Associate Professor
Department e-mail: admiss@mcgregor.edu
School Web address: www.mcgregor.edu
Institutional accreditation: North Central Association of
    Colleges and Schools

Admissions Requirements

Is a minimum undergraduate GPA required? No
Is provisional admission available? No
Is an admissions interview required? Yes
Can pre-requisite course work be waived? No
Are international students eligible to apply? Yes
Is the TOEFL required for international students? No

Program Delivery

Software requirements: Netscape 4.0 and above or Internet
    Explorer 4.x and above, or AOL 4.0 and above
Is the library accessible to students? Yes
Are computers accessible to students? Yes

Remote Sites

Other branches of the institution: No
Other college campuses: Yes
Students' homes: Yes
Work sites: Yes
Libraries: Yes
Elementary/Secondary schools: No
Community-based organizations: Yes
Correctional institutions: No

On-Campus Requirements

Is an on-campus component required? Yes
On-campus course work: Yes
On-campus admissions interview: No
On-campus program orientation: Yes
On-campus exams: No
On-campus thesis defense: No

Tuition & Fees

In-state tuition per credit: $2,416
Application fee: $50
Can it be waived? No
Average yearly cost of books: $900

Financial Aid

Is financial aid available to full-time students? Yes
Is financial aid available to part-time students? No
Are academic scholarships available? No
Assistance programs available to students: Federal Stafford Loan, Federal Work-Study Program

Arizona State University

College of Extended Education
Distance Learning Technology
PO Box 870501
Tempe, AZ 85287-0501
Contact: Elizabeth Craft, Director
Department e-mail: distance@asu.edu
Department Web address: www.dlt.asu.edu
School Web address: www.asu.edu
Institutional accreditation: North Central Association of Colleges and Schools

Subjects Offered

Accounting, art education, art history, analysis and systems, chemical engineering, construction, computer science and engineering, English, family studies, finance, foreign languages, cultural geography, gerontology, humanities, industrial engineering, Latin, management, nursing, public affairs, physics, urban and environmental planning, recreation

Admissions Requirements

Is a minimum undergraduate GPA required? Yes
Is provisional admission available? Yes
Is an admissions interview required? No
Are international students eligible to apply? Yes
Is the TOEFL required for international students? Yes
What is the minimum TOEFL score required? 550

Program Delivery

Primary method of program delivery: Web
Two-way audio, one-way video: Yes
One-way pre-recorded video: Yes
Audio: Yes
Hardware requirements: 90 MHz Intel Pentium processor, 32MB of RAM (64MB recommended)
Software requirements: Operating system: Windows 95/98/NT, current browser—Microsoft Internet Explorer 4.02 or Netscape 4.5 or better
Is the library accessible to students? Yes
Are computers accessible to students? Yes

Remote Sites

Other branches of the institution: Yes
Other college campuses: Yes
Students' homes: Yes
Work sites: Yes
Libraries: No
Elementary/Secondary schools: No
Community-based organizations: No
Correctional institutions: No

On-Campus Requirements

Is an on-campus component required? No

Tuition & Fees

In-state tuition per credit: $2,346
Out-of-state tuition per credit: $9,802
Average yearly cost of books: $600

Financial Aid

Is financial aid available to full-time students? Yes
Is financial aid available to part-time students? Yes
Are academic scholarships available? Yes
Assistance programs available to students: Federal Stafford Loan, Federal Perkins Loan, Federal Work-Study Program, in-state student aid programs, veterans' assistance

Arkansas Tech University

Office of Academic Affairs
Virtual Learning Center
Russellville, AR 72801
Contact: John Gale, Director of the Virtual Learning Center
Department e-mail: gabriel.esteban@mail.atu.edu
Department Web address: www.vlc.atu.edu
School Web address: www.atu.edu
Institutional accreditation: North Central Association of Colleges and Schools

Subjects Offered

Administrative law, e-mail and the Internet, journalism, liberal arts

Admissions Requirements

Is a minimum undergraduate GPA required? Yes
Is provisional admission available? Yes
Is an admissions interview required? No
Can pre-requisite course work be waived? No
Are international students eligible to apply? Yes
Is the TOEFL required for international students? Yes
What is the minimum TOEFL score required? 500

Program Delivery

Primary method of program delivery: Web
Two-way interactive video: Yes
Two-way audio, one-way video: No
One-way live video: No
One-way pre-recorded video: Yes
Audio graphics: No
Audio: No
Hardware requirements: IBM PC Compatible 486-66 or Macintosh 68040
Software requirements: Netscape Navigator or Internet Explorer and Microsoft Word or Word Perfect
Is the library accessible to students? Yes
Are computers accessible to students? Yes

Remote Sites

Other branches of the institution: No
Other college campuses: Yes
Students' homes: No
Work sites: No
Libraries: No
Elementary/Secondary schools: Yes
Community-based organizations: Yes
Correctional institutions: No

On-Campus Requirements

Is an on-campus component required? No

Tuition & Fees

In-state tuition per credit: $116
Out-of-state tuition per credit: $232
Average yearly cost of books: $400

Financial Aid

Is financial aid available to full-time students? Yes
Is financial aid available to part-time students? Yes
Are academic scholarships available? Yes
Assistance programs available to students: Federal Stafford Loan, Federal Perkins Loan, Federal Plus Loan, Federal Pell Grant, Federal Work-Study Program, in-state student aid programs, veterans' assistance

Athabasca University, Centre for Innovative Management

Centre for Innovative Management/Graduate Management Programs
301, 22 Sir Winston Churchill Avenue
St. Albert, AB, Canada T8N 1B4
Contact: Dr. Lindsay Redpath, Director

Department Web address: www.athabascau.ca/mba
School Web address: www.athabascau.ca
Institutional accreditation: Association of Universities and Colleges of Canada

Subjects Offered

Strategic management, analytical tools, human resource management, financial accounting, marketing management, operations management, managerial accounting, information technology strategy, strategy and organizational analysis, business economics and society, human factors in information technology, project management for IT projects, electronic commerce

Admissions Requirements

Is provisional admission available? Yes
Is an admissions interview required? No
Are international students eligible to apply? Yes
Is the TOEFL required for international students? Yes

Program Delivery

Primary method of program delivery: Web
Hardware requirements: Pentium 166 MHz, 32MB Memory, 1 GB free space hard drive, Windows 95/98/NT 4.0, monitor 256 colors, 56KBPS modem
Is the library accessible to students? Yes
Are computers accessible to students? No

Remote Sites

Students' homes: Yes
Work sites: Yes

On-Campus Requirements

Is an on-campus component required? No

Tuition & Fees

Application fee: $165
Can it be waived? No

Financial Aid

Is financial aid available to full-time students? No
Is financial aid available to part-time students? No
Are academic scholarships available? No

Atlantic University

Building 3300, Suite 100
397 Little Neck Road
Virginia Beach, VA 23452
Contact: Herk Stokely, CEO
Department e-mail: registrar@atlanticuniv.edu
School Web address: www.atlanticuniv.edu
Institutional accreditation: Distance Education and Training Council

Subjects Offered

Consciousness and intuition, holistic health and holistic living, sacred literature, visual arts, archetypal studies, women and the transpersonal perspective

Admissions Requirements

Is a minimum undergraduate GPA required? Yes
Is provisional admission available? Yes
Is an admissions interview required? No
Can pre-requisite course work be waived? Yes
Are international students eligible to apply? Yes
Is the TOEFL required for international students? Yes
What is the minimum TOEFL score required? 550

Program Delivery

Primary method of program delivery: Text
Two-way interactive video: No
Two-way audio, one-way video: Yes
One-way live video: No
One-way pre-recorded video: Yes
Audio graphics: No
Audio: Yes
Is the library accessible to students? Yes
Are computers accessible to students? No

Remote Sites

Other branches of the institution: No
Other college campuses: No
Students' homes: Yes
Work sites: No
Libraries: Yes
Elementary/Secondary schools: No
Community-based organizations: No
Correctional institutions: No

On-Campus Requirements

Is an on-campus component required? No

Tuition & Fees

In-state tuition per credit: $510
Average yearly cost of books: $300

Financial Aid

Is financial aid available to full-time students? No
Is financial aid available to part-time students? No
Are academic scholarships available? Yes

Auburn University

Distance Learning
204 Mell Hall
Auburn University, AL 36849
Contact: Richard Alekna, Director

Department e-mail: audl@auburn.edu
Department Web address: www.auburn.edu/outreach/dl
School Web address: www.auburn.edu
Institutional accreditation: Southern Association of Colleges and Schools

Admissions Requirements

Is a minimum undergraduate GPA required? Yes
Is provisional admission available? No
Is an admissions interview required? No
Can pre-requisite course work be waived? No
Are international students eligible to apply? No

Program Delivery

Primary method of program delivery: Remote site
Two-way interactive video: No
Two-way audio, one-way video: No
One-way live video: No
One-way pre-recorded video: Yes
Audio graphics: No
Audio: Yes
Is the library accessible to students? Yes
Are computers accessible to students? Yes

Remote Sites

Other branches of the institution: No
Other college campuses: Yes
Students' homes: Yes
Work sites: Yes
Libraries: Yes
Elementary/Secondary schools: No
Community-based organizations: Yes
Correctional institutions: No

On-Campus Requirements

Is an on-campus component required? Yes
On-campus course work: No
On-campus admissions interview: No
On-campus program orientation: No
On-campus exams: Yes
On-campus thesis defense: Yes

Tuition & Fees

In-state tuition per credit: $296
Out-of-state tuition per credit: $296
Average yearly cost of books: $400

Financial Aid

Is financial aid available to full-time students? Yes
Is financial aid available to part-time students? No
Are academic scholarships available? Yes

Baker College Center for Graduate Studies

1050 West Bristol Road
Flint, MI 48507
Contact: Chuck Gurden, Director of Graduate and On-Line Admissions
Department e-mail: gurden_c@corpfl.baker.edu
Department Web address: online.baker.edu
School Web address: www.baker.edu
Institutional accreditation: North Central Association of Colleges and Schools

Admissions Requirements

Is a minimum undergraduate GPA required? Yes
Is provisional admission available? Yes
Is an admissions interview required? No
Can pre-requisite course work be waived? No
Are international students eligible to apply? Yes
Is the TOEFL required for international students? Yes
What is the minimum TOEFL score required? 550

Program Delivery

Primary method of program delivery: Web
Two-way interactive video: No
Two-way audio, one-way video: No
One-way live video: No
One-way pre-recorded video: No
Audio graphics: No
Audio: No
Software requirements: Word processing, spreadsheet, Internet service provider
Is the library accessible to students? Yes
Are computers accessible to students? No

Remote Sites

Other branches of the institution: Yes
Other college campuses: No
Students' homes: Yes
Work sites: Yes
Libraries: Yes
Elementary/Secondary schools: No
Community-based organizations: No
Correctional institutions: No

On-Campus Requirements

Is an on-campus component required? No

Tuition & Fees

In-state tuition per credit: $228
Out-of-state tuition per credit: $228
Average yearly cost of books: $18

Financial Aid

Is financial aid available to full-time students? Yes
Is financial aid available to part-time students? Yes
Are academic scholarships available? No
Assistance programs available to students: Federal Stafford Loan, veterans' assistance

Bellvue University

College of Distributed Learning
1000 Galvin Road South
Bellvue, NE 68005
Contact: Dr. Christine Beischel, Dean, College of Distributed Learning
Department e-mail: kathy@bellvue.edu
Department Web address: bellvue.edu
School Web address: bellvue.edu
Institutional accreditation: North Central Association of Colleges and Schools

Subjects Offered

Business administration, computer information, management

Admissions Requirements

Is a minimum undergraduate GPA required? Yes
Is provisional admission available? Yes
Is an admissions interview required? No
Can pre-requisite course work be waived? No
Are international students eligible to apply? Yes
Is the TOEFL required for international students? Yes
What is the minimum TOEFL score required? 550

Program Delivery

Primary method of program delivery: Web
Two-way interactive video: No
Two-way audio, one-way video: No
One-way live video: No
One-way pre-recorded video: Yes
Audio graphics: Yes
Audio: Yes
Hardware requirements: For Mac: G3 processor or higher, 32MB of RAM or higher, OS 8 or higher, 56KBPS modem or higher, sound card/speakers, same for PC except Windows 95 or higher
Software requirements: Microsoft Office (Word, Excel, PowerPoint), Internet browser (Microsoft Internet Explorer 4.0 or higher, Netscape Navigator 4.0 or higher)
Is the library accessible to students? Yes
Are computers accessible to students? No

Remote Sites

Other branches of the institution: Yes
Students' homes: Yes

On-Campus Requirements

Is an on-campus component required? No

Tuition & Fees

In-state tuition per credit: $280
Out-of-state tuition per credit: $280
Average yearly cost of books: $130

Financial Aid

Is financial aid available to full-time students? Yes
Is financial aid available to part-time students? Yes
Are academic scholarships available? Yes
Assistance programs available to students: Federal Stafford
   Loan, Federal Work-Study Program, veterans' assistance

Bethel Seminary

In Ministry Program
3949 Bethel Drive
St. Paul, MN 55112
Contact: Dr. Greg Bourgond, Director of Instructional
   Technology
Department e-mail: g-bourgound@bethel.edu
School Web address: www.bethel.edu
Institutional accreditation: North Central Association of
   Colleges and Schools; Association of Theological Schools

Admissions Requirements

Is a minimum undergraduate GPA required? Yes
Is provisional admission available? Yes
Can pre-requisite course work be waived? No
Are international students eligible to apply? Yes
Is the TOEFL required for international students? Yes
What is the minimum TOEFL score required? 550

Program Delivery

Primary method of program delivery: Web
Two-way interactive video: Yes
Two-way audio, one-way video: No
One-way live video: No
One-way pre-recorded video: Yes
Audio graphics: No
Audio: No
Hardware requirements: Windows, Pentium (133MHz),
   28.8KBPS modem, CD-ROM
Software requirements: Microsoft Word 97, Netscape 3.0
   or better, RealPlayer, Adobe Acrobat Reader 2.1 or better
Is the library accessible to students? Yes
Are computers accessible to students? Yes

Remote Sites

Other branches of the institution: Yes
Other college campuses: No
Students' homes: Yes
Work sites: Yes
Libraries: No
Elementary/Secondary schools: No
Community-based organizations: No
Correctional institutions: No

On-Campus Requirements

Is an on-campus component required? Yes

Tuition & Fees

In-state tuition per credit: $160
Out-of-state tuition per credit: $160
Average yearly cost of books: $760

Financial Aid

Is financial aid available to full-time students? Yes
Is financial aid available to part-time students? Yes
Are academic scholarships available? No
Assistance programs available to students: Federal Stafford
   Loan

Binghamton University

EngiNet
Watson School, PO Box 6000
Binghamton, NY 13902
Contact: Ronald S. Carlson, Director of EngiNet
Department e-mail: jkinzer@binghaton.edu
School Web address: www.enginet.bingamton.edu

Subjects Offered

Computer science, electrical engineering, system science
   and industrial engineering

Admissions Requirements

Is provisional admission available? Yes
Is an admissions interview required? No
Can pre-requisite course work be waived? No
Are international students eligible to apply? No

Program Delivery

Primary method of program delivery: Web
Two-way interactive video: No
Two-way audio, one-way video: No
One-way live video: Yes
One-way pre-recorded video: No
Audio graphics: Yes
Audio: Yes

Is the library accessible to students? Yes
Are computers accessible to students? No

Remote Sites

Students' homes: Yes
Work sites: Yes

On-Campus Requirements

Is an on-campus component required? No

Tuition & Fees

In-state tuition per credit: $213
Out-of-state tuition per credit: $351

Financial Aid

Is financial aid available to full-time students? Yes
Is financial aid available to part-time students? Yes
Are academic scholarships available? No
Assistance programs available to students: Federal Stafford
  Loan, Federal Perkins Loan, Federal Plus Loan, Federal
  Work-Study Program, in-state student aid programs,
  veterans' assistance

Boise State University

Extended Studies
1910 University Drive
Boise, ID 83725
Contact: Janet Atkinson, Director, Distance Education
Department e-mail: jatkinso@boisestate.edu
Department Web address: www.boisestate.edu/conted
School Web address: www.boisestate.edu
Institutional accreditation: Northwest Association of
  Schools and Colleges

Subjects Offered

Instructional and performance technology, educational
  technology, accounting, art, biology, engineering,
  computer science, education, English, Spanish,
  geography, history, business, health science, music,
  nursing

Admissions Requirements

Is a minimum undergraduate GPA required? Yes
Is provisional admission available? Yes
Is an admissions interview required? No
Can pre-requisite course work be waived? Yes
Are international students eligible to apply? Yes
Is the TOEFL required for international students? No

Program Delivery

Two-way interactive video: Yes
Two-way audio, one-way video: Yes

One-way pre-recorded video: Yes
Audio: Yes
Is the library accessible to students? Yes
Are computers accessible to students? No

Remote Sites

Other branches of the institution: Yes
Other college campuses: Yes
Students' homes: Yes
Work sites: Yes
Libraries: Yes
Elementary/Secondary schools: Yes
Community-based organizations: Yes
Correctional institutions: No

On-Campus Requirements

Is an on-campus component required? No

Financial Aid

Is financial aid available to full-time students? Yes
Is financial aid available to part-time students? No
Are academic scholarships available? Yes

Boston University

Manufacturing Engineering
ICV Program
Boston, MA 02215
Contact: Professor Merrill Ebner, Faculty Coordinator
Department e-mail: icv@bu.edu
Department Web address: www.bu.edu/mfg/dlp
School Web address: www.bu.edu
Institutional accreditation: Association Board for Engineer-
  ing and Technology

Subjects Offered

Manufacturing engineering

Admissions Requirements

Is provisional admission available? No
Is an admissions interview required? No
Can pre-requisite course work be waived? No
Are international students eligible to apply? Yes
Is the TOEFL required for international students? Yes

Program Delivery

Two-way interactive video: Yes
Is the library accessible to students? Yes
Are computers accessible to students? Yes

Remote Sites

Other branches of the institution: Yes
Work sites: Yes

On-Campus Requirements

Is an on-campus component required? No

Tuition & Fees

In-state tuition per credit: $772
Application fee: $40
Can it be waived? No
Average yearly cost of books: $300

Financial Aid

Is financial aid available to full-time students? No
Is financial aid available to part-time students? No
Are academic scholarships available? No

Bradley University

Continuing Education
1501 West Bradley Avenue
Peoria, IL 61625
Contact: Susan Manley, Program Director
Department e-mail: cepd@bradley.edu
Department Web address: www.bradley.edu/continue
School Web address: www.bradley.edu
Institutional accreditation: North Central Association of Colleges and Schools

Admissions Requirements

Is a minimum undergraduate GPA required? Yes
Is provisional admission available? Yes
Is an admissions interview required? No
Is the TOEFL required for international students? Yes
What is the minimum TOEFL score required? 550

Program Delivery

Primary method of program delivery: Remote site
Two-way interactive video: Yes
Two-way audio, one-way video: Yes
One-way live video: Yes
One-way pre-recorded video: Yes
Audio graphics: No
Audio: No
Is the library accessible to students? Yes
Are computers accessible to students? Yes

Remote Sites

Other branches of the institution: No
Other college campuses: No
Students' homes: Yes
Work sites: Yes
Libraries: No
Elementary/Secondary schools: No
Community-based organizations: No
Correctional institutions: No

On-Campus Requirements

Is an on-campus component required? Yes

Tuition & Fees

Application fee: $40
Can it be waived? No
Average yearly additional fees: $100

Financial Aid

Is financial aid available to full-time students? Yes
Is financial aid available to part-time students? Yes
Are academic scholarships available? Yes
Assistance programs available to students: Federal Stafford Loan

Brenau University

Business Administration and Mass Communications
Online Education
One Centennial Circle
Gainesville, GA 30501
Contact: William Fox, Associate Professor of Business Administration
Department e-mail: wfox@lib.brenau.edu
Department Web address: www.brenau.edu/busdiv
School Web address: www.brenau.edu
Institutional accreditation: Southern Association of Colleges and Schools

Subjects Offered

Accounting, marketing, management

Admissions Requirements

Is a minimum undergraduate GPA required? Yes
Is provisional admission available? Yes
Is an admissions interview required? Yes
Can pre-requisite course work be waived? No
Are international students eligible to apply? Yes
Is the TOEFL required for international students? Yes
What is the minimum TOEFL score required? 550

Program Delivery

Primary method of program delivery: Web
Two-way interactive video: No
Two-way audio, one-way video: No
One-way live video: No
One-way pre-recorded video: No
Audio graphics: No
Audio: Yes
Hardware requirements: Pentium and 56KBPS modem recommended
Software requirements: Microsoft Office 97 or later version, Internet service provider

Is the library accessible to students? Yes
Are computers accessible to students? Yes

Remote Sites

Other branches of the institution: No
Other college campuses: No
Students' homes: Yes
Work sites: Yes
Libraries: No
Elementary/Secondary schools: No
Community-based organizations: No
Correctional institutions: No

On-Campus Requirements

Is an on-campus component required? No

Tuition & Fees

In-state tuition per credit: $335
Out-of-state tuition per credit: $335
Average yearly cost of books: $700

Financial Aid

Is financial aid available to full-time students? Yes
Is financial aid available to part-time students? Yes
Are academic scholarships available? Yes
Assistance programs available to students: Federal Stafford
   Loan, Federal Perkins Loan, Federal Plus Loan, Federal
   Work-Study Program, in-state student aid programs,
   veterans' assistance

California Institute of Integral Studies

School for Consciousness and Transformation
1453 Mission Street
San Francisco, CA 94103
Contact: Elizabeth Campbell, Program Director
Department e-mail: lizc@ciis.edu
School Web address: www.ciis.edu
Institutional accreditation: Western Association of Schools
   and Colleges

Subjects Offered

Humanities, organizational development, adult learning
   theory, systems theory, gross cultural studies, social
   change, spiritual perspectives, women's studies,
   sociology, group dynamics, leadership

Admissions Requirements

Is an admissions interview required? Yes
Can pre-requisite course work be waived? No
Are international students eligible to apply? Yes
Is the TOEFL required for international students? Yes

Program Delivery

Primary method of program delivery: Web
One-way pre-recorded video: Yes
Is the library accessible to students? Yes
Are computers accessible to students? No

Remote Sites

Students' homes: Yes

On-Campus Requirements

Is an on-campus component required? Yes
On-campus course work: Yes
On-campus program orientation: Yes
On-campus thesis defense: Yes

Tuition & Fees

In-state tuition per credit: $578
Average yearly cost of books: $600
Average yearly additional fees: $65

Financial Aid

Is financial aid available to full-time students? Yes
Are academic scholarships available? Yes
Assistance programs available to students: Federal Stafford
   Loan, veterans' assistance

California State University, Domiguez Hills—Quality Assurance Program

Division of Extended Education
Center for Mediated Instruction and Distance Learning
1000 East Victoria
Carson, CA 90747
Contact: Dr. Warren Ashley, Director, Center for Mediated
   and Instruction Distance Learning
Department Web address: www.csudh.edu/
   dominguezonline
School Web address: www.csudh.edu
Institutional accreditation: Western Association of Schools
   and Colleges

Subjects Offered

Assistive technology, purchasing, production and inventory
   control, quality assurance

Admissions Requirements

Is provisional admission available? Yes
Is an admissions interview required? No
Can pre-requisite course work be waived? No
Are international students eligible to apply? Yes

Is the TOEFL required for international students? Yes
What is the minimum TOEFL score required? 550

Program Delivery

Hardware requirements: Pentium I, 32MB of RAM,
28.8KBPS modem
Software requirements: Internet Explorer or Netscape 4.0,
Windows 95
Is the library accessible to students? Yes
Are computers accessible to students? Yes

Remote Sites

Students' homes: Yes

On-Campus Requirements

Is an on-campus component required? No

Tuition & Fees

In-state tuition per credit: $145
Out-of-state tuition per credit: $145
Average yearly cost of books: $500

Financial Aid

Is financial aid available to full-time students? Yes
Is financial aid available to part-time students? Yes
Are academic scholarships available? Yes

California State University, Dominguez Hills— Humanities Program

Division of Extended Education
Center for Mediated Instruction and Distance Learning
1000 East Victoria Street
Carson, CA 90747
Contact: Dr. Warren Ashley, Director, Center for Mediated
Instruction and Distance Learning
Department Web address: www.csudh.edu/
dominguezonline
School Web address: www.csudh.edu
Institutional accreditation: Western Association of Schools
and Colleges

Subjects Offered

Humanities

Admissions Requirements

Is a minimum undergraduate GPA required? Yes
Is provisional admission available? Yes
Is an admissions interview required? No
Can pre-requisite course work be waived? No
Are international students eligible to apply? Yes

Is the TOEFL required for international students? Yes
What is the minimum TOEFL score required? 550

Program Delivery

Primary method of program delivery: Text
Is the library accessible to students? Yes
Are computers accessible to students? Yes

Remote Sites

Students' homes: Yes

On-Campus Requirements

Is an on-campus component required? No

Tuition & Fees

In-state tuition per credit: $135
Out-of-state tuition per credit: $135
Average yearly cost of books: $500

Financial Aid

Is financial aid available to full-time students? Yes
Is financial aid available to part-time students? Yes
Are academic scholarships available? Yes

California State University, Northridge— Communication Disorders and Sciences

18111 Nordhoff Avenue
Northridge, CA 91330-8279
Contact: Dr. Karen Jones Green, Coordinator
Department e-mail: communication.disorders@csun.edu
Department Web address: exloracle.csun.edu/cds
School Web address: www.csun.edu
Institutional accreditation: Western Association of Schools
and Colleges

Subjects Offered

Computer applications, research, interviewing and
counseling, clinical practice, neuroanatomy, aphasia,
voice, fluency, phonology, neurogenics, structural
audiology, educational psychology.

Admissions Requirements

Is a minimum undergraduate GPA required? Yes
Is provisional admission available? No
Is an admissions interview required? Yes
Can pre-requisite course work be waived? No
Are international students eligible to apply? Yes
Is the TOEFL required for international students? No

Program Delivery

Primary method of program delivery: Web
Two-way interactive video: No
Two-way audio, one-way video: No
One-way live video: No
One-way pre-recorded video: No
Audio graphics: Yes
Audio: Yes
Is the library accessible to students? Yes
Are computers accessible to students? No

Remote Sites

Other branches of the institution: No
Other college campuses: No
Students' homes: Yes
Work sites: Yes
Libraries: Yes
Elementary/Secondary schools: Yes
Community-based organizations: Yes
Correctional institutions: No

On-Campus Requirements

Is an on-campus component required? No

Tuition & Fees

Application fee: $55
Can it be waived? No

Financial Aid

Is financial aid available to full-time students? Yes
Are academic scholarships available? No
Assistance programs available to students: Federal Stafford
   Loan, Federal Perkins Loan, Federal Plus Loan, Federal
   Work-Study Program, in-state student aid programs,
   veterans' assistance

California State University, Dominguez Hills— Behavioral Science Program

Division of Extended Education
Center for Mediated Instruction and Distance Education
1000 East Victoria
Carson, CA 90747
Contact: Dr. Warren Ashley, Director, Center for Mediated
   Instruction and Distance Education
Department Web address: www.csudh.edu/
   dominguezonline
School Web address: www.csudh.edu

Institutional accreditation: Western Association of Schools
   and Colleges

Subjects Offered

Behavioral science

Admissions Requirements

Is a minimum undergraduate GPA required? Yes
Is provisional admission available? Yes
Is an admissions interview required? No
Can pre-requisite course work be waived? No
Are international students eligible to apply? Yes
Is the TOEFL required for international students? Yes
What is the minimum TOEFL score required? 550

Program Delivery

Two-way audio, one-way video: Yes
Hardware requirements: Pentium I, 32MB of RAM,
   28.8KBPS modem
Software requirements: Windows 95, Netscape Navigator
   or Internet Explorer 4.0
Is the library accessible to students? Yes
Are computers accessible to students? Yes

Remote Sites

Students' homes: Yes

On-Campus Requirements

Is an on-campus component required? No

Tuition & Fees

In-state tuition per credit: $170
Out-of-state tuition per credit: $170
Average yearly cost of books: $500

Financial Aid

Is financial aid available to full-time students? Yes
Is financial aid available to part-time students? Yes
Are academic scholarships available? Yes

Campbellsville University

1 University Drive
Campbellsville, KY 42718
School Web address: www.campbellsville.edu
Institutional accreditation: Southern Association of
   Colleges and Schools

Subjects Offered

Educational assessment, cognitive psychology

Admissions Requirements

Is a minimum undergraduate GPA required? Yes
Is provisional admission available? Yes

Is an admissions interview required? No
Can pre-requisite course work be waived? Yes
Are international students eligible to apply? Yes
Is the TOEFL required for international students? Yes
What is the minimum TOEFL score required? 500

Program Delivery

Primary method of program delivery: Web

On-Campus Requirements

Is an on-campus component required? No

Tuition & Fees

In-state tuition per credit: $255
Average yearly additional fees: $120

Capella University—School of Business

222 South 9th Street
Minneapolis, MN 55402
Contact: Susan Saxton, PhD, Dean, School of Business
Department e-mail: info@capella.edu
School Web address: www.capellauniversity.edu
Institutional accreditation: North Central Association of
    Colleges and Schools

Subjects Offered

Brand management, communications technology, e-
    business, entrepreneurship, finance, human resource
    management, information technology, international
    business, leadership, marketing

Admissions Requirements

Is a minimum undergraduate GPA required? Yes
Is provisional admission available? Yes
Is an admissions interview required? No
Are international students eligible to apply? Yes
Is the TOEFL required for international students? Yes
What is the minimum TOEFL score required? 550

Program Delivery

Primary method of program delivery: Web
Two-way interactive video: No
Two-way audio, one-way video: No
One-way live video: No
One-way pre-recorded video: No
Audio graphics: Yes
Audio: Yes
Hardware requirements: Pentium processor 133 MHz
    (Mac-180), 32MB of RAM, 200MB of hard disk space,
    CD-ROM drive, 28.8KBPS modem, multimedia
    capability, video card (800 x 600)

Software requirements: Windows 95/98/2000 or NT,
    Acrobat Reader, Internet browser 4.0 or higher,
    RealPlayer 7, Word/WordPerfect, e-mail. Mac OS 8.0 or
    later
Is the library accessible to students? Yes

Remote Sites

Other branches of the institution: No
Other college campuses: No
Students' homes: Yes
Work sites: No
Libraries: Yes
Elementary/Secondary schools: No
Community-based organizations: No
Correctional institutions: No

On-Campus Requirements

Is an on-campus component required? Yes

Tuition & Fees

Application fee: $50
Can it be waived? No
Average yearly cost of books: $400
Average yearly additional fees: $350

Capella University—School of Human Services

222 South 9th Street
Minneapolis, MN 55402
Contact: Robert Ford, PhD, Dean, School of Human
    Services
Department e-mail: info@capella.edu
School Web address: www.capellauniversity.edu
Institutional accreditation: North Central Association of
    Colleges and Schools

Subjects Offered

Educational assessment, cognitive psychology

Admissions Requirements

Is a minimum undergraduate GPA required? Yes
Is provisional admission available? Yes
Can pre-requisite course work be waived? Yes
Are international students eligible to apply? Yes
Is the TOEFL required for international students? Yes
What is the minimum TOEFL score required? 550

Program Delivery

Primary method of program delivery: Web
Two-way interactive video: No
Two-way audio, one-way video: No

One-way live video: No
One-way pre-recorded video: No
Audio graphics: Yes
Audio: Yes
Is the library accessible to students? Yes
Are computers accessible to students? No

Remote Sites

Other branches of the institution: No
Other college campuses: No
Students' homes: Yes
Work sites: No
Libraries: Yes
Elementary/Secondary schools: No
Community-based organizations: No
Correctional institutions: No

On-Campus Requirements

Is an on-campus component required? Yes
On-campus course work: Yes
On-campus admissions interview: No
On-campus program orientation: No
On-campus exams: No
On-campus thesis defense: No

Tuition & Fees

In-state tuition per credit: $231
Application fee: $50
Can it be waived? No
Average yearly cost of books: $400

Financial Aid

Is financial aid available to full-time students? Yes
Is financial aid available to part-time students? Yes
Are academic scholarships available? No
Assistance programs available to students: Federal Stafford
  Loan, in-state student aid programs, veterans' assistance

Capella University—School of Psychology

222 South 9th Street
Minneapolis, MN 55402
Contact: Brian Austin, PhD, Dean
Department e-mail: info@capella.edu
School Web address: www.capellauniversity.edu
Institutional accreditation: North Central Association of
  Colleges and Schools

Subjects Offered

Family psychology, health psychology, organizational
  psychology, sports psychology, educational psychology,
  clinical psychology, addiction psychology

Admissions Requirements

Is a minimum undergraduate GPA required? Yes
Is provisional admission available? Yes
Is an admissions interview required? Yes
Can pre-requisite course work be waived? Yes
Are international students eligible to apply? Yes
Is the TOEFL required for international students? Yes
What is the minimum TOEFL score required? 550

Program Delivery

Primary method of program delivery: Web
Two-way interactive video: No
Two-way audio, one-way video: No
One-way live video: No
One-way pre-recorded video: No
Audio graphics: Yes
Audio: Yes
Is the library accessible to students? Yes
Are computers accessible to students? No

Remote Sites

Other branches of the institution: No
Other college campuses: No
Students' homes: Yes
Libraries: Yes

On-Campus Requirements

Is an on-campus component required? Yes
On-campus course work: Yes
On-campus admissions interview: No
On-campus program orientation: No
On-campus exams: No
On-campus thesis defense: No

Tuition & Fees

In-state tuition per credit: $260
Out-of-state tuition per credit: $260
Average yearly cost of books: $600

Financial Aid

Is financial aid available to full-time students? Yes
Is financial aid available to part-time students? Yes
Are academic scholarships available? No
Assistance programs available to students: Federal Stafford
  Loan, in-state student aid programs, veterans' assistance

Capella University—School of Education and Professional Development

222 South 9th Street
Minneapolis, MN 55402
Contact: Dr. Elizabeth Bruch, Dean, School of Education and Professional Development
Department e-mail: info@capella.edu
School Web address: www.capellauniversity.edu
Institutional accreditation: North Central Association of Colleges and Schools

Subjects Offered

Teaching: training online, instructional design for online learning, adult education, educational administration

Admissions Requirements

Is a minimum undergraduate GPA required? Yes
Is provisional admission available? Yes
Is an admissions interview required? Yes
Are international students eligible to apply? Yes
Is the TOEFL required for international students? Yes
What is the minimum TOEFL score required? 550

Program Delivery

Primary method of program delivery: Web
Two-way interactive video: No
Two-way audio, one-way video: No
One-way live video: No
One-way pre-recorded video: No
Audio graphics: Yes
Audio: Yes
Is the library accessible to students? Yes
Are computers accessible to students? No

Remote Sites

Other branches of the institution: No
Other college campuses: No
Students' homes: Yes
Work sites: No
Libraries: Yes
Elementary/Secondary schools: No
Community-based organizations: No
Correctional institutions: No

On-Campus Requirements

Is an on-campus component required? Yes
On-campus course work: No
On-campus admissions interview: No
On-campus program orientation: No
On-campus exams: No
On-campus thesis defense: No

Tuition & Fees

In-state tuition per credit: $231
Application fee: $50
Can it be waived? No
Average yearly cost of books: $400

Financial Aid

Is financial aid available to full-time students? Yes
Is financial aid available to part-time students? Yes
Are academic scholarships available? No
Assistance programs available to students: Federal Stafford Loan, in-state student aid programs, veterans' assistance

Capitol College

Graduate School
11301 Springfield Road
Laurel, MD 20708
Contact: Ken Crockett, Director, Graduate Admissions
Department e-mail: gradadmit@capitol-college.edu
Department Web address: www.capitol-college.edu/academics/grad/default.htm
School Web address: www.capitol-college.edu
Institutional accreditation: Middle States Association of Colleges and Schools

Subjects Offered

Internet architecture, e-commerce, information and telecommunications systems, technology management

Admissions Requirements

Is a minimum undergraduate GPA required? Yes
Is provisional admission available? Yes
Is an admissions interview required? No
Can pre-requisite course work be waived? Yes
Are international students eligible to apply? Yes
Is the TOEFL required for international students? Yes
What is the minimum TOEFL score required? 600

Program Delivery

Primary method of program delivery: Web
One-way live video: Yes
Audio: Yes
Hardware requirements: Pentium 166 with 64MB of RAM, sound card with speakers or headphones and microphone
Software requirements: Windows 95/98 or NT
Is the library accessible to students? No
Are computers accessible to students? No

Remote Sites

Other college campuses: Yes

Tuition & Fees

In-state tuition per credit: $336
Out-of-state tuition per credit: $336
Average yearly cost of books: $600

Financial Aid

Is financial aid available to full-time students? Yes
Is financial aid available to part-time students? Yes
Are academic scholarships available? No
Assistance programs available to students: Federal Stafford
    Loan, Federal Perkins Loan, veterans' assistance

Carlow College

Division of Nursing—Graduate
3333 Fifth Avenue
Pittsburgh, PA 15213
Contact: Susan Sterrett, Graduate Program Director
Department e-mail: ssterret@carlow.edu
School Web address: www.carlow.edu
Institutional accreditation: Middle States Association of
    Colleges and Schools

Subjects Offered

Nursing theories, health policy, epidemiology, conceptual
    basis of community health, nursing case management,
    advanced physical assessment, chronic care home
    management, advanced pathophysiology

Admissions Requirements

Is a minimum undergraduate GPA required? Yes
Is provisional admission available? Yes
Is an admissions interview required? Yes
Can pre-requisite course work be waived? No
Are international students eligible to apply? Yes

Program Delivery

Primary method of program delivery: Remote site
Is the library accessible to students? Yes
Are computers accessible to students? Yes

Remote Sites

Other branches of the institution: Yes
Students' homes: Yes
Work sites: Yes
Libraries: Yes

On-Campus Requirements

Is an on-campus component required? No

Financial Aid

Is financial aid available to full-time students? Yes
Is financial aid available to part-time students? Yes
Are academic scholarships available? Yes
Assistance programs available to students: Federal Stafford
    Loan, Federal Perkins Loan, Federal Plus Loan, Federal
    Work-Study Program, in-state student aid programs

Carnegie Mellon University—Master of Science in Computational Finance

Graduate School of Industrial Administration
Schenley Park
Pittsburgh, PA 15213
Contact: Richard L. Bryant, Director, Computational
    Finance Program
Department e-mail: nmlo@andrew.cmu.edu
Department Web address: student.gsia.cmu.edu/msce/
School Web address: www.cmu.edu
Institutional accreditation: AACSB—The International
    Association for Management Education

Subjects Offered

Finance, statistics, mathematics, information technology

Admissions Requirements

Is a minimum undergraduate GPA required? No
Is provisional admission available? No
Can pre-requisite course work be waived? No
Are international students eligible to apply? Yes
Is the TOEFL required for international students? Yes

Program Delivery

Primary method of program delivery: Remote site
Two-way interactive video: Yes
Two-way audio, one-way video: No
One-way live video: No
One-way pre-recorded video: No
Audio graphics: Yes
Audio: Yes
Is the library accessible to students? Yes
Are computers accessible to students? Yes

Remote Sites

Other branches of the institution: Yes
Other college campuses: No
Students' homes: No
Work sites: No
Libraries: No

Elementary/Secondary schools: No
Community-based organizations: No
Correctional institutions: No

On-Campus Requirements

Is an on-campus component required? No

Tuition & Fees

Application fee: $60
Can it be waived? No

Financial Aid

Is financial aid available to full-time students? Yes
Is financial aid available to part-time students? Yes
Are academic scholarships available? No
Assistance programs available to students: Federal Stafford
Loan, Federal Perkins Loan, Federal Work-Study
Program

Carnegie Mellon University—MBA

Graduate School of Industrial Administration
5000 Forbes Avenue
Pittsburgh, PA 15213
Contact: Dr. Ilker Baybars, Senior Deputy Dean and
Professor
Department e-mail: baybars@andrew.cmu.edu
Department Web address: www.gsia.cmu.edu
School Web address: www.cmu.edu
Institutional accreditation: AACSB—The International
Association for Management Education

Subjects Offered

Business

Admissions Requirements

Is provisional admission available? No
Is an admissions interview required? Yes
Can pre-requisite course work be waived? No
Are international students eligible to apply? Yes
Is the TOEFL required for international students? Yes

Program Delivery

Primary method of program delivery: Remote site
Two-way interactive video: Yes
Hardware requirements: Fax machine, PictureTEL
Software requirements: We provide distance learning
students with computers fully configured with all the
software they will need
Is the library accessible to students? Yes
Are computers accessible to students? Yes

Remote Sites

Work sites: Yes

On-Campus Requirements

Is an on-campus component required? No

Tuition & Fees

In-state tuition per credit: $1,668
Out-of-state tuition per credit: $1,668

Catholic Distance University

120 East Colonial Highway
Hamilton, VA 20158-9012
Contact: Rev. Leonard Obloy, Dean of Graduate Programs
Department e-mail: cdu@cdu.edu
School Web address: www.cdu.edu
Institutional accreditation: Distance Education and
Training Council

Subjects Offered

Religious studies

Admissions Requirements

Is a minimum undergraduate GPA required? No
Is provisional admission available? No
Is an admissions interview required? No
Can pre-requisite course work be waived? Yes
Are international students eligible to apply? Yes
Is the TOEFL required for international students? No

Program Delivery

Primary method of program delivery: Text
Two-way interactive video: No
Two-way audio, one-way video: No
One-way live video: No
One-way pre-recorded video: No
Audio graphics: No
Audio: No
Is the library accessible to students? Yes
Are computers accessible to students? No

Remote Sites

Other branches of the institution: No
Other college campuses: No
Students' homes: Yes
Work sites: No
Libraries: Yes
Elementary/Secondary schools: No
Community-based organizations: No
Correctional institutions: No

On-Campus Requirements

Is an on-campus component required? No

Tuition & Fees

In-state tuition per credit: $210
Out-of-state tuition per credit: $210
Application fee: $100
Can it be waived? No
Average yearly cost of books: $200

Financial Aid

Is financial aid available to full-time students? No
Is financial aid available to part-time students? No
Are academic scholarships available? No

Central Michigan University

College of Extended Learning
Distance/Distributed Learning
Central Michigan University, CEL- DDL
Mt. Pleasant, MI 48859
Contact: William Rugg, Director
Department e-mail: celinfo@mail.cel.cmich.edu
Department Web address: www.ddl.cmich.edu
School Web address: www.cmich.edu
Institutional accreditation: North Central Association of
    Colleges and Schools

Subjects Offered

Communications disorders, master of science in adminis-
    tration, marketing, computer science, journalism

Admissions Requirements

Is a minimum undergraduate GPA required? Yes
Is provisional admission available? Yes
Is an admissions interview required? No
Can pre-requisite course work be waived? Yes
Are international students eligible to apply? Yes
Is the TOEFL required for international students? Yes
What is the minimum TOEFL score required? 550

Program Delivery

Primary method of program delivery: Web
Hardware requirements: Pentium-class computer (or
    equivalent Macintosh), 28.8KBPS or faster modem or
    other Internet connections, 256-color display monitor
Software requirements: JAVA-compatible browser (Internet
    Explorer or Netscape 4 or higher), full Internet access
    and an e-mail address
Is the library accessible to students? Yes
Are computers accessible to students? No

Remote Sites

Other branches of the institution: Yes
Other college campuses: Yes
Students' homes: Yes
Work sites: Yes
Libraries: Yes
Elementary/Secondary schools: Yes

On-Campus Requirements

Is an on-campus component required? No

Tuition & Fees

In-state tuition per credit: $231
Out-of-state tuition per credit: $231
Average yearly cost of books: $50

Financial Aid

Is financial aid available to full-time students? Yes
Is financial aid available to part-time students? Yes
Are academic scholarships available? Yes
Assistance programs available to students: Federal Stafford
    Loan, veterans' assistance

Central Missouri State University

Office of Extended Campus
Distance Learning
Humphreys 403
Warrensburg, MO 64093
Contact: Debbie Bassore, Assistant Director for Distance
    Learning
Department e-mail: extcamp@cmsuvmb.cmsu.edu
Department Web address: www.cmsu.edu/extcamp
School Web address: www.cmsu.edu
Institutional accreditation: North Central Association of
    Colleges and Schools

Subjects Offered

Child and family development, library science and
    information services, dietetics and nutrition, nursing,
    special education, physical education, speech communi-
    cation, safety science and technology, computer
    information systems, technology and occupational
    education, curriculum and instruction, teaching English
    as a second language, criminal justice

Admissions Requirements

Is a minimum undergraduate GPA required? Yes
Is provisional admission available? Yes
Is an admissions interview required? No
Can pre-requisite course work be waived? No

Are international students eligible to apply? Yes
Is the TOEFL required for international students? Yes
What is the minimum TOEFL score required? 550

Program Delivery

Primary method of program delivery: Remote site
Two-way interactive video: Yes
Hardware requirements: Computer with minimum
    33.3KBPS modem
Software requirements: varies
Is the library accessible to students? Yes
Are computers accessible to students? Yes

Remote Sites

Other branches of the institution: Yes
Other college campuses: Yes
Students' homes: Yes
Work sites: Yes
Elementary/Secondary schools: Yes
Community-based organizations: Yes

Tuition & Fees

In-state tuition per credit: $210
Out-of-state tuition per credit: $210

Financial Aid

Is financial aid available to full-time students? Yes
Is financial aid available to part-time students? Yes
Are academic scholarships available? Yes
Assistance programs available to students: Federal Stafford
    Loan, Federal Perkins Loan, Federal Plus Loan, Federal
    Pell Grant, Federal Work-Study Program, in-state
    student aid programs, veterans' assistance

Chadron State College

Extended Campus Programs
100 Main Street
Chadron, NE 69337
Contact: Steve Taylor, Assistant Vice President of Extended
    Campus Programs
Department e-mail: alangford@csc.edu
Department Web address: www.csc.edu/ecampus.htm
School Web address: www.csc.edu
Institutional accreditation: North Central Association of
    Colleges and Schools

Subjects Offered

Accounting, management, counseling, marketing, criminal
    justice, philosophy, education, psychology, family and
    consumer science, information management systems,
    math

Admissions Requirements

Is a minimum undergraduate GPA required? Yes
Is provisional admission available? Yes
Is an admissions interview required? No
Can pre-requisite course work be waived? No
Are international students eligible to apply? Yes
Is the TOEFL required for international students? Yes
What is the minimum TOEFL score required? 600

Program Delivery

Primary method of program delivery: Remote site
Two-way interactive video: Yes
Is the library accessible to students? Yes
Are computers accessible to students? No

Remote Sites

Other branches of the institution: No
Other college campuses: Yes
Students' homes: No
Work sites: No
Libraries: No
Elementary/Secondary schools: No
Community-based organizations: No
Correctional institutions: No

On-Campus Requirements

Is an on-campus component required? No

Tuition & Fees

In-state tuition per credit: $125
Out-of-state tuition per credit: $208
Average yearly cost of books: $600

Financial Aid

Is financial aid available to full-time students? Yes
Is financial aid available to part-time students? Yes
Are academic scholarships available? Yes
Assistance programs available to students: Federal Stafford
    Loan, Federal Perkins Loan, Federal Work-Study
    Program, veterans' assistance

Clarkson College

Graduate Nursing
Distance Learning
101 South 42nd Street
Omaha, NE 68131
Contact: Dr. Mac Timmons, Director of Graduate Nursing
School Web address: www.clarksoncollege.edu
Institutional accreditation: North Central Association of
    Colleges and Schools

Subjects Offered

Family nurse practitioner, nursing education, nursing administration

Admissions Requirements

Is a minimum undergraduate GPA required? Yes
Is provisional admission available? Yes
Is an admissions interview required? No
Can pre-requisite course work be waived? No
Are international students eligible to apply? Yes
Is the TOEFL required for international students? Yes
What is the minimum TOEFL score required? 600

Program Delivery

Primary method of program delivery: Web
Two-way interactive video: No
Two-way audio, one-way video: No
One-way live video: Yes
One-way pre-recorded video: Yes
Audio graphics: Yes
Audio: Yes
Is the library accessible to students? Yes
Are computers accessible to students? Yes

Remote Sites

Other branches of the institution: No
Other college campuses: No
Students' homes: Yes
Work sites: Yes
Libraries: No
Elementary/Secondary schools: No
Community-based organizations: No
Correctional institutions: No

On-Campus Requirements

Is an on-campus component required? Yes
On-campus exams: Yes
On-campus thesis defense: Yes

Tuition & Fees

In-state tuition per credit: $334
Out-of-state tuition per credit: $334
Average yearly cost of books: $500

Financial Aid

Is financial aid available to full-time students? Yes
Is financial aid available to part-time students? Yes
Are academic scholarships available? No
Assistance programs available to students: Federal Stafford Loan, veterans' assistance

Cleveland State University

Off-Campus Academic Programs
1860 East 22nd Street, RT 1209
Cleveland, OH 44114-4435
Contact: M. Judith Crocker, EdD, Director
Department e-mail: j.crocker@csuohio.edu
Department Web address: www.csuohio.edu/offcampus
School Web address: www.csuohio.edu
Institutional accreditation: North Central Association of Colleges and Schools

Subjects Offered

Education, philosophy, urban studies, public administration, nursing, geology, computer uses in education, education technology

Admissions Requirements

Is a minimum undergraduate GPA required? Yes
Is provisional admission available? Yes
Are international students eligible to apply? Yes
Is the TOEFL required for international students? Yes
What is the minimum TOEFL score required? 550

Program Delivery

Primary method of program delivery: Web
Two-way interactive video: Yes
Hardware requirements: Mac or PC
Software requirements: Netscape, Internet Explorer or other Internet browser
Is the library accessible to students? Yes
Are computers accessible to students? No

Remote Sites

Other college campuses: Yes
Students' homes: Yes
Work sites: Yes
Elementary/Secondary schools: Yes

On-Campus Requirements

Is an on-campus component required? Yes
On-campus course work: Yes

Tuition & Fees

In-state tuition per credit: $228
Out-of-state tuition per credit: $451
Average yearly cost of books: $25

Financial Aid

Is financial aid available to full-time students? Yes
Is financial aid available to part-time students? Yes
Are academic scholarships available? Yes
Assistance programs available to students: Federal Stafford

Loan, Federal Perkins Loan, Federal Plus Loan, Federal Work-Study Program, veterans' assistance

College of St. Scholastica

Education Department
Master of Education via Distance Learning Program
1200 Kenwod Avenue
Duluth, MN 55811
Contact: Jo Olsen Murray, Director of Graduate Education Programs
Department e-mail: jmurray@css.edu
Department Web address: www.csss.edu/med/
School Web address: www.css.edu
Institutional accreditation: North Central Association of Colleges and Schools

Subjects Offered

Curriculum and instruction

Admissions Requirements

Is a minimum undergraduate GPA required? Yes
Is provisional admission available? Yes
Is an admissions interview required? No
Can pre-requisite course work be waived? No
Are international students eligible to apply? Yes
Is the TOEFL required for international students? No

Program Delivery

Primary method of program delivery: Text
One-way pre-recorded video: Yes
Software requirements: Access to Internet
Is the library accessible to students? Yes
Are computers accessible to students? Yes

Remote Sites

Students' homes: Yes
Libraries: Yes

On-Campus Requirements

Is an on-campus component required? Yes
On-campus program orientation: Yes

Tuition & Fees

In-state tuition per credit: $265
Out-of-state tuition per credit: $265
Average yearly cost of books: $300

Financial Aid

Is financial aid available to full-time students? Yes
Is financial aid available to part-time students? Yes
Are academic scholarships available? No

Assistance programs available to students: Federal Stafford Loan, in-state student aid programs, veterans' assistance

College of the Southwest

6610 Lovington Highway
Institutional accreditation: North Central Association of Colleges and Schools

Admissions Requirements

Is a minimum undergraduate GPA required? Yes
Is provisional admission available? Yes
Is an admissions interview required? Yes
Can pre-requisite course work be waived? No

Program Delivery

Primary method of program delivery: Remote site
Two-way interactive video: Yes
Is the library accessible to students? Yes
Are computers accessible to students? Yes

Remote Sites

Other branches of the institution: Yes
Other college campuses: No
Students' homes: No
Work sites: No
Libraries: No
Elementary/Secondary schools: Yes
Community-based organizations: No
Correctional institutions: No

On-Campus Requirements

Is an on-campus component required? No

Tuition & Fees

In-state tuition per credit: $158
Out-of-state tuition per credit: $158

Financial Aid

Is financial aid available to full-time students? Yes
Is financial aid available to part-time students? Yes
Are academic scholarships available? Yes
Assistance programs available to students: Federal Stafford Loan, Federal Work-Study Program, veterans' assistance

Colorado State University

Division of Educational Outreach
Distance Degree Program
Spruce Hall
Fort Collins, CO 80523-1040
Contact: Arietta Wiedmann, PhD, Director of Extended Studies

Department e-mail: info@learn.colostate.edu
Department Web address: www.csu2learn.colostate.edu
School Web address: www.colostate.edu
Institutional accreditation: North Central Association of
 Colleges and Schools

Subjects Offered

Agricultural sciences, bioresource and agricultural
 engineering, business administration, business management, civil engineering, computer science, electrical
 engineering, chemical engineering, mechanical engineering, statistics

Admissions Requirements

Is a minimum undergraduate GPA required? Yes
Can pre-requisite course work be waived? Yes
Are international students eligible to apply? Yes
Is the TOEFL required for international students? Yes

Program Delivery

Two-way interactive video: Yes
One-way pre-recorded video: Yes
Hardware requirements: Pentium
Software requirements: Internet and e-mail access
Is the library accessible to students? Yes
Are computers accessible to students? No

Remote Sites

Other college campuses: Yes
Work sites: Yes
Libraries: Yes

On-Campus Requirements

Is an on-campus component required? No

Tuition & Fees

Application fee: $30
Can it be waived? No

Financial Aid

Is financial aid available to full-time students? Yes
Is financial aid available to part-time students? Yes
Are academic scholarships available? No
Assistance programs available to students: Federal Stafford
 Loan, veterans' assistance

Columbia International University

Columbia Extension
PO Box 3122
Columbia, SC 29203-3122
Department e-mail: extoff@ciu.edu

Department Web address: www.ciuextension.com
School Web address: www.ciu.edu
Institutional accreditation: Southern Association of
 Colleges and Schools

Subjects Offered

Bible, theology, Muslim studies, education, christian
 education, intercultural studies, evangelism, Greek,
 church history, ministry studies, missions

Admissions Requirements

Is a minimum undergraduate GPA required? Yes
Is provisional admission available? Yes
Can pre-requisite course work be waived? Yes
Are international students eligible to apply? Yes
Is the TOEFL required for international students? Yes
What is the minimum TOEFL score required? 550

Program Delivery

Primary method of program delivery: Text
One-way pre-recorded video: Yes
Is the library accessible to students? Yes
Are computers accessible to students? Yes

Remote Sites

Other branches of the institution: Yes

On-Campus Requirements

Is an on-campus component required? Yes
On-campus course work: Yes

Tuition & Fees

In-state tuition per credit: $169
Out-of-state tuition per credit: $169
Average yearly cost of books: $1,040

Columbia University

School of Engineering and Applied Science
Columbia Video Network
540 Mudd Building, MC 4719
500 West 120th Street
New York, NY 10027
Contact: Grace Chung, Executive Director
Department e-mail: cvn@cvn.columbia.edu
Department Web address: www.cvn.columbia.edu
School Web address: www.columbia.edu
Institutional accreditation: Middle States Association of
 Colleges and Schools

Subjects Offered

Computer science, information systems, electrical
 engineering, telecommunications engineering, industrial

engineering/operations research, financial engineering, engineering and management systems, business, mechanical engineering, material science, earth and environmental engineering, wireless and mobile communications, new media engineering, multimedia networking, lightwave engineering

Admissions Requirements

Is a minimum undergraduate GPA required? Yes
Is provisional admission available? No
Is an admissions interview required? No
Can pre-requisite course work be waived? Yes
Are international students eligible to apply? Yes
Is the TOEFL required for international students? Yes

Program Delivery

Primary method of program delivery: Web
Two-way interactive video: Yes
Two-way audio, one-way video: No
One-way live video: Yes
One-way pre-recorded video: Yes
Audio graphics: No
Audio: Yes
Hardware requirements: 56KBPS modem, Pentium
    processor, 32MB of RAM
Software requirements: Windows Media Player and/or
    RealPlayer

On-Campus Requirements

Is an on-campus component required? No

Tuition & Fees

In-state tuition per credit: $951
Out-of-state tuition per credit: $951
Average yearly cost of books: $50

Financial Aid

Is financial aid available to full-time students? No
Is financial aid available to part-time students? No
Are academic scholarships available? No

Columbus State University

4225 University Avenue
Columbus, GA 31907
Contact: Dr. Vladimir Zanev, Chair, Computer Science
    Department
Department Web address: www.cs.colstate.edu/
    graduate.htm
School Web address: www.colstate.edu
Institutional accreditation: Southern Association of
    Colleges and Schools

Subjects Offered

Computer science

Admissions Requirements

Is a minimum undergraduate GPA required? Yes
Is provisional admission available? Yes
Is an admissions interview required? No
Can pre-requisite course work be waived? Yes
Are international students eligible to apply? Yes
Is the TOEFL required for international students? Yes
What is the minimum TOEFL score required? 550

Program Delivery

Primary method of program delivery: Web
Hardware requirements: See specifications at
    www.csuonline.edu
Software requirements: See specifications at
    www.csuonline.edu
Is the library accessible to students? Yes
Are computers accessible to students? Yes

Remote Sites

Students' homes: Yes
Work sites: Yes

On-Campus Requirements

Is an on-campus component required? No

Tuition & Fees

In-state tuition per credit: $228
Out-of-state tuition per credit: $510
Average yearly cost of books: $300
Average yearly additional fees: $25

Financial Aid

Is financial aid available to full-time students? Yes
Is financial aid available to part-time students? Yes
Are academic scholarships available? Yes
Assistance programs available to students: Federal Stafford
    Loan, Federal Perkins Loan, Federal Plus Loan, Federal
    Work-Study Program, veterans' assistance

Concordia University— St. Paul

School of Human Services
275 Synicate Street North
St. Paul, MN 55104-5494
Contact: Jim Ollhoff, Dean
Department e-mail: cshs@csp.edu
School Web address: www.cshs.csp.edu
Institutional accreditation: North Central Association of
    Colleges and Schools

Subjects Offered

Early childhood, school-age care, youth development, family studies, leadership

Admissions Requirements

Is provisional admission available? Yes
Is an admissions interview required? No
Can pre-requisite course work be waived? No
Are international students eligible to apply? Yes
Is the TOEFL required for international students? Yes
What is the minimum TOEFL score required? 600

Program Delivery

Hardware requirements: Pentium processor, 28.8KBPS modem or faster
Software requirements: Windows 95, IBM or compatible, e-mail that supports attachments
Is the library accessible to students? Yes
Are computers accessible to students? Yes

Remote Sites

Students' homes: Yes
Work sites: Yes

On-Campus Requirements

Is an on-campus component required? Yes
On-campus course work: Yes
On-campus program orientation: Yes

Tuition & Fees

In-state tuition per credit: $250
Out-of-state tuition per credit: $250
Average yearly cost of books: $100

Financial Aid

Is financial aid available to full-time students? Yes
Are academic scholarships available? No
Assistance programs available to students: Federal Stafford Loan, Federal Perkins Loan, Federal Plus Loan, veterans' assistance

Concordia University— Wisconsin

Distance Learning Graduate Programs
12800 North Lake Shore Drive
Mequon, WI 53097
Contact: David W. Borst, Director
School Web address: www.cuw.edu
Institutional accreditation: North Central Association of Colleges and Schools

Subjects Offered

Education administration, education counseling, education reading, education curriculum and instruction, nursing

Admissions Requirements

Is a minimum undergraduate GPA required? Yes
Is provisional admission available? Yes
Can pre-requisite course work be waived? No
Are international students eligible to apply? No

Program Delivery

Primary method of program delivery: Text
Two-way interactive video: Yes
One-way pre-recorded video: Yes
Is the library accessible to students? Yes
Are computers accessible to students? No

Remote Sites

Other branches of the institution: Yes

On-Campus Requirements

Is an on-campus component required? Yes
On-campus course work: Yes
On-campus thesis defense: Yes

Tuition & Fees

In-state tuition per credit: $325
Out-of-state tuition per credit: $325
Average yearly cost of books: $100

Financial Aid

Is financial aid available to full-time students? Yes
Is financial aid available to part-time students? Yes
Are academic scholarships available? No
Assistance programs available to students: Federal Stafford Loan, veterans' assistance

Connecticut State University System

Online CSU
CSU System Office
39 Woodland Street
Hartford, CT 06118-2337
Contact: Robin Worley, Executive Officer Online CSU
Department e-mail: worleyr@sysoff.ctstateu.edu
School Web address: www.onlinecsu.ctstateu.edu
Institutional accreditation: New England Association of Schools and Colleges; The Board of Governors of Higher Education of Connecticut

Subjects Offered

Education, nursing, business, library science

Admissions Requirements

Is a minimum undergraduate GPA required? Yes
Is provisional admission available? Yes
Is an admissions interview required? No
Can pre-requisite course work be waived? No
Are international students eligible to apply? Yes
Is the TOEFL required for international students? Yes
What is the minimum TOEFL score required? 550

Program Delivery

Primary method of program delivery: Web
Two-way interactive video: No
Two-way audio, one-way video: No
One-way live video: No
One-way pre-recorded video: Yes
Audio graphics: Yes
Audio: Yes
Hardware requirements: 90 MHz Pentium Processor (604 Power PC Mac) 32MB of RAM, 28.8KBPS modem, sound card
Software requirements: Windows 95, 98, NT, RealPlayer
Is the library accessible to students? Yes
Are computers accessible to students? Yes

Remote Sites

Other branches of the institution: Yes
Other college campuses: Yes
Students' homes: Yes
Work sites: Yes
Libraries: Yes
Elementary/Secondary schools: Yes
Community-based organizations: Yes
Correctional institutions: Yes

On-Campus Requirements

Is an on-campus component required? No

Tuition & Fees

In-state tuition per credit: $250
Out-of-state tuition per credit: $250
Average yearly cost of books: $100

Financial Aid

Is financial aid available to full-time students? Yes
Is financial aid available to part-time students? Yes
Are academic scholarships available? Yes
Assistance programs available to students: Federal Stafford Loan, Federal Perkins Loan, Federal Plus Loan, Federal Work-Study Program, in-state student aid programs, veterans' assistance

Cornerstone University

Grand Rapids Baptist Seminary
Extension Study
1001 East Beltline Northeast
Grand Rapids, MI 49525-5897
Contact: Peter G. Osborn, Director of Graduate Admissions
Department e-mail: grbs@cornerstone.edu
Department Web address: www.grbs.edu
School Web address: www.grbs.edu
Institutional accreditation: North Central Association of Colleges and Schools

Subjects Offered

Bible, ministry, theology

Admissions Requirements

Is a minimum undergraduate GPA required? Yes
Is provisional admission available? Yes
Is an admissions interview required? No
Can pre-requisite course work be waived? Yes
Are international students eligible to apply? Yes
Is the TOEFL required for international students? Yes
What is the minimum TOEFL score required? 575

Program Delivery

Primary method of program delivery: Text
Two-way interactive video: No
Two-way audio, one-way video: No
One-way live video: No
One-way pre-recorded video: No
Audio graphics: No
Audio: Yes
Hardware requirements: none
Software requirements: none
Is the library accessible to students? Yes
Are computers accessible to students? Yes

Remote Sites

Other branches of the institution: No
Other college campuses: No
Students' homes: Yes
Work sites: No
Libraries: No
Elementary/Secondary schools: No
Community-based organizations: No
Correctional institutions: No

On-Campus Requirements

Is an on-campus component required? Yes
On-campus course work: Yes
On-campus admissions interview: No

On-campus program orientation: No
On-campus exams: No
On-campus thesis defense: No

Tuition & Fees

In-state tuition per credit: $277
Out-of-state tuition per credit: $277
Average yearly cost of books: $800

Financial Aid

Is financial aid available to full-time students? Yes
Is financial aid available to part-time students? Yes
Are academic scholarships available? Yes
Assistance programs available to students: Federal Stafford
  Loan, veterans' assistance

Dakota State University

Office of Distance Education
201A Mundt Library
Madison, SD 57042
Contact: Deb Gearhart, Director of Distance Education
Department e-mail: dsuinfo@pluto.dsu.edu
Department Web address: www.courses.dsu.edu/disted/
School Web address: www.dsu.edu
Institutional accreditation: North Central Association of
  Colleges and Schools

Admissions Requirements

Is provisional admission available? Yes
Is an admissions interview required? No
Are international students eligible to apply? Yes
Is the TOEFL required for international students? Yes
What is the minimum TOEFL score required? 550

Program Delivery

Primary method of program delivery: Web
Two-way interactive video: Yes
Is the library accessible to students? Yes
Are computers accessible to students? No

On-Campus Requirements

Is an on-campus component required? No

Tuition & Fees

In-state tuition per credit: $170
Out-of-state tuition per credit: $170

Financial Aid

Is financial aid available to full-time students? Yes

Dalhousie University

Office of Instructional Development and Technology
Distributed Education
Halifax, NS, Canada B3H 3J5
Contact: Alan Wright, Executive Director
Department e-mail: de@dal.ca
Department Web address: www.dal.ca/de
School Web address: www.dal.ca

Subjects Offered

Occupational therapy, business administration, nursing,
  social work

Admissions Requirements

Is a minimum undergraduate GPA required? Yes
Is provisional admission available? No
Can pre-requisite course work be waived? Yes
Are international students eligible to apply? Yes
What is the minimum TOEFL score required? 580

Program Delivery

Primary method of program delivery: Web
Audio graphics: Yes
Audio: Yes
Hardware requirements: PC: Pentium 133 MHz, 16MB of
  RAM, 10MB of hard drive space, 28.8KBPS modem
  Mac: PowerPC 601, 100 MHz, 32MB of RAM, 10MB
  of hard drive space, 28.8KBPS modem
Software requirements: Web browser: Netscape 4.0 or
  better, Internet Explorer 4.01 or better
Is the library accessible to students? Yes
Are computers accessible to students? Yes

Remote Sites

Other branches of the institution: Yes
Other college campuses: Yes
Students' homes: Yes
Work sites: Yes

On-Campus Requirements

Is an on-campus component required? Yes
On-campus program orientation: Yes
On-campus exams: Yes
On-campus thesis defense: Yes

Tuition & Fees

Average yearly cost of books: $1,000

Financial Aid

Is financial aid available to full-time students? Yes
Are academic scholarships available? Yes

Dallas Baptist University

Online Education
3000 Mountain Creek Parkway
Dallas, TX 75211
Contact: Kaye Shelton, Faculty Systems Coordinator
Department e-mail: online@dbu.edu
Department Web address: www.dbuonline.org
School Web address: www.dbu.edu
Institutional accreditation: Southern Association of
  Colleges and Schools

Subjects Offered

Accounting, economics, management, management
  information systems, marketing, e-commerce

Admissions Requirements

Is a minimum undergraduate GPA required? Yes
Is provisional admission available? Yes
Can pre-requisite course work be waived? Yes
Are international students eligible to apply? Yes
Is the TOEFL required for international students? Yes
What is the minimum TOEFL score required? 550

Program Delivery

Primary method of program delivery: Web
Two-way interactive video: No
Two-way audio, one-way video: No
One-way live video: No
One-way pre-recorded video: Yes
Audio graphics: Yes
Audio: Yes
Hardware requirements: Mac PowerPC (minimum 604) or
  PC-90 MHz Pentium processor or faster, 32MB of
  RAM, 28.8KBPS modem or faster, sound card, speakers.
Software requirements: Windows 95/98/NT, Mac OS 8.1
  or later, JAVA-capable browser, RealPlayer
Is the library accessible to students? Yes
Are computers accessible to students? Yes

Remote Sites

Other branches of the institution: No
Other college campuses: No
Students' homes: Yes
Work sites: Yes
Libraries: Yes
Elementary/Secondary schools: No
Community-based organizations: No
Correctional institutions: No

On-Campus Requirements

Is an on-campus component required? No

Tuition & Fees

In-state tuition per credit: $355
Out-of-state tuition per credit: $355
Average yearly cost of books: $250

Financial Aid

Is financial aid available to full-time students? Yes
Is financial aid available to part-time students? Yes
Are academic scholarships available? Yes
Assistance programs available to students: Federal Stafford
  Loan, Federal Perkins Loan, Federal Plus Loan, Federal
  Work-Study Program, in-state student aid programs,
  veterans' assistance

Dallas Theological Seminary

External Studies
3909 Swiss Avenue
Dallas, TX 75204
Contact: Ben Scott, Director of External Studies
Department e-mail: externalstudies@dts.edu
Department Web address: www.dts.edu/externalstudies
School Web address: www.dts.edu
Institutional accreditation: Southern Association of
  Colleges and Schools

Subjects Offered

Bible, theology, world missions, christian education

Admissions Requirements

Is a minimum undergraduate GPA required? Yes
Is provisional admission available? Yes
Can pre-requisite course work be waived? Yes
Are international students eligible to apply? Yes
Is the TOEFL required for international students? Yes
What is the minimum TOEFL score required? 575

Program Delivery

Primary method of program delivery: Remote site
Two-way interactive video: No
Two-way audio, one-way video: No
One-way live video: No
One-way pre-recorded video: Yes
Audio graphics: No
Audio: Yes
Software requirements: Internet Explorer or Netscape
  Navigator Web browser
Is the library accessible to students? Yes
Are computers accessible to students? Yes

Remote Sites

Other branches of the institution: Yes
Other college campuses: Yes

Students' homes: No
Work sites: No
Libraries: Yes
Elementary/Secondary schools: No
Community-based organizations: No
Correctional institutions: No

On-Campus Requirements

Is an on-campus component required? No

Tuition & Fees

In-state tuition per credit: $290
Out-of-state tuition per credit: $290
Average yearly cost of books: $400

Financial Aid

Is financial aid available to full-time students? Yes
Is financial aid available to part-time students? Yes
Are academic scholarships available? No
Assistance programs available to students: Veterans'
    assistance

Drexel University College of Information, Science, and Technology

3141 Chestnut Street
Philadelphia, PA 19104
Department e-mail: info@cis.drexel.edu
School Web address: www.cis.drexel.edu
Institutional accreditation: Middle States Association of
    Colleges and Schools

Subjects Offered

Library science, information science, information systems,
    competitive intelligence

Admissions Requirements

Is a minimum undergraduate GPA required? Yes
Is provisional admission available? Yes
Is an admissions interview required? No
Can pre-requisite course work be waived? Yes
Are international students eligible to apply? Yes
Is the TOEFL required for international students? Yes
What is the minimum TOEFL score required? 600

Program Delivery

Primary method of program delivery: Web
Hardware requirements: Pentium Processor, 16MB of
    RAM, 350MB disk, CD-ROM, 28.8KBPS modem, 600
    x 800 pixel monitor, Windows 95/98/NT, JAVA-enabled
    browser

Software requirements: MSIS: Lotus notes, MS Office,
    Visio, Internet browser. CI/MS: MS Office, drawing
    tool, Internet browser, e-mail
Is the library accessible to students? Yes

On-Campus Requirements

Is an on-campus component required? No

Tuition & Fees

In-state tuition per credit: $472
Out-of-state tuition per credit: $472
Average yearly cost of books: $250

Financial Aid

Is financial aid available to full-time students? No
Is financial aid available to part-time students? No
Are academic scholarships available? No

Duke University—Cross Continent

Fuqua School of Business
Executive MBA Programs
Box 90120, 1 Towerview
Durham, NC 27708
Contact: Alison Hubbard Ashton, Associate Dean for
    EMBA Programs
Department Web address: www.fuqua.duke.edu
School Web address: www.duke.edu
Institutional accreditation: AACSB—The International
    Association for Management Education

Subjects Offered

Financial management, economics, probability and
    statistics, decision models, marketing, managerial
    effectiveness, corporate strategy, operations management,
    accounting, managerial economics

Admissions Requirements

Is a minimum undergraduate GPA required? No
Is provisional admission available? No
Is an admissions interview required? No
Can pre-requisite course work be waived? No
Are international students eligible to apply? Yes
Is the TOEFL required for international students? Yes
What is the minimum TOEFL score required? 600

Program Delivery

One-way pre-recorded video: Yes
Audio: Yes
Is the library accessible to students? Yes
Are computers accessible to students? No

Remote Sites

Other branches of the institution: Yes
Students' homes: Yes
Work sites: Yes

On-Campus Requirements

Is an on-campus component required? Yes
On-campus course work: Yes
On-campus program orientation: Yes

Tuition & Fees

Application fee: $150
Can it be waived? No

Financial Aid

Is financial aid available to full-time students? Yes
Is financial aid available to part-time students? Yes
Are academic scholarships available? No
Assistance programs available to students: Federal Stafford
    Loan, veterans' assistance

Duke University—Global Executive

Fuqua School of Business
Executive MBA Programs
1 Towerview Drive
Durham, NC 27708
Contact: Alison Hubbard Ashton, Associate Dean for
    EMBA Programs
Department Web address: www.fuqua.duke.edu
School Web address: www.duke.edu
Institutional accreditation: AACSB—The International
    Association for Management Education

Subjects Offered

Corporate strategy, operations management, accounting,
    managerial economics, financial management, econom-
    ics, probability and statistics, decision models, market-
    ing, managerial effectiveness

Admissions Requirements

Is provisional admission available? No
Can pre-requisite course work be waived? No
Are international students eligible to apply? Yes
Is the TOEFL required for international students? No

Program Delivery

One-way pre-recorded video: Yes
Audio: Yes
Is the library accessible to students? Yes
Are computers accessible to students? No

Remote Sites

Other branches of the institution: Yes
Students' homes: Yes
Work sites: Yes

On-Campus Requirements

Is an on-campus component required? Yes
On-campus course work: Yes

Financial Aid

Is financial aid available to full-time students? Yes
Is financial aid available to part-time students? Yes
Are academic scholarships available? No
Assistance programs available to students: Federal Stafford
    Loan, veterans' assistance

Duquesne University— Division of Continuing Education

600 Forbes Avenue
210 Rockwell Hall
Pittsburgh, PA 15282
Department e-mail: coned@duq.edu
Department Web address: coned.duq.edu
School Web address: www.duq.edu
Institutional accreditation: Middle States Association of
    Colleges and Schools

Admissions Requirements

Is a minimum undergraduate GPA required? No
Is provisional admission available? Yes
Is an admissions interview required? Yes
Are international students eligible to apply? Yes
What is the minimum TOEFL score required? 550

Program Delivery

Primary method of program delivery: Web
Hardware requirements: Pentium processor, 32 MB of
    RAM, 3GB hard drive, 33.6KBPS modem
Software requirements: Windows 95
Is the library accessible to students? Yes
Are computers accessible to students? Yes

On-Campus Requirements

Is an on-campus component required? No

Tuition & Fees

In-state tuition per credit: $453
Out-of-state tuition per credit: $453
Average yearly cost of books: $25

Financial Aid

Is financial aid available to full-time students? Yes

Is financial aid available to part-time students? Yes

Are academic scholarships available? No

Assistance programs available to students: Federal Stafford Loan, Federal Perkins Loan, Federal Work-Study Program, veterans' assistance

Duquesne University—Mary Pappert School of Music

600 Forbes Avenue

Pittsburgh, PA 15282

Contact: Judith Bowman, PhD, Associate Professor of Music Education and Music Technology

Department Web address: www.duq.edu/music/music.html

School Web address: www.duq.edu

Institutional accreditation: Middle States Association of Colleges and Schools

Subjects Offered

Research and bibliography, philosophy of music education, psychology of music teaching and learning, music education research, music curriculum design

Admissions Requirements

Is a minimum undergraduate GPA required? Yes

Is provisional admission available? No

Can pre-requisite course work be waived? No

Are international students eligible to apply? Yes

Is the TOEFL required for international students? Yes

What is the minimum TOEFL score required? 500

Program Delivery

Primary method of program delivery: Web

Two-way interactive video: No

Two-way audio, one-way video: No

One-way live video: No

One-way pre-recorded video: No

Audio graphics: Yes

Audio: No

Hardware requirements: Windows 95/Mac OS 8, 33.6 modem, 32MB of RAM, 3GB hard drive, CD-ROM drive and sound capabilities

Software requirements: Current Web browser and plug-ins

Is the library accessible to students? Yes

Are computers accessible to students? Yes

Remote Sites

Other branches of the institution: No

Other college campuses: No

Students' homes: Yes

Work sites: No

Libraries: No

Elementary/Secondary schools: No

Community-based organizations: No

Correctional institutions: No

On-Campus Requirements

Is an on-campus component required? Yes

On-campus course work: Yes

On-campus admissions interview: No

On-campus program orientation: No

On-campus exams: No

On-campus thesis defense: Yes

Tuition & Fees

In-state tuition per credit: $591

Out-of-state tuition per credit: $591

Average yearly cost of books: $200

Financial Aid

Is financial aid available to full-time students? No

Is financial aid available to part-time students? No

Are academic scholarships available? No

Duquesne University— Mylan School of Pharmacy

Life Long Learning

600 Forbes Avenue, Bayer Learning Center

Pittsburgh, PA 15282

Contact: Dr. Therese Poirier, Professor of Clinical Pharmacy, Director, Life Long Learning

Department e-mail: poirier@duq.edu

School Web address: www.duq.edu

Institutional accreditation: American Council on Pharmaceutical Education

Subjects Offered

Pharmacy

Admissions Requirements

Is a minimum undergraduate GPA required? Yes

Is provisional admission available? No

Can pre-requisite course work be waived? No

Are international students eligible to apply? Yes

Is the TOEFL required for international students? Yes

What is the minimum TOEFL score required? 600

Program Delivery

Primary method of program delivery: Web

Two-way interactive video: No

Two-way audio, one-way video: No

One-way live video: No
One-way pre-recorded video: No
Audio graphics: Yes
Audio: Yes
Hardware requirements: First-class PC system running at least Windows 98
Software requirements: Microsoft Office suite, Internet
Is the library accessible to students? Yes
Are computers accessible to students? Yes

Remote Sites

Other branches of the institution: No
Other college campuses: No
Students' homes: Yes
Work sites: Yes
Libraries: No
Elementary/Secondary schools: No
Community-based organizations: No
Correctional institutions: No

On-Campus Requirements

Is an on-campus component required? Yes
On-campus course work: Yes
On-campus admissions interview: No
On-campus program orientation: Yes
On-campus exams: No
On-campus thesis defense: No

Tuition & Fees

In-state tuition per credit: $501
Out-of-state tuition per credit: $501
Average yearly cost of books: $100

Financial Aid

Is financial aid available to full-time students? Yes
Is financial aid available to part-time students? Yes
Are academic scholarships available? No
Assistance programs available to students: Federal Stafford Loan, Federal Perkins Loan, Federal Plus Loan, veterans' assistance

Duquesne University— School of Education

Program in Instructional Technology
600 Forbes Avenue
Pittsburgh, PA 15282
Contact: Dr. Lawrence A. Tomei, Director
Department e-mail: tomei@duq.edu
Department Web address: www.education.duq.edu
School Web address: www.duq.edu

Institutional accreditation: Middle States Association of Colleges and Schools

Subjects Offered

Technology and education, instructional technology, teaching with technology across the curriculum, distance learning course design

Admissions Requirements

Is a minimum undergraduate GPA required? Yes
Is provisional admission available? Yes
Is an admissions interview required? No
Can pre-requisite course work be waived? Yes
Are international students eligible to apply? Yes
Is the TOEFL required for international students? No

Program Delivery

Primary method of program delivery: Web
One-way pre-recorded video: Yes
Hardware requirements: Multimedia-capable Macintosh or Windows 98/2000
Software requirements: Microsoft Office, Multimedia utilities, Internet browser
Is the library accessible to students? Yes
Are computers accessible to students? Yes

Remote Sites

Other branches of the institution: No
Other college campuses: Yes
Students' homes: Yes
Work sites: No
Libraries: No
Elementary/Secondary schools: Yes
Community-based organizations: No
Correctional institutions: No

On-Campus Requirements

Is an on-campus component required? No

Tuition & Fees

In-state tuition per credit: $588
Out-of-state tuition per credit: $588
Average yearly cost of books: $65

Financial Aid

Is financial aid available to full-time students? Yes
Is financial aid available to part-time students? Yes
Are academic scholarships available? Yes
Assistance programs available to students: Federal Stafford Loan, Federal Perkins Loan, Federal Work-Study Program, veterans' assistance

Duquesne University— School of Nursing

Center for Distance Learning
600 Forbes Avenue
Pittsburgh, PA 15282
Contact: Dr. Kathleen Gaberson, Chair
Department e-mail: simmer@duq.edu
Department Web address: www.nursing.duq.edu
School Web address: www.duq.edu
Institutional accreditation: Middle States Association of Colleges and Schools

Subjects Offered

Nursing informatics, operating room/perioperative nursing, nursing education, nursing administration, mental health/psychiatric nursing, transcultural nursing, history and philosophy of science, nurse practitioner, nursing theory development, nursing research methods, bioethics, advanced pharmacology, advanced pathophysiology, health promotion

Admissions Requirements

Is a minimum undergraduate GPA required? Yes
Is provisional admission available? Yes
Is an admissions interview required? Yes
Can pre-requisite course work be waived? Yes
Are international students eligible to apply? Yes
Is the TOEFL required for international students? Yes
What is the minimum TOEFL score required? 550

Program Delivery

Primary method of program delivery: Web
Hardware requirements: Pentium Processor, PowerPC processor or better, 32MB of RAM, 3GB hard drive, 33.6KBPS modem, CD-ROM drive, sound card, printer
Software requirements: Windows 95 or later, Mac OS 8.0 or later, Word Perfect or Word, database, spreadsheet, and presentation graphics
Is the library accessible to students? Yes
Are computers accessible to students? Yes

Remote Sites

Students' homes: Yes
Work sites: Yes

On-Campus Requirements

Is an on-campus component required? Yes
On-campus course work: Yes
On-campus admissions interview: No
On-campus program orientation: Yes
On-campus exams: Yes
On-campus thesis defense: No

Tuition & Fees

In-state tuition per credit: $588
Out-of-state tuition per credit: $588
Average yearly cost of books: $400

Financial Aid

Is financial aid available to full-time students? Yes
Is financial aid available to part-time students? Yes
Are academic scholarships available? Yes
Assistance programs available to students: Federal Stafford Loan, Federal Perkins Loan, Federal Plus Loan, Federal Work-Study Program, veterans' assistance

East Carolina University— Librarianship, Educational Technology, and Distance Education

102 Joyner East
Greenville, NC 27858
Contact: Diane Kester, Department Chair
Department e-mail: kesterd@mail.ecu.edu
Department Web address: www.soe.ecu.edu/lset/default
School Web address: www.ecu.edu

Admissions Requirements

Is a minimum undergraduate GPA required? Yes
Is provisional admission available? No
Is an admissions interview required? No
Can pre-requisite course work be waived? No
Are international students eligible to apply? Yes

Financial Aid

Is financial aid available to full-time students? Yes
Is financial aid available to part-time students? Yes

East Carolina University— School of Allied Health Sciences

Communication Sciences and Disorders
Greenville, NC 27858
Contact: Robert A. Muzzarelli, Director, Distance Education Program
Department e-mail: muzzarellir@mail.ecu.edu
Department Web address: www.csdl.ah.ecu.edu
School Web address: www.ecu.edu

Subjects Offered

Speech-language pathology

Admissions Requirements

Is a minimum undergraduate GPA required? Yes
Is provisional admission available? Yes
Is an admissions interview required? No
Can pre-requisite course work be waived? No
Are international students eligible to apply? Yes
Is the TOEFL required for international students? Yes

Program Delivery

Two-way interactive video: No
Two-way audio, one-way video: No
One-way live video: No
One-way pre-recorded video: Yes
Hardware requirements: PC: 200 MHz, Intel Pentium
   processor, 64MB of RAM, 100MB RAM, 16 bit
   soundcard and speakers, 65,000 color video display card,
   56KBPS modem
Software requirements: Word processor, Windows 95/98,
   Web browser, Internet service provider, e-mail
Is the library accessible to students? Yes

Remote Sites

Students' homes: Yes

On-Campus Requirements

Is an on-campus component required? Yes
On-campus course work: Yes
On-campus admissions interview: No
On-campus program orientation: No
On-campus exams: No
On-campus thesis defense: No

Financial Aid

Is financial aid available to part-time students? No
Are academic scholarships available? No

East Carolina University— School of Human Environmental Sciences

Nutrition and Hospitality Management
Greenville, NC 27858
Contact: Dr. Evelyn Farrior, Distance Education
   Coordinator
Department e-mail: farriore@mail.ecu.edu
Department Web address: www.ecu.edu/hes/home.htm
School Web address: www.ecu.edu

Subjects Offered

Nutrition and dietetics

Admissions Requirements

Is a minimum undergraduate GPA required? Yes
Is provisional admission available? No
Is an admissions interview required? No
Can pre-requisite course work be waived? No
Are international students eligible to apply? Yes

Tuition & Fees

In-state tuition per credit: $61
Out-of-state tuition per credit: $127

Financial Aid

Is financial aid available to full-time students? Yes
Is financial aid available to part-time students? Yes

East Carolina University— School of Industry and Technology

Rawl Building
Greenville, NC 27858
Contact: Dr. Charles Coddington, Department Chair
Department e-mail: coddingtonc@mail.ecu.edu
Department Web address: www.sit.ecu.edu/gradp
School Web address: www.ecu.edu

Admissions Requirements

Is a minimum undergraduate GPA required? Yes
Is provisional admission available? No
Is an admissions interview required? No
Can pre-requisite course work be waived? No
Are international students eligible to apply? Yes

Tuition & Fees

In-state tuition per credit: $61
Out-of-state tuition per credit: $127

Financial Aid

Is financial aid available to full-time students? Yes
Is financial aid available to part-time students? Yes

East Carolina University— School of Nursing

Greenville, NC 27858
Contact: Dr. Phyllis Turner, Associate Dean Graduate
   Nursing Program
Department e-mail: turnerp@mail.ecu.edu

Department Web address: www.ecu.edu/nursing
School Web address: www.ecu.edu
Institutional accreditation: Southern Association of
Colleges and Schools

Subjects Offered

Nursing

Admissions Requirements

Is a minimum undergraduate GPA required? Yes
Is provisional admission available? No
Is an admissions interview required? Yes
Can pre-requisite course work be waived? No
Are international students eligible to apply? Yes
Is the TOEFL required for international students? Yes

Program Delivery

Two-way interactive video: No
Two-way audio, one-way video: No
One-way live video: No
One-way pre-recorded video: No
Audio graphics: No
Audio: No
Hardware requirements: 200 MHz Pentium, 32MB of
RAM, 33 KBPS modem, sound card, speakers, 10x CD-
ROM player
Software requirements: Windows 95/98/2000, Microsoft
Office 97, antivirus, Internet browser
Is the library accessible to students? Yes

On-Campus Requirements

Is an on-campus component required? Yes
On-campus course work: No
On-campus admissions interview: Yes
On-campus program orientation: Yes
On-campus exams: Yes
On-campus thesis defense: No

Tuition & Fees

In-state tuition per credit: $576
Out-of-state tuition per credit: $2,541
Average yearly cost of books: $800

Financial Aid

Is financial aid available to full-time students? Yes
Is financial aid available to part-time students? Yes
Are academic scholarships available? Yes
Assistance programs available to students: Federal Stafford
Loan, Federal Perkins Loan

Eastern Kentucky University

Office of Extended Programs
521 Lancaster Avenue
Richmond, KY 40475
Contact: Dr. Kenneth R. Nelson, Director of Extended
Programs
Department Web address: www.extendedprograms.eku.edu
School Web address: www.eku.edu
Institutional accreditation: Southern Association of
Colleges and Schools

Subjects Offered

Counseling, criminal justice, education-various areas,
library, occupational therapy, nursing

Admissions Requirements

Is a minimum undergraduate GPA required? Yes
Is provisional admission available? Yes
Are international students eligible to apply? Yes
Is the TOEFL required for international students? Yes
What is the minimum TOEFL score required? 550

Program Delivery

Two-way interactive video: Yes
Two-way audio, one-way video: Yes
One-way live video: No
One-way pre-recorded video: No
Audio graphics: No
Audio: No
Hardware requirements: Depends upon course
requirements
Software requirements: Varies depending upon course
requirements, Blackboard is our primary course
management tool
Is the library accessible to students? Yes
Are computers accessible to students? Yes

Remote Sites

Other branches of the institution: Yes
Other college campuses: Yes
Students' homes: Yes
Work sites: No
Libraries: No
Elementary/Secondary schools: Yes
Community-based organizations: No
Correctional institutions: No

Tuition & Fees

In-state tuition per credit: $153
Out-of-state tuition per credit: $418
Average yearly cost of books: $600

Financial Aid

Is financial aid available to full-time students? Yes
Is financial aid available to part-time students? Yes
Are academic scholarships available? Yes
Assistance programs available to students: Federal Stafford
Loan, Federal Perkins Loan, Federal Work-Study
Program, veterans' assistance

Embry-Riddle Aeronautical University

Department of Distance Learning
600 South Clyde Morris Boulevard
Daytona Beach, FL 32114-3900
Contact: Wm. Francis Herleshy III, Chair
Department Web address: www.ec.erau.edu/ddl
School Web address: www.erau-edu
Institutional accreditation: Southern Association of
Colleges and Schools

Admissions Requirements

Is an admissions interview required? No

Program Delivery

Primary method of program delivery: Web
One-way pre-recorded video: Yes
Hardware requirements: Any computer with capability of
accessing the Internet
Software requirements: Windows 95 or better
Is the library accessible to students? Yes
Are computers accessible to students? Yes

On-Campus Requirements

Is an on-campus component required? No

Tuition & Fees

In-state tuition per credit: $305
Out-of-state tuition per credit: $305

Financial Aid

Is financial aid available to full-time students? Yes
Is financial aid available to part-time students? Yes
Are academic scholarships available? No
Assistance programs available to students: Federal Stafford
Loan, Federal Work-Study Program

Empire State College—The State University of New York

Office of Graduate Studies
28 Union Avenue
Saratoga Springs, NY 12866
Contact: Dr. Meredith Brown, Dean of Graduate Studies
Department e-mail: grad@esc.edu
Department Web address: www.esc.edu/grad
School Web address: www.esc.edu
Institutional accreditation: New York State Education
Department; State University of New York

Subjects Offered

Business, human services, labor, management, human
resources, marketing, criminal justice, labor law, health
care policy, HIV/AIDS policy, community and
government, strategic management, education policy,
public policy

Admissions Requirements

Is a minimum undergraduate GPA required? No
Is provisional admission available? Yes
Is an admissions interview required? No
Can pre-requisite course work be waived? No
Are international students eligible to apply? Yes
Is the TOEFL required for international students? Yes
What is the minimum TOEFL score required? 600

Program Delivery

Primary method of program delivery: Text
Is the library accessible to students? Yes

On-Campus Requirements

Is an on-campus component required? Yes
On-campus course work: Yes
On-campus program orientation: Yes
On-campus exams: Yes

Tuition & Fees

In-state tuition per credit: $213
Out-of-state tuition per credit: $351
Average yearly cost of books: $600

Financial Aid

Is financial aid available to full-time students? Yes
Is financial aid available to part-time students? Yes
Are academic scholarships available? Yes
Assistance programs available to students: Federal Stafford
Loan, Federal Perkins Loan, Federal Work-Study
Program, in-state student aid programs

Excelsior College—Master of Liberal Studies

7 Columbia Circle
Albany, NY 12203
Contact: Daniel Eisenberg, Associate Dean
Department e-mail: mls@excelsior.edu
Department Web address: www.excelsior.edu/mls
School Web address: www.excelsior.edu
Institutional accreditation: Middle States Association of Colleges and Schools

Subjects Offered

Interdisciplinary liberal studies

Admissions Requirements

Is a minimum undergraduate GPA required? No
Is provisional admission available? Yes
Is an admissions interview required? No
Are international students eligible to apply? Yes
Is the TOEFL required for international students? No

Program Delivery

Primary method of program delivery: Web
Is the library accessible to students? Yes

Remote Sites

Students' homes: Yes

On-Campus Requirements

Is an on-campus component required? No

Tuition & Fees

In-state tuition per credit: $275
Out-of-state tuition per credit: $275
Average yearly cost of books: $150

Financial Aid

Is financial aid available to full-time students? Yes
Is financial aid available to part-time students? Yes
Are academic scholarships available? No
Assistance programs available to students: In-state student aid programs, veterans' assistance

Excelsior College—Master of Science in Nursing

7 Columbia Circle
Albany, NY 12203
Contact: Deborah Sopczyk, Director
Department e-mail: msn@excelsior.edu
Department Web address: www.excelsior.edu/msn
School Web address: www.excelsior.edu
Institutional accreditation: Middle States Association of Colleges and Schools, National League for Nursing

Subjects Offered

Nursing, health care informatics

Admissions Requirements

Is a minimum undergraduate GPA required? No
Is provisional admission available? Yes
Is an admissions interview required? No
Are international students eligible to apply? Yes
Is the TOEFL required for international students? No

Program Delivery

Primary method of program delivery: Web
Software requirements: Lotus Learning Space
Is the library accessible to students? Yes

Remote Sites

Students' homes: Yes

On-Campus Requirements

Is an on-campus component required? No

Tuition & Fees

In-state tuition per credit: $300
Out-of-state tuition per credit: $300
Average yearly cost of books: $150

Financial Aid

Is financial aid available to full-time students? Yes
Is financial aid available to part-time students? Yes
Assistance programs available to students: In-state student aid programs, veterans' assistance

The Fielding Institute

2112 Santa Barbara Street
Santa Barbara, CA 93105
Department e-mail: admissions @fielding.edu
School Web address: www.fielding.edu
Institutional accreditation: Western Association of Schools and Colleges

Admissions Requirements

Is a minimum undergraduate GPA required? Yes
Is provisional admission available? No
Is an admissions interview required? Yes
Can pre-requisite course work be waived? No
Are international students eligible to apply? Yes
Is the TOEFL required for international students? No

Program Delivery

Primary method of program delivery: Text
Two-way interactive video: No
Two-way audio, one-way video: No
One-way live video: No
One-way pre-recorded video: No
Audio graphics: No
Audio: No
Software requirements: Any that provides access to e-mail and the Internet
Is the library accessible to students? Yes
Are computers accessible to students? Yes

Remote Sites

Other branches of the institution: No
Other college campuses: No
Students' homes: Yes
Work sites: Yes
Libraries: Yes
Elementary/Secondary schools: No
Community-based organizations: No
Correctional institutions: No

On-Campus Requirements

On-campus program orientation: Yes
On-campus thesis defense: Yes

Tuition & Fees

In-state tuition per credit: $13,400

Financial Aid

Is financial aid available to full-time students? Yes
Assistance programs available to students: Federal Stafford Loan, veterans' assistance

Fairleigh Dickinson University

Office of Educational Technology
1000 River Road
Teaneck, NJ 07666
Contact: Ellen Spaldo, Assistant Provost for Educational Technology
Department e-mail: edtech@mailbox.fdu.edu
School Web address: fdu.edu
Institutional accreditation: AACSB—The International Association for Management Education

Subjects Offered

Biology, history, computer science, psychology, chemistry, nursing, management information systems, taxation, electrical engineering, education, criminal justice, corporate communications, economics, art, Spanish, English

Admissions Requirements

Is a minimum undergraduate GPA required? No
Is provisional admission available? Yes
Is an admissions interview required? No
Can pre-requisite course work be waived? Yes
Are international students eligible to apply? Yes
Is the TOEFL required for international students? Yes
What is the minimum TOEFL score required? 500

Program Delivery

Primary method of program delivery: Web
Two-way interactive video: Yes
Two-way audio, one-way video: No
One-way live video: No
One-way pre-recorded video: No
Audio graphics: No
Audio: No
Is the library accessible to students? Yes
Are computers accessible to students? Yes

Remote Sites

Other branches of the institution: Yes
Other college campuses: Yes
Students' homes: Yes
Work sites: Yes
Libraries: No
Elementary/Secondary schools: No
Community-based organizations: No
Correctional institutions: No

On-Campus Requirements

Is an on-campus component required? No

Tuition & Fees

In-state tuition per credit: $597
Out-of-state tuition per credit: $597
Average yearly cost of books: $625

Financial Aid

Is financial aid available to full-time students? Yes
Is financial aid available to part-time students? Yes
Are academic scholarships available? Yes
Assistance programs available to students: Federal Stafford Loan, Federal Perkins Loan, Federal Plus Loan, Federal Pell Grant, Federal Work-Study Program, veterans' assistance

Florida State University

Office for Distributed and Distance Learning

Subjects Offered

Criminolgy, information studies, open and distance learning, mechanical engineering

Admissions Requirements

Is a minimum undergraduate GPA required? Yes
Is provisional admission available? Yes
Is an admissions interview required? No
Can pre-requisite course work be waived? No
Are international students eligible to apply? Yes
Is the TOEFL required for international students? Yes
What is the minimum TOEFL score required? 550

Program Delivery

Primary method of program delivery: Web
Two-way interactive video: No
One-way live video: Yes
Audio: Yes

Remote Sites

Students' homes: Yes

Tuition & Fees

In-state tuition per credit: $153
Out-of-state tuition per credit: $532
Average yearly cost of books: $100

Financial Aid

Is financial aid available to part-time students? Yes
Are academic scholarships available? Yes
Assistance programs available to students: Federal Stafford Loan, Federal Perkins Loan, Federal Plus Loan

Franciscan University of Steubanville

Distance Learning
1235 University Boulevard
Steubanville, OH 43952
Contact: Rev. Mr. Dominic Cerrato, Director of Distance Learning
Department e-mail: distance@franuniv.edu
School Web address: www.franuniv.edu
Institutional accreditation: North Central Association of Colleges and Schools

Subjects Offered

Theology

Admissions Requirements

Is a minimum undergraduate GPA required? Yes
Is provisional admission available? Yes
Is an admissions interview required? No
Can pre-requisite course work be waived? No
Are international students eligible to apply? Yes
Is the TOEFL required for international students? Yes
What is the minimum TOEFL score required? 550

Program Delivery

Audio: Yes
Is the library accessible to students? No
Are computers accessible to students? No

On-Campus Requirements

Is an on-campus component required? Yes
On-campus course work: Yes
On-campus admissions interview: No
On-campus program orientation: No
On-campus exams: No
On-campus thesis defense: No

Tuition & Fees

In-state tuition per credit: $175
Out-of-state tuition per credit: $175
Average yearly cost of books: $640

Financial Aid

Is financial aid available to full-time students? No
Is financial aid available to part-time students? No
Are academic scholarships available? No

Franklin Pierce Law Center

Education Law Institute
2 White Street
Concord, NH 03301
Contact: Sara E. Redfield, Professor
Department e-mail: sredfield@fplc.edu
Department Web address: www.edlawfplc.edu
School Web address: www.fplc.edu
Institutional accreditation: American Bar Association

Subjects Offered

Education law

Admissions Requirements

Is provisional admission available? Yes
Is an admissions interview required? Yes
Can pre-requisite course work be waived? Yes
Are international students eligible to apply? Yes
Is the TOEFL required for international students? Yes
What is the minimum TOEFL score required? 550

Program Delivery

Primary method of program delivery: Web
Two-way interactive video: No
Two-way audio, one-way video: No
One-way live video: No
One-way pre-recorded video: Yes
Audio graphics: Yes
Audio: Yes
Software requirements: No specific software needed other than current browser
Is the library accessible to students? Yes
Are computers accessible to students? Yes

Remote Sites

Other branches of the institution: No
Other college campuses: No
Students' homes: Yes
Work sites: Yes
Libraries: No
Elementary/Secondary schools: No
Community-based organizations: No

On-Campus Requirements

Is an on-campus component required? Yes
On-campus course work: Yes
On-campus admissions interview: No
On-campus program orientation: No
On-campus exams: No
On-campus thesis defense: No

Tuition & Fees

In-state tuition per credit: $375
Out-of-state tuition per credit: $375
Average yearly cost of books: $100

Financial Aid

Is financial aid available to full-time students? Yes
Is financial aid available to part-time students? Yes
Are academic scholarships available? Yes

Georgia Institute of Technology

Continuing Education and Outreach
Center for Distance Learning
620 Cherry Street, ESM G-6
Atlanta, GA 30332-0240
Contact: Dr. Joseph Boland, Director, Center for Distance Learning
Department e-mail: cdl@conted.swann.gatech.edu
Department Web address: www.conted.gatech.edu/distance
School Web address: www.gatech.edu

Institutional accreditation: Southern Association of Colleges and Schools

Subjects Offered

Environmental engineering, health physics/radiological engineering, electrical and computer engineering, industrial systems engineering, mechanical engineering, mathematics

Admissions Requirements

Is a minimum undergraduate GPA required? Yes
Is provisional admission available? No
Is an admissions interview required? No
Can pre-requisite course work be waived? No
Are international students eligible to apply? Yes
Is the TOEFL required for international students? Yes

Program Delivery

Primary method of program delivery: Web
Two-way interactive video: Yes
One-way pre-recorded video: Yes
Is the library accessible to students? Yes
Are computers accessible to students? Yes

Remote Sites

Other branches of the institution: Yes
Students' homes: Yes
Work sites: Yes

On-Campus Requirements

Is an on-campus component required? No

Tuition & Fees

In-state tuition per credit: $530
Out-of-state tuition per credit: $530
Average yearly cost of books: $1,000

Financial Aid

Is financial aid available to full-time students? Yes
Is financial aid available to part-time students? Yes
Are academic scholarships available? No
Assistance programs available to students: Federal Stafford Loan, Federal Perkins Loan, Federal Plus Loan, veterans' assistance

Gordon-Conwell Theological Seminary

Ockenga Institute
Semlink
130 Essex Street
South Hamilton, MA 01982

Contact: David Horn, Director, Semlink Program and Shoemaker Center

Department e-mail: semlink@gcts.edu

Department Web address: www.gcts.edu/semlink

School Web address: www.gcts.edu

Institutional accreditation: Association of Theological Schools

Subjects Offered

Biblical studies, ethics, theology, church history, counseling, missions

Admissions Requirements

Is a minimum undergraduate GPA required? Yes

Is provisional admission available? Yes

Is an admissions interview required? No

Can pre-requisite course work be waived? Yes

Are international students eligible to apply? Yes

Is the TOEFL required for international students? Yes

What is the minimum TOEFL score required? 550

Program Delivery

Primary method of program delivery: Text

Two-way interactive video: No

Two-way audio, one-way video: No

One-way live video: No

One-way pre-recorded video: Yes

Audio graphics: Yes

Audio: Yes

Hardware requirements: 28.8KBPS modem, CD-ROM

Software requirements: Web browser, word processor, RealPlayer

Is the library accessible to students? Yes

Are computers accessible to students? Yes

Remote Sites

Other branches of the institution: Yes

Other college campuses: Yes

Students' homes: Yes

Work sites: Yes

Libraries: Yes

Elementary/Secondary schools: No

Community-based organizations: Yes

Correctional institutions: Yes

On-Campus Requirements

Is an on-campus component required? No

Tuition & Fees

In-state tuition per credit: $331

Average yearly cost of books: $1,000

Financial Aid

Is financial aid available to full-time students? Yes

Is financial aid available to part-time students? No

Are academic scholarships available? Yes

Assistance programs available to students: Federal Stafford Loan, Federal Perkins Loan, Federal Work-Study Program, veterans' assistance

Goucher College

Center for Graduate and Professional Studies

1021 Dulaney Valley Road

Baltimore, MD 21204

Contact: Debbie Culbertson, Executive Director

Department e-mail: center@goucher.edu

Department Web address: www.goucher.edu/center

School Web address: www.goucher.edu

Institutional accreditation: Middle States Association of Colleges and Schools

Subjects Offered

Historic preservation, creative nonfiction, arts administration

Admissions Requirements

Is provisional admission available? No

Is an admissions interview required? No

Can pre-requisite course work be waived? No

Are international students eligible to apply? Yes

Is the TOEFL required for international students? Yes

Program Delivery

Two-way interactive video: No

Two-way audio, one-way video: No

One-way live video: No

One-way pre-recorded video: No

Audio graphics: No

Audio: No

Hardware requirements: Intel-based Pentium PC with at least a 277MB processor, minimum of 64 RAM (128 is better), 3GB hard drive, 56.6KBPS modem

Software requirements: Internet Explorer 5 or Netscape Navigator 4.5 or better, Windows 98

Remote Sites

Other branches of the institution: No

Other college campuses: No

Students' homes: Yes

Work sites: No

Libraries: No

Elementary/Secondary schools: No

Community-based organizations: No

Correctional institutions: No

On-Campus Requirements

On-campus course work: Yes
On-campus admissions interview: No
On-campus program orientation: No
On-campus exams: Yes
On-campus thesis defense: Yes

Tuition & Fees

In-state tuition per credit: $515
Out-of-state tuition per credit: $515
Average yearly cost of books: $50

Financial Aid

Is financial aid available to full-time students? Yes
Is financial aid available to part-time students? Yes
Are academic scholarships available? No
Assistance programs available to students: Federal Stafford Loan, Federal Perkins Loan, Federal Plus Loan, veterans' assistance

Graceland University— Family Nurse Practitioner

Division of Health Care Professions
1 University Place
Lamoni, IA 50140
Contact: Sharon M. Kirkpatrick, PhD, Provost
Department e-mail: iec@graceland.edu
Institutional accreditation: North Central Association of Colleges and Schools

Subjects Offered

Nursing

Admissions Requirements

Is a minimum undergraduate GPA required? Yes
Is provisional admission available? No
Is an admissions interview required? No
Can pre-requisite course work be waived? No
Are international students eligible to apply? Yes
Is the TOEFL required for international students? Yes
What is the minimum TOEFL score required? 550

Program Delivery

Primary method of program delivery: Text
Two-way interactive video: No
Two-way audio, one-way video: No
One-way live video: No
One-way pre-recorded video: Yes
Audio graphics: No
Audio: No

Is the library accessible to students? Yes
Are computers accessible to students? No

Remote Sites

Other branches of the institution: No
Other college campuses: No
Students' homes: Yes
Work sites: Yes
Libraries: No

On-Campus Requirements

Is an on-campus component required? Yes
On-campus course work: Yes
On-campus admissions interview: No
On-campus program orientation: No
On-campus exams: Yes
On-campus thesis defense: No

Tuition & Fees

Application fee: $80
Can it be waived? No
Average yearly cost of books: $1,000

Graceland University— Master of Arts in Religion

1 University Place
Lamoni, IA 50140
Contact: Sharon M. Kirkpatrick, PhD, Provost
Department e-mail: iec@graceland.edu
Institutional accreditation: North Central Association of Colleges and Schools

Subjects Offered

Religion

Admissions Requirements

Is a minimum undergraduate GPA required? Yes
Is provisional admission available? Yes
Can pre-requisite course work be waived? Yes
Are international students eligible to apply? Yes
Is the TOEFL required for international students? Yes
What is the minimum TOEFL score required? 550

Program Delivery

Primary method of program delivery: Remote site
Two-way interactive video: No
Two-way audio, one-way video: No
One-way live video: No
One-way pre-recorded video: Yes
Audio graphics: Yes
Audio: Yes

Is the library accessible to students? Yes
Are computers accessible to students? Yes

Remote Sites

Other branches of the institution: No
Other college campuses: No
Students' homes: No
Work sites: Yes
Libraries: Yes
Elementary/Secondary schools: No
Community-based organizations: Yes
Correctional institutions: No

On-Campus Requirements

Is an on-campus component required? Yes
On-campus course work: Yes
On-campus admissions interview: No
On-campus program orientation: No
On-campus exams: Yes
On-campus thesis defense: No

Tuition & Fees

In-state tuition per credit: $170
Application fee: $30
Can it be waived? No
Average yearly cost of books: $550

Financial Aid

Is financial aid available to full-time students? No
Is financial aid available to part-time students? No
Are academic scholarships available? No

Graceland University— Master of Education

1 University Place
Lamoni, IA 50140
Contact: Sharon M. Kirkpatrick, PhD, Provost
Department e-mail: iec@graceland.edu
Institutional accreditation: North Central Association of
    Colleges and Schools

Subjects Offered

Education

Admissions Requirements

Is a minimum undergraduate GPA required? Yes
Is provisional admission available? Yes
Can pre-requisite course work be waived? No
Are international students eligible to apply? Yes
Is the TOEFL required for international students? Yes
What is the minimum TOEFL score required? 550

Program Delivery

Primary method of program delivery: Remote site
Two-way interactive video: No
Two-way audio, one-way video: No
One-way live video: No
One-way pre-recorded video: No
Audio graphics: Yes
Audio: Yes
Is the library accessible to students? Yes
Are computers accessible to students? No

Remote Sites

Other branches of the institution: No
Other college campuses: No
Students' homes: No
Work sites: Yes
Libraries: No
Elementary/Secondary schools: Yes
Community-based organizations: No
Correctional institutions: No

On-Campus Requirements

Is an on-campus component required? Yes
On-campus course work: Yes
On-campus program orientation: Yes
On-campus exams: Yes

Tuition & Fees

In-state tuition per credit: $290
Application fee: $30
Average yearly cost of books: $300

Financial Aid

Is financial aid available to full-time students? Yes
Is financial aid available to part-time students? Yes
Are academic scholarships available? Yes
Assistance programs available to students: Veterans'
    assistance

Graceland University— Master of Science in Nursing

1 University Place
Lamoni, IA 50140
Contact: Sharon M. Kirkpatrick, Provost
Department e-mail: iec@graceland.edu
Institutional accreditation: North Central Association of
    Colleges and Schools

Subjects Offered

Nursing

Admissions Requirements

Is a minimum undergraduate GPA required? Yes
Is provisional admission available? No
Can pre-requisite course work be waived? No
Are international students eligible to apply? Yes
Is the TOEFL required for international students? Yes
What is the minimum TOEFL score required? 550

Program Delivery

Primary method of program delivery: Text
Two-way interactive video: No
Two-way audio, one-way video: No
One-way live video: No
One-way pre-recorded video: Yes
Audio graphics: No
Audio: No
Is the library accessible to students? Yes
Are computers accessible to students? No

Remote Sites

Other branches of the institution: No
Other college campuses: No
Students' homes: Yes
Work sites: Yes
Libraries: Yes
Elementary/Secondary schools: No

On-Campus Requirements

Is an on-campus component required? Yes
On-campus course work: Yes
On-campus exams: Yes
On-campus thesis defense: Yes

Tuition & Fees

Application fee: $80
Average yearly cost of books: $1,000

Financial Aid

Is financial aid available to full-time students? Yes
Is financial aid available to part-time students? Yes
Are academic scholarships available? Yes
Assistance programs available to students: Veterans'
    assistance

Henley Management College

Graduate Business Studies
Greenlands
Henley-on-Thames, Oxon, England RT9 3AU
Contact: Richard McBain, Director of Studies, Distance
    Learning MBA
Department e-mail: mba@henleymc.ac.uk
Department Web address: www.henley.ac.uk/mba
School Web address: www.henleymc.ac.uk

Subjects Offered

Accounting and finance, human resources, marketing,
    information systems, operations management, strategic
    management, strategic direction, business transforma-
    tion, foundations of management

Admissions Requirements

Is provisional admission available? No
Is an admissions interview required? No
Can pre-requisite course work be waived? No
Are international students eligible to apply? Yes
Is the TOEFL required for international students? No

Program Delivery

Primary method of program delivery: Web
Is the library accessible to students? Yes
Are computers accessible to students? Yes

Remote Sites

Other branches of the institution: Yes
Other college campuses: No
Students' homes: Yes
Work sites: Yes
Libraries: No
Elementary/Secondary schools: No
Community-based organizations: No
Correctional institutions: No

On-Campus Requirements

Is an on-campus component required? Yes
On-campus course work: Yes
On-campus program orientation: Yes
On-campus exams: Yes

Financial Aid

Is financial aid available to full-time students? No
Is financial aid available to part-time students? No
Are academic scholarships available? No

Idaho State University

Institutional Research
Media/Distance Learning Center
741 South 7th Avenue
Pocatello, ID 83209
Contact: Randy Gaines, Manager
Department e-mail: blaicath@isu.edu
Department Web address: www.isu.edu/departments/instres/
School Web address: www.isu.edu
Institutional accreditation: Northwest Association of Schools and Colleges

Subjects Offered

Biology, education, English, history, library, math, physical education, political science, sociology, art, chemistry, geology, health education, nursing, philosophy, physics, politics, pharmacology, speech/speech pathology, theatre, adult education, anthropology, management/finance, women's studies

Admissions Requirements

Is a minimum undergraduate GPA required? No
Is provisional admission available? Yes
Is an admissions interview required? No
Can pre-requisite course work be waived? Yes
Are international students eligible to apply? Yes
Is the TOEFL required for international students? Yes
What is the minimum TOEFL score required? 500

Program Delivery

Primary method of program delivery: Remote site
Two-way interactive video: Yes
Two-way audio, one-way video: Yes
One-way live video: Yes
One-way pre-recorded video: Yes
Audio: Yes
Is the library accessible to students? Yes
Are computers accessible to students? Yes

Remote Sites

Other branches of the institution: Yes
Other college campuses: Yes
Elementary/Secondary schools: Yes
Community-based organizations: Yes

On-Campus Requirements

Is an on-campus component required? No

Tuition & Fees

In-state tuition per credit: $159
Out-of-state tuition per credit: $249
Average yearly cost of books: $600
Average yearly additional fees: $30

Financial Aid

Is financial aid available to full-time students? Yes
Is financial aid available to part-time students? Yes
Are academic scholarships available? Yes
Assistance programs available to students: Federal Stafford Loan, Federal Perkins Loan, Federal Plus Loan, Federal Work-Study Program, in-state student aid programs, veterans' assistance

Illinois Institute of Technology

IIT Online Client Service
3300 South Federal
Chicago, IL 60616-3793
Contact: Holly Pryor Harris, Director, Client Service
Department e-mail: holli.pryorharris@iit.edu
Department Web address: www.iit-online.itt.edu
School Web address: www.iit.edu
Institutional accreditation: North Central Association of Colleges and Schools

Admissions Requirements

Is a minimum undergraduate GPA required? Yes
Is provisional admission available? Yes
Is an admissions interview required? No
Can pre-requisite course work be waived? No
Are international students eligible to apply? Yes
Is the TOEFL required for international students? Yes

Program Delivery

Primary method of program delivery: Web
One-way pre-recorded video: Yes
Audio: Yes
Hardware requirements: Varies by program
Software requirements: Varies by program
Is the library accessible to students? Yes
Are computers accessible to students? Yes

Remote Sites

Students' homes: Yes
Work sites: Yes

Tuition & Fees

In-state tuition per credit: $590
Out-of-state tuition per credit: $590
Average yearly cost of books: $750

Financial Aid

Is financial aid available to full-time students? Yes
Is financial aid available to part-time students? Yes
Are academic scholarships available? Yes
Assistance programs available to students: Federal Stafford Loan, Federal Perkins Loan, veterans' assistance

Imperial College At WYE, University of London

External Programme
Ashford, Kent TN255AH England
Contact: Dr. J.G. Kydd, Director Professor
Department e-mail: epadmin@ic.ac.uk
Department Web address: www.wye.ac.uk/ep
School Web address: www.wye.ac.uk
Institutional accreditation: University of London

Subjects Offered

Environment, biodiversity, sustainable agriculture, applied economics, agribusiness and food management

Admissions Requirements

Is a minimum undergraduate GPA required? No
Is provisional admission available? Yes
Is an admissions interview required? No
Can pre-requisite course work be waived? No
Are international students eligible to apply? Yes
Is the TOEFL required for international students? Yes
What is the minimum TOEFL score required? 500

Program Delivery

Primary method of program delivery: Text
Hardware requirements: None is obligatory
Software requirements: None is obligatory
Is the library accessible to students? No
Are computers accessible to students? No

Remote Sites

Students' homes: Yes
Work sites: Yes

On-Campus Requirements

Is an on-campus component required? No

Financial Aid

Is financial aid available to full-time students? No
Is financial aid available to part-time students? No
Are academic scholarships available? Yes

Indiana College Network (ICN)

714 North Senate Avenue
Indianapolis, IN 46202
Department e-mail: info@icn.org
School Web address: www.icn.org

Admissions Requirements

Is a minimum undergraduate GPA required? Yes
Is an admissions interview required? No
Are international students eligible to apply? Yes

Program Delivery

Primary method of program delivery: Web
Two-way interactive video: Yes
Two-way audio, one-way video: Yes
One-way pre-recorded video: Yes

Remote Sites

Other branches of the institution: Yes
Students' homes: Yes
Work sites: Yes
Libraries: Yes
Elementary/Secondary schools: Yes
Community-based organizations: Yes
Correctional institutions: Yes

Financial Aid

Is financial aid available to full-time students? Yes
Are academic scholarships available? Yes

Indiana State University

Lifelong Learning
Office of Student Services
Erickson Hall, Room 210-211
Terre Haute, IN 47809
Contact: Harry K. Barnes, Director
Department e-mail: studentservices@indstate.edu
Department Web address: indstate.edu/distance
School Web address: web.indstate.edu
Institutional accreditation: North Central Association of Colleges and Schools

Subjects Offered

Criminal law proceedings, criminal theory, law and society, criminology, cellular development, cell and tissue culture, plant taxonomy, embryology, endocrinology, public administration, research methods, public personnel administration, conflict resolution, communication disorders, special education, counseling, curriculum instruction and media technology, library materials, library management, educational psychology, educational leadership, administration and foundations, elementary and early childhood education, health and safety, recreation and sports management, nursing, electronics and computer technology, industrial and mechanical technology, industrial technology education, manufacturing and construction technology

Admissions Requirements

Is a minimum undergraduate GPA required? Yes
Is provisional admission available? Yes
Is an admissions interview required? No
Can pre-requisite course work be waived? Yes
Are international students eligible to apply? Yes
Is the TOEFL required for international students? Yes
What is the minimum TOEFL score required? 550

Program Delivery

Primary method of program delivery: Web
Two-way interactive video: Yes
Two-way audio, one-way video: Yes
One-way live video: Yes
One-way pre-recorded video: Yes
Audio: Yes
Hardware requirements: Windows 95/98, Pentium I, II, III, 32MB of RAM, 56.6KBPS modem, 100MB of free disk space; Macintosh System 8 or above
Software requirements: Netscape or Internet Explorer browser (4.x or higher), word processor (MS Word preferred)
Is the library accessible to students? Yes
Are computers accessible to students? Yes

Remote Sites

Other branches of the institution: No
Other college campuses: Yes
Students' homes: Yes
Work sites: Yes
Libraries: Yes
Elementary/Secondary schools: Yes
Community-based organizations: Yes
Correctional institutions: Yes

On-Campus Requirements

Is an on-campus component required? Yes
On-campus course work: Yes
On-campus admissions interview: No
On-campus program orientation: No
On-campus exams: Yes
On-campus thesis defense: Yes

Tuition & Fees

In-state tuition per credit: $154
Out-of-state tuition per credit: $154
Average yearly cost of books: $35

Financial Aid

Is financial aid available to full-time students? Yes
Is financial aid available to part-time students? Yes
Are academic scholarships available? Yes
Assistance programs available to students: Federal Stafford Loan, Federal Perkins Loan, Federal Plus Loan, Federal Work-Study Program, veterans' assistance

Indiana University

Indiana University System
Office of Distributed Education
ES 2129 902 West New York Street
Indianapolis, IN 46202-5157
Contact: Erwin Boschmann, Associate Vice President
Department e-mail: scs@indiana.edu
Department Web address: www.indiana.edu/~iude/
School Web address: www.indiana.edu
Institutional accreditation: North Central Association of Colleges and Schools

Subjects Offered

Adult education, area ethnic and cultural studies, business, curriculum and instruction, education, education administration, educational psychology, educational research, electrical engineering, English, environmental science, fine arts, health profession, health and physical fitness, instructional media, library and information systems, nursing, physiology, public administration, special education, teacher education, telecommunications, therapeutic recreation

Admissions Requirements

Is a minimum undergraduate GPA required? Yes
Is provisional admission available? Yes
Can pre-requisite course work be waived? No
Are international students eligible to apply? Yes
Is the TOEFL required for international students? Yes

Program Delivery

Primary method of program delivery: Web
Two-way interactive video: Yes
Two-way audio, one-way video: Yes
Hardware requirements: Varies by course
Software requirements: Varies by course
Is the library accessible to students? Yes
Are computers accessible to students? Yes

Remote Sites

Other branches of the institution: Yes
Other college campuses: Yes
Students' homes: Yes
Work sites: Yes
Libraries: Yes
Elementary/Secondary schools: Yes
Community-based organizations: Yes

On-Campus Requirements

On-campus course work: Yes
On-campus program orientation: Yes

Tuition & Fees

In-state tuition per credit: $169
Out-of-state tuition per credit: $169
Application fee: $45

Financial Aid

Is financial aid available to full-time students? Yes
Is financial aid available to part-time students? Yes
Are academic scholarships available? Yes
Assistance programs available to students: Federal Stafford Loan, Federal Perkins Loan, Federal Work-Study Program, in-state student aid programs, veterans' assistance

Indiana Wesleyan University

Center for Distributed Learning
4301 South Washington Street
Marion, IN 46953
Contact: Dr. Hank Kelly, Director of Distance Education
Department e-mail: hkelly@indwes.edu
School Web address: www.indwes.edu
Institutional accreditation: North Central Association of Colleges and Schools; National Council for Accreditation of Teacher Education

Subjects Offered

Education, business

Admissions Requirements

Is a minimum undergraduate GPA required? Yes
Is provisional admission available? Yes
Is an admissions interview required? No
Can pre-requisite course work be waived? Yes
Are international students eligible to apply? Yes
Is the TOEFL required for international students? Yes
What is the minimum TOEFL score required? 550

Program Delivery

Primary method of program delivery: Web
Two-way interactive video: No
Two-way audio, one-way video: No
One-way live video: No
One-way pre-recorded video: No
Audio graphics: No
Audio: No
Software requirements: Netscape Navigator or Internet Explorer version 4.0 or higher, Microsoft Office 95 or newer
Is the library accessible to students? Yes
Are computers accessible to students? Yes

Remote Sites

Other branches of the institution: No
Other college campuses: No
Students' homes: No
Work sites: No
Libraries: No
Elementary/Secondary schools: No
Community-based organizations: No
Correctional institutions: No

On-Campus Requirements

Is an on-campus component required? Yes
On-campus course work: Yes
On-campus admissions interview: No
On-campus program orientation: No
On-campus exams: No
On-campus thesis defense: No

Tuition & Fees

In-state tuition per credit: $365
Out-of-state tuition per credit: $285
Average yearly cost of books: $725

Financial Aid

Is financial aid available to full-time students? Yes
Is financial aid available to part-time students? Yes
Are academic scholarships available? No
Assistance programs available to students: Federal Stafford Loan, veterans' assistance

Institute of Transpersonal Psychology

Global Program
744 San Antonio Road
Palo Alto, CA 94303
Contact: Michael Hutton, PhD, Program Chair
Department e-mail: itpinfo@itp.edu

Department Web address: www.itp.edu
School Web address: www.itp.edu
Institutional accreditation: Western Association of Schools and Colleges

Subjects Offered

Psychology, creative expression, spirituality, ecology, religion, women's studies, health, fitness, stress reduction, counseling

Admissions Requirements

Is provisional admission available? Yes
Can pre-requisite course work be waived? Yes
Are international students eligible to apply? Yes
Is the TOEFL required for international students? Yes
What is the minimum TOEFL score required? 530

Program Delivery

Primary method of program delivery: Web
Hardware requirements: Computer, modem, printer
Is the library accessible to students? Yes
Are computers accessible to students? No

Remote Sites

Community-based organizations: Yes

On-Campus Requirements

Is an on-campus component required? Yes
On-campus course work: Yes
On-campus admissions interview: No
On-campus program orientation: Yes
On-campus exams: No
On-campus thesis defense: No

Tuition & Fees

In-state tuition per credit: $355
Out-of-state tuition per credit: $355
Average yearly cost of books: $300

Financial Aid

Is financial aid available to full-time students? Yes
Is financial aid available to part-time students? Yes
Are academic scholarships available? Yes
Assistance programs available to students: Federal Stafford Loan, Federal Perkins Loan, in-state student aid programs

Iowa State University

Extended and Continuing Education
102 Scheman
Ames, IA 50011-1112

Contact: Ann Hill Duin, Associate Provost and Director of Extended and Continuing Education
Department e-mail: conted@iastate.edu
Department Web address: www.lifelearner.iastate.edu
School Web address: www.iastate.edu
Institutional accreditation: North Central Association of Colleges and Schools

Subjects Offered

Agriculture, family and consumer sciences, engineering, liberal arts and sciences

Admissions Requirements

Is a minimum undergraduate GPA required? Yes
Is provisional admission available? Yes
Is an admissions interview required? No
Can pre-requisite course work be waived? Yes
Are international students eligible to apply? Yes
Is the TOEFL required for international students? Yes

Program Delivery

Primary method of program delivery: Remote site
Two-way interactive video: Yes
Two-way audio, one-way video: No
One-way live video: No
One-way pre-recorded video: Yes
Audio graphics: No
Audio: No
Is the library accessible to students? Yes
Are computers accessible to students? Yes

Remote Sites

Other branches of the institution: No
Other college campuses: Yes
Students' homes: Yes
Work sites: Yes
Libraries: Yes
Elementary/Secondary schools: Yes
Community-based organizations: Yes
Correctional institutions: No

On-Campus Requirements

Is an on-campus component required? No

Tuition & Fees

In-state tuition per credit: $192
Out-of-state tuition per credit: $192

Financial Aid

Is financial aid available to full-time students? Yes
Is financial aid available to part-time students? Yes
Are academic scholarships available? Yes
Assistance programs available to students: Federal Stafford

Loan, Federal Perkins Loan, Federal Plus Loan, Federal Work-Study Program, in-state student aid programs, veterans' assistance

Jacksonville State University

Department of Distance Learning
700 Pelham Road North
Jacksonville, AL 36265
Contact: Franklin King, Director of Distance Learning
Department e-mail: dlinfo@jsucc.jsu.edu
School Web address: www.jsu.edu/depart/distance
Institutional accreditation: Southern Association of Colleges and Schools

Subjects Offered

Finance, political science, management, special education, emergency management, education, business administration, marketing, educational psychology, economics, nursing

Admissions Requirements

Is a minimum undergraduate GPA required? No
Is provisional admission available? Yes
Can pre-requisite course work be waived? No
Are international students eligible to apply? Yes
Is the TOEFL required for international students? Yes
What is the minimum TOEFL score required? 500

Program Delivery

Primary method of program delivery: Web
Two-way interactive video: Yes
Two-way audio, one-way video: No
One-way live video: Yes
One-way pre-recorded video: Yes
Audio graphics: No
Audio: Yes
Hardware requirements: 28.8KBPS modem, 150 MHz processor, minimum 16MB of RAM, monitor capable of 800 x 600 resolution
Software requirements: Netscape Navigator 4.0 or higher, Microsoft Internet Explorer 4.0 or higher, or equivalent browser
Is the library accessible to students? Yes
Are computers accessible to students? Yes

Remote Sites

Other branches of the institution: Yes
Other college campuses: Yes
Students' homes: Yes
Work sites: Yes
Libraries: Yes
Elementary/Secondary schools: Yes

Community-based organizations: No
Correctional institutions: No

On-Campus Requirements

Is an on-campus component required? No

Tuition & Fees

In-state tuition per credit: $132
Out-of-state tuition per credit: $264
Average yearly cost of books: $600

Financial Aid

Is financial aid available to full-time students? Yes
Is financial aid available to part-time students? Yes
Are academic scholarships available? Yes
Assistance programs available to students: Federal Stafford Loan, Federal Perkins Loan, Federal Plus Loan, Federal Pell Grant, Federal Work-Study Program, in-state student aid programs, veterans' assistance

Johns Hopkins University School of Hygiene and Public Health

Distance Education Division
615 North Wolfe Street
Baltimore, MD 21205
Contact: Sukon Kanchanaraksa, PhD, Director of Distance Education Division
Department e-mail: distance@jhsph.edu
Department Web address: www.distance.jhsph.edu
School Web address: www.jhsph.edu
Institutional accreditation: Council on Education for Public Health

Subjects Offered

Biostatistics, environmental health, epidemiology, health policy and management, international health, population and family health sciences, molecular microbiology and immunology

Admissions Requirements

Is a minimum undergraduate GPA required? No
Is provisional admission available? Yes
Is an admissions interview required? No
Can pre-requisite course work be waived? Yes
Are international students eligible to apply? Yes
Is the TOEFL required for international students? Yes
What is the minimum TOEFL score required? 550

Program Delivery

Primary method of program delivery: Web
One-way pre-recorded video: Yes
Audio graphics: Yes
Audio: Yes
Hardware requirements: 200 MHz Pentium w/64MB of RAM, CD-ROM, sound card and speakers, 56KBPS modem, printer
Software requirements: Microsoft Office 2000 Professional Edition
Is the library accessible to students? Yes
Are computers accessible to students? Yes

Remote Sites

Other branches of the institution: No
Other college campuses: No
Students' homes: Yes
Work sites: Yes
Libraries: Yes
Elementary/Secondary schools: No
Community-based organizations: No
Correctional institutions: No

On-Campus Requirements

Is an on-campus component required? Yes
On-campus course work: Yes
On-campus admissions interview: No
On-campus program orientation: Yes
On-campus exams: No
On-campus thesis defense: No

Tuition & Fees

In-state tuition per credit: $513
Out-of-state tuition per credit: $513
Average yearly cost of books: $100

Financial Aid

Is financial aid available to full-time students? Yes
Is financial aid available to part-time students? Yes
Are academic scholarships available? No
Assistance programs available to students: Federal Perkins Loan, Federal Work-Study Program, in-state student aid programs, veterans' assistance

Jones International University

9697 East Mineral Avenue
Englewood, CO 80112
Contact: Dr. Pamela Pease, President
Department e-mail: info@jonesinternational.edu

School Web address: www.jonesinternational.edu
Institutional accreditation: North Central Association of Colleges and Schools

Subjects Offered

Business communication

Admissions Requirements

Is a minimum undergraduate GPA required? Yes
Is provisional admission available? No
Is an admissions interview required? No
Can pre-requisite course work be waived? Yes
Are international students eligible to apply? Yes
Is the TOEFL required for international students? Yes
What is the minimum TOEFL score required? 550

Program Delivery

Hardware requirements: Pentium processor with at least 133 MHz, 16MB of RAM, VGH 256-color monitor 28.8KBPS modem
Software requirements: Netscape Navigator version 3 or 4, or Internet Explorer version 4.01. Some courses: 3-chat, Adobe Acrobat Reader and RealPlayer
Is the library accessible to students? Yes
Are computers accessible to students? No

Remote Sites

Other branches of the institution: No
Other college campuses: No
Students' homes: Yes
Work sites: Yes
Libraries: Yes
Elementary/Secondary schools: No
Community-based organizations: No
Correctional institutions: No

On-Campus Requirements

Is an on-campus component required? No

Tuition & Fees

In-state tuition per credit: $242
Out-of-state tuition per credit: $242
Average yearly cost of books: $840

Financial Aid

Is financial aid available to full-time students? Yes
Is financial aid available to part-time students? Yes
Are academic scholarships available? No
Assistance programs available to students: Veterans' assistance

Keller Graduate School of Management

Online Education Center
One Tower Lane
Oakbrook Terrace, IL 60181
Contact: Larry Rubly, Director of Online Education
Development
Department Web address: online.keller.edu
School Web address: www.keller.edu
Institutional accreditation: North Central Association of
Colleges and Schools

Admissions Requirements

Is a minimum undergraduate GPA required? No
Is provisional admission available? Yes
Is an admissions interview required? Yes
Can pre-requisite course work be waived? Yes
Are international students eligible to apply? Yes
Is the TOEFL required for international students? No

Program Delivery

Primary method of program delivery: Web
Two-way interactive video: No
Two-way audio, one-way video: No
One-way live video: No
One-way pre-recorded video: Yes
Audio graphics: No
Audio: Yes
Hardware requirements: 100 MHz Pentium PC, 32MB of
RAM, CD-ROM, sound and video card, 28.8KBPS
modem
Software requirements: MS Office suite, Windows 98,
Internet Explorer 5.5
Is the library accessible to students? Yes
Are computers accessible to students? Yes

Remote Sites

Other branches of the institution: Yes
Other college campuses: No
Students' homes: Yes
Work sites: Yes
Libraries: Yes
Elementary/Secondary schools: No
Community-based organizations: No
Correctional institutions: No

On-Campus Requirements

Is an on-campus component required? No

Tuition & Fees

In-state tuition per credit: $382
Average yearly cost of books: $600

Financial Aid

Is financial aid available to full-time students? Yes
Is financial aid available to part-time students? Yes
Are academic scholarships available? No
Assistance programs available to students: Federal Stafford
Loan, veterans' assistance

Kettering University

Office of Graduate Studies
1700 West Third Avenue
Flint, MI 48504-4898
Contact: Tony Hain, PhD, Dean of Graduate Studies
Department e-mail: bbedore@kettering.edu
Department Web address: www.kettering.edu/acad/grad/
School Web address: www.kettering.edu
Institutional accreditation: North Central Association of
Colleges and Schools

Subjects Offered

Finance and economics, quantitative skills and computer
application, management and administration, manufacturing engineering, operations analysis, industrial and
manufacturing engineering, mechanical design,
automotive systems engineering

Admissions Requirements

Is a minimum undergraduate GPA required? Yes
Is provisional admission available? Yes
Is an admissions interview required? No
Can pre-requisite course work be waived? No
Are international students eligible to apply? Yes
Is the TOEFL required for international students? Yes
What is the minimum TOEFL score required? 570

Program Delivery

Primary method of program delivery: Remote site
Two-way interactive video: No
Two-way audio, one-way video: Yes
One-way live video: No
One-way pre-recorded video: Yes
Audio graphics: No
Audio: No
Hardware requirements: TV/VCR and Internet access
Is the library accessible to students? No
Are computers accessible to students? No

Remote Sites

Other branches of the institution: No
Other college campuses: Yes
Students' homes: Yes
Work sites: Yes

Libraries: No
Elementary/Secondary schools: No
Community-based organizations: No
Correctional institutions: No

On-Campus Requirements

Is an on-campus component required? No

Tuition & Fees

In-state tuition per credit: $427
Out-of-state tuition per credit: $427
Average yearly cost of books: $45

Financial Aid

Is financial aid available to full-time students? Yes
Is financial aid available to part-time students? Yes
Are academic scholarships available? No
Assistance programs available to students: Federal Stafford Loan, Federal Perkins Loan, Federal Plus Loan, in-state student aid programs, veterans' assistance

Knowledge Systems Institute

Computer and Information Sciences
3420 Main Street
Skokie, IL 60076
Contact: Judy Pan, Executive Director
Department e-mail: office@ksi.edu
School Web address: www.ksi.edu
Institutional accreditation: Illinois Board of Higher Education

Subjects Offered

Information systems design, software project management, database management systems, JAVA programming, theory of computation, independent study, programming languages, data mining, advanced operating systems, thesis research, computer networks, knowledge engineering

Admissions Requirements

Is a minimum undergraduate GPA required? No
Is provisional admission available? Yes
Is an admissions interview required? Yes
Can pre-requisite course work be waived? Yes
Are international students eligible to apply? Yes
Is the TOEFL required for international students? Yes
What is the minimum TOEFL score required? 550

Program Delivery

Primary method of program delivery: Web
Two-way interactive video: Yes

Audio: Yes
Hardware requirements: PC
Software requirements: Windows 95 or higher (98, 2000, NT), Internet connection with Netscape Navigator 2.0 or higher
Is the library accessible to students? Yes
Are computers accessible to students? Yes

Remote Sites

Other branches of the institution: No
Other college campuses: No
Students' homes: Yes
Work sites: No
Libraries: No
Elementary/Secondary schools: No
Community-based organizations: No
Correctional institutions: No

On-Campus Requirements

Is an on-campus component required? Yes
On-campus course work: No
On-campus admissions interview: Yes
On-campus program orientation: No
On-campus exams: Yes
On-campus thesis defense: Yes

Tuition & Fees

In-state tuition per credit: $295
Out-of-state tuition per credit: $295
Average yearly cost of books: $600

Financial Aid

Is financial aid available to full-time students? Yes
Is financial aid available to part-time students? Yes
Are academic scholarships available? No
Assistance programs available to students: Federal Stafford Loan, Federal Plus Loan, Federal Work-Study Program, veterans' assistance

Lakehead University

Part-time and Distance Education
Regional Centre 0009, 955 Oliver Road
Thunder Bay, Ontario, Canada P7B 5E1
Contact: Gwen Wojoa, Director
Department e-mail: parttime@lakeheadu.ca
School Web address: www.lakeheadu.ca
Institutional accreditation: Council of Ontario Universities

Subjects Offered

Education, social work, forestry

Admissions Requirements

Is a minimum undergraduate GPA required? Yes
Is an admissions interview required? No
Can pre-requisite course work be waived? No
Are international students eligible to apply? Yes
Is the TOEFL required for international students? Yes
What is the minimum TOEFL score required? 550

Program Delivery

Primary method of program delivery: Web
Two-way interactive video: Yes
Two-way audio, one-way video: Yes
One-way live video: Yes
One-way pre-recorded video: No
Audio graphics: Yes
Audio: Yes
Hardware requirements: PC with Windows 95/98 or PowerMac, connection to Internet—Netscape or Internet Explorer 4 or more recent
Is the library accessible to students? Yes
Are computers accessible to students? Yes

Remote Sites

Other branches of the institution: Yes
Other college campuses: Yes
Students' homes: Yes
Work sites: Yes
Libraries: Yes
Elementary/Secondary schools: Yes
Community-based organizations: Yes

On-Campus Requirements

Is an on-campus component required? Yes
On-campus course work: Yes
On-campus thesis defense: Yes

Tuition & Fees

In-state tuition per credit: $1,949
Out-of-state tuition per credit: $3,600

Financial Aid

Is financial aid available to full-time students? Yes
Is financial aid available to part-time students? Yes
Are academic scholarships available? Yes
Assistance programs available to students: Federal Stafford Loan, Federal Work-Study Program, in-state student aid programs

Lehigh University

Office of Distance Education
205 Johnson Hall
36 University Drive
Bethlehem, PA 18015
Contact: Peg Kercsmar, Manager, Distance Education
Department e-mail: mak5@lehigh.edu
Department Web address: www.distance.lehigh.edu
School Web address: www2.lehigh.edu
Institutional accreditation: Middle States Association of Colleges and Schools

Subjects Offered

Chemistry, chemical engineering, biological sciences, quality engineering, manufacturing systems engineering, business administration, polymers science and engineering, environmental engineering, pharmaceutical sciences

Admissions Requirements

Is a minimum undergraduate GPA required? Yes
Is provisional admission available? Yes
Is an admissions interview required? No
Can pre-requisite course work be waived? Yes
Are international students eligible to apply? Yes
Is the TOEFL required for international students? Yes
What is the minimum TOEFL score required? 550

Program Delivery

Two-way audio, one-way video: Yes
Hardware requirements: Satellite: PC and proprietary receiver. Streaming Video: PC minimum 133 MHz, 64MB of RAM, 56KBPS modem or high-speed connection
Software requirements: Satellite reception: Windows 95 or later operating system. For streaming video: RealPlayer, Adobe Acrobat, Netscape 4.0 or higher
Is the library accessible to students? Yes
Are computers accessible to students? Yes

Remote Sites

Other college campuses: Yes
Students' homes: Yes
Work sites: Yes

On-Campus Requirements

Is an on-campus component required? No

Tuition & Fees

In-state tuition per credit: $590
Out-of-state tuition per credit: $590
Average yearly cost of books: $30

Financial Aid

Is financial aid available to part-time students? No
Are academic scholarships available? No
Assistance programs available to students: Federal Stafford
Loan, Federal Perkins Loan, Federal Plus Loan

Louisiana State University and A&M

Centers for Excellence in Learning and Teaching
Center for Distance Education
118 Hines Hall
Baton Rouge, LA 70803
Contact: Tammy E. Adams, Director
Department e-mail: tadams3@lsu.edu
Department Web address: www.cde.lsu.edu
School Web address: www.lsu.edu

Admissions Requirements

Is a minimum undergraduate GPA required? Yes
Are international students eligible to apply? Yes

Program Delivery

Two-way interactive video: Yes
Two-way audio, one-way video: No
One-way live video: No
One-way pre-recorded video: Yes
Audio graphics: No
Audio: No

Remote Sites

Other branches of the institution: Yes
Other college campuses: Yes
Students' homes: Yes
Work sites: Yes
Libraries: No
Elementary/Secondary schools: Yes
Community-based organizations: Yes
Correctional institutions: No

Financial Aid

Is financial aid available to full-time students? Yes
Is financial aid available to part-time students? Yes
Are academic scholarships available? Yes
Assistance programs available to students: Federal Stafford
Loan, Federal Perkins Loan, Federal Plus Loan, Federal
Work-Study Program, in-state student aid programs,
veterans' assistance

Loyola University New Orleans

Loyola Institute for Ministry
6363 St. Charles Avenue, Campus Box 67
New Orleans, LA 70118
Contact: Dr. Barbara Fleischer, Director
Department e-mail: lim@loyno.edu
Department Web address: www.loyno.edu/lim/extension
School Web address: www.loyno.edu
Institutional accreditation: Southern Association of
Colleges and Schools

Subjects Offered

Religious education, pastoral studies, christian spirituality,
small christian communities, religion and ecology,
pastoral administration, marketplace ministries

Admissions Requirements

Is a minimum undergraduate GPA required? Yes
Is provisional admission available? Yes
Are international students eligible to apply? Yes

Program Delivery

Primary method of program delivery: Remote site
One-way pre-recorded video: Yes
Audio: Yes
Is the library accessible to students? Yes
Are computers accessible to students? No

Remote Sites

Work sites: Yes
Elementary/Secondary schools: Yes

Tuition & Fees

In-state tuition per credit: $232
Out-of-state tuition per credit: $232
Application fee: $20
Average yearly cost of books: $90

Financial Aid

Is financial aid available to part-time students? No
Are academic scholarships available? No
Assistance programs available to students: Veterans'
assistance

Lutheran Theological Seminary at Philadelphia

7301 Germantown Avenue
Philadelphia, PA 19119
Contact: Richard N. Stewart

Department e-mail: rstewart@ltsp.edu
School Web address: www.ltsp.edu
Institutional accreditation: Middle States Association of
Colleges and Schools

Subjects Offered

Theology, ministry

Admissions Requirements

Is a minimum undergraduate GPA required? Yes
Is provisional admission available? Yes
Can pre-requisite course work be waived? No
Are international students eligible to apply? Yes
Is the TOEFL required for international students? Yes
What is the minimum TOEFL score required? 550

Program Delivery

Primary method of program delivery: Web
Two-way interactive video: Yes
Two-way audio, one-way video: No
One-way live video: Yes
One-way pre-recorded video: Yes
Audio graphics: Yes
Audio: Yes
Hardware requirements: Computer with CD-ROM
56KBPS modem, Internet access
Software requirements: Microsoft Word 97
Are computers accessible to students? No

Remote Sites

Other branches of the institution: Yes
Other college campuses: Yes
Students' homes: Yes
Work sites: Yes
Libraries: No
Elementary/Secondary schools: No
Community-based organizations: Yes
Correctional institutions: No

On-Campus Requirements

Is an on-campus component required? Yes
On-campus course work: Yes
On-campus admissions interview: No
On-campus program orientation: Yes
On-campus exams: Yes
On-campus thesis defense: Yes

Tuition & Fees

In-state tuition per credit: $825
Out-of-state tuition per credit: $825
Average yearly cost of books: $500

Financial Aid

Is financial aid available to full-time students? Yes
Is financial aid available to part-time students? No
Are academic scholarships available? Yes
Assistance programs available to students: Federal Stafford
Loan

Marist College

School of Management
Poughkeepsie, NY 12601-1387
Contact: Siamack Shojai, PhD, Associate Dean
School Web address: www.marist.edu
Institutional accreditation: Middle States Association of
Colleges and Schools; New York State Education
Department

Admissions Requirements

Is a minimum undergraduate GPA required? Yes
Is provisional admission available? Yes
Is an admissions interview required? No
Can pre-requisite course work be waived? Yes
Are international students eligible to apply? Yes
What is the minimum TOEFL score required? 550

Program Delivery

Primary method of program delivery: Web
One-way pre-recorded video: Yes
Audio: Yes
Hardware requirements: Pentium III, modem
Software requirements: Microsoft Office 2000
Is the library accessible to students? Yes
Are computers accessible to students? Yes

Remote Sites

Other branches of the institution: Yes
Libraries: Yes

On-Campus Requirements

Is an on-campus component required? No

Tuition & Fees

In-state tuition per credit: $462
Out-of-state tuition per credit: $462
Average yearly cost of books: $500

Financial Aid

Is financial aid available to full-time students? Yes
Is financial aid available to part-time students? Yes
Are academic scholarships available? Yes
Assistance programs available to students: Federal Stafford
Loan

Mary Grove College

Graduate Admission and Student Services
Master in the Art of Teaching
8425 West McNichols
Detroit, MI 48221
Contact: Dr. Ednice Jordan, MAT Director
Department e-mail: ejordan@marygrove.edu
School Web address: marygrove.edu
Institutional accreditation: North Central Association of
Colleges and Schools

Subjects Offered

Education

Admissions Requirements

Is provisional admission available? Yes
Is an admissions interview required? No
Can pre-requisite course work be waived? No
Are international students eligible to apply? Yes
Is the TOEFL required for international students? Yes

Program Delivery

Primary method of program delivery: Web
Two-way audio, one-way video: Yes
One-way live video: Yes
Is the library accessible to students? Yes
Are computers accessible to students? No

Remote Sites

Students' homes: Yes
Work sites: Yes

On-Campus Requirements

Is an on-campus component required? No

Tuition & Fees

In-state tuition per credit: $250
Out-of-state tuition per credit: $250
Average yearly cost of books: $70

Financial Aid

Is financial aid available to full-time students? Yes
Is financial aid available to part-time students? Yes
Are academic scholarships available? Yes
Assistance programs available to students: Federal Stafford
Loan, in-state student aid programs, veterans' assistance

Medical College of Wisconsin

Department of Preventive Medicine
MPH Degree Programs
8701 Watertown Plank Road
Milwaukee, WI 53226
Contact: William W. Greaves MD, MSPH, Chair,
Department of Preventive Medicine, Director, MPH
Programs
Department e-mail: mph@mcw.edu
Department Web address: instruct.mcw.edu/premed
School Web address: www.mcw.edu
Institutional accreditation: North Central Association of
Colleges and Schools

Subjects Offered

Occupational medicine, health services administration,
general preventive medicine and public health

Admissions Requirements

Is a minimum undergraduate GPA required? No
Is provisional admission available? No
Is an admissions interview required? No
Can pre-requisite course work be waived? No
Are international students eligible to apply? Yes
Is the TOEFL required for international students? Yes

Program Delivery

Primary method of program delivery: Text
Two-way interactive video: No
Two-way audio, one-way video: No
One-way live video: No
One-way pre-recorded video: No
Audio graphics: No
Audio: No
Hardware requirements: PC Pentium or Pentium II, 32MB
of RAM, Mac System 7.1 or higher
Software requirements: Web browser, Word processor
packages, e-mail, Netscape Navigator 4.0 or higher
Is the library accessible to students? Yes
Are computers accessible to students? No

Remote Sites

Other branches of the institution: No
Other college campuses: No
Students' homes: Yes
Work sites: Yes
Libraries: No
Elementary/Secondary schools: No
Community-based organizations: No
Correctional institutions: No

On-Campus Requirements

Is an on-campus component required? Yes
On-campus course work: No
On-campus admissions interview: No
On-campus program orientation: Yes
On-campus exams: No
On-campus thesis defense: No

Tuition & Fees

In-state tuition per credit: $555
Out-of-state tuition per credit: $555
Average yearly cost of books: $100

Financial Aid

Is financial aid available to full-time students? No
Is financial aid available to part-time students? No
Are academic scholarships available? No

Michigan State University

Outreach Instructional Programs
23 Kellogg Center
East Lansing, MI 48824
Contact: Dr. Barbara Fails, Director of Outreach
    Instruction
Department e-mail: gotomsu@ms.edu
Department Web address: www.vu.msu.edu
School Web address: www.msu.edu
Institutional accreditation: North Central Association of
    Colleges and Schools

Subjects Offered

Chemical engineering, Braille literacy, education of
    students with severe and multiple disabilities, profes-
    sional roles in special education, high school high
    acheiver courses, ecological economics, economics,
    math, introduction to programming, introdution to the
    information society, telecommunications, teacher
    education, food law, computer science, nursing, resource
    development, geography, advanced placement courses
    for high school students

Admissions Requirements

Is provisional admission available? Yes
Are international students eligible to apply? Yes
Is the TOEFL required for international students? Yes

Program Delivery

Primary method of program delivery: Web
Hardware requirements: Intel-based Pentium PC, 16MB
    RAM, 28.8KBPS modem or higher, or Macintosh
    compatible system

Software requirements: Internet explorer 4.0 or higher,
    Netscape Navigator 4.0, Windows NT, 95, or 98
Is the library accessible to students? Yes
Are computers accessible to students? Yes

Remote Sites

Other branches of the institution: Yes
Other college campuses: Yes
Students' homes: Yes
Elementary/Secondary schools: Yes

On-Campus Requirements

Is an on-campus component required? No

Tuition & Fees

In-state tuition per credit: $237
Out-of-state tuition per credit: $479
Average yearly cost of books: $1,046

Financial Aid

Is financial aid available to full-time students? Yes
Is financial aid available to part-time students? Yes
Are academic scholarships available? Yes
Assistance programs available to students: Veterans'
    assistance

Michigan Technological University

Extended University Programs
1400 Townsend Drive
Houghton, MI 49931
Contact: Marti Banks Sikarskie, Program Director
Department e-mail: nclose@mtu.edu
Department Web address: www.admin.mtu.edu/eup
School Web address: www.mtu.edu
Institutional accreditation: North Central Association of
    Colleges and Schools

Subjects Offered

Bs in surveying, ms mechanical engineering, phd mechani-
    cal engineering, phd chemistry, phd electrical engineer-
    ing, designing engineer certificate

Admissions Requirements

Is a minimum undergraduate GPA required? Yes
Is provisional admission available? Yes
Is an admissions interview required? No
Can pre-requisite course work be waived? Yes
Are international students eligible to apply? Yes
Is the TOEFL required for international students? Yes
What is the minimum TOEFL score required? 550

Program Delivery

Primary method of program delivery: Remote site
One-way pre-recorded video: Yes
Hardware requirements: Course-specific
Software requirements: Course-specific
Is the library accessible to students? Yes
Are computers accessible to students? No

Remote Sites

Work sites: Yes

On-Campus Requirements

Is an on-campus component required? Yes
On-campus program orientation: Yes

Tuition & Fees

Application fee: $35
Can it be waived? Yes
Average yearly cost of books: $900

Financial Aid

Is financial aid available to full-time students? Yes
Is financial aid available to part-time students? Yes
Are academic scholarships available? Yes
Assistance programs available to students: Federal Stafford
  Loan, Federal Perkins Loan, Federal Plus Loan, Federal
  Work-Study Program, in-state student aid programs,
  veterans' assistance

Middle Tennessee State University

Continuing Studies and Public Service
Academic Outreach and Distance Learning
MTSU
1301 East Main Street
Murfreesboro, TN 37132
Contact: Dianne Zeh, Director
Department e-mail: dzeh@mtsu.edu
Department Web address: www.mtsu.edu/~contstud/
School Web address: www.mtsu.edu

Subjects Offered

Education, math, management, political science, aerospace,
  nutrition

Admissions Requirements

Is a minimum undergraduate GPA required? Yes
Is provisional admission available? Yes
Is an admissions interview required? No
Can pre-requisite course work be waived? Yes

Are international students eligible to apply? Yes
Is the TOEFL required for international students? Yes

Program Delivery

Primary method of program delivery: Web
Two-way interactive video: Yes
Is the library accessible to students? Yes

Remote Sites

Other college campuses: Yes
Work sites: Yes
Elementary/Secondary schools: Yes

Tuition & Fees

In-state tuition per credit: $157
Out-of-state tuition per credit: $400
Average yearly cost of books: $320

Financial Aid

Is financial aid available to full-time students? Yes
Is financial aid available to part-time students? Yes
Are academic scholarships available? Yes
Assistance programs available to students: Federal Stafford
  Loan, Federal Perkins Loan, Federal Plus Loan, Federal
  Work-Study Program, in-state student aid programs,
  veterans' assistance

Mississippi State University—Geosciences

108 Hilburn Hall PO Box 5448
Mississippi State, MS 39762
Contact: Dr. Mark Binkley, Professor
Department e-mail: bailey@geosci.msstate.edu
Department Web address: msstate.edu/dept/geosciences/
  distance.html
School Web address: msstate.edu
Institutional accreditation: Southern Association of
  Colleges and Schools

Subjects Offered

Meteorology, geology, oceanography, geography

Admissions Requirements

Is a minimum undergraduate GPA required? Yes
Is provisional admission available? Yes
Is an admissions interview required? No
Can pre-requisite course work be waived? No
Are international students eligible to apply? Yes
Is the TOEFL required for international students? No

Program Delivery

Primary method of program delivery: Web
One-way pre-recorded video: Yes
Hardware requirements: Computer with 64MB of RAM and 56KBPS modem
Software requirements: Internet browser
Is the library accessible to students? Yes
Are computers accessible to students? No

Remote Sites

Other branches of the institution: No
Other college campuses: No
Students' homes: No
Work sites: No
Libraries: No
Elementary/Secondary schools: No
Community-based organizations: No
Correctional institutions: No

On-Campus Requirements

Is an on-campus component required? No

Tuition & Fees

In-state tuition per credit: $173
Application fee: $25
Can it be waived? Yes
Average yearly cost of books: $2,400

Financial Aid

Is financial aid available to full-time students? Yes
Is financial aid available to part-time students? Yes
Are academic scholarships available? No
Assistance programs available to students: Federal Stafford Loan, Federal Perkins Loan, Federal Plus Loan, veterans' assistance

Mississippi State University—Division of Continuing Education

PO Box 5247
Mississippi State, MS 39762
Contact: Duke West, Manager of Distance Education
Department Web address: www.msstate.edu/dept/ced
School Web address: www.msstate.edu
Institutional accreditation: Southern Association of Colleges and Schools

Subjects Offered

Elementary education, public policy, health education and health promotion, counselor education, community college leadership, vocational teacher licensure

Admissions Requirements

Is a minimum undergraduate GPA required? Yes
Is provisional admission available? Yes
Is an admissions interview required? No
Can pre-requisite course work be waived? No
Are international students eligible to apply? Yes
Is the TOEFL required for international students? Yes
What is the minimum TOEFL score required? 550

Program Delivery

Primary method of program delivery: Remote site
Two-way interactive video: Yes
Two-way audio, one-way video: No
One-way live video: No
One-way pre-recorded video: Yes
Audio graphics: No
Audio: No
Is the library accessible to students? Yes
Are computers accessible to students? Yes

Remote Sites

Other branches of the institution: Yes
Other college campuses: Yes
Students' homes: Yes
Work sites: Yes
Libraries: Yes
Elementary/Secondary schools: Yes
Community-based organizations: Yes
Correctional institutions: Yes

On-Campus Requirements

Is an on-campus component required? Yes
On-campus course work: Yes
On-campus admissions interview: No
On-campus program orientation: No
On-campus exams: No
On-campus thesis defense: Yes

Tuition & Fees

In-state tuition per credit: $167
Out-of-state tuition per credit: $172
Average yearly cost of books: $500

Financial Aid

Is financial aid available to full-time students? Yes
Is financial aid available to part-time students? Yes
Are academic scholarships available? No
Assistance programs available to students: Federal Stafford

Loan, Federal Perkins Loan, Federal Plus Loan, veterans' assistance

Mississippi State University—Department of Engineering

Engineering Off-Campus Graduate Program
Box 9544
Mississippi State, MS 39762-9544
Contact: Dr. Bob Taylor, Associate Dean for Academics and Administration
Department e-mail: distance_education@engr.msstate.edu
Department Web address: www.engr.msstate.edu
School Web address: www.msstate.edu
Institutional accreditation: Southern Association of Colleges and Schools

Subjects Offered

Civil engineering, chemical engineering, electrical and computer engineering, industrial engineering, mechanical engineering, computer science

Admissions Requirements

Is a minimum undergraduate GPA required? Yes
Is provisional admission available? Yes
Is an admissions interview required? No
Can pre-requisite course work be waived? Yes
Are international students eligible to apply? Yes
Is the TOEFL required for international students? Yes
What is the minimum TOEFL score required? 550

Program Delivery

Primary method of program delivery: Remote site
Two-way interactive video: Yes
Two-way audio, one-way video: No
One-way live video: No
One-way pre-recorded video: Yes
Audio graphics: No
Audio: No
Hardware requirements: Pentium processor or better, modem, printer
Software requirements: RealPlayer, Adobe Acrobat Reader
Is the library accessible to students? Yes
Are computers accessible to students? Yes

Remote Sites

Other branches of the institution: Yes
Other college campuses: No
Students' homes: No
Work sites: Yes

Libraries: No
Elementary/Secondary schools: No
Community-based organizations: No
Correctional institutions: No

On-Campus Requirements

Is an on-campus component required? No

Tuition & Fees

Out-of-state tuition per credit: $295
Average yearly cost of books: $200

Montana State University—Bozeman

Intercollege Programs for Science Education
Burns Telecommunications Center
401 Linfield Hall
Bozeman, MT 59717-2805
Contact: Dr. Carol Thoresen, Director, IPSE
Department e-mail: thoresen@montana.edu
School Web address: www.montana.edu
Institutional accreditation: Northwest Association of Schools and Colleges

Subjects Offered

Education, biology, chemistry, microbiology, plant science, environmental science, physics, earth science, astronomy, mathematics

Admissions Requirements

Is a minimum undergraduate GPA required? Yes
Is provisional admission available? Yes
Is an admissions interview required? No
Can pre-requisite course work be waived? No
Are international students eligible to apply? Yes
Is the TOEFL required for international students? Yes
What is the minimum TOEFL score required? 550

Program Delivery

Primary method of program delivery: Web
Hardware requirements: Internet access via local Internet provider
Software requirements: Windows 95 or later, Mac OS 7.1 or later
Is the library accessible to students? Yes
Are computers accessible to students? No

Remote Sites

Other branches of the institution: No
Other college campuses: No
Students' homes: Yes

Work sites: Yes
Libraries: No
Elementary/Secondary schools: No
Community-based organizations: No
Correctional institutions: No

On-Campus Requirements

Is an on-campus component required? Yes
On-campus course work: Yes
On-campus admissions interview: No
On-campus program orientation: Yes
On-campus exams: No
On-campus thesis defense: No

Tuition & Fees

In-state tuition per credit: $150
Out-of-state tuition per credit: $150
Average yearly cost of books: $50

Financial Aid

Is financial aid available to full-time students? Yes
Is financial aid available to part-time students? Yes
Are academic scholarships available? Yes
Assistance programs available to students: Federal Stafford Loan, Federal Perkins Loan, Federal Plus Loan, veterans' assistance

Montana Tech of the University of Montana

1300 West Park Street
Butte, MT 59701
Contact: Dr. Kumar Ganesan, Department Head, Environmental Engineering
Department e-mail: kganesan@mtech.edu
Department Web address: www.mtech.edu/mpem
School Web address: www.mtech.edu
Institutional accreditation: Northwest Association of Schools and Colleges

Subjects Offered

Environment engineering, industrial hygiene, project engineering management

Admissions Requirements

Is a minimum undergraduate GPA required? Yes
Is provisional admission available? Yes
Is an admissions interview required? No
Can pre-requisite course work be waived? No
Are international students eligible to apply? Yes
Is the TOEFL required for international students? Yes
What is the minimum TOEFL score required? 525

Program Delivery

Primary method of program delivery: Web
Two-way interactive video: No
Two-way audio, one-way video: No
One-way live video: No
One-way pre-recorded video: No
Audio graphics: Yes
Audio: Yes
Hardware requirements: Pentium II, 64MB of RAM, 28.8KBPS modem
Software requirements: Windows 98, Internet Explorer 4.0 or more recent
Is the library accessible to students? Yes
Are computers accessible to students? Yes

On-Campus Requirements

Is an on-campus component required? No

Tuition & Fees

In-state tuition per credit: $200
Out-of-state tuition per credit: $475
Average yearly cost of books: $400

Financial Aid

Is financial aid available to full-time students? Yes
Is financial aid available to part-time students? Yes
Are academic scholarships available? Yes
Assistance programs available to students: Federal Stafford Loan, Federal Perkins Loan, Federal Plus Loan, Federal Work-Study Program, in-state student aid programs, veterans' assistance

Mount Saint Vincent University

Distance Learning and Continuing Education
166 Bedford Highway
Halifax, NS, Canada B3H 2J6
Contact: Dr. Peggy Watts, Director of Distance Learning Continuing Education
Department e-mail: distance@msvu.ca
School Web address: www.msva.ca
Institutional accreditation: Maritime Provinces Higher Education Council

Admissions Requirements

Is a minimum undergraduate GPA required? Yes
Is provisional admission available? Yes
Is an admissions interview required? No
Are international students eligible to apply? Yes
Is the TOEFL required for international students? Yes

Program Delivery

Primary method of program delivery: Web
Audio: Yes
Is the library accessible to students? Yes
Are computers accessible to students? Yes

Remote Sites

Other college campuses: Yes
Students' homes: Yes
Community-based organizations: Yes

On-Campus Requirements

Is an on-campus component required? No

Financial Aid

Is financial aid available to full-time students? Yes
Are academic scholarships available? Yes

National Technological University

Admissions and Records
700 Centre Avenue
Fort Collins, CO 80526
Contact: Jeanne Breiner, Director of Admissions
Department e-mail: jeanne@ntu.edu
School Web address: www.ntu.edu
Institutional accreditation: North Central Association of
    Colleges and Schools

Subjects Offered

Engineering, business administration, management

Admissions Requirements

Is a minimum undergraduate GPA required? Yes
Is provisional admission available? Yes
Is an admissions interview required? No
Can pre-requisite course work be waived? Yes
Are international students eligible to apply? Yes
Is the TOEFL required for international students? No

Program Delivery

Two-way interactive video: No
Two-way audio, one-way video: No
One-way live video: Yes
One-way pre-recorded video: Yes
Audio graphics: No
Audio: No
Is the library accessible to students? No
Are computers accessible to students? No

Remote Sites

Other branches of the institution: No
Other college campuses: Yes
Students' homes: Yes
Work sites: Yes
Libraries: No
Elementary/Secondary schools: No
Community-based organizations: No
Correctional institutions: No

On-Campus Requirements

Is an on-campus component required? No

Tuition & Fees

In-state tuition per credit: $625
Out-of-state tuition per credit: $625
Average yearly cost of books: $50

Financial Aid

Is financial aid available to full-time students? No
Is financial aid available to part-time students? No
Are academic scholarships available? No

New Jersey City University

Continuing Education
2039 Kennedy Boulevard
Jersey City, NJ 07305
Contact: Betsey McPeake, Director of Continuing
    Education
Department e-mail: conted@njcu.edu
Department Web address: newlearning.njcu.edu
School Web address: www.njcu.edu
Institutional accreditation: Middle States Association of
    Colleges and Schools

Program Delivery

Primary method of program delivery: Web
Two-way interactive video: No
Two-way audio, one-way video: No
One-way live video: No
One-way pre-recorded video: No
Audio graphics: Yes
Audio: Yes
Hardware requirements: Computer with Macintosh or
    Windows operating system, 32MB of RAM, 33.3KBPS
    modem
Software requirements: Microsoft Internet Explorer or
    Netscape Navigator versions 4.0 or higher

Remote Sites

Other branches of the institution: No
Other college campuses: No

Students' homes: Yes
Work sites: Yes
Libraries: Yes
Elementary/Secondary schools: Yes
Community-based organizations: Yes
Correctional institutions: No

On-Campus Requirements

Is an on-campus component required? No

Tuition & Fees

In-state tuition per credit: $728

New Jersey Institute of Technology

Continuing Professional Education
University Heights
Newark, NJ 07102
Contact: Dr. Gale Spak, Associate Vice President
Department e-mail: dl@njit.edu
Department Web address: cpe.njit.edu
School Web address: www.njit.edu
Institutional accreditation: Middle States Association of
    Colleges and Schools

Subjects Offered

Computer science, mathematics, English, electrical
    engineering, humanities, economics, finance, manage-
    ment information systems, accounting, chemical
    engineering, environmental science, marketing

Admissions Requirements

Is a minimum undergraduate GPA required? Yes
Is provisional admission available? No
Is an admissions interview required? No
Can pre-requisite course work be waived? Yes
Are international students eligible to apply? Yes
Is the TOEFL required for international students? Yes
What is the minimum TOEFL score required? 550

Program Delivery

Primary method of program delivery: Web
Two-way interactive video: Yes
Two-way audio, one-way video: Yes
One-way live video: Yes
One-way pre-recorded video: Yes
Audio graphics: Yes
Audio: Yes
Hardware requirements: Pentium II computer with
    Internet access and sound card

Is the library accessible to students? Yes
Are computers accessible to students? Yes

Remote Sites

Other branches of the institution: Yes
Other college campuses: Yes
Students' homes: No
Work sites: No
Libraries: No
Elementary/Secondary schools: No
Community-based organizations: No
Correctional institutions: No

On-Campus Requirements

Is an on-campus component required? No

Tuition & Fees

In-state tuition per credit: $406
Out-of-state tuition per credit: $558
Average yearly cost of books: $300

Financial Aid

Is financial aid available to full-time students? Yes
Is financial aid available to part-time students? Yes
Are academic scholarships available? Yes
Assistance programs available to students: Federal Stafford
    Loan, Federal Perkins Loan, Federal Plus Loan, Federal
    Work-Study Program, in-state student aid programs,
    veterans' assistance

New Mexico State University

Distance Education and Weekend College
MSC 3WEC
Box 30001
Las Cruces, NM 88003-8001
Contact: Dr. Lynford L. Ames, Associate Vice President for
    Community Colleges
Department e-mail: distance@nmsu.edu
Department Web address: www.nmsu.edu/~distance
School Web address: www.nmsu.edu

Subjects Offered

Accounting, management, marketing, economics, electrical
    engineering, industrial engineering, mechanical
    engineering; waste management education and research
    consortium, counseling and educational psychology,
    curriculum and instruction, educational management
    and development, special education, educational
    technologies, nursing, government

Admissions Requirements

Is provisional admission available? Yes
Can pre-requisite course work be waived? No
Are international students eligible to apply? Yes
Is the TOEFL required for international students? Yes

Program Delivery

Primary method of program delivery: Remote site
Two-way interactive video: Yes
Two-way audio, one-way video: Yes
One-way live video: Yes
One-way pre-recorded video: Yes
Audio graphics: No
Audio: No

Remote Sites

Other branches of the institution: Yes
Other college campuses: Yes
Students' homes: Yes
Work sites: Yes
Libraries: No
Elementary/Secondary schools: Yes
Community-based organizations: No
Correctional institutions: No

On-Campus Requirements

Is an on-campus component required? No
On-campus thesis defense: Yes

Tuition & Fees

In-state tuition per credit: $135
Out-of-state tuition per credit: $225

Financial Aid

Is financial aid available to full-time students? Yes
Is financial aid available to part-time students? Yes
Are academic scholarships available? Yes
Assistance programs available to students: Federal Stafford
  Loan, Federal Perkins Loan, Federal Plus Loan, Federal
  Work-Study Program, in-state student aid programs,
  veterans' assistance

North Dakota State University

Institutional Analysis
1301 12th Avenue North
Fargo, ND 58105
Contact: Dr. Richard Chenoweth
School Web address: www.ndsu.edu
Institutional accreditation: North Central Association of
  Colleges and Schools

Subjects Offered

Managerial accounting, operations management, world
  technology, agricultural law, aircraft component failure
  analysis, aircraft design/aircraft corrosion, aircraft
  structural repair, business, cardiovascular engineering,
  career counseling and testing, character education,
  education, family trauma and burnout, composition
  materials manufacturing, internet for educators,
  accounting, forensic psychology, geology, geography,
  mathematics

Admissions Requirements

Is provisional admission available? Yes
Can pre-requisite course work be waived? No
Are international students eligible to apply? Yes
Is the TOEFL required for international students? Yes
What is the minimum TOEFL score required? 525

Program Delivery

Primary method of program delivery: Remote site
Two-way interactive video: Yes
Two-way audio, one-way video: No
One-way live video: No
One-way pre-recorded video: No
Audio graphics: No
Audio: No
Is the library accessible to students? Yes
Are computers accessible to students? No

Remote Sites

Other branches of the institution: Yes
Other college campuses: Yes
Students' homes: No
Work sites: Yes
Libraries: Yes
Elementary/Secondary schools: Yes
Community-based organizations: Yes

On-Campus Requirements

Is an on-campus component required? No

Tuition & Fees

In-state tuition per credit: $134
Out-of-state tuition per credit: $330
Average yearly cost of books: $30

Financial Aid

Is financial aid available to full-time students? Yes
Is financial aid available to part-time students? Yes
Are academic scholarships available? Yes
Assistance programs available to students: Federal Stafford
  Loan, Federal Perkins Loan, Federal Plus Loan, Federal
  Work-Study Program

Northern Kentucky University

Credit Continuing Education and Distance Learning
Nunn Drive
Highland Heights, KY 41099
Contact: Barbara Hedges, Director
Department e-mail: hedgesb@nku.edu
Department Web address: www.nku.edu/~conted
School Web address: www.nku.edu
Institutional accreditation: Southern Association of Colleges and Schools

Subjects Offered

Education, technology, social work, nursing

Admissions Requirements

Is a minimum undergraduate GPA required? Yes
Is provisional admission available? Yes
Is an admissions interview required? No
Can pre-requisite course work be waived? No
Are international students eligible to apply? Yes
Is the TOEFL required for international students? Yes
What is the minimum TOEFL score required? 550

Program Delivery

Primary method of program delivery: Remote site
Two-way interactive video: Yes
Two-way audio, one-way video: No
One-way live video: No
One-way pre-recorded video: Yes
Audio graphics: No
Audio: No
Software requirements: Internet access
Is the library accessible to students? Yes
Are computers accessible to students? Yes

Remote Sites

Other branches of the institution: Yes
Other college campuses: Yes
Students' homes: Yes
Work sites: Yes
Libraries: No
Elementary/Secondary schools: Yes
Community-based organizations: Yes
Correctional institutions: No

Tuition & Fees

Application fee: $25
Can it be waived? Yes
Average yearly additional fees: $360

Financial Aid

Is financial aid available to full-time students? Yes
Is financial aid available to part-time students? No
Are academic scholarships available? Yes
Assistance programs available to students: Federal Stafford Loan, Federal Perkins Loan, Federal Work-Study Program, veterans' assistance

Northwestern State University

Electronic Learning Systems
210 Roy Hall
Natchitoches, LA 71495
Contact: Darlene Williams, Electronic Learning Systems Coordinator
Department e-mail: e_learning@nsula.edu
Department Web address: www.nsula.edu/cldec
School Web address: www.nsula.edu
Institutional accreditation: Southern Association of Colleges and Schools

Subjects Offered

Early childhood education, adult education, educational leadership, education, educational technology, library information science, special education

Admissions Requirements

Is a minimum undergraduate GPA required? Yes
Is provisional admission available? Yes
Is an admissions interview required? No
Can pre-requisite course work be waived? No
Are international students eligible to apply? Yes
Is the TOEFL required for international students? Yes
What is the minimum TOEFL score required? 500

Program Delivery

Primary method of program delivery: Web
Two-way interactive video: Yes
Two-way audio, one-way video: No
One-way live video: No
One-way pre-recorded video: Yes
Audio graphics: No
Audio: No
Hardware requirements: 16MB or better, 28.8KBPS modem or better
Software requirements: Browser (Internet Explorer 4 or better), MS Word, Windows 95/98/NT
Is the library accessible to students? Yes
Are computers accessible to students? Yes

Remote Sites

Other branches of the institution: Yes
Other college campuses: Yes
Students' homes: Yes
Work sites: Yes
Libraries: Yes
Elementary/Secondary schools: Yes
Community-based organizations: Yes
Correctional institutions: No

On-Campus Requirements

Is an on-campus component required? No

Tuition & Fees

Out-of-state tuition per credit: $218
Average yearly cost of books: $500

Financial Aid

Is financial aid available to full-time students? Yes
Is financial aid available to part-time students? Yes
Are academic scholarships available? Yes
Assistance programs available to students: Federal Stafford
   Loan, Federal Perkins Loan, Federal Plus Loan, Federal
   Work-Study Program, in-state student aid programs,
   veterans' assistance

Norwich University

Vermont College of Norwich University
36 College Street
Montpelier, VT 05602
Contact: Craig Crist-Evans, Director of Adult Admissions
Department e-mail: vcadmis@norwich.edu
School Web address: www.norwich.edu/vermontcollege
Institutional accreditation: New England Association of
   Schools and Colleges

Admissions Requirements

Is provisional admission available? Yes
Are international students eligible to apply? Yes
Is the TOEFL required for international students? Yes
What is the minimum TOEFL score required? 600

Program Delivery

Two-way interactive video: No
Two-way audio, one-way video: No
One-way live video: No
One-way pre-recorded video: No
Audio graphics: No
Audio: Yes
Is the library accessible to students? Yes
Are computers accessible to students? Yes

Remote Sites

Other branches of the institution: Yes
Other college campuses: Yes
Students' homes: Yes
Work sites: Yes
Libraries: Yes
Elementary/Secondary schools: Yes
Community-based organizations: No
Correctional institutions: Yes

On-Campus Requirements

Is an on-campus component required? Yes
On-campus course work: Yes
On-campus admissions interview: No
On-campus program orientation: Yes
On-campus exams: No
On-campus thesis defense: Yes

Financial Aid

Is financial aid available to full-time students? Yes
Is financial aid available to part-time students? Yes
Are academic scholarships available? Yes
Assistance programs available to students: Federal Stafford
   Loan, Federal Perkins Loan, Federal Plus Loan, Federal
   Work-Study Program, in-state student aid programs,
   veterans' assistance

Nova Southeastern University

School of Computer and Information Sciences
6100 Griffin Road
Fort Lauderdale, FL 33314
Department e-mail: scisinfo@nova.edu
Department Web address: www.scis.nova.edu
School Web address: www.nova.edu
Institutional accreditation: Southern Association of
   Colleges and Schools

Admissions Requirements

Is provisional admission available? Yes
Is an admissions interview required? No
Are international students eligible to apply? Yes
Is the TOEFL required for international students? Yes
What is the minimum TOEFL score required? 550

Program Delivery

Hardware requirements: Pentium II or higher, 28.8KBPS
   modem, full duplex sound card with speaker/head-
   phones and microphone, SVG monitor (1024 x 768)
Software requirements: Windows 95 or higher
Is the library accessible to students? Yes

On-Campus Requirements

Is an on-campus component required? No

Tuition & Fees

In-state tuition per credit: $395
Out-of-state tuition per credit: $395
Average yearly cost of books: $50

Financial Aid

Is financial aid available to full-time students? Yes
Is financial aid available to part-time students? Yes
Are academic scholarships available? Yes

Oklahoma State University

University Extension
Office of Distance Education
470 Student Union
Stillwater, OK 74078-7065
Contact: Bill Cooper, Interim Director of Distance
    Learning
Department e-mail: ext-dl@okstate.edu
Department Web address: www.okstate.edu/outreach/
    distance/
School Web address: pio.okstate.edu
Institutional accreditation: North Central Association of
    Colleges and Schools

Subjects Offered

Arts and sciences, business, engineering, education, human
    environmental sciences, agriculture

Admissions Requirements

Is a minimum undergraduate GPA required? Yes
Is provisional admission available? No
Can pre-requisite course work be waived? No
Are international students eligible to apply? Yes
Is the TOEFL required for international students? Yes
What is the minimum TOEFL score required? 550

Program Delivery

Two-way interactive video: Yes
Two-way audio, one-way video: No
One-way live video: Yes
One-way pre-recorded video: Yes
Audio graphics: No
Audio: Yes
Hardware requirements: PC or Mac
Is the library accessible to students? Yes
Are computers accessible to students? Yes

Remote Sites

Other branches of the institution: Yes
Other college campuses: Yes
Students' homes: Yes
Work sites: Yes
Libraries: Yes
Elementary/Secondary schools: Yes
Community-based organizations: Yes
Correctional institutions: Yes

On-Campus Requirements

Is an on-campus component required? No

Tuition & Fees

In-state tuition per credit: $190
Out-of-state tuition per credit: $350
Average yearly cost of books: $25

Financial Aid

Is financial aid available to full-time students? Yes
Is financial aid available to part-time students? No
Are academic scholarships available? No
Assistance programs available to students: Veterans'
    assistance

Olivet Nazarene University

School of Graduate and Adult Studies
PO Box 592
Kankakee, IL 60901-0592
Contact: Dr. Carol Maxson, Associate Dean for Graduate
    and Adult Studies
School Web address: www.olivet.edu
Institutional accreditation: North Central Association of
    Colleges and Schools

Subjects Offered

Education

Admissions Requirements

Is a minimum undergraduate GPA required? No
Is provisional admission available? No
Is an admissions interview required? Yes
Are international students eligible to apply? Yes
Is the TOEFL required for international students? Yes
What is the minimum TOEFL score required? 550

Program Delivery

Primary method of program delivery: Text
Two-way interactive video: No
Two-way audio, one-way video: No
One-way live video: No
One-way pre-recorded video: Yes

Audio graphics: No
Audio: No
Software requirements: Word processing, spreadsheet, presentation programs, Internet and e-mail, Windows 95/98
Is the library accessible to students? Yes
Are computers accessible to students? Yes

Remote Sites

Other branches of the institution: No
Other college campuses: No
Students' homes: Yes
Work sites: Yes
Libraries: Yes
Elementary/Secondary schools: Yes
Community-based organizations: No
Correctional institutions: No

On-Campus Requirements

Is an on-campus component required? No

Tuition & Fees

In-state tuition per credit: $221
Out-of-state tuition per credit: $221
Average yearly cost of books: $200

Financial Aid

Is financial aid available to full-time students? Yes
Are academic scholarships available? No
Assistance programs available to students: Federal Stafford Loan, veterans' assistance

Ottawa University

1001 South Cedar #43
Ottawa, KS 66067-3399
School Web address: www.ottawa.edu
Institutional accreditation: North Central Association of Colleges and Schools

Subjects Offered

Human resources

Admissions Requirements

Is a minimum undergraduate GPA required? Yes
Is provisional admission available? Yes
Is an admissions interview required? No
Are international students eligible to apply? Yes

Program Delivery

Primary method of program delivery: Web
Hardware requirements: Internet connection

Software requirements: Netscape or Internet Explorer (recent versions), Office 97 or higher
Is the library accessible to students? Yes
Are computers accessible to students? Yes

On-Campus Requirements

Is an on-campus component required? Yes
On-campus course work: Yes

Tuition & Fees

In-state tuition per credit: $330
Out-of-state tuition per credit: $330
Average yearly cost of books: $50

Financial Aid

Is financial aid available to full-time students? Yes
Is financial aid available to part-time students? Yes
Are academic scholarships available? No
Assistance programs available to students: Federal Stafford Loan, veterans' assistance

Prairie Graduate School

Prairie Distance Education
PO Box 4000
Three Hills, AB, Canada T0M 2N0
Contact: Dr. Arnold L. Stauffer, Associate Dean
Department e-mail: distance.ed@pbi.ab.ca
Department Web address: www.pbi.ab.ca/distanceed
School Web address: www.pbi.ab.ca
Institutional accreditation: Associate Member Association of Theological Schools

Subjects Offered

Bible, bible language, theology, history, church ministries, leadership, personal development, world mission, field education

Admissions Requirements

Is a minimum undergraduate GPA required? Yes
Is provisional admission available? Yes
Is an admissions interview required? No
Can pre-requisite course work be waived? Yes
Are international students eligible to apply? Yes
Is the TOEFL required for international students? Yes
What is the minimum TOEFL score required? 600

Program Delivery

Primary method of program delivery: Text
One-way pre-recorded video: Yes
Audio: Yes
Is the library accessible to students? Yes
Are computers accessible to students? No

Remote Sites

Students' homes: Yes
Community-based organizations: Yes

On-Campus Requirements

Is an on-campus component required? No

Tuition & Fees

In-state tuition per credit: $145
Out-of-state tuition per credit: $145
Average yearly cost of books: $600

Financial Aid

Is financial aid available to full-time students? No
Are academic scholarships available? No

Prescott College

Admissions Office
Master of Arts Program
220 Grove Avenue
Prescott, AZ 86301
Contact: Steve Walters, Dean of the Adult Degree
    Programs
Department e-mail: admissions@prescott.edu
School Web address: www.prescott.edu
Institutional accreditation: North Central Association of
    Colleges and Schools

Subjects Offered

Adventure education, counseling psychology, education,
    environmental studies, humanities

Admissions Requirements

Is a minimum undergraduate GPA required? No
Is provisional admission available? No
Can pre-requisite course work be waived? No
Are international students eligible to apply? Yes
Is the TOEFL required for international students? Yes
What is the minimum TOEFL score required? 550

Program Delivery

Primary method of program delivery: Text
Is the library accessible to students? Yes
Are computers accessible to students? Yes

Remote Sites

Other branches of the institution: Yes
Other college campuses: No
Students' homes: Yes
Work sites: Yes
Libraries: Yes
Elementary/Secondary schools: Yes

Community-based organizations: Yes
Correctional institutions: Yes

On-Campus Requirements

Is an on-campus component required? Yes
On-campus program orientation: Yes

Tuition & Fees

In-state tuition per credit: $275
Out-of-state tuition per credit: $275
Average yearly cost of books: $400

Financial Aid

Is financial aid available to full-time students? Yes
Is financial aid available to part-time students? No
Are academic scholarships available? Yes
Assistance programs available to students: Federal Stafford
    Loan, Federal Perkins Loan, Federal Plus Loan, Federal
    Work-Study Program, in-state student aid programs,
    veterans' assistance

Rensselaer Polytechnic Institute

Office of Professional & Distance Education
CII Suite 4011
110 8th Street
Troy, NY 12180-3590
Contact: Kim Scalzo, Director Professional & Distance
    Education Programs
Department e-mail: rsvp@rpi.edu
Department Web address: rsvp.rpi.edu
School Web address: www.rpi.edu
Institutional accreditation: Engineering: EAC, Accredita-
    tion Board for Engineering and Technology; Manage-
    ment: AACSB—The International Association for
    Management Education, Middle States Association of
    Colleges and Schools

Subjects Offered

Computer science, management technology, information
    technology, electronical engineering, mechanical
    engineering, technical communications

Admissions Requirements

Is a minimum undergraduate GPA required? Yes
Is provisional admission available? No
Is an admissions interview required? No
Can pre-requisite course work be waived? Yes
Are international students eligible to apply? Yes
Is the TOEFL required for international students? Yes
What is the minimum TOEFL score required? 550

Program Delivery

Primary method of program delivery: Remote site
Two-way interactive video: Yes
Two-way audio, one-way video: Yes
One-way live video: Yes
One-way pre-recorded video: Yes
Hardware requirements: Varies by program
Software requirements: Varies by program
Is the library accessible to students? Yes
Are computers accessible to students? Yes

Remote Sites

Other branches of the institution: Yes
Students' homes: Yes
Work sites: Yes

On-Campus Requirements

Is an on-campus component required? No

Tuition & Fees

In-state tuition per credit: $700
Out-of-state tuition per credit: $700

Rochester Institute of Technology

Graduate Enrollment Services
Office of Distance Learning
58 Lomb Memorial Drive
Rochester, NY 14623
Contact: Diane Ellison, Director of Graduate Enrollment
    Services
Department e-mail: gradinfo@rit.edu
Department Web address: www.rit.edu/grad
School Web address: www.rit.edu
Institutional accreditation: Middle States Association of
    Colleges and Schools

Subjects Offered

Statistical quality, integrated health systems, health systems
    finance, software development and management, applied
    statistics, health systems administration, cross disciplin-
    ary professional studies, microelectronics manufacturing
    engineering, imaging science, information technology

Admissions Requirements

Is a minimum undergraduate GPA required? No
Is provisional admission available? Yes
Is an admissions interview required? No
Can pre-requisite course work be waived? Yes
Are international students eligible to apply? Yes

Is the TOEFL required for international students? Yes
What is the minimum TOEFL score required? 550

Program Delivery

Primary method of program delivery: Web
Two-way interactive video: Yes
Two-way audio, one-way video: Yes
One-way live video: No
One-way pre-recorded video: Yes
Audio graphics: No
Audio: Yes
Hardware requirements: Pentium 133 or above, Windows
    95/98/NT/2000, 64MB of RAM, Power Mac OS 7 or
    higher
Software requirements: Web browser (Netscape Navigator
    4.0/Internet Explorer 4.0 or higher)
Is the library accessible to students? Yes
Are computers accessible to students? Yes

Remote Sites

Other branches of the institution: No
Other college campuses: No
Students' homes: Yes
Work sites: Yes
Libraries: No
Elementary/Secondary schools: Yes
Community-based organizations: No
Correctional institutions: No

Tuition & Fees

In-state tuition per credit: $565
Application fee: $40
Can it be waived? Yes
Average yearly cost of books: $500

Financial Aid

Is financial aid available to full-time students? Yes
Is financial aid available to part-time students? Yes
Are academic scholarships available? Yes
Assistance programs available to students: Federal Stafford
    Loan, Federal Perkins Loan, Federal Plus Loan, in-state
    student aid programs, veterans' assistance

Saint Francis College

Department of Physician Assistant Science
Master of Medical Science Research
117 Evergreen Drive, 105 Sullivan Hall
Loretto, PA 15940-0600
Contact: Dr. William Duryea, Director, MMS program
Department e-mail: bduryea@sfpa.edu
Department Web address: www.sfcpa.edu/newsfc/
    academic/graduate/mmshome.html

School Web address: www.sfcpa.edu

Institutional accreditation: Middle States Association of Colleges and Schools

Subjects Offered

Research methods, pharmacology, healthcare systems and management, practician for underserved, seminar in medical topics, clinical residency, medical ethics

Admissions Requirements

Is provisional admission available? Yes

Is an admissions interview required? No

Can pre-requisite course work be waived? No

Are international students eligible to apply? Yes

Is the TOEFL required for international students? No

Program Delivery

Primary method of program delivery: Web

Two-way interactive video: Yes

Audio: Yes

Hardware requirements: Minimum Pentium I with modem and speakers

Software requirements: Software to enable Internet access, and reception of audio/videostreams

Is the library accessible to students? Yes

Are computers accessible to students? No

Remote Sites

Other college campuses: Yes

On-Campus Requirements

Is an on-campus component required? No

Tuition & Fees

In-state tuition per credit: $483

Out-of-state tuition per credit: $483

Average yearly cost of books: $250

Financial Aid

Is financial aid available to full-time students? No

Are academic scholarships available? No

Saint Joseph's College

Graduate and Professional Studies

278 Whitesbridge Road

Standish, ME 04084

Contact: Dr. Susan Neshitt, Dean Graduate and Professional Studies

School Web address: sjc.edu

Institutional accreditation: New England Association of Schools and Colleges

Subjects Offered

Health care, pastoral studies, education, nursing

Admissions Requirements

Is a minimum undergraduate GPA required? Yes

Is provisional admission available? Yes

Is an admissions interview required? No

Can pre-requisite course work be waived? Yes

Are international students eligible to apply? Yes

Is the TOEFL required for international students? Yes

What is the minimum TOEFL score required? 550

Program Delivery

Primary method of program delivery: Text

Audio: Yes

Hardware requirements: PC with 486 processor, 16MB RAM, 200MB hard drive, 28.8KBPS modem

Software requirements: Word 6.0, a current Internet browser

Is the library accessible to students? Yes

Are computers accessible to students? Yes

Remote Sites

Other college campuses: Yes

Students' homes: No

Libraries: Yes

On-Campus Requirements

Is an on-campus component required? Yes

On-campus course work: Yes

Tuition & Fees

In-state tuition per credit: $235

Out-of-state tuition per credit: $235

Average yearly cost of books: $100

Financial Aid

Is financial aid available to full-time students? Yes

Is financial aid available to part-time students? Yes

Assistance programs available to students: Federal Stafford Loan, veterans' assistance

Saint Mary of the Wood College

Registrar

School Web address: www.smwc.edu

Institutional accreditation: North Central Association of Colleges and Schools

Admissions Requirements

Is a minimum undergraduate GPA required? Yes
Is provisional admission available? Yes
Is an admissions interview required? No
Can pre-requisite course work be waived? No
Is the TOEFL required for international students? Yes
What is the minimum TOEFL score required? 500

Program Delivery

Primary method of program delivery: Text
Is the library accessible to students? Yes
Are computers accessible to students? No

On-Campus Requirements

Is an on-campus component required? Yes
On-campus course work: Yes
On-campus program orientation: Yes

Tuition & Fees

In-state tuition per credit: $325
Out-of-state tuition per credit: $325
Average yearly cost of books: $35

Financial Aid

Is financial aid available to full-time students? Yes
Is financial aid available to part-time students? Yes
Are academic scholarships available? Yes
Assistance programs available to students: Federal Stafford
    Loan, veterans' assistance

Saint Peter's College

Academic Affairs
2641 Kennedy Boulevard
Jersey City, NJ 07643
School Web address: www.spc.edu

Admissions Requirements

Is a minimum undergraduate GPA required? Yes

Program Delivery

Two-way interactive video: Yes
One-way pre-recorded video: Yes

On-Campus Requirements

Is an on-campus component required? Yes
On-campus course work: Yes

Tuition & Fees

In-state tuition per credit: $477
Application fee: $30

Financial Aid

Assistance programs available to students: Federal Stafford
    Loan, Federal Perkins Loan, Federal Plus Loan, Federal
    Work-Study Program, in-state student aid programs,
    veterans' assistance

Salve Regina University

Extension Study
Graduate Extension Study
100 Ochre Paint Avenue
Newport, RI 02840
Contact: Debra Mitchell, Associate Director
Department e-mail: mitcheld@salve.edu
Department Web address: salve.edu.geshome.html
School Web address: salve.edu
Institutional accreditation: New England Association of
    Schools and Colleges

Subjects Offered

Human development, international resources, manage-
    ment, fellow risk management

Admissions Requirements

Is a minimum undergraduate GPA required? No
Is provisional admission available? Yes
Is an admissions interview required? No
Can pre-requisite course work be waived? No
Are international students eligible to apply? Yes
Is the TOEFL required for international students? Yes
What is the minimum TOEFL score required? 550

Program Delivery

Primary method of program delivery: Text
Is the library accessible to students? Yes
Are computers accessible to students? Yes

On-Campus Requirements

Is an on-campus component required? Yes
On-campus course work: Yes

Tuition & Fees

In-state tuition per credit: $350
Out-of-state tuition per credit: $350
Average yearly cost of books: $750

Financial Aid

Is financial aid available to full-time students? Yes
Is financial aid available to part-time students? Yes
Are academic scholarships available? No
Assistance programs available to students: Federal Stafford
    Loan

San Diego State University

Academic Affairs
Office of Distributed Learning
5500 Campanile Drive
San Diego, CA 92182-8010
Contact: Treacy Lau, Principal Coordinator of Distributed
Learning
Department e-mail: dl@sdsu.edu
Department Web address: sdsu.edu/dl
School Web address: sdsu.edu
Institutional accreditation: Western Association of Schools
and Colleges

Subjects Offered

Education technology, business administration, rehabilitation counseling, teacher education, social work

Program Delivery

Two-way interactive video: No
Two-way audio, one-way video: No
One-way live video: No
One-way pre-recorded video: No
Audio graphics: No
Audio: Yes
Is the library accessible to students? Yes
Are computers accessible to students? Yes

Remote Sites

Other branches of the institution: No
Other college campuses: No
Students' homes: Yes
Work sites: Yes
Libraries: No
Elementary/Secondary schools: No
Community-based organizations: No
Correctional institutions: No

Financial Aid

Is financial aid available to full-time students? Yes
Is financial aid available to part-time students? Yes
Are academic scholarships available? Yes
Assistance programs available to students: Federal Stafford
Loan, Federal Perkins Loan, Federal Work-Study
Program, in-state student aid programs, veterans'
assistance

Seton Hall University

Seton World Wide
400 South Orange Avenue
South Orange, NJ 07079
Contact: Philip Disalvio, Director

Department e-mail: setonworldwide@shu.edu
Department Web address: www.setonworldwide.net
School Web address: www.shu.edu
Institutional accreditation: Middle States Association of
Colleges and Schools

Admissions Requirements

Is a minimum undergraduate GPA required? Yes
Is provisional admission available? Yes
Can pre-requisite course work be waived? Yes
Are international students eligible to apply? Yes
Is the TOEFL required for international students? Yes

Program Delivery

Primary method of program delivery: Web
Two-way interactive video: No
Two-way audio, one-way video: No
One-way live video: Yes
One-way pre-recorded video: Yes
Audio graphics: Yes
Audio: Yes
Hardware requirements: PC: 90 MHz Pentium processor,
32MB of RAM, 28.8KBPS modem, sound card,
speakers; Mac OS 8.1 or later
Software requirements: Microsoft Internet Explorer 5.0 or
higher (4.5 Mac)
Is the library accessible to students? Yes
Are computers accessible to students? Yes

Remote Sites

Other branches of the institution: No
Other college campuses: No
Students' homes: Yes
Work sites: Yes
Libraries: Yes
Elementary/Secondary schools: Yes
Community-based organizations: Yes
Correctional institutions: No

On-Campus Requirements

Is an on-campus component required? Yes
On-campus course work: No
On-campus admissions interview: No
On-campus program orientation: Yes
On-campus exams: No
On-campus thesis defense: No

Tuition & Fees

Application fee: $50
Can it be waived? No

Financial Aid

Is financial aid available to full-time students? Yes
Is financial aid available to part-time students? Yes
Are academic scholarships available? Yes
Assistance programs available to students: Veterans'
assistance

Southern Christian University

Center of Institutional Research
Extended Learning
1200 Taylor Road
Montgomery, AL 36117
Contact: Dr. Rex A. Turner Jr., President
Department e-mail: admissions@southernchristian.edu
School Web address: www.southernchristian.edu
Institutional accreditation: Southern Association of
Colleges and Schools

Admissions Requirements

Is provisional admission available? Yes
Is an admissions interview required? No
Can pre-requisite course work be waived? No
Are international students eligible to apply? Yes
Is the TOEFL required for international students? Yes
What is the minimum TOEFL score required? 500

Program Delivery

Primary method of program delivery: Web
One-way live video: Yes
Hardware requirements: 200 MHz Intel Pentium processor
or equivalent, 32–64MB of RAM; 56.6KBPS modem
Software requirements: Microsoft Word, Adobe Acrobat
Reader 4.0, RealPlayer 7.0, Windows 95 operating
system
Is the library accessible to students? Yes

Remote Sites

Students' homes: Yes
Work sites: Yes
Libraries: Yes

On-Campus Requirements

Is an on-campus component required? No

Tuition & Fees

In-state tuition per credit: $360
Out-of-state tuition per credit: $360
Average yearly cost of books: $400

Financial Aid

Is financial aid available to full-time students? Yes
Is financial aid available to part-time students? Yes
Are academic scholarships available? Yes
Assistance programs available to students: Federal Stafford
Loan, Federal Plus Loan, Federal Work-Study Program,
veterans' assistance

Southern Illinois University, Edwardsville

Graduate Admissions
Edwardsville, IL 62026
Department e-mail: admis@siue.edu
Department Web address: www.admis.siue.edu
School Web address: www.siue.edu
Institutional accreditation: North Central Association of
Colleges and Schools

Admissions Requirements

Is a minimum undergraduate GPA required? Yes
Is provisional admission available? Yes
Is an admissions interview required? No
Are international students eligible to apply? Yes
Is the TOEFL required for international students? Yes
What is the minimum TOEFL score required? 550

Subjects Offered

Business, nursing, education

Program Delivery

Primary method of program delivery: Remote site
Two-way interactive video: Yes
Software requirements: Internet
Is the library accessible to students? Yes
Are computers accessible to students? Yes

Remote Sites

Other college campuses: Yes

On-Campus Requirements

Is an on-campus component required? No

Tuition & Fees

Application fee: $25
Can it be waived? No

Financial Aid

Is financial aid available to full-time students? Yes
Is financial aid available to part-time students? Yes
Are academic scholarships available? Yes

Assistance programs available to students: Federal Perkins Loan, Federal Plus Loan, Federal Work-Study Program, in-state student aid programs, veterans' assistance

Southern Methodist University

School of Engineering & Applied Science
Distance Education
PO Box 750335
Dallas, TX 75275-0335
Contact: Stephanie Dye, Associate Director, Distance Education
Department e-mail: sdye@seas.smu.edu
Department Web address: www.seas.smu.edu
School Web address: www.smu.edu
Institutional accreditation: Southern Association of Colleges and Schools

Subjects Offered

Telecommunications, manufacturing systems management, software engineering, computer science, engineering management, electrical engineering, systems engineeering, mechanical engineering, environmental systems management

Admissions Requirements

Is a minimum undergraduate GPA required? Yes
Is provisional admission available? Yes
Is an admissions interview required? No
Can pre-requisite course work be waived? No
Are international students eligible to apply? Yes
Is the TOEFL required for international students? Yes
What is the minimum TOEFL score required? 550

Program Delivery

Two-way interactive video: No
Two-way audio, one-way video: No
One-way live video: No
One-way pre-recorded video: Yes
Audio graphics: No
Audio: No
Is the library accessible to students? Yes
Are computers accessible to students? No

Remote Sites

Other branches of the institution: Yes
Other college campuses: No
Students' homes: Yes
Work sites: Yes
Libraries: No
Elementary/Secondary schools: No

Community-based organizations: No
Correctional institutions: No

On-Campus Requirements

Is an on-campus component required? No

Tuition & Fees

In-state tuition per credit: $733
Out-of-state tuition per credit: $733
Average yearly cost of books: $100

Financial Aid

Is financial aid available to full-time students? No
Is financial aid available to part-time students? No
Are academic scholarships available? No

Southwest Missouri State University—College of Business Administration

Department of Academic Outreach
901 South National Avenue
Springfield, MO 65804
Contact: Steve Robinette, Director of Academic Outreach
Department e-mail: ce@smsu.edu
Department Web address: www.coba.smsu.edu
School Web address: www.smsu.edu
Institutional accreditation: AACSB—The International Association for Management Education

Subjects Offered

Accounting, computer information systems, economics, finance, management, marketing, quantitative business analysis

Admissions Requirements

Is a minimum undergraduate GPA required? Yes
Is provisional admission available? Yes
Is an admissions interview required? No
Can pre-requisite course work be waived? Yes
Are international students eligible to apply? Yes
Is the TOEFL required for international students? Yes
What is the minimum TOEFL score required? 550

Program Delivery

Two-way interactive video: Yes
Two-way audio, one-way video: No
One-way live video: No
One-way pre-recorded video: Yes
Audio graphics: No
Audio: No
Hardware requirements: Pentium

Software requirements: Frames-compatible browser, Microsoft Office

Remote Sites

Other branches of the institution: Yes
Other college campuses: Yes
Students' homes: No
Work sites: No
Libraries: No
Elementary/Secondary schools: Yes
Community-based organizations: No
Correctional institutions: No

On-Campus Requirements

Is an on-campus component required? Yes
On-campus course work: Yes
On-campus admissions interview: No
On-campus program orientation: Yes
On-campus exams: No
On-campus thesis defense: No

Tuition & Fees

In-state tuition per credit: $345
Out-of-state tuition per credit: $345

Financial Aid

Is financial aid available to full-time students? Yes
Is financial aid available to part-time students? Yes
Are academic scholarships available? Yes
Assistance programs available to students: Federal Stafford Loan, Federal Perkins Loan, Federal Plus Loan, Federal Work-Study Program, in-state student aid programs, veterans' assistance

Southwest Missouri State University—Graduate College

Academic Outreach and Continuing Education
901 South National Avenue
Springfield, MO 65804
Contact: Dr. Frank Einhellig, Dean of the Graduate College
Department e-mail: graduatecollege@smsu.edu
Department Web address: www.smsu.edu/grad
School Web address: www.smsu.edu
Institutional accreditation: North Central Association of Colleges and Schools

Subjects Offered

Accounting, communication and the mass media, communication sciences and disorders, economics, instructional media technology, psychology, sociology, business administration, elementary education, social work, administrative studies, computer information systems

Admissions Requirements

Is a minimum undergraduate GPA required? Yes
Is provisional admission available? Yes
Can pre-requisite course work be waived? Yes
Are international students eligible to apply? Yes
Is the TOEFL required for international students? Yes
What is the minimum TOEFL score required? 550

Program Delivery

Primary method of program delivery: Remote site
Two-way interactive video: Yes
Hardware requirements: 166 MHz Intel Pentium processor, 32MB of RAM, 28.8KBPS modem, 16 bit sound card and speakers, 65,000-color video, CD-ROM
Software requirements: Windows 95 Operating system (or Mac OS 8.1 or greater), Internet connection (Internet Explorer 4.0)
Is the library accessible to students? Yes
Are computers accessible to students? Yes

Remote Sites

Other branches of the institution: Yes
Other college campuses: Yes

On-Campus Requirements

Is an on-campus component required? No

Tuition & Fees

In-state tuition per credit: $121
Out-of-state tuition per credit: $242
Average yearly cost of books: $50

Financial Aid

Is financial aid available to full-time students? Yes
Is financial aid available to part-time students? Yes
Are academic scholarships available? Yes
Assistance programs available to students: Federal Stafford Loan, Federal Perkins Loan, Federal Work-Study Program, veterans' assistance

Spertus Institute of Jewish Studies

618 South Michigan
Chicago, IL 60605
Contact: Dr. Dean Bell, Associate Dean
Department e-mail: college@spertus.edu

School Web address: www.spertus.edu
Institutional accreditation: North Central Association of Colleges and Schools

Subjects Offered

Jewish theology, religion of biblical Israel, medieval judaism, Jewish ethics, Jewish mysticism, encountering the Holocaust

Admissions Requirements

Is provisional admission available? Yes
Can pre-requisite course work be waived? No
Are international students eligible to apply? Yes

Program Delivery

Primary method of program delivery: Text
Two-way interactive video: No
Two-way audio, one-way video: No
One-way live video: No
One-way pre-recorded video: Yes
Audio graphics: No
Audio: Yes
Is the library accessible to students? Yes
Are computers accessible to students? No

On-Campus Requirements

Is an on-campus component required? Yes
On-campus course work: Yes

Tuition & Fees

In-state tuition per credit: $200
Out-of-state tuition per credit: $200
Average yearly cost of books: $50

Financial Aid

Is financial aid available to full-time students? Yes
Is financial aid available to part-time students? Yes
Are academic scholarships available? Yes
Assistance programs available to students: Federal Stafford Loan

State University of New York at New Paltz

Extension & Distance Learning
75 South Manheim Boulevard, Suite 9
New Paltz, NY 12561
Contact: Helise Winters, Coordinator, Extension & Distance Learning
Department Web address: www.newpaltz.edu/ continuing_ed
School Web address: www.newpaltz.edu

Institutional accreditation: Middle States Association of Colleges and Schools

Subjects Offered

Education/elementary, ed studies, nursing

Admissions Requirements

Is a minimum undergraduate GPA required? Yes
Can pre-requisite course work be waived? Yes
Are international students eligible to apply? Yes
Is the TOEFL required for international students? Yes

Program Delivery

Primary method of program delivery: Web
Two-way interactive video: Yes
Two-way audio, one-way video: No
One-way live video: No
One-way pre-recorded video: No
Audio graphics: No
Audio: No
Hardware requirements: Pentium processor, 32MB RAM, 28.8KBPS modem
Software requirements: Windows 98, 95 or NT, Macintosh System 8 or higher
Is the library accessible to students? Yes
Are computers accessible to students? Yes

Remote Sites

Other college campuses: Yes
Students' homes: Yes

On-Campus Requirements

Is an on-campus component required? Yes

Tuition & Fees

In-state tuition per credit: $213
Out-of-state tuition per credit: $351
Application fee: $50
Can it be waived? No
Average yearly cost of books: $60
Average yearly additional fees: $54

Financial Aid

Is financial aid available to full-time students? Yes
Is financial aid available to part-time students? Yes
Assistance programs available to students: Federal Stafford Loan, Federal Perkins Loan, in-state student aid programs

Stevens Institute of Technology

The Graduate School
Castle Point On Hudson
Hoboken, NJ 07030
Contact: Robert Ubell, Director, Web-based Distance
    Learning
Department e-mail: webcampus@stevens-tech.edu
Department Web address: www.stevens-tech.edu
School Web address: www.webcampus.stevens.edu
Institutional accreditation: Middle States Communication
    Higher Education

Subjects Offered

Computer science, telecommunications, wireless, project
    management, technology management, science
    education

Admissions Requirements

Is a minimum undergraduate GPA required? Yes
Is provisional admission available? No
Is an admissions interview required? No
Can pre-requisite course work be waived? No
Are international students eligible to apply? Yes
Is the TOEFL required for international students? Yes

Program Delivery

Primary method of program delivery: Web
Two-way interactive video: No
Two-way audio, one-way video: No
One-way live video: No
One-way pre-recorded video: No
Audio graphics: No
Audio: No
Is the library accessible to students? Yes
Are computers accessible to students? No

Remote Sites

Other branches of the institution: No
Other college campuses: Yes
Students' homes: No
Work sites: Yes
Libraries: No
Elementary/Secondary schools: No
Community-based organizations: No
Correctional institutions: No

On-Campus Requirements

Is an on-campus component required? No

Tuition & Fees

Application fee: $50
Can it be waived? No
Average yearly cost of books: $200
Average yearly additional fees: $80

Financial Aid

Is financial aid available to full-time students? Yes
Is financial aid available to part-time students? No
Are academic scholarships available? Yes
Assistance programs available to students: Federal Perkins
    Loan, Federal Plus Loan

Strayer University

Strayer Online
PO Box 487
Newington, VA 22122
Contact: Allen Durgin, Coordinator
Department e-mail: axd@strayer.edu
Department Web address: www.strayer.edu/online/frtr.htm
School Web address: www.strayer.edu
Institutional accreditation: Middle States Association of
    Colleges and Schools

Admissions Requirements

Is a minimum undergraduate GPA required? Yes
Is provisional admission available? Yes
Is an admissions interview required? No
Can pre-requisite course work be waived? Yes
Are international students eligible to apply? Yes
Is the TOEFL required for international students? Yes
What is the minimum TOEFL score required? 550

Program Delivery

Primary method of program delivery: Web
Audio: Yes
Hardware requirements: 300 MHz, 64MB RAM, sound
    card and speakers
Software requirements: All free downloads from website
Is the library accessible to students? Yes
Are computers accessible to students? No

Remote Sites

Students' homes: Yes

On-Campus Requirements

Is an on-campus component required? No

Tuition & Fees

In-state tuition per credit: $280
Out-of-state tuition per credit: $280
Average yearly cost of books: $800

Financial Aid

Is financial aid available to full-time students? Yes
Is financial aid available to part-time students? Yes
Are academic scholarships available? Yes
Assistance programs available to students: Federal Stafford
Loan, Federal Plus Loan, veterans' assistance

Suffolk University

Online Program
Beacon Hill & Ashburton Place, 11th Floor
Boston, MA 02108-2770
Contact: Dr. Mawdudur Rahman, Professor & Director
Online Programs
Department e-mail: cmaher@suffolk.edu
Department Web address: www.suffolkmba.org
School Web address: www.suffolk.edu
Institutional accreditation: AACSB—The International
Association for Management Education; National
Association of Schools of Public Affairs and
Administration

Subjects Offered

Accounting, information technology, business, investments, commerce, management, economics, marketing,
entrepreneurship, statistics, finance, taxation, human
resource management

Admissions Requirements

Is a minimum undergraduate GPA required? No
Is provisional admission available? No
Can pre-requisite course work be waived? Yes
Are international students eligible to apply? Yes
Is the TOEFL required for international students? Yes
What is the minimum TOEFL score required? 550

Program Delivery

Primary method of program delivery: Web
Two-way interactive video: No
Two-way audio, one-way video: No
One-way live video: No
One-way pre-recorded video: Yes
Audio graphics: Yes
Audio: Yes
Hardware requirements: Recommend Pentium computer,
28.8KBPS modem
Software requirements: Microsoft Windows 95, Office 97
Professional edition, RealPlayer
Is the library accessible to students? Yes
Are computers accessible to students? Yes

Remote Sites

Other branches of the institution: No
Other college campuses: No
Students' homes: Yes
Work sites: Yes
Libraries: Yes
Elementary/Secondary schools: No
Community-based organizations: No
Correctional institutions: No

On-Campus Requirements

Is an on-campus component required? No

Tuition & Fees

In-state tuition per credit: $649
Out-of-state tuition per credit: $649
Average yearly cost of books: $280

Financial Aid

Is financial aid available to full-time students? Yes
Is financial aid available to part-time students? Yes
Are academic scholarships available? Yes
Assistance programs available to students: Federal Stafford
Loan, Federal Perkins Loan, Federal Plus Loan, Federal
Work-Study Program, in-state student aid programs,
veterans' assistance

Syracuse University

Continuing Education
Independent Study Degree Education
700 University Avenue, Suite 326
Syracuse, NY 13244
Contact: Robert M. Colley, Director, Distance Education
Department e-mail: suisdp@uc.syr.edu
Department Web address: suce.syr.edu/distanced
School Web address: www.syr.edu

Admissions Requirements

Is a minimum undergraduate GPA required? No
Is provisional admission available? No
Is an admissions interview required? No
Can pre-requisite course work be waived? Yes
Is the TOEFL required for international students? Yes
What is the minimum TOEFL score required? 550

Program Delivery

Primary method of program delivery: Web
Hardware requirements: Pentium computer
Is the library accessible to students? Yes
Are computers accessible to students? Yes

Remote Sites

Other branches of the institution: Yes
Students' homes: Yes
Work sites: Yes
Libraries: Yes

Tuition & Fees

In-state tuition per credit: $613
Out-of-state tuition per credit: $613
Average yearly cost of books: $300

Temple Baptist Seminary

Distance Learning
1815 Union Avenue
Chattanooga, TN 37404
Contact: Carlos Casteel, Enrollment Counselor
Department e-mail: tbsinfo@templebaptistseminary.edu
School Web address: www.templebaptistseminary.edu
Institutional accreditation: TRACS

Subjects Offered

Hermeneutics, theology, homifetics, apologetics, christian
education, church history, missions, bible content/old
and new testament, pastoral theology

Admissions Requirements

Is a minimum undergraduate GPA required? Yes
Is provisional admission available? Yes
Is an admissions interview required? No
Are international students eligible to apply? Yes
Is the TOEFL required for international students? Yes
What is the minimum TOEFL score required? 550

Program Delivery

Primary method of program delivery: Remote site
Two-way interactive video: No
Two-way audio, one-way video: No
One-way live video: No
One-way pre-recorded video: Yes
Audio graphics: No
Audio: Yes
Is the library accessible to students? No
Are computers accessible to students? No

Remote Sites

Other branches of the institution: No
Other college campuses: No
Students' homes: Yes
Work sites: No
Libraries: No
Elementary/Secondary schools: No

Community-based organizations: No
Correctional institutions: No

On-Campus Requirements

Is an on-campus component required? Yes
On-campus course work: Yes
On-campus admissions interview: No
On-campus program orientation: No
On-campus exams: No
On-campus thesis defense: Yes

Tuition & Fees

In-state tuition per credit: $150
Out-of-state tuition per credit: $150
Average yearly cost of books: $300
Average yearly additional fees: $35

Financial Aid

Is financial aid available to full-time students? Yes
Is financial aid available to part-time students? Yes
Are academic scholarships available? Yes
Assistance programs available to students: Veterans'
assistance

Texas A&M University

School of Nursing and Health Science
6300 Ocean Drive
Corpus Christi, TX 78412
Contact: Dr. Rebecca Jones, Director of the SONHS
School Web address: www.tamucc.edu
Institutional accreditation: Southern Association of
Colleges and Schools, National League for Nursing

Subjects Offered

Nursing administration, family nurse practitioner

Admissions Requirements

Is a minimum undergraduate GPA required? Yes
Is provisional admission available? Yes
Is an admissions interview required? No
Can pre-requisite course work be waived? No
Are international students eligible to apply? Yes
Is the TOEFL required for international students? Yes

Program Delivery

Primary method of program delivery: Remote site
Two-way interactive video: Yes
Hardware requirements: A computer capable of opening
e-mail and attachments
Software requirements: E-mail and Microsoft Word
Is the library accessible to students? Yes
Are computers accessible to students? Yes

Remote Sites

Other branches of the institution: No
Other college campuses: Yes
Students' homes: No
Work sites: No
Libraries: No
Elementary/Secondary schools: No
Community-based organizations: No
Correctional institutions: No

Tuition & Fees

In-state tuition per credit: $230
Out-of-state tuition per credit: $230
Average yearly cost of books: $250

Financial Aid

Is financial aid available to full-time students? Yes
Is financial aid available to part-time students? Yes
Are academic scholarships available? Yes
Assistance programs available to students: Federal Stafford
Loan, Federal Perkins Loan, Federal Plus Loan, Federal
Work-Study Program, in-state student aid programs,
veterans' assistance

Texas Christian University

2800 South University
PO Box 297024
Ft. Worth, TX 76133
Contact: Leo W. Muuson, Associate Vice Chancellor For
Academic Support
Department Web address: www.tcuglobal.edu
School Web address: www.tcu.edu
Institutional accreditation: Southern Association of
Colleges and Schools

Subjects Offered

Theology, ministry

Admissions Requirements

Is a minimum undergraduate GPA required? No
Is provisional admission available? No
Is an admissions interview required? No
Can pre-requisite course work be waived? No
Are international students eligible to apply? Yes
Is the TOEFL required for international students? No

Program Delivery

Primary method of program delivery: Web
Two-way interactive video: No
Two-way audio, one-way video: No
One-way live video: No
One-way pre-recorded video: No

Audio graphics: No
Audio: No
Hardware requirements: PC: 90MHz Pentium or higher,
32MB of RAM. Mac: 604 Power PC, 32MB of RAM
Software requirements: Windows 95/98/NT, Mac OS 8.1
Explorer 5.0 or higher (PC), 4.5 or higher (Mac)
Is the library accessible to students? Yes
Are computers accessible to students? Yes

Remote Sites

Other branches of the institution: No
Other college campuses: No
Students' homes: Yes
Work sites: Yes
Libraries: Yes
Elementary/Secondary schools: No
Community-based organizations: Yes
Correctional institutions: Yes

On-Campus Requirements

Is an on-campus component required? No

Tuition & Fees

In-state tuition per credit: $390
Out-of-state tuition per credit: $390
Average yearly cost of books: $150

Financial Aid

Is financial aid available to full-time students? Yes
Is financial aid available to part-time students? Yes
Are academic scholarships available? Yes
Assistance programs available to students: Federal Stafford
Loan, Federal Perkins Loan, Federal Plus Loan, in-state
student aid programs, veterans' assistance

Texas Wesleyan University

Department of Graduate Studies in Education
1201 Wesleyan Street
Fort Worth, TX 76105-1536
Contact: Dr. Joy Edwards, Department of Graduate
Studies in Education
Department e-mail: edgrad@txwes.edu
School Web address: www.txwes.edu
Institutional accreditation: Southern Association of
Colleges and Schools

Admissions Requirements

Is provisional admission available? No
Can pre-requisite course work be waived? No
Are international students eligible to apply? Yes
Is the TOEFL required for international students? Yes
What is the minimum TOEFL score required? 550

Program Delivery

One-way pre-recorded video: Yes
Audio: Yes
Hardware requirements: VCR, computer
Software requirements: Student must have access to e-mail
Is the library accessible to students? Yes
Are computers accessible to students? No

Remote Sites

Students' homes: Yes

On-Campus Requirements

Is an on-campus component required? No

Tuition & Fees

In-state tuition per credit: $200
Application fee: $40
Can it be waived? No
Average yearly cost of books: $750

Financial Aid

Is financial aid available to full-time students? Yes
Is financial aid available to part-time students? Yes
Are academic scholarships available? No
Assistance programs available to students: Federal Stafford
    Loan

Thomas Edison State College

Office of Graduate Studies
101 West State Street
Trenton, NJ 08608-1176
Department e-mail: info-msm@tesc.edu
School Web address: www.tesc.edu
Institutional accreditation: Middle States Association of
    Colleges and Schools

Admissions Requirements

Is a minimum undergraduate GPA required? No
Is provisional admission available? No
Is an admissions interview required? No
Can pre-requisite course work be waived? No
Are international students eligible to apply? Yes
Is the TOEFL required for international students? Yes
What is the minimum TOEFL score required? 550

Program Delivery

Primary method of program delivery: Web
Two-way interactive video: No
Two-way audio, one-way video: No
One-way live video: No

One-way pre-recorded video: No
Audio graphics: No
Audio: No
Software requirements: Internet browser, e-mail
Is the library accessible to students? Yes

Remote Sites

Other branches of the institution: No
Other college campuses: No
Students' homes: No
Work sites: No
Libraries: No
Elementary/Secondary schools: No
Community-based organizations: No
Correctional institutions: No

On-Campus Requirements

Is an on-campus component required? Yes
On-campus course work: No
On-campus admissions interview: No
On-campus program orientation: Yes
On-campus exams: No
On-campus thesis defense: No

Tuition & Fees

In-state tuition per credit: $298
Out-of-state tuition per credit: $298
Average yearly cost of books: $900

Financial Aid

Is financial aid available to part-time students? Yes
Are academic scholarships available? No
Assistance programs available to students: Federal Stafford
    Loan

Trinity Lutheran Seminary

Continuing Education and Distance Education
2199 Main Street
Columbus, OH 43209
Contact: Ward Cornett III, Director of Continuing
    Education and Distance Learning
Department e-mail: wcornett@trinity.capital.edu
School Web address: trinity.capital.edu
Institutional accreditation: Association of Theological
    Schools

Subjects Offered

Theology, ethics, church history, bible

Admissions Requirements

Is provisional admission available? Yes
Is an admissions interview required? Yes

Can pre-requisite course work be waived? Yes
Are international students eligible to apply? Yes
Is the TOEFL required for international students? No

Program Delivery

Two-way interactive video: Yes
One-way pre-recorded video: Yes
Is the library accessible to students? Yes
Are computers accessible to students? Yes

Remote Sites

Other branches of the institution: Yes
Other college campuses: Yes
Students' homes: Yes
Libraries: Yes
Elementary/Secondary schools: Yes
Community-based organizations: Yes
Correctional institutions: Yes

On-Campus Requirements

Is an on-campus component required? Yes
On-campus course work: Yes
On-campus thesis defense: Yes

Tuition & Fees

In-state tuition per credit: $400
Out-of-state tuition per credit: $700

Financial Aid

Is financial aid available to full-time students? Yes
Is financial aid available to part-time students? Yes
Are academic scholarships available? Yes

Trinity University

Health Care Administration
715 Stadium Drive
San Antonio, TX 78212-7200
Contact: Williams C. McCaughrin, PhD, Chair
Department e-mail: hca@trinity.edu
Department Web address: trinity.edu/departments/
    healthcare
School Web address: trinity.edu
Institutional accreditation: Southern Association of
    Colleges and Schools

Subjects Offered

Health care administration

Admissions Requirements

Is a minimum undergraduate GPA required? Yes
Is provisional admission available? Yes
Is an admissions interview required? No

Can pre-requisite course work be waived? No
Are international students eligible to apply? Yes
Is the TOEFL required for international students? Yes
What is the minimum TOEFL score required? 600

Program Delivery

Primary method of program delivery: Text
Two-way interactive video: No
Two-way audio, one-way video: No
One-way live video: No
One-way pre-recorded video: No
Audio graphics: No
Audio: Yes
Hardware requirements: IBM-compatible computer
Software requirements: Internet access
Is the library accessible to students? Yes
Are computers accessible to students? Yes

Remote Sites

Other branches of the institution: No
Other college campuses: No
Students' homes: Yes
Work sites: Yes
Libraries: No
Elementary/Secondary schools: No
Community-based organizations: No
Correctional institutions: No

On-Campus Requirements

Is an on-campus component required? Yes
On-campus course work: Yes
On-campus admissions interview: No
On-campus program orientation: Yes
On-campus exams: No
On-campus thesis defense: No

Tuition & Fees

In-state tuition per credit: $652
Out-of-state tuition per credit: $652
Average yearly cost of books: $250

Financial Aid

Is financial aid available to full-time students? No
Is financial aid available to part-time students? No
Are academic scholarships available? No

The Union Institute

Graduate College
440 East McMillan Street
Cincinnati, OH 45206
Department e-mail: admissions@tui.edu
School Web address: www.tui.edu

Institutional accreditation: North Central Association of Colleges and Schools

Admissions Requirements

Is a minimum undergraduate GPA required? No
Is provisional admission available? No
Is an admissions interview required? No
Are international students eligible to apply? Yes
Is the TOEFL required for international students? No

Program Delivery

Audio: Yes
Is the library accessible to students? Yes
Are computers accessible to students? No

Remote Sites

Students' homes: Yes

On-Campus Requirements

Is an on-campus component required? Yes
On-campus course work: Yes
On-campus program orientation: Yes

Tuition & Fees

Application fee: $50
Can it be waived? Yes
Average yearly cost of books: $2,100

Financial Aid

Is financial aid available to full-time students? Yes
Is financial aid available to part-time students? No
Are academic scholarships available? Yes
Assistance programs available to students: Federal Stafford Loan, Federal Perkins Loan, Federal Plus Loan, Federal Work-Study Program

United States Sports Academy

Continuing Education and Distance Learning
One Academy Drive
Daphne, AL 36526
Contact: Dr. Gordon Strong, Director, Continuing Education and Distance Learning
Department e-mail: academy@ussa.edu
School Web address: www.ussa.edu
Institutional accreditation: Southern Association of Colleges and Schools

Subjects Offered

Sport administration and finance, sport marketing, professional writing and research, contemporary issues in sport, sport business and personnel management, sport public relations and fund raising, sport facilities, sport law and risk management, sport psychology, sport coaching methodology, sport biomechanics, sport conditioning and nutrition, sports medicine, communications and organizational leadership, sport and travel tourism, sport agency, exercise physiology

Admissions Requirements

Is a minimum undergraduate GPA required? Yes
Is provisional admission available? Yes
Is an admissions interview required? No
Can pre-requisite course work be waived? No
Are international students eligible to apply? Yes
Is the TOEFL required for international students? Yes
What is the minimum TOEFL score required? 550

Program Delivery

Primary method of program delivery: Text
Two-way interactive video: No
Two-way audio, one-way video: No
One-way live video: No
One-way pre-recorded video: Yes
Audio graphics: No
Audio: Yes
Software requirements: E-mail
Is the library accessible to students? Yes
Are computers accessible to students? Yes

Remote Sites

Other branches of the institution: No
Other college campuses: No
Students' homes: Yes
Work sites: No
Libraries: No
Elementary/Secondary schools: No
Community-based organizations: No
Correctional institutions: No

On-Campus Requirements

Is an on-campus component required? Yes
On-campus course work: No
On-campus admissions interview: No
On-campus program orientation: No
On-campus exams: Yes
On-campus thesis defense: Yes

Tuition & Fees

In-state tuition per credit: $350
Out-of-state tuition per credit: $350
Average yearly cost of books: $1,500

Financial Aid

Is financial aid available to full-time students? Yes
Is financial aid available to part-time students? Yes
Are academic scholarships available? No
Assistance programs available to students: Federal Stafford
Loan, Federal Perkins Loan, Federal Work-Study
Program, veterans' assistance

University of Alabama

Division of Distance Education
Box 870388
Tuscaloosa, AL 35487-0388
Contact: Dr. Carroll Tingle, Director of Distance
Education
Department e-mail: disted@ccs.us.edu
Department Web address: bama.disted.ua.edu
School Web address: www.ua.edu
Institutional accreditation: Southern Association of
Colleges and Schools

Subjects Offered

American studies, astronomy, athletic coaching, biology,
chemical engineering, classics, computer science,
consumer sciences, counselor education, criminal justice,
economics, English, finance, geography, German,
history, human development and family studies, human
environmental sciences, human nutrition and hospitality
management, journalism, library studies, management

Program Delivery

Primary method of program delivery: Text
Two-way interactive video: Yes
One-way live video: Yes
One-way pre-recorded video: Yes
Hardware requirements: 486 processor
Software requirements: Netscape 3.0 or higher
Is the library accessible to students? Yes
Are computers accessible to students? Yes

Remote Sites

Other branches of the institution: Yes
Other college campuses: Yes
Students' homes: Yes
Work sites: Yes
Elementary/Secondary schools: Yes

On-Campus Requirements

Is an on-campus component required? No

Financial Aid

Is financial aid available to full-time students? Yes
Are academic scholarships available? Yes

Assistance programs available to students: Federal Perkins
Loan, Federal Work-Study Program, veterans' assistance

University of Arizona

Extended University
Distance Learning
PO Box 210158
Tucson, AZ 85721-0158
Contact: Marsha Ham, Program Developer
Department e-mail: distance@u.arizona.edu
Department Web address: www.eu.arizona.edu/dist/
School Web address: www.arizona.edu

Subjects Offered

Engineering, optical sciences, information resources,
information resources and library science

Admissions Requirements

Is a minimum undergraduate GPA required? Yes
Is provisional admission available? Yes
Is an admissions interview required? No
Can pre-requisite course work be waived? Yes
Are international students eligible to apply? Yes
Is the TOEFL required for international students? Yes

Program Delivery

One-way live video: Yes
One-way pre-recorded video: Yes
Is the library accessible to students? Yes
Are computers accessible to students? No

Remote Sites

Students' homes: Yes
Work sites: Yes

On-Campus Requirements

Is an on-campus component required? Yes

Financial Aid

Is financial aid available to full-time students? No
Is financial aid available to part-time students? No
Are academic scholarships available? No

University of Baltimore

Admissions Office
1420 North Charles Street
Baltimore, MD 21201
Department e-mail: admissions@ubmail.ubalt.edu
Department Web address: www.ubonline.edu
School Web address: www.ubalt.edu

Institutional accreditation: Middle States Association of Colleges and Schools

Subjects Offered

Finance, economics, marketing, operations research, accounting, information systems

Admissions Requirements

Is a minimum undergraduate GPA required? No
Is provisional admission available? Yes
Is an admissions interview required? No
Can pre-requisite course work be waived? Yes
Are international students eligible to apply? Yes

Program Delivery

Primary method of program delivery: Web
Software requirements: Microsoft Office
Is the library accessible to students? Yes

On-Campus Requirements

Is an on-campus component required? No

Tuition & Fees

In-state tuition per credit: $282
Out-of-state tuition per credit: $420
Average yearly cost of books: $700

University of Bridgeport

Office of Distance Education
303 University Avenue
Bridgeport, CT 06601
Contact: Michael Giampaoli, Director of Distance Education
Department e-mail: ubonline@bridgeport.edu
Department Web address: www.bridgeport.edu/disted/index.html
School Web address: www.bridgeport.edu
Institutional accreditation: New England Association for Schools and Colleges

Subjects Offered

Nutrition

Admissions Requirements

Is a minimum undergraduate GPA required? Yes
Is provisional admission available? Yes
Is an admissions interview required? No
Can pre-requisite course work be waived? No
Are international students eligible to apply? Yes
Is the TOEFL required for international students? Yes
What is the minimum TOEFL score required? 550

Program Delivery

Primary method of program delivery: Web
Hardware requirements: Pentium or Mac OS 8.1
Software requirements: MS Office
Is the library accessible to students? Yes
Are computers accessible to students? Yes

Remote Sites

Libraries: Yes

On-Campus Requirements

Is an on-campus component required? Yes
On-campus exams: Yes

Tuition & Fees

In-state tuition per credit: $370
Out-of-state tuition per credit: $370
Average yearly cost of books: $400

Financial Aid

Is financial aid available to full-time students? Yes
Is financial aid available to part-time students? No
Assistance programs available to students: Federal Stafford Loan

University of California, Santa Barbara

Off-Campus Studies
Santa Barbara, CA 93106
Contact: Howard Adamson, Manager/Systems Engineer
Department e-mail: ocs@els.ucsb.edu
School Web address: www.ocs.xlrn.ucsb.edu
Institutional accreditation: Western Association of Schools and Colleges

Subjects Offered

Computer science, electrical and computer engineering

Admissions Requirements

Is provisional admission available? No
Is an admissions interview required? Yes
Can pre-requisite course work be waived? No
Are international students eligible to apply? No

Program Delivery

Two-way interactive video: Yes
One-way live video: Yes
One-way pre-recorded video: Yes
Is the library accessible to students? Yes
Are computers accessible to students? Yes

Remote Sites

Other branches of the institution: Yes
Other college campuses: No
Students' homes: No
Work sites: No
Libraries: No
Elementary/Secondary schools: No
Community-based organizations: No
Correctional institutions: No

On-Campus Requirements

Is an on-campus component required? Yes
On-campus course work: No
On-campus admissions interview: Yes
On-campus program orientation: No
On-campus exams: Yes
On-campus thesis defense: Yes

Tuition & Fees

Average yearly cost of books: $300

Financial Aid

Is financial aid available to full-time students? Yes
Is financial aid available to part-time students? Yes
Are academic scholarships available? Yes
Assistance programs available to students: Federal Stafford Loan, Federal Perkins Loan, Federal Plus Loan, Federal Pell Grant, Federal Work-Study Program, in-state student aid programs, veterans' assistance

University of Central Arkansas

Division of Continuing Education
201 Donaghey Avenue
McCastlain Hall, Suite 101
Conway, AR 72035
Contact: Kim Bradford
Department e-mail: rebeccar@ecom.uca.edu
Department Web address: www.uca.edu/conted
School Web address: www.uca.edu
Institutional accreditation: National Council for Accreditation of Teacher Education

Subjects Offered

Health sciences, media library science, educational leadership, physical therapy, nursing, special education

Admissions Requirements

Is a minimum undergraduate GPA required? Yes
Is provisional admission available? Yes
Is an admissions interview required? No
Can pre-requisite course work be waived? No
Are international students eligible to apply? Yes
Is the TOEFL required for international students? Yes
What is the minimum TOEFL score required? 550

Program Delivery

Primary method of program delivery: Web
Two-way interactive video: Yes
Software requirements: Most recent version of Internet browsers
Is the library accessible to students? Yes
Are computers accessible to students? Yes

Remote Sites

Other branches of the institution: No
Other college campuses: Yes
Elementary/Secondary schools: Yes

On-Campus Requirements

Is an on-campus component required? Yes
On-campus course work: Yes
On-campus admissions interview: No
On-campus program orientation: No
On-campus exams: Yes
On-campus thesis defense: Yes

Tuition & Fees

In-state tuition per credit: $168
Out-of-state tuition per credit: $325
Average yearly cost of books: $25

Financial Aid

Is financial aid available to full-time students? Yes
Is financial aid available to part-time students? Yes
Are academic scholarships available? No
Assistance programs available to students: Federal Stafford Loan, Federal Perkins Loan, Federal Plus Loan, Federal Work-Study Program, veterans' assistance

University of Colorado at Boulder

Division of Continuing Education
Center for Advanced Training in Engineering and Computer Science
ECOT Room 127, Campus Box 435
Boulder, CO 80309-0435
Contact: Vince Micucci, Director
Department e-mail: catecs-info@colorado.edu
Department Web address: www.colorado.edu/catecs
School Web address: www.colorado.edu

Institutional accreditation: North Central Association of Colleges and Schools

Subjects Offered

Aerospace engineering, electrical and computer science, mechanical engineering, computer science, engineering management, telecommunications

Admissions Requirements

Is a minimum undergraduate GPA required? Yes
Is provisional admission available? Yes
Can pre-requisite course work be waived? Yes
Are international students eligible to apply? Yes
Is the TOEFL required for international students? Yes
What is the minimum TOEFL score required? 530

Program Delivery

Primary method of program delivery: Remote site
Two-way audio, one-way video: Yes
Hardware requirements: Computer and modem
Software requirements: Internet, e-mail

Remote Sites

Work sites: Yes
Libraries: Yes

On-Campus Requirements

Is an on-campus component required? No

Tuition & Fees

In-state tuition per credit: $400
Out-of-state tuition per credit: $400
Average yearly cost of books: $1,000

Financial Aid

Is financial aid available to full-time students? Yes
Is financial aid available to part-time students? Yes
Are academic scholarships available? No
Assistance programs available to students: Federal Stafford Loan, Federal Perkins Loan, veterans' assistance

University of Colorado at Colorado Springs

Graduate School of Business Administration
Distance MBA
1420 Austin Bluffs Parkway
Colorado Springs, CO 80933-7150
Contact: Karen S. Sangermano, Program Manager for Distance Education
Department e-mail: busadvsr@mail.uccs.edu

Department Web address: web.uccs.edu/business/ambamain.htm
School Web address: www.uccs.edu

Subjects Offered

Business administration—general, business administration—finance

Admissions Requirements

Is provisional admission available? Yes
Is an admissions interview required? No
Can pre-requisite course work be waived? Yes
Are international students eligible to apply? Yes
Is the TOEFL required for international students? Yes
What is the minimum TOEFL score required? 550

Program Delivery

Primary method of program delivery: Web
Two-way interactive video: No
Two-way audio, one-way video: No
One-way live video: No
One-way pre-recorded video: Yes
Audio graphics: No
Audio: No
Hardware requirements: Pentium, 28.8KBPS modem
Software requirements: Adobe Acrobat Reader, Netscape Navigator or Internet Explorer 4.0 or higher
Is the library accessible to students? No
Are computers accessible to students? No

Remote Sites

Other branches of the institution: No
Other college campuses: No
Students' homes: Yes
Work sites: No
Libraries: No
Elementary/Secondary schools: No
Community-based organizations: No
Correctional institutions: No

On-Campus Requirements

Is an on-campus component required? No

Tuition & Fees

In-state tuition per credit: $400
Out-of-state tuition per credit: $400
Average yearly cost of books: $200

Financial Aid

Is financial aid available to full-time students? No
Is financial aid available to part-time students? No
Are academic scholarships available? No

University of Denver

Extended Learning
2211 South Josephine Street
Denver, CO 80208
Contact: Lisa Mattiace, Vice President of External
Relations
Department e-mail: tlennon@du.edu
School Web address: www.learning.du.edu
Institutional accreditation: North Central Association of
Colleges and Schools

Subjects Offered

Environmental policy management, computer information
science, telecommunications, liberal studies, geographic
information systems, applied communications

Admissions Requirements

Is a minimum undergraduate GPA required? Yes
Is provisional admission available? Yes
Can pre-requisite course work be waived? Yes
Are international students eligible to apply? Yes
Is the TOEFL required for international students? Yes
What is the minimum TOEFL score required? 550

Program Delivery

Primary method of program delivery: Remote site
Two-way interactive video: Yes
Two-way audio, one-way video: Yes
One-way live video: Yes
One-way pre-recorded video: Yes
Audio graphics: Yes
Audio: Yes
Hardware requirements: 486 166 MHz, 28.8KBPS
modem, sound card, VGA color (256 colors), SVGA
Software requirements: Netscape or Internet Explorer
Is the library accessible to students? Yes
Are computers accessible to students? No

Remote Sites

Other branches of the institution: Yes

On-Campus Requirements

Is an on-campus component required? No

Tuition & Fees

In-state tuition per credit: $314
Out-of-state tuition per credit: $314

University of Durham

Business School
DL Programme Office
Mill Hill Lane
Durham, UK DH1 3LB
Contact: Professor R. Dixon, Director, DL Programmes
Department e-mail: mbadl.eng@durham.ac.uk
Department Web address: www.dur.ac.uk/udbs
School Web address: www.dur.ac.uk
Institutional accreditation: Association of MBAs

Subjects Offered

Business administration, management

Admissions Requirements

Is provisional admission available? Yes
Is an admissions interview required? No
Are international students eligible to apply? Yes
Is the TOEFL required for international students? Yes

Program Delivery

Primary method of program delivery: Text
Two-way interactive video: No
Two-way audio, one-way video: No
One-way live video: No
One-way pre-recorded video: No
Audio graphics: No
Audio: No
Software requirements: Microsoft Office
Is the library accessible to students? No
Are computers accessible to students? No

Remote Sites

Other branches of the institution: No
Other college campuses: No
Students' homes: Yes
Work sites: No
Libraries: No
Elementary/Secondary schools: No
Community-based organizations: No
Correctional institutions: No

On-Campus Requirements

Is an on-campus component required? Yes
On-campus course work: Yes
On-campus admissions interview: No
On-campus program orientation: Yes
On-campus exams: No
On-campus thesis defense: No

Financial Aid

Is financial aid available to full-time students? No
Is financial aid available to part-time students? No
Are academic scholarships available? No

University of Florida

Department of Communication Disorders and Distance
　Learning Program
PO Box 100174
1600 Southwest Archer Road
Gainesville, FL 32610
Contact: Janet M. Caffee, Director
Department e-mail: jcaffee@hp.ufl.edu
Department Web address: www.intelicus.com/aud/
　index.htm
School Web address: www.ufl.edu
Institutional accreditation: Southern Association of
　Colleges and Schools

Subjects Offered

Applied auditory electrophysiology, cochlear implants and
　assistive technology, audiologic assessment in a medical
　setting, principles of amplification, occupational and
　environmental hearing conservation, balance disorders:
　evaluation and treatment, audiologic rehabilitation,
　counseling, business and professional issues in hearing
　health

Admissions Requirements

Is a minimum undergraduate GPA required? Yes
Is provisional admission available? Yes
Is an admissions interview required? No
Can pre-requisite course work be waived? No
Are international students eligible to apply? Yes
Is the TOEFL required for international students? Yes
What is the minimum TOEFL score required? 550

Program Delivery

Primary method of program delivery: Web
One-way pre-recorded video: Yes
Hardware requirements: Computer, 200 MHz, 32MB of
　RAM, 1GB free hard disk space, SVGA 256-color
　monitor
Software requirements: Windows 95 or higher, MS Office
　97, Internet access, e-mail address, Netscape Navigator 4
　or higher or Internet Explorer 5 or higher

Remote Sites

Other college campuses: Yes
Work sites: Yes

On-Campus Requirements

Is an on-campus component required? No

Tuition & Fees

Application fee: $20
Can it be waived? No

Financial Aid

Is financial aid available to full-time students? Yes
Is financial aid available to part-time students? Yes
Are academic scholarships available? No
Assistance programs available to students: Federal Stafford
　Loan, veterans' assistance

University of Houston

Division of Distance and Continuing Education
4242 South Mason Road
Houston, TX 77077
Contact: Dr. Marshall Schott, Associate Director of
　Distance Education
Department e-mail: deadvisor@uh.edu
Department Web address: www.uh.edu/udistance/
School Web address: www.uh.edu
Institutional accreditation: Southern Association of
　Colleges and Schools

Admissions Requirements

Is a minimum undergraduate GPA required? Yes
Are international students eligible to apply? Yes
Is the TOEFL required for international students? Yes
What is the minimum TOEFL score required? 537

Program Delivery

Primary method of program delivery: Remote site
Two-way interactive video: Yes
Two-way audio, one-way video: Yes
One-way live video: Yes
One-way pre-recorded video: No
Audio graphics: No
Audio: No
Is the library accessible to students? Yes
Are computers accessible to students? Yes

Remote Sites

Other branches of the institution: Yes
Other college campuses: Yes
Students' homes: Yes
Work sites: Yes
Libraries: No
Elementary/Secondary schools: No
Community-based organizations: No
Correctional institutions: No

On-Campus Requirements

Is an on-campus component required? No

Tuition & Fees

In-state tuition per credit: $268
Out-of-state tuition per credit: $422

Financial Aid

Is financial aid available to full-time students? Yes
Is financial aid available to part-time students? Yes
Are academic scholarships available? Yes
Assistance programs available to students: Federal Stafford Loan, Federal Perkins Loan, Federal Plus Loan, Federal Work-Study Program, in-state student aid programs, veterans' assistance

University of Idaho

Engineering Outreach
PO Box 441014
Moscow, ID 83844-1014
Contact: Dr. Barry Willis, Associate Dean of Outreach
Department e-mail: outreach@uidaho.edu
Department Web address: www.uidaho.edu/evo/
School Web address: www.uidaho.edu
Institutional accreditation: Northwest Association of Schools and Colleges

Subjects Offered

Biological and agricultural engineering, business, civil engineering, computer engineering, computer science, education, electrical engineering, engineering management, general engineering, geological engineering, hydrology, mathematics, mechanical engineering, metallurgical engineering, mining engineering, psychology, statistics

Admissions Requirements

Is a minimum undergraduate GPA required? Yes
Is provisional admission available? Yes
Is an admissions interview required? No
Can pre-requisite course work be waived? Yes
Are international students eligible to apply? Yes
Is the TOEFL required for international students? Yes
What is the minimum TOEFL score required? 550

Program Delivery

Primary method of program delivery: Web
Two-way interactive video: Yes
Two-way audio, one-way video: No
One-way live video: Yes
One-way pre-recorded video: Yes

Audio graphics: No
Audio: No
Software requirements: Internet and e-mail
Is the library accessible to students? Yes
Are computers accessible to students? Yes

Remote Sites

Other branches of the institution: Yes
Other college campuses: Yes
Students' homes: Yes
Work sites: Yes
Libraries: No
Elementary/Secondary schools: No
Community-based organizations: No
Correctional institutions: No

On-Campus Requirements

Is an on-campus component required? No

Tuition & Fees

In-state tuition per credit: $377
Out-of-state tuition per credit: $377
Average yearly cost of books: $35

Financial Aid

Is financial aid available to full-time students? Yes
Is financial aid available to part-time students? No
Are academic scholarships available? Yes
Assistance programs available to students: Federal Stafford Loan, Federal Perkins Loan, Federal Plus Loan, veterans' assistance

University of London Extension

External Programme
Information Centre, Senate House, Malet House
London, UK WC1E 7HU
Department e-mail: enquiries@external.lon.ac.uk
School Web address: www.lon.ac.uk/external

Subjects Offered

Agriculture, business administration, dentistry, drugs and alcohol, economics, education, finance, food industry, geography, health systems management, infectious diseases, livestock health, occupational psychology, organizational behavior, public policy

Program Delivery

Primary method of program delivery: Text

Financial Aid

Is financial aid available to full-time students? No
Is financial aid available to part-time students? No
Are academic scholarships available? No

University of Maryland, Baltimore County

Center for Distance Learning
1000 Hilltop Circle
Baltimore, MD 21250
Contact: Mary Cerrio, Assistant Director of Distance
 Learning
Department e-mail: connect@umbc.edu
Department Web address: continuinged.umbc.edu/
 distanceed
School Web address: umbc.edu
Institutional accreditation: Middle States Commission of
 Higher Learning

Subjects Offered

Education, economics, language, film, ehs, e-commerce,
 information systems

Admissions Requirements

Is a minimum undergraduate GPA required? Yes
Is provisional admission available? Yes
Is an admissions interview required? No
Can pre-requisite course work be waived? Yes
Are international students eligible to apply? Yes
Is the TOEFL required for international students? Yes
What is the minimum TOEFL score required? 550

Program Delivery

Primary method of program delivery: Web
Hardware requirements: Pentium-class processor,
 250MHz, 56KBPS modem, sound card with speakers,
 64MB of RAM, Windows 98 or Macintosh OS 8.5
Software requirements: Discipline-specific
Is the library accessible to students? Yes
Are computers accessible to students? Yes

Remote Sites

Other branches of the institution: Yes
Other college campuses: Yes
Students' homes: Yes
Work sites: Yes
Libraries: Yes
Elementary/Secondary schools: Yes
Community-based organizations: Yes
Correctional institutions: No

On-Campus Requirements

Is an on-campus component required? No

Tuition & Fees

In-state tuition per credit: $278
Out-of-state tuition per credit: $470
Average yearly cost of books: $1,200

Financial Aid

Is financial aid available to full-time students? Yes
Is financial aid available to part-time students? Yes
Are academic scholarships available? Yes
Assistance programs available to students: Federal Stafford
 Loan, Federal Perkins Loan, Federal Plus Loan, Federal
 Pell Grant, Federal Work-Study Program, in-state
 student aid programs, veterans' assistance

University of Maryland, College Park

Instructional Television System/Reliability Engineering
College Park, MD 20742
Contact: Dr. Arnold Seigel/Dr. Marvin Roush, Directors
Department e-mail: itv@eng.umd.edu
Department Web address: www.itv.umd.edu
School Web address: www.umcp.edu
Institutional accreditation: Middle State Commission of
 Higher Learning

Subjects Offered

Reliability engineering

Admissions Requirements

Is a minimum undergraduate GPA required? Yes
Is provisional admission available? Yes
Is an admissions interview required? No
Can pre-requisite course work be waived? Yes
Are international students eligible to apply? Yes
Is the TOEFL required for international students? Yes
What is the minimum TOEFL score required? 575

Program Delivery

Primary method of program delivery: Remote site
Two-way audio, one-way video: Yes
One-way live video: No
One-way pre-recorded video: Yes
Is the library accessible to students? Yes

Remote Sites

Other branches of the institution: Yes
Other college campuses: Yes

Students' homes: Yes
Work sites: Yes

On-Campus Requirements

Is an on-campus component required? No

Tuition & Fees

In-state tuition per credit: $649
Out-of-state tuition per credit: $649
Average yearly cost of books: $50

Financial Aid

Is financial aid available to full-time students? Yes
Is financial aid available to part-time students? Yes
Are academic scholarships available? Yes
Assistance programs available to students: Federal Stafford Loan, Federal Perkins Loan, Federal Plus Loan, Federal Work-Study Program, in-state student aid programs

University of Missouri— Center for Distance and Independent Study

136 Clark Hall
Columbia, MO 65211-4200
Contact: Dr. Evan Smith, University and Non-credit Coordinator
Department e-mail: cdis@missouri.edu
Department Web address: www.cdis.missouri.edu
School Web address: www.missouri.edu
Institutional accreditation: North Central Association of Colleges and Schools

Subjects Offered

Animal sciences, classical studies, communication, criminology and criminal justice, economics, education, English, health services management, history, human development and family studies, management, marketing, parks, recreation and tourism, pest management, philosophy, physics, plant pathology, political science, psychology, sociology, women studies

Admissions Requirements

Can pre-requisite course work be waived? Yes
Are international students eligible to apply? Yes

Program Delivery

Primary method of program delivery: Text
Two-way interactive video: No
Two-way audio, one-way video: No
One-way live video: No
One-way pre-recorded video: No

Audio graphics: No
Audio: Yes
Is the library accessible to students? Yes
Are computers accessible to students? No

Remote Sites

Other branches of the institution: No
Other college campuses: No
Students' homes: No
Work sites: No
Libraries: No
Elementary/Secondary schools: No
Community-based organizations: No
Correctional institutions: No

Tuition & Fees

In-state tuition per credit: $173
Out-of-state tuition per credit: $173
Application fee: $15
Can it be waived? No

Financial Aid

Is financial aid available to full-time students? No
Is financial aid available to part-time students? No
Are academic scholarships available? No

University of Missouri— Columbia

MU Direct: Continuing and Distance Education
102 Whitten Hall
Columbia, MO 65211
Contact: Linda Cupp, Director
Department e-mail: mudirect@missouri.edu
Department Web address: mudirect.missouri.edu
School Web address: www.missouri.edu
Institutional accreditation: North Central Association of Colleges and Schools

Subjects Offered

Library science, educational administration, education, education-literacy, journalism-media management, agriculture economics, community development, nursing

Admissions Requirements

Is a minimum undergraduate GPA required? Yes
Is provisional admission available? Yes
Are international students eligible to apply? Yes
Is the TOEFL required for international students? Yes

Program Delivery

Primary method of program delivery: Web
Two-way interactive video: No
Two-way audio, one-way video: No
One-way live video: No
One-way pre-recorded video: No
Audio graphics: No
Audio: No
Hardware requirements: PC: Pentium 166 MHz, 64MB of RAM, 2GB hard drive, 28.8KBPS modem, CD-ROM drive, Windows 98. Macintosh: comparable features
Software requirements: Netscape Navigator 4.05 or Internet Explorer 4.0, Microsoft Office
Is the library accessible to students? Yes
Are computers accessible to students? Yes

Remote Sites

Other branches of the institution: Yes
Other college campuses: Yes
Students' homes: Yes
Work sites: Yes
Libraries: Yes
Elementary/Secondary schools: Yes
Community-based organizations: Yes
Correctional institutions: No

On-Campus Requirements

On-campus course work: Yes
On-campus admissions interview: No
On-campus program orientation: Yes
On-campus exams: No
On-campus thesis defense: No

Tuition & Fees

In-state tuition per credit: $173
Out-of-state tuition per credit: $173
Application fee: $25
Can it be waived? No

Financial Aid

Is financial aid available to full-time students? Yes
Is financial aid available to part-time students? Yes
Are academic scholarships available? Yes
Assistance programs available to students: Federal Stafford Loan, in-state student aid programs, veterans' assistance

University of Montana—Missoula

Continuing Education
External Degree Programs
32 Campus Drive
Missoula, MT 59812
Contact: Dr. Sharon Alexander, Dean of Continuing Education
Department e-mail: mjones@selway.umt.edu
Department Web address: www.umt.edu/ccesp
School Web address: www.umt.edu
Institutional accreditation: Northwest Association of Schools and Colleges

Subjects Offered

Geography, business administration, educational leadership, counselor education, library media, curriculum and instruction, public administration

Admissions Requirements

Is a minimum undergraduate GPA required? Yes
Is provisional admission available? Yes
Is an admissions interview required? No
Are international students eligible to apply? Yes
Is the TOEFL required for international students? Yes
What is the minimum TOEFL score required? 525

Program Delivery

Primary method of program delivery: Remote site
Two-way interactive video: Yes
Two-way audio, one-way video: No
One-way live video: No
One-way pre-recorded video: Yes
Audio graphics: No
Audio: No

Remote Sites

Other branches of the institution: Yes
Other college campuses: Yes
Students' homes: Yes
Work sites: Yes
Libraries: Yes
Elementary/Secondary schools: Yes
Community-based organizations: Yes
Correctional institutions: No

On-Campus Requirements

Is an on-campus component required? No

Tuition & Fees

In-state tuition per credit: $200
Out-of-state tuition per credit: $450
Average yearly cost of books: $500
Are academic scholarships available? No

University of Nebraska—Lincoln

Academic Telecommunications
Nebraska Center for Continuing Education
Room 334
33rd and Holdrege Streets
Lincoln, NE 68583-9805
Contact: Nancy Aden, Director
Department e-mail: atc3@unl.edu
Department Web address: dcs.unl.edu/telecom/
School Web address: unl.edu
Institutional accreditation: North Central Association of
    Colleges and Schools

Subjects Offered

Agriculture, journalism and mass communications,
    agronomy, statistics, business administration, special
    education, education, textiles, clothing and design,
    engineering, entomology, human resources and family
    sciences

Admissions Requirements

Is provisional admission available? Yes
Are international students eligible to apply? Yes
Is the TOEFL required for international students? Yes
What is the minimum TOEFL score required? 500

Program Delivery

Primary method of program delivery: Web
Two-way interactive video: Yes
Two-way audio, one-way video: Yes
One-way live video: Yes
One-way pre-recorded video: Yes
Audio graphics: No
Audio: Yes
Hardware requirements: Program-specific
Software requirements: Program-specific
Is the library accessible to students? Yes
Are computers accessible to students? No

Remote Sites

Other branches of the institution: Yes
Other college campuses: Yes
Students' homes: Yes
Work sites: Yes

Libraries: Yes
Elementary/Secondary schools: Yes
Community-based organizations: Yes
Correctional institutions: No

On-Campus Requirements

Is an on-campus component required? Yes

Tuition & Fees

In-state tuition per credit: $122
Out-of-state tuition per credit: $122
Average yearly cost of books: $35

Financial Aid

Is financial aid available to full-time students? Yes
Is financial aid available to part-time students? Yes
Are academic scholarships available? Yes
Assistance programs available to students: Federal Stafford
    Loan, Federal Perkins Loan, Federal Plus Loan, Federal
    Work-Study Program, in-state student aid programs,
    veterans' assistance

University of Nevada, Las Vegas

Distance Education & Creative Services
4505 Maryland Parkway
Las Vegas, NV 89154-1038
Contact: Charlotte Farr, Director
Department e-mail: distanceed@ccmail.nevada.edu
Department Web address: www.unlv.edu/infotech/distance
    education
School Web address: www.unlv.edu
Institutional accreditation: Northwest Association of
    Schools and Colleges

Subjects Offered

Criminal justice, education, English, hotel administration,
    nursing, theatre

Admissions Requirements

Is a minimum undergraduate GPA required? Yes
Is provisional admission available? Yes
Can pre-requisite course work be waived? No
Are international students eligible to apply? Yes
Is the TOEFL required for international students? Yes
What is the minimum TOEFL score required? 550

Program Delivery

Primary method of program delivery: Web
Two-way interactive video: Yes
One-way pre-recorded video: Yes

Audio: Yes
Hardware requirements: Pentium, Internet access
Software requirements: Word processor, Netscape
Navigator browser
Is the library accessible to students? Yes
Are computers accessible to students? Yes

Remote Sites

Other college campuses: Yes
Students' homes: Yes
Elementary/Secondary schools: Yes

On-Campus Requirements

Is an on-campus component required? No

Tuition & Fees

In-state tuition per credit: $100
Out-of-state tuition per credit: $205
Average yearly cost of books: $700

Financial Aid

Is financial aid available to full-time students? Yes
Are academic scholarships available? Yes
Assistance programs available to students: Federal Stafford
Loan, Federal Perkins Loan, Federal Work-Study
Program, veterans' assistance

University of Nevada—Reno

College of Extended Studies
Independent Learning Program
PO Box 14429
Reno, NV 89507
Contact: Kerri Garcia, Director
Department e-mail: istudy@unc.nevada.edu
Department Web address: ww.dce.unr.edu/istudy/
School Web address: www.unr.edu
Institutional accreditation: Northwest Association of
Schools and Colleges

Subjects Offered

Basque, educational leadership, human development and
family studies

Program Delivery

Two-way interactive video: No
Two-way audio, one-way video: No
One-way live video: No
One-way pre-recorded video: Yes
Audio graphics: No
Audio: No
Hardware requirements: for online courses: computer with
modem and access to the Internet

Software requirements: e-mail and Internet access, word
processing software
Is the library accessible to students? No
Are computers accessible to students? No

On-Campus Requirements

On-campus course work: No

Financial Aid

Is financial aid available to full-time students? Yes
Is financial aid available to part-time students? Yes
Are academic scholarships available? Yes
Assistance programs available to students: Federal Plus
Loan, veterans' assistance

University of North Dakota

Division of Continuing Education
Extended Degree Programs
PO Box 9021
Gustafson Hall, UND
Grand Forks, ND 58202
Contact: Lynette Krenelka, Director of Extended Degree
Programs
Department e-mail: ext_degree@mail.und.nodak.edu
Department Web address: www.conted.und.edu
School Web address: www.und.nodak.edu
Institutional accreditation: North Central Association of
Colleges and Schools

Subjects Offered

Fine arts, occupational therapy, accounting, French,
nutrition and dietetics, anthropology, geography, visual
arts, atmospheric sciences, geology, Spanish, business
and vocational education, history, sociology, chemical
engineering, humanities, psychology, economics, music,
Norwegian, English language and literature

Admissions Requirements

Is a minimum undergraduate GPA required? Yes
Is provisional admission available? Yes
Is an admissions interview required? No
Can pre-requisite course work be waived? No
Are international students eligible to apply? Yes
Is the TOEFL required for international students? Yes
What is the minimum TOEFL score required? 550

Program Delivery

Primary method of program delivery: Remote site
Two-way interactive video: Yes
Two-way audio, one-way video: Yes
One-way live video: No
One-way pre-recorded video: Yes

Audio graphics: No
Audio: No
Hardware requirements: varies according to program
Software requirements: varies according to program
Is the library accessible to students? Yes
Are computers accessible to students? Yes

Remote Sites

Other college campuses: Yes
Students' homes: Yes
Work sites: Yes
Elementary/Secondary schools: Yes

On-Campus Requirements

Is an on-campus component required? Yes
On-campus course work: Yes
On-campus admissions interview: No
On-campus program orientation: No
On-campus exams: No
On-campus thesis defense: Yes

Tuition & Fees

In-state tuition per credit: $140
Out-of-state tuition per credit: $313
Average yearly cost of books: $500

Financial Aid

Is financial aid available to full-time students? Yes
Is financial aid available to part-time students? No
Are academic scholarships available? Yes
Assistance programs available to students: Federal Stafford
   Loan, Federal Perkins Loan, Federal Plus Loan, Federal
   Work-Study Program, in-state student aid programs,
   veterans' assistance

University of Notre Dame

Executive Education
126 Mendoza College of Business
Notre Dame, IN 46556
Contact: Dr. Barry Van Dyck
Department e-mail: emba@nd.edu
Department Web address: www.nd.edu/~execprog
School Web address: www.nd.edu
Institutional accreditation: AACSB—The International
   Association for Management Education

Subjects Offered

Organizational behavior, international business, business
   conditions analysis, legal environment of business,
   financial accounting for managers, financial management, statistics for managers, marketing management,
   tactics for effective leaders, operations management,

economics of the firm, strategic management information system, managerial accounting and council,
   investments with a global perspective

Admissions Requirements

Is provisional admission available? No
Is an admissions interview required? Yes
Can pre-requisite course work be waived? Yes
Are international students eligible to apply? Yes
Is the TOEFL required for international students? Yes

Program Delivery

Primary method of program delivery: Remote site
Two-way interactive video: Yes
Hardware requirements: Varies
Software requirements: Varies
Is the library accessible to students? Yes
Are computers accessible to students? Yes

Remote Sites

Work sites: Yes

On-Campus Requirements

Is an on-campus component required? Yes
On-campus course work: Yes
On-campus program orientation: Yes

Tuition & Fees

Application fee: $50

Financial Aid

Is financial aid available to full-time students? Yes
Assistance programs available to students: Federal Stafford
   Loan, Federal Perkins Loan, Federal Plus Loan, Federal
   Work-Study Program

University of Pennsylvania— School of Engineering

Penn Online
Philadelphia, PA 19104
Contact: Dwight L. Jaggard, Professor
Department e-mail: jaggard@seas.upenn.edu
Department Web address: www.seas.upenn.edu/grad/
   pennonline.html
School Web address: www.upenn.edu
Institutional accreditation: Middle States Association of
   Colleges and Schools

Subjects Offered

Electrical engineering, systems engineering, telecommunications and networking

Admissions Requirements

Is provisional admission available? Yes
Is an admissions interview required? No
Can pre-requisite course work be waived? No
Are international students eligible to apply? Yes
Is the TOEFL required for international students? Yes
What is the minimum TOEFL score required? 600

Program Delivery

Primary method of program delivery: Web
Hardware requirements: PC or Macintosh
Software requirements: Adobe Acrobat Reader, Real Audio
 Player, PowerPoint
Is the library accessible to students? Yes
Are computers accessible to students? Yes

Remote Sites

Students' homes: Yes
Work sites: Yes

On-Campus Requirements

Is an on-campus component required? No

Tuition & Fees

Application fee: $65
Can it be waived? No

Financial Aid

Is financial aid available to full-time students? No
Is financial aid available to part-time students? No
Are academic scholarships available? No

University of Pennsylvania— School of Nursing

Distance Learning Program
420 Guardian Drive
Philadelphia, PA 19104-6096
Institutional accreditation: Middle States Association of
 Colleges and Schools

Subjects Offered

Nursing

Admissions Requirements

Is provisional admission available? Yes
Is an admissions interview required? Yes
Can pre-requisite course work be waived? No
Are international students eligible to apply? Yes
Is the TOEFL required for international students? Yes
What is the minimum TOEFL score required? 550

Program Delivery

Two-way interactive video: Yes
Two-way audio, one-way video: No
One-way live video: No
One-way pre-recorded video: Yes
Audio: Yes
Hardware requirements: Computer with 56KBPS modem
Software requirements: Internet access
Is the library accessible to students? Yes

Remote Sites

Other branches of the institution: No
Other college campuses: Yes
Students' homes: Yes
Work sites: Yes
Libraries: Yes
Elementary/Secondary schools: No
Community-based organizations: No
Correctional institutions: No

On-Campus Requirements

Is an on-campus component required? Yes
On-campus course work: Yes
On-campus admissions interview: No
On-campus program orientation: Yes
On-campus exams: No

Tuition & Fees

Average yearly cost of books: $840
Average yearly additional fees: $65

Financial Aid

Is financial aid available to full-time students? Yes
Is financial aid available to part-time students? Yes
Are academic scholarships available? Yes
Assistance programs available to students: Federal Stafford
 Loan, Federal Perkins Loan, Federal Plus Loan, Federal
 Work-Study Program, veterans' assistance

University of Phoenix Online

3157 East Elwood Street
Phoenix, AZ 85034
Contact: Michael Berkowitz, National Director of
 Enrollment
Department e-mail: online@apollogrp.edu
Department Web address: online.uophx.edu
School Web address: online.uophx.edu
Institutional accreditation: North Central Association of
 Colleges and Schools

Subjects Offered

Business, e-business, management, information technology, technology management, information systems, education, nursing, accounting

Admissions Requirements

Is a minimum undergraduate GPA required? Yes
Is provisional admission available? Yes
Is an admissions interview required? No
Can pre-requisite course work be waived? Yes
Are international students eligible to apply? Yes
Is the TOEFL required for international students? Yes
What is the minimum TOEFL score required? 580

Program Delivery

Hardware requirements: Pentium or better with at least 32MB of RAM, 1.5 GB or larger hard drive, SVGA monitor, Internet connection of 28.8KBPS or better
Software requirements: Windows 95 or better, browser and e-mail software are provided by University of Phoenix Online
Is the library accessible to students? Yes
Are computers accessible to students? No

On-Campus Requirements

Is an on-campus component required? No

Tuition & Fees

In-state tuition per credit: $485
Application fee: $85
Can it be waived? No
Average yearly cost of books: $900

Financial Aid

Is financial aid available to full-time students? Yes
Is financial aid available to part-time students? No
Are academic scholarships available? Yes
Assistance programs available to students: Federal Stafford Loan, Federal Perkins Loan, Federal Plus Loan, veterans' assistance

University of St. Francis

500 North Wilcox Street
Joliet, IL 60435
Department Web address: stfrancis.edu/online/index.htm
School Web address: stfrancis.edu
Institutional accreditation: North Central Association of Colleges and Schools

Admissions Requirements

Is a minimum undergraduate GPA required? Yes
Is provisional admission available? No
Is an admissions interview required? No
Can pre-requisite course work be waived? Yes
Are international students eligible to apply? Yes
What is the minimum TOEFL score required? 550

Program Delivery

Primary method of program delivery: Web
Hardware requirements: IBM-compatible 56KBPS modem
Software requirements: Microsoft Office 97
Is the library accessible to students? Yes
Are computers accessible to students? Yes

On-Campus Requirements

Is an on-campus component required? No

Tuition & Fees

In-state tuition per credit: $425
Out-of-state tuition per credit: $425
Average yearly cost of books: $1,000

Financial Aid

Is financial aid available to full-time students? No
Is financial aid available to part-time students? No
Are academic scholarships available? No

University of Sarasota

5250 17th Street
Sarasota, FL 34240
Contact: Linda Voltz, Director of Enrollment
Department e-mail: linda-voltz@embanet.com
School Web address: sarasota.edu
Institutional accreditation: Southern Association of Colleges and Schools

Admissions Requirements

Is a minimum undergraduate GPA required? Yes
Is provisional admission available? No
Is an admissions interview required? No
Can pre-requisite course work be waived? No
Are international students eligible to apply? Yes
Is the TOEFL required for international students? Yes
What is the minimum TOEFL score required? 500

Program Delivery

Primary method of program delivery: Web
Two-way interactive video: No
Two-way audio, one-way video: No
One-way live video: No
One-way pre-recorded video: No
Audio graphics: No
Audio: No

Is the library accessible to students? Yes
Are computers accessible to students? Yes

Remote Sites

Other branches of the institution: Yes
Other college campuses: No
Students' homes: Yes
Work sites: No
Libraries: No
Elementary/Secondary schools: No
Community-based organizations: No
Correctional institutions: No

On-Campus Requirements

Is an on-campus component required? Yes
On-campus course work: Yes
On-campus admissions interview: No
On-campus program orientation: No
On-campus exams: No
On-campus thesis defense: Yes

Tuition & Fees

Out-of-state tuition per credit: $397
Average yearly cost of books: $800

Financial Aid

Is financial aid available to full-time students? Yes
Is financial aid available to part-time students? Yes
Are academic scholarships available? No
Assistance programs available to students: Federal Stafford
  Loan, Federal Perkins Loan, veterans' assistance

University of South Carolina

Darla Moore School of Business
MBA Program
University of South Carolina
1705 College Street, Room 510, SC 29208
Contact: Paul B. Yazel, Managing Director of MBA
  Programs
Department e-mail: mba@darla.badm.sc.edu
Department Web address: www.business.sc.edu/mba
School Web address: www.sc.edu
Institutional accreditation: Southern Association of
  Colleges and Schools

Subjects Offered

Accounting, international business, finance, e-commerce,
  marketing, operations management, economics,
  management, management science, management
  informations systems

Admissions Requirements

Is a minimum undergraduate GPA required? No
Is provisional admission available? No
Can pre-requisite course work be waived? No
Are international students eligible to apply? Yes
Is the TOEFL required for international students? Yes
What is the minimum TOEFL score required? 600

Program Delivery

Primary method of program delivery: Remote site
Two-way audio, one-way video: Yes
Hardware requirements: Varies—must have regular access
  to Internet and e-mail
Software requirements: Varies—must have regular access to
  Internet and e-mail
Is the library accessible to students? Yes
Are computers accessible to students? Yes

Remote Sites

Other branches of the institution: Yes
Other college campuses: Yes
Students' homes: Yes
Work sites: Yes
Libraries: Yes
Elementary/Secondary schools: Yes
Community-based organizations: Yes

On-Campus Requirements

Is an on-campus component required? Yes
On-campus course work: Yes
On-campus admissions interview: No
On-campus program orientation: Yes
On-campus exams: Yes
On-campus thesis defense: No

Tuition & Fees

In-state tuition per credit: $209
Out-of-state tuition per credit: $209
Average yearly cost of books: $100

Financial Aid

Is financial aid available to part-time students? No
Are academic scholarships available? No

University of Southern Mississippi

Continuing Education & Distance Learning (CEOL)
Hattiesburg, MS 39406-5136
Contact: Sue Pace, Director (CEDL)
Department e-mail: distance.learning@usm.edu

Department Web address: www.cice.usm.edu
School Web address: www.usm.edu
Institutional accreditation: Southern Association of
Colleges and Schools

Subjects Offered

Adult education, research and foundation (education),
child development, software engineering technology,
community health sciences, special education, geography, technical and occupational education, nutrition and
food systems, nursing

Program Delivery

Primary method of program delivery: Web
Two-way interactive video: No
Two-way audio, one-way video: No
One-way live video: No
One-way pre-recorded video: No
Audio graphics: No
Audio: No
Hardware requirements: IBM/Pentium with 32MB of
RAM, 2GHz of hard drive space, monitor, sound card,
CD-ROM, speakers. Apple/Macintosh: Power-PC
machine, 32MB of RAM
Software requirements: No special software requirements
for general online courses/some courses do have special
software courses
Is the library accessible to students? Yes
Are computers accessible to students? Yes

Remote Sites

Other branches of the institution: Yes
Other college campuses: Yes
Students' homes: Yes
Work sites: Yes
Libraries: Yes
Elementary/Secondary schools: Yes
Community-based organizations: Yes
Correctional institutions: Yes

On-Campus Requirements

Is an on-campus component required? No

Tuition & Fees

In-state tuition per credit: $158
Out-of-state tuition per credit: $376
Average yearly cost of books: $25

Financial Aid

Is financial aid available to full-time students? Yes
Assistance programs available to students: Federal Perkins
Loan, Federal Work-Study Program

University of Tennessee at Martin

Extended Campus and Continuing Education
Martin, TN 38238
Contact: William Duffy, Director
Department e-mail: ecce@utm.edu
Department Web address: www.utm.edu~ecce/
School Web address: www.utm.edu
Institutional accreditation: Southern Association of
Colleges and Schools

Subjects Offered

Management, accounting, finance, business law, marketing,
economics, elementary and secondary education,
educational foundations, educational evaluation,
educational psychology and guidance

Admissions Requirements

Is a minimum undergraduate GPA required? Yes
Is provisional admission available? Yes
Is an admissions interview required? No
Can pre-requisite course work be waived? No
Are international students eligible to apply? Yes
Is the TOEFL required for international students? Yes
What is the minimum TOEFL score required? 525

Program Delivery

Primary method of program delivery: Remote site
Two-way interactive video: Yes
Two-way audio, one-way video: No
One-way live video: No
One-way pre-recorded video: No
Audio graphics: No
Audio: No
Is the library accessible to students? Yes
Are computers accessible to students? Yes

Remote Sites

Other branches of the institution: No
Other college campuses: Yes
Students' homes: No
Work sites: Yes
Libraries: No
Elementary/Secondary schools: No
Community-based organizations: No
Correctional institutions: No

On-Campus Requirements

Is an on-campus component required? No

Tuition & Fees

In-state tuition per credit: $194
Out-of-state tuition per credit: $500
Average yearly cost of books: $25

Financial Aid

Is financial aid available to full-time students? Yes
Is financial aid available to part-time students? Yes
Are academic scholarships available? Yes
Assistance programs available to students: Federal Stafford
Loan, Federal Perkins Loan, Federal Plus Loan, Federal
Pell Grant, Federal Work-Study Program, in-state
student aid programs, veterans' assistance

University of Toledo

Division of Distance Learning
2801 West Bancroft
Toledo, OH 43606
Contact: Karen Rhoda, PhD, Interim Director of Distance
Learning
Department e-mail: utdl@utoledo.edu
Department Web address: www.ucollege.utoledo.edu/dilrn/
htm
School Web address: www.utoledo.edu

Subjects Offered

Political science, history, geography, health education,
philosophy, master in liberal studies, curriculum and
instructional education technology, special education,
theory and science foundations

Admissions Requirements

Is a minimum undergraduate GPA required? Yes
Is provisional admission available? Yes
Is an admissions interview required? No
Are international students eligible to apply? Yes
Is the TOEFL required for international students? Yes

Program Delivery

Primary method of program delivery: Web
Two-way interactive video: Yes
Two-way audio, one-way video: No
One-way live video: No
One-way pre-recorded video: Yes
Audio graphics: No
Audio: No
Hardware requirements: 486, 100MHz, 16MB RAM,
28.8KBPS modem
Software requirements: Windows 95 or higher, or Mac
equivalent

Remote Sites

Other branches of the institution: Yes
Other college campuses: Yes
Students' homes: Yes
Work sites: Yes
Libraries: Yes
Elementary/Secondary schools: Yes
Community-based organizations: Yes
Correctional institutions: No

On-Campus Requirements

Is an on-campus component required? No

Tuition & Fees

In-state tuition per credit: $242
Out-of-state tuition per credit: $523

Financial Aid

Is financial aid available to full-time students? Yes
Is financial aid available to part-time students? Yes
Are academic scholarships available? Yes
Assistance programs available to students: Federal Stafford
Loan, Federal Perkins Loan, Federal Plus Loan, Federal
Work-Study Program, in-state student aid programs,
veterans' assistance

University of Virginia

Educational Technologies
104 Midmont Lane
Charlottesville, VA 22904
Contact: John Payne, Director, Educational Technologies
Department e-mail: jpayne@virginia.edu
Department Web address: www.uvace.virginia.edu
School Web address: www.virginia.edu

Subjects Offered

Engineering, nursing, education, procurement and
contacts, accounting, human resources, technology
leadership

Admissions Requirements

Is a minimum undergraduate GPA required? Yes
Is provisional admission available? Yes
Is an admissions interview required? No
Can pre-requisite course work be waived? Yes
Are international students eligible to apply? Yes
Is the TOEFL required for international students? Yes

Program Delivery

Primary method of program delivery: Remote site
Two-way interactive video: Yes

Is the library accessible to students? Yes
Are computers accessible to students? No

Remote Sites

Other branches of the institution: Yes
Other college campuses: Yes
Work sites: Yes

On-Campus Requirements

Is an on-campus component required? No

University of Wisconsin— Milwaukee

Distance Learning and Instructional Support
PO Box 413
Milwaukee, WI 53120
Contact: Nancy Morris, Manager, DLIS
Department Web address: www.uwm.edu/
   universityoutreach/dluwm
School Web address: www.uwm.edu

Subjects Offered

Allied health, business and management, e-commerce,
   library and information science, nursing

Admissions Requirements

Is a minimum undergraduate GPA required? Yes
Is provisional admission available? Yes
Can pre-requisite course work be waived? Yes
Are international students eligible to apply? Yes
Is the TOEFL required for international students? Yes
What is the minimum TOEFL score required? 500

Program Delivery

Two-way interactive video: Yes
Two-way audio, one-way video: Yes
One-way live video: Yes
One-way pre-recorded video: Yes
Audio graphics: Yes
Audio: Yes
Hardware requirements: PC/Mac, modem 33.6KBPS
   modem, sound card
Software requirements: MS Office, Netscape/Internet
   Explorer
Is the library accessible to students? Yes
Are computers accessible to students? No

Remote Sites

Other branches of the institution: Yes
Other college campuses: Yes
Students' homes: Yes

Work sites: Yes
Libraries: Yes
Elementary/Secondary schools: Yes
Community-based organizations: Yes
Correctional institutions: Yes

Tuition & Fees

Average yearly cost of books: $600

Financial Aid

Is financial aid available to full-time students? Yes
Is financial aid available to part-time students? Yes
Are academic scholarships available? Yes
Assistance programs available to students: Federal Stafford
   Loan, Federal Perkins Loan, Federal Plus Loan, Federal
   Pell Grant, Federal Work-Study Program, in-state
   student aid programs, veterans' assistance

University of Wisconsin— Platteville

Distance Learning Center
B12 Karrmann Library
1 University Plaza
Platteville, WI 53818-3099
Department e-mail: disted@uwplatt.edu
Department Web address: www.uwplatt.edu/~disted
School Web address: www.uwplatt.edu
Institutional accreditation: North Central Association of
   Colleges and Schools

Subjects Offered

Accounting, business administration, communication,
   computer science, criminal justice, economics, English,
   engineering—civil, industrial, mechanical, environmental, industrial studies, mathematics, political science,
   project management, psychology, sociology

Admissions Requirements

Is a minimum undergraduate GPA required? Yes
Is provisional admission available? Yes
Can pre-requisite course work be waived? No
Are international students eligible to apply? Yes
Is the TOEFL required for international students? Yes
What is the minimum TOEFL score required? 500

Program Delivery

Primary method of program delivery: Web
Hardware requirements: PC: Pentium 133 processor,
   32MB of RAM, color monitor-256 colors, sound card
   and speakers, CD-ROM, VGA, 56KBPS modem

Software requirements: Windows 95/98/NT, Internet
Explorer 4.5 (or later)/Netscape Navigator 4.0 (or later),
Adobe Acrobat, RealPlayer, IBM TechExplorer
Is the library accessible to students? Yes
Are computers accessible to students? No

Remote Sites

Students' homes: Yes
Work sites: Yes

On-Campus Requirements

Is an on-campus component required? No

Tuition & Fees

In-state tuition per credit: $486
Out-of-state tuition per credit: $650
Average yearly cost of books: $45

Financial Aid

Is financial aid available to full-time students? Yes
Is financial aid available to part-time students? Yes
Are academic scholarships available? No
Assistance programs available to students: Federal Stafford
Loan

University of Wisconsin— Whitewater

On-Line MBA
College of Business and Economics
800 West Main Street
Whitewater, WI 53190
Contact: Donald Zahn, Associate Dean of College of
Business and Economics
Department e-mail: gradbus@mail.uww.edu
Department Web address: www.academics.uww.edu/
business/business.htm
School Web address: www.uww.edu
Institutional accreditation: North Central Association of
Colleges and Schools

Subjects Offered

Business communications, accounting foundations,
business and professional communications, economics
foundations, legal environment of business, strategic
management, international management, marketing,
advanced statistical methods, international business,
management of technology, financial markets, training
and development, managerial economics

Admissions Requirements

Is a minimum undergraduate GPA required? Yes
Is provisional admission available? Yes
Is an admissions interview required? No
Can pre-requisite course work be waived? Yes
Are international students eligible to apply? Yes
Is the TOEFL required for international students? Yes
What is the minimum TOEFL score required? 550

Program Delivery

Primary method of program delivery: Web
Two-way interactive video: No
Two-way audio, one-way video: No
One-way live video: No
One-way pre-recorded video: Yes
Audio graphics: Yes
Audio: Yes
Hardware requirements: Pentium 133, 28.8KBPS modem,
32MB of RAM
Software requirements: Windows 95 or higher
Is the library accessible to students? Yes
Are computers accessible to students? Yes

Remote Sites

Other branches of the institution: Yes
Other college campuses: Yes
Students' homes: Yes
Work sites: Yes
Libraries: Yes
Elementary/Secondary schools: No
Community-based organizations: No
Correctional institutions: No

On-Campus Requirements

Is an on-campus component required? No

Tuition & Fees

In-state tuition per credit: $261
Out-of-state tuition per credit: $758
Average yearly cost of books: $15

Financial Aid

Is financial aid available to full-time students? Yes
Is financial aid available to part-time students? No
Are academic scholarships available? No
Assistance programs available to students: Federal Stafford
Loan, Federal Perkins Loan, Federal Work-Study
Program

Virginia Commonwealth University

Distance Education
901 Park Avenue, Suite B-30
PO Box 843008
Richmond, Virginia 23284-3008
Contact: Sonja Moore, Director of Distance Education
Department e-mail: somoore@vcu.edu
School Web address: www.vcu.edu
Institutional accreditation: Southern Association of Colleges and Schools

Subjects Offered

Occupational therapy, pharmacy, rehabilitation counseling, criminal justice, sociology and anthropology, physics, philosophy, health administration, allied health, gerontology

Program Delivery

Primary method of program delivery: Web
Two-way interactive video: Yes
Two-way audio, one-way video: Yes
One-way pre-recorded video: Yes
Audio: Yes
Is the library accessible to students? Yes

Remote Sites

Other college campuses: Yes
Students' homes: Yes
Work sites: Yes
Community-based organizations: Yes
Correctional institutions: Yes

On-Campus Requirements

On-campus course work: Yes
On-campus program orientation: Yes
On-campus exams: Yes

Financial Aid

Is financial aid available to full-time students? Yes
Is financial aid available to part-time students? Yes
Are academic scholarships available? Yes
Assistance programs available to students: Federal Stafford Loan, Federal Perkins Loan, Federal Plus Loan, Federal Work-Study Program, in-state student aid programs, veterans' assistance

Wheaton College Graduate School

Distance Learning
501 College Avenue
Wheaton, IL 60187-5593
Contact: Douglas Milford, Director
Department e-mail: distance.learning@wheaton.edu
Department Web address: www.wheaton.edu/ distancelearning/
School Web address: www.wheaton.edu
Institutional accreditation: North Central Association of Colleges and Schools

Subjects Offered

Biblical studies, theological studies, missions studies

Admissions Requirements

Are international students eligible to apply? Yes
Is the TOEFL required for international students? Yes
What is the minimum TOEFL score required? 550

Program Delivery

Audio: Yes
Hardware requirements: Pentium-class computer (for online classes)
Software requirements: Internet browser, RealPlayer, Adobe Acrobat (for online classes)

On-Campus Requirements

Is an on-campus component required? No

Tuition & Fees

In-state tuition per credit: $260
Out-of-state tuition per credit: $260
Average yearly cost of books: $360

Financial Aid

Is financial aid available to part-time students? No
Are academic scholarships available? No

Indexes

Alphabetical List of Undergraduate Schools

Alphabetical List of Graduate Schools

V

W

ABOUT THE AUTHORS

Dr. Paul Jay Edelson

Dr. Edelson is Dean of the School of Professional Development at the State University of New York (SUNY) at Stony Brook. He has published four books, *Rethinking Leadership in Adult and Continuing Education* (1992), *Higher Education's Role in Retraining Displaced Professionals* (1997), *Enhancing Creativity in Adult and Continuing Education* (1999), and *Weiterbildung in den USA* (2000) as well as over eighty articles on leadership, academic planning, electronic distance learning, and creativity. He teaches graduate courses at Stony Brook and at Teachers College, Columbia University. He attended the City University of New York (BA), the University of Minnesota, and New York University (MA, PhD).

Dr. Jerry Ice

Dr. Ice is the Chief Academic Officer of Thomas Edison State College in New Jersey. He received his doctorate in Administration and Supervision from Fordham University. Many of his publications have focused on the educational needs and goals of adults returning to college. During Dr. Ice's tenure at Thomas Edison, a number of innovative programs have been implemented, including the National Institute for Experiential Learning, the Computer Assisted Lifelong Learning (CALL) Network, and the CALL-PC Loan program for underserved students.

Notes

Notes

Notes

Notes

Notes

Notes

Notes

Notes

Expert Advice

www.review.com

Talk About It

www.review.com

Pop Surveys

Paying for it

www.review.com

www.review.com

The Princeton Review

Getting in

Word du Jour

www.review.com

Find-O-Rama School & Career Search

www.review.com

Finding it

Best Schools

www.review.com

FIND US...

International

Hong Kong
4/F Sun Hung Kai Centre
30 Harbour Road, Wan Chai,
Hong Kong
Tel: (011)85-2-517-3016

Japan
Fuji Building 40, 15-14
Sakuragaokacho, Shibuya Ku,
Tokyo 150, Japan
Tel: (011)81-3-3463-1343

Korea
Tae Young Bldg, 944-24,
Daechi- Dong, Kangnam-Ku
The Princeton Review- ANC
Seoul, Korea 135-280,
South Korea
Tel: (011)82-2-554-7763

Mexico City
PR Mex S De RL De Cv
Guanajuato 228 Col. Roma
06700 Mexico D.F., Mexico
Tel: 525-564-9468

Montreal
666 Sherbrooke St.
West, Suite 202
Montreal, QC H3A 1E7 Canada
Tel: (514) 499-0870

Pakistan
1 Bawa Park - 90 Upper Mall
Lahore, Pakistan
Tel: (011)92-42-571-2315

Spain
Pza. Castilla, 3 - 5° A, 28046
Madrid, Spain
Tel: (011)341-323-4212

Taiwan
155 Chung Hsiao East Road
Section 4 - 4th Floor,
Taipei R.O.C., Taiwan
Tel: (011)886-2-751-1243

Thailand
Building One, 99 Wireless Road
Bangkok, Thailand 10330
Tel: (662) 256-7080

Toronto
1240 Bay Street, Suite 300
Toronto M5R 2A7 Canada
Tel: (800) 495-7737
Tel: (716) 839-4391

locations

National (U.S.)

We have over 60 offices around the United States and run courses in over 400 sites. For courses and locations within the U.S. call 1 (800) 2/Review and you will be routed to the nearest office.

MORE EXPERT ADVICE FROM THE PRINCETON REVIEW

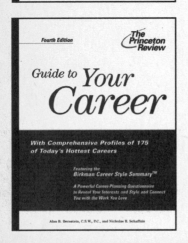

I f you want to give yourself the best chances for getting into the graduate school of your choice, we can help you get higher test scores, make the most informed choices, and make the most of your experience once you get there. We can also help you make the career move that will let you use your skills and education to their best advantage.

CRACKING THE GRE
2002 EDITION
0-375-76196-9 $20.00

CRACKING THE GRE SAMPLE TESTS ON CD-ROM
2002 EDITION
0-375-76197-7 $31.00

CRACKING THE GRE BIOLOGY
3RD EDITION
0-375-75615-9 $18.00

CRACKING THE GRE CHEMISTRY
0-375-75346-X $16.00

CRACKING THE GRE LITERATURE
3RD EDITION
0-375-75617-5 $18.00

CRACKING THE GRE MATH
0-375-75399-0 $18.00

CRACKING THE GRE PSYCHOLOGY
5TH EDITION
0-375-75398-2 $18.00

VERBAL WORKOUT FOR THE GRE
0-679-77890-X $16.00

THE BEST GRADUATE PROGRAMS: ENGINEERING
2ND EDITION
0-375-75205-6 $21.00

THE BEST GRADUATE PROGRAMS: HUMANITIES AND SOCIAL SCIENCES
2ND EDITION
0-375-75203-X $25.00

THE BEST GRADUATE PROGRAMS: PHYSICAL AND BIOLOGICAL SCIENCES
2ND EDITION
0-375-75204-8 $25.00

GUIDE TO YOUR CAREER
4TH EDITION
0-375-75620-5 $21.00

GUIDE TO CAREERS IN THE HEALTH PROFESSIONS
0-375-76158-6 $24.95